The Alabama & the Kearsarge

WILLIAM MARVEL

CIVIL WAR AMERICA   Gary W. Gallagher, editor

The Alabama & the Kearsarge

The Sailor's Civil War

The

University

of North

Carolina

Press

Chapel Hill

& London

© 1996 The University of North Carolina Press

All rights reserved

Manufactured in the United States of America

The paper in this book meets the guidelines for
permanence and durability of the Committee on
Production Guidelines for Book Longevity of the
Council on Library Resources.

Library of Congress Cataloging-in-Publication Data
Marvel, William. The Alabama and the Kearsarge:
the sailor's Civil War / by William Marvel.
p. cm. — (Civil War America)
Includes bibliographical references (p.) and index.
ISBN 0-8078-2294-9 (alk. paper)
1. United States—History—Civil War, 1861–1865—
Naval operations. 2. Alabama (Ship) 3. Kearsage
(Sloop) 4. United States. Navy—History—Civil
War, 1861–1865. 5. United States. Navy—Military
life. 6. Confederate States of America. Navy—Military
life. I. Title. II. Series.
E591.M3   1996   96-11144
973.7'54—dc20   CIP

00 99 98 97 96   5 4 3 2 1

For Dolly Marvel,
and her sailor

CONTENTS

MAPS AND ILLUSTRATIONS

A section of illustrations follows page 125.

Soldier life in the Civil War has been examined in all its aspects, from the rigors of camp, march, and battlefield to the details of diet, disease, and diversion. On the other hand sailors, especially the blue-water variety, have been largely ignored save for those who wore gold braid. Namelessly clad in dark, baggy uniforms, the seamen of either side led an uncomfortable, exhausting, and monotonous existence and returned home with little if any fanfare, often succumbing at an early age to ailments encountered aboard ship. They tended to be poorer than their rifle-toting counterparts, and their lives ashore more often ended in obscurity. Few of them left memoirs, and almost none of those manuscripts found print. The long, cold days and nights on deck or the sweltering, smokey watches in the engine rooms went undescribed, forgotten by those who showed such interest in the campaigns on land. Curiosity about the experience of the common sailor was one of the principal motives behind this book.

Another incentive lay in the absence of a judicious and thorough investigation into the history of either the CSS *Alabama* or the USS *Kearsarge*. Three memoirs written by *Alabama* officers offered biased interpretations (and in one instance dubious credibility), and one account by an alleged crewman proved perfectly fraudulent; most secondary works on the ship's career to date have been based on such sources. The *Kearsarge* enjoyed no book-length treatment save an imaginative work by a former Marine corporal. Even a recent book on the *Alabama* that appeared during the preparation of this manuscript provided almost nothing in the way of new source material—instead merely forwarding an uncritical repetition of the standard collection of postwar reminiscences and secondary works, replete with repetitions of old mistakes with a few new ones thrown in to muddle the tale.

As I discovered some years ago, the surest way to uncover the real story of a time past is to go straight to the contemporary manuscripts. Wartime diaries and letters have helped in the development of new and more dependable interpretations of certain characters and events, but the careers of the *Alabama* and the *Kearsarge* posed a significant problem because such truly primary sources were so few. The crew of the *Kearsarge* produced a handful of diaries, but some of those seem to have been revised or expanded after the war, while one—Austin Quinby's journal—was so heavily reworked as to challenge its reliability. Aboard the *Alabama*, only two officer's journals survive, and sometimes they contradict each other. A few letters also address conditions on either ship. Careful use of these few private accounts and official documents (themselves occasionally suspect) did, however, seem to yield a more detailed and believable picture of saltwater Yankees and Confederates than was left behind by aging former officers intent on the security of their reputations.

A number of people assisted in the research for this book, most notably two tireless correspondents. Dick Winslow, of Rye, New Hampshire, sent me every scrap of related material that he encountered in his own research on the Portsmouth Naval Shipyard, while Maurice Rigby answered many questions about *Alabama* crewmen and gave me a guided tour of Liverpool. Douglas Stein, curator of the G. W. Blunt White Library at Mystic Seaport, and his assistant Leah Prescott assisted me with the three *Kearsarge* journals in that repository's vault, and Barry Zerby of the National Archives found much of the naval material held in that institution. Bill Erwin at Duke University and David Moltke-Hansen of the Southern Historical Collection, at the University of North Carolina, proved as helpful as ever. At the University of Alabama Jerry Oldshue, of the W. S. Hoole Special Collections Library, cordially accommodated me with various manuscripts and rare books, while in Montgomery Norwood A. Kerr, of the Alabama Department of Archives and History, gathered up Raphael Semmes's journals and some related manuscripts. Overseas research was expedited by a number of sympathetic curators, as well, especially Robert A. H. Smith, assistant keeper of manuscripts at the British Library. Clive Powell and John Graves, at the National Maritime Museum in Greenwich, did some long-distance research for me, and Erik Le Marisquier, interim conservator at the Service Historique de la Marine à Cherbourg, provided some pertinent material besides helping me to decipher old maps of the naval station at that place. I am also grateful to Mme. Huyghues Des Etages, conservator of manuscripts at the Musée de la Marine, in Paris.

Preliminary planning for a book like this began with my first crossing of the English Channel, in 1979. Two solid years of research and writing, however, never took me closer to the sea than the estuary at Mystic Seaport. Herman Melville once observed from the crosstrees of a whaler that long reflection on deep water can be a dangerous and unpredictable thing, but salt air seemed a necessary ingredient. The entire project has assumed a new flavor as a result of consummation within sight of beaches washed by water the *Alabama* and the *Kearsarge* both crossed.

Wells, Maine
October 13, 1994

The Alabama & the Kearsarge

Moor your boys to that best of harbors, the hearth-stone.

—Herman Melville, *White Jacket*

CHAPTER ONE

Escape

Alone on a wide wide sea.
—Coleridge, "Rime of the Ancient Mariner"

Under the bright yellow gaze of the three-quarter moon a small, trim bark with bare spars cut the muddy waters of the lower Mississippi River. Languid smoke drifted from the funnel ahead of its mainmast. The black ship's wake lapped at ribbonlike riverbanks on either side, beyond which lay miles of wetlands that cartographers called "trembling prairie." The wheezy throbbing of the steamer's engine disturbed an occasional heron, or egret, flocks of which nested in reedbeds just beyond the river's edge.

At 3:00 this sweltering morning of June 19, 1861, the first hint of twilight lay half an hour away, so the mosquito-tormented deck watch of the Confederate States cruiser *Sumter* did not see the riverbanks disappear as the prow of their ship approached the last dogleg in the Mississippi's tortuous 2,500-mile journey to the Gulf of Mexico. An hour later, as the boatswain's mate tripped the capstan and the anchor splashed into murky water, the lurking shapes of two forts emerged from the darkness. Nearer, on the right bank, sat Fort Jackson, and across the river Fort St. Phillip—both of them perched on soggy soil carried there over the centuries from the plains, the prairies, and the northern forests. Towering cypress trees draped in Spanish moss threatened to recapture these two hostile islands of humanity, while vines and hyacinths crept softly toward the red brick casemates, their roots feeding from soil that may have been dislodged by the boots of de Soto's men, or La Salle's.

Powerful Union warships lurked off the delta, and Commander Raphael

3

Semmes, the spare, frail-looking, fifty-one-year-old skipper of the *Sumter*, wished to familiarize his crew with the ship's five guns before venturing into open water. The shadow of the big forts seemed a likely spot. After conferring briefly with the forts' chief officers, Semmes watched as the lieutenants began gun drill.[1]

The captain had spent nearly thirty-five years in the service of the U.S. Navy, from his appointment as a midshipman in 1826. A native of Maryland, he had settled his family in Alabama in 1841, and he considered himself loyal to that state when the secession crisis struck. Alabama seceded on January 11, 1861, but Commander Semmes lingered on duty as secretary of the U.S. Lighthouse Board until February 14, when a representative of the Committee on Naval Affairs of the new Confederate Congress asked him to repair to Montgomery: the next morning Semmes resigned his commission, and his war had begun.

Semmes ruled his ships with firm discipline, maintaining an austere distance from his subordinates, but he did not typify the naval martinet of his day. Though bold and adventurous, he was an omnivorous reader who devoted the endless hours at sea to books on law, literature, and history. He had served ashore with Winfield Scott during the campaign to Mexico City, scrambling over the Mexican fortifications with the infantry, and his fluent Spanish had come in handy when the generals began looking for interpreters. As captain of the brig *Somers*, he had barely survived the sinking of his ship in a gale off the Mexican coast. In the months between cruises, Semmes had studied law and was admitted to the Alabama bar, practicing at Mobile. His legal training would prove valuable to the Confederacy.[2]

Under Semmes's supervision, the *Sumter* had but recently been transformed from the packet boat *Habana* into a warship, and the reinforced deck still bore the scars where, sixty days before, passenger cabins had adorned it for the trade between New Orleans and Havana. Of the twenty-two officers and ninety-two crewmen, few had ever served on a man-of-war. In the wardroom only the lieutenants could claim much experience, most notably John McIntosh Kell, the executive officer. Kell had spent half his thirty-eight years in the service of the United States and the Confederate navies. He had served through the Mexican War and had sailed around the world, going to Japan with Commodore Perry. A dozen years before he joined the *Sumter* he had been court-martialed on a trumped-up charge of disobedience, and despite the best efforts of his legal counsel (the same Raphael Semmes under whom he now served) he had been convicted and dismissed from the service. Late in 1850 Kell was reinstated, however, and he served for another ten years before the secession of Georgia, his native state. The red-haired Scotsman still wore the old blue uniform of the U.S.

Navy, but with different buttons. He also wore a new beard, which he vowed not to trim until the new Confederacy won its independence. Kell would sail with Semmes for exactly three more years from this day.[3]

For three days the 500-ton *Sumter* remained anchored off Fort Jackson as the green gun crews learned their new trade. The creak of gun tackles carried across the broad, rippling river, followed by the shrill squeal of the 8-inch pivot gun as its carriage wheels ground around the fresh-laid track. Occasionally a gun would belch a blank cartridge at the far shore, and for a time Semmes had them fire live rounds at floating targets, no doubt to the dismay of the waterfowl inhabiting the marshes on the other side.

While the crews practiced, their captain plied his glass to the south, hoping for a chance to bolt for the open sea and begin complying with his orders from the secretary of the navy, who bade him to "do the enemy's commerce the greatest injury in the shortest time." From the masthead the view carried a good twenty miles over the alluvial plain, and downstream Semmes could distinguish Pass à l'Outre, the northeastern passageway through the delta. In the distance beyond he could just make out the silhouette of a ship, which he supposed to be the USS *Brooklyn*, a twenty-four-gun frigate that outweighed the *Sumter* four to one. The USS *Powhatan* was also reported to be hovering about the delta passes, and Semmes seemed pessimistic about his chances of escape.[4]

As the setting sun emblazoned Fort St. Phillip on June 21, word arrived that the *Powhatan* was gone, chasing sails that had approached the passes. Semmes thought he might be able to feint his way past one ship, which would have to sail the outside of a circle around him, and he immediately ordered steam. By 10:30 the *Sumter* reached the Head of Passes, where the three major avenues of the delta intersected, but the keeper of the lighthouse there said there were no pilots on duty. An impatient Semmes asked the captain of the privateer *Ivy* to sail down to the lighthouse at Southwest Pass and find a pilot, but the next morning the *Ivy* returned without one. Semmes therefore sent an ultimatum to the master of the pilots' association to come aboard with his pilots or be arrested; some of them came, but by the time Semmes was ready to run the gantlet he could see the *Powhatan* back at anchor, with the *Brooklyn* in sight.

Trapped for the moment, Semmes improved his time by sending detachments to the lighthouses at Pass à l'Outre and South Pass, from which they took the lamps and destroyed the oil. He deposited the lamps with the keeper at Head of Passes lighthouse, congratulating himself that the enemy could no longer avail himself of these landmarks. With so tight a blockade, he reasoned, Confederate commerce could reap no benefit from the beacons.[5]

For the next week the *Sumter* clung to its anchorage at the Head of Passes, the gun crews growing gradually more familiar with their cumbersome weapons. When Semmes was satisfied with their artillery training, he set them to drill with revolvers and cutlasses. That sort of exercise in the steaming delta days left officers and men alike drenched in sweat, driving them to bucket river water aboard for bathing and an occasional draught— for no one wasted fresh water on a gunboat. The Mississippi hosted myriad microbes, however, and those who imbibed any of it came down with diarrhea. That was the extent of illness, though, and—contrary to the captain's apparent expectations—fever did not seize the crew. Only the paymaster's clerk fell so ill that Semmes had to put him ashore.[6]

The *Powhatan* swung around to the mouth of Southwest Pass, while the *Brooklyn* lingered at Pass à l'Outre. On the morning of June 29 the lookout called down that the *Brooklyn* had disappeared, and the engine room raised steam to run that chute, but a few miles down the channel the Federal warship appeared at her usual place: the *Sumter* had merely dragged her anchor during the night, putting a few treetops between the *Brooklyn* and the lookout's eye. A disappointed Semmes ordered the ship about, grumbling over the waste of coal.

Two hours after midnight a supply ship stopped to replenish the *Sumter*'s coal bunkers, continuing on afterward to Pass à l'Outre. The ship returned from there at 10:30 in the morning, sending a boat over with news that the *Brooklyn* was out of sight. Again Semmes called for steam, and the *Sumter* plowed toward the gulf once more. The pilot, whom Semmes had kept aboard all that week, suddenly disavowed any knowledge of Pass à l'Outre, claiming familiarity with only the Southwest Pass. Disgusted, Semmes hoisted his jack to signal for another pilot, but he anticipated that none would come, in which case he intended to take her through on his own dim memory of the bar. Luck clung to him this day, though, and a pilot did rush aboard the little warship as she passed the pilot station, where the pilot's wife stood waving him to his work.

Just then the *Brooklyn* appeared south of the bar, seven or eight miles away, hurrying back to her station. The race was on. The Yankee vessel gained half the distance to its prey, but came no closer than four miles. In an effort to supplement his engines the *Brooklyn*'s skipper set his sails, so Semmes sent his own men aloft to unfurl the *Sumter*'s sheets. To lighten ship he directed his marines to dismantle the 24-pounder howitzer that the commander of the forts had given him, but in strict recognition of the proprieties he convened an impromptu board of survey among his three senior lieutenants before pitching the gun overboard. Despite the frigate's reputation for speed, the little Confederate cruiser slowly pulled away from her, running first north-northeast but curving ever eastward toward open water. By 3:30 in the afternoon the growing distance told the inevitable tale, and the *Brooklyn* sheered off to the north, after other game. All hands on the Confederate ship scurried into the rigging to cheer their infant flag, and Semmes invited his officers into the wardroom for a celebratory sip of wine.[7]

After the hot, heavy delta air the Southern sailors drank deep of the cool ocean breezes. Their first night at sea passed beneath starlit skies, and the next day gentle west winds died to calm as the sun set. Not a sail did they spot, but early in the evening a great shining comet appeared in the heavens, in the general direction of Tallahassee; the *Sumter*, meanwhile, held her helm for the tip of Cuba.

Neither did they sight another vessel on July 2, though they rounded Cape San Antonio in the Yucatan Channel. Early on the afternoon of July 3 the lookout called two sails, and the *Sumter* made for a brig that turned out to be Spanish. Shearing off then to the other vessel, a bark somewhat larger than the *Sumter*, Semmes fired a shot that brought her to and sent the U.S. colors to her peak. Semmes dropped the British flag that he sailed under and raised the Stars and Bars. A boarding party found the bark to be the *Golden Rocket* of Bangor, Maine: she had come down in ballast, looking for sugar to transport north. Her astounded master learned that his ship was to be burned, and after stripping the prize of its useful cordage, sails, and other stores, the prize crew broke up the cabin and forecastle furniture and kindled the blaze. The match was set at 10:00 that night, and the Yankee captain watched from the deck of the *Sumter* as the flames engulfed his ship. The blaze lighted the sea for miles, burning well into the morning of the old Independence Day.[8]

On the same June 19 that brought the *Sumter* to the forts, the hollow, staccato rattle of steel on oak echoed across the Piscataqua River from an island between Maine and New Hampshire, where carpenters at the Portsmouth Navy Yard hacked away with adzes and broadaxes at the first few timbers of two new warships destined for Federal service. The keel of one, called the *Kearsarge*, lay sprouting its ribs on the open-air railway while a larger one, the *Ossipee*, went together in the ship-house nearby. Less than four weeks before, some sixty carpenters and laborers had been laid off here for lack of work, but since then the secretary of the navy had ordered several dozen gunboats. Now 900 workmen flitted busily about under the supervision of Constructor Isaiah Hanscom, carving out the frames of the two new sloops and refitting the fifty-gun frigate *Santee*. With the usual optimism of a contractor starting a new job, the supervisor expected to have the first of the new ships launched "in three months or so."[9]

The navy secretary, Gideon Welles, had found himself stuck for names to apply to all these new ships. Wishing the vessels to wear a distinctly American air, he lit upon the notion of giving them Indian names, and he asked those around him to offer some ideas. His own wife suggested "Juniata," for the river near her birthplace, and such a ship went under construction at the Philadelphia Navy Yard. Assistant Secretary Gustavus Fox approached his chief with the name "Kearsarge," which he said his own wife proposed in honor of a 3,268-foot mountain in the towns of Bartlett and Chatham, of her native New Hampshire, which she could see from her summertime hotel room in North Conway. Welles therefore applied that name to one of the new ships in the stocks at Portsmouth. At first he misspelled it "Kearsage," but Treasury Secretary Salmon P. Chase, another New Hampshire native, corrected him.[10]

The *Kearsarge* would be but one element in the government's plan to strangle the Confederacy with a blockade of its ports. Mighty ships would stand at the mouths of every Southern harbor just as the *Brooklyn* and the *Powhatan* had waited off the Mississippi Delta for Semmes and the *Sumter*. With no real manufacturing base, the South had been dependent upon the North and Europe for virtually everything but food and slaves, and everyone in Washington supposed that, if the blockade were effective it would not be long before the insurgent states collapsed.

Establishing such a blockade required a lot of armed vessels, however, and the U.S. Navy had only ninety ships in commission when the war began. Of these, most were overseas, under repair, or otherwise unavailable for duty. Only fourteen vessels—two of them storeships and one a tender— constituted the entire Home Squadron. Secretary Welles armed a wide assortment of tugs and coastal packets to harry blockade runners, for almost anything with a weapon aboard posed a threat to merchant ships whose only defense was speed, and he hastened the return of those warships that wandered abroad. He ordered new gunboats of different types, and shipbuilders hounded him for these plums; New Hampshire Senator John P. Hale lobbied him in particular for Toby & Littlefield, of Portsmouth, promising that they would be as prompt as anyone. Navy yard superintendents from Philadelphia to Portsmouth meanwhile rushed the refitting of the two dozen ships laid up under their care and the completion of the new ones for which the government had contracted.

At Portsmouth the old sailing sloops *Marion* and *Dale* were sent back to sea by the second week in July, and the frigate *Sabine* came in for repairs. Six hundred men worked on the *Kearsarge* and the *Ossipee*. By the end of July the frame of the *Kearsarge* was complete—a couple of weeks later than originally expected. Her timbers had been bolted through and through, and long iron bands had been fastened diagonally up and down her sides, crossing each other to resist any racking of the ship's skeleton.

Through August carpenters clambered up staging to affix white oak planks to the sides of the *Kearsarge*, with Constructor Hanscom hurrying them all the more after he learned that the navy intended to build two more sidewheel steamers here. He watched anxiously on September 11 while his crews, pelted by a daylong downpour, slid the bare hulk down the rails into the drydock, where some of them began paneling the ship's belly with copper sheeting while others laid the keel of one of the sidewheelers on the vacated railway. By October 5 the *Kearsarge*'s bottom was sheathed, and workmen flooded the drydock. The mastless vessel floated out to dock with the other ships, where carpenters crawled into her dark, echoing bowels to raise the interior bulkheads, to seal the future magazine in three layers of oak interspersed with sheets of lead, and to finish off the cabin and wardroom. She had already attained her length of 201′ 4″ at the keel, and her beam width of 33′ 10″. From main deck to keel she measured 16′, and when her engines and riggings were in place she would weigh 1,031 tons, representing three-quarters of a million board feet of yellow pine, white oak, and live oak. Fully loaded, the *Kearsarge* would draw about 14′ of water.[11]

It was dangerous work at the yard, particularly for the new men who flocked to Portsmouth and Kittery for the flurry of jobs. Experienced observers at the yard saw relatively few accidents, for all the sudden activity, but some blood did mar the making of the new steamers. One artisan who was turning a piece of oak had his arm badly broken when the stick flew out of the lathe, and, on the morning after the *Kearsarge* went into the drydock, a Maine carpenter who had been hired only three days before cut his foot almost completely off with an axe.[12]

That same June found British workmen framing another ship a thousand leagues to the east, on the banks of the Mersey River. James Dunwoody Bulloch, a thirty-eight-year-old native of Savannah, Georgia, had landed in England early that month as an agent for the Confederacy, coming by way of Montreal, Detroit, and Montgomery, Alabama. He arrived with the rank of lieutenant in the Confederate States Navy, and his mission was to provide his new nation with fighting ships, but, three weeks before he stepped off in Liverpool, Queen Victoria had issued a proclamation of neutrality that made his job all the more difficult.

Commander Bulloch managed wonderfully, despite a lack of funds and the complications of British neutrality. He knew ships and shipping well, having entered the U.S. Navy as a midshipman at sixteen and served in it until he was thirty. Thereafter he had commanded merchant vessels in the coastal trade between New York and New Orleans, and his broad experiences yielded a resourcefulness that he would need in his new calling.

The balding young officer approached William C. Miller & Sons, Liverpool shipbuilders, about a wooden screw steamer of some 700 tons. The founder of the firm presented him with a drawing of a British gunboat with the strong deck and expansive crew quarters Bulloch sought. They expanded the drawing to lend the ship a sleeker silhouette and increased the rigging to give her greater canvas, and thus better speed. Then Bulloch visited the nearby Fawcett, Preston and Co., with whom he contracted for the design of the engines and the overall construction of the ship. Among the modifications these engineers made was an arrangement for disconnecting and lifting the propeller, that the ship might save coal by sailing without either steam or drag. It was a provision of neutrality that no belligerent vessel could replenish its bunkers in a neutral port more frequently than once in three months; Britain's declaration of neutrality had been followed by similar proclamations in nations across Europe and even in South America, and Bulloch supposed that any Southern vessel should be prepared to wait a long time between coalings. As camels were considered the ships of the desert, Confederate cruisers would have to be camels of the sea.

Through all of this Bulloch also had to consider, of course, that no neutral shipbuilder could knowingly produce an armed vessel for one of the belligerents. In order to save his contractors from violating their country's laws, Bulloch acted as an individual, dropping no hint of his true employers, and he made no effort to arm the ship in British territory. He suggested that she was destined for an Italian company, and to enhance that suspicion he engaged an agent of a Palermo mercantile firm to supervise the details of construction. Bulloch supposed that the builders were wise to the final destination of their ship by the time construction was well under way; he may not have feared any treachery on their part because they seemed willing to ask no questions, but he left them the legal luxury of knowing nothing definite about his intentions. U.S. diplomats in England deemed Liverpool a hotbed of Confederate sympathy, and that may have been true, but Bulloch was taking no chances: while the craft stood in the stocks he called her *Oreto*, to further the Italian fiction. Until this ship crossed Britain's marine league, no British subject would know that her name was to be the *Florida*.[13]

Even before he had concluded his arrangements on the first ship, Bulloch crossed the Mersey, where he took a tour of the Birkenhead Ironworks. He met William and John Laird, Jr., of John Laird & Sons, and discussed with them the construction of "wooden despatch vessels." These builders, who owned an expansive and prolific yard, talked freely with him, and in July they agreed to draw up plans for a ship of Bulloch's specifications. The Confederate agent wished her to be bigger than the *Oreto*, with a keel length of 211'6"—220' overall—and a beam of 31'8". She would draw an average of 15' of water, with a depth of 17'8", and would weigh more than 1,040 tons. With two engines making 300 horsepower and extra canvas capacity this vessel should be fleet; like her predecessor across the estuary, she would be able to lift her propeller for clear sailing. Again Bulloch allowed his contractors the pretense of ignorance, but it did not take a shipbuilder to deduce that a vessel designed with a magazine, three shell rooms, and numerous shot racks was not meant for the tea trade.[14]

Thus far Bulloch had been operating on credit alone, committing his government to a price of £45,628 for the *Oreto*. Late in July the Confederate account in England saw its first deposit, and on the first day of August, 1861, Bulloch signed a £47,500 contract with the Lairds for the new ship, which would be the 290th they had built in their facility. For the present the new vessel would go by that number, 290, rather than any name, but to history she would be known as the *Alabama*.[15]

CHAPTER TWO

Pursuit

It was that fatal and perfidious bark
Built in th' eclipse, and rigged with curses dark.
—Milton, "Lycidas"

October frosts had gilded the trees by the time a schooner turned up the Piscataqua River with the USS *Kearsarge*'s engines. For eight days the riggers labored to swing them aboard the new ship and guide them between the yawning timbers, while two supervisors shouted orders and called for caution: the largest block weighed forty-three tons, they said. The two engines came from the Hartford foundry of Woodruff and Beach, and their horizontal pistons stood as tall as a powder monkey. Driven by two main boilers and an auxiliary of the tubular variety, Martin's patent, they produced 400 horsepower.[1]

To command this rapid vessel, Secretary Welles chose forty-five-year-old Charles Whipple Pickering, a Portsmouth native who had spent most of his life in the navy. Appointed a midshipman when he was only six years old, he had sailed his first cruise aboard the USS *Cyane* under his uncle during James Monroe's presidency; thirty years later he served as executive officer of that same vessel. A commander since 1855, he was, like Raphael Semmes, on lighthouse duty as 1861 began, and when the guns turned on Fort Sumter he held the Key West station. Pickering sailed up the coast to collect his welcome new orders, which Welles signed on November 1; on November 5 the new skipper debarked at the Portsmouth yard and reported to the commandant, Captain George F. Pearson. He found the new ship without spars, rigging, or crew.[2]

Pickering's arrival opened the crew list, and the commandant gave him a quota of men for each department. Besides his wardroom and steerage officers, he would need deck hands, an engineer department, and petty officers. First came the appointments for the chiefs of departments, and for their own crews. On November 8 Pickering greeted his chief engineer, William H. Cushman, and told him he might ship thirty-one men—ten first-class firemen, seven second-class, and fourteen coal heavers. Cushman set about looking for the men, but he already had a notion of asking for five more, and eventually the Navy Department would allow him to have them. Besides the enlisted men, Cushman already enjoyed the aid of First Assistant Engineer James Whittaker, Second Assistant Engineer William H. Badlam, and three third assistant engineers. Cushman had been in the navy since 1855, while Whittaker and Badlam had also been to sea before, but the three below them had never seen naval service.[3]

Secretary Welles prodded the shipyard commandant to finish his ships, and the *Ossipee* slid into the water on November 16. Unlike the neglected and somewhat smaller *Kearsarge*, the *Ossipee* enjoyed a regular christening, complete with a senator, the district congressman, the former governor, and a couple of ladies—including the wife of Henry McFarland, a Concord newspaper publisher who claimed to have suggested this ship's name as well as that of the *Kearsarge*. Mrs. McFarland and the other lady offered the traditional liquid blessing, and the *Ossipee* bobbed into the river. Meanwhile the *Kearsarge*'s officers advertised for sailors, and they began trickling in.[4]

The New England states had spent the previous seven months scouring their populations for soldiers, and most of the region's excess patriotism had been expended to fill infantry regiments, artillery batteries, and cavalry companies. The sea had always drawn young men with images of exotic foreign places, but now the drudgery for which the army was so well known was overshadowed by the opportunity for battlefield glory, and for the hesitant recruit there was the more practical allure of a hundred-dollar enlistment bounty. The navy could offer nothing so tempting, and then there was the notorious shipboard discipline that Herman Melville had exposed: thanks in part to Melville's *White Jacket*, published in 1850, officers could no longer strike or flog sailors (or hang them, as one American captain did in 1842), but hand and leg irons, the straitjacket, or the sweatbox with a bread-and-water diet remained a handy response to any recalcitrance from Jack Tar. The war itself had also spurred additional shipping that sharpened competition for sailors with the merchant service, so the *Kearsarge*'s muster roll grew slowly.

Five weeks before his twenty-first birthday, a stocky textile worker named William Wainwright left his home in Exeter, New Hampshire, and took the cars for Portsmouth. That day—November 21, 1861—the Cheshire-born immigrant signed on as a coal heaver in William Cushman's engineer department, and that afternoon he returned to Exeter to tell his parents. Five days later he packed a duffel bag and headed for the navy yard, where he climbed aboard the *Kearsarge* for the first time. He discovered an old friend aboard the ship and chatted briefly with him, but the hammocks and galley were not yet ready for the crew members so Wainwright rowed back to Portsmouth to rent a room in a boardinghouse.

The next morning Wainwright went back aboard, finding the vessel crawling with machinists, riggers, and carpenters. To his dismay, he was chosen for the crew of the boat that plied back and forth from Portsmouth each day, transporting officers, and the assignment prompted him to register the first of many complaints that would litter his three-year journal of wartime service. The next day, November 28, he began his regular duties.[5]

Joining Wainwright that cold November day was Charles Poole, a housepainter from Bowdoinham, Maine, who had signed on as soon as he saw a poster appealing for men—also exaggerating his age slightly to an officer who probably cared little. Poole, too, shipped as a coal heaver for three years, and he was also picked to man the officer's boat. He, Wainwright, and a half-dozen other oarsmen pulled across the bay to the *Kearsarge* that morning and started wiping down the engines, which had not yet been started. That evening, back in Portsmouth, Poole secured a room at the City Hotel for $3.50 a week.[6]

By the first week in December the shipyard workforce had doubled again. The payroll included 2,134 names now, and most of those men lived on the Portsmouth side of the river. They swarmed over the ships, reconditioning and refitting old ones like the *Santee* and the *Sabine* even as the four new steamers lay under construction. On December 13 the *Portsmouth* went back into commission, and the next day a new double-ender steamer dipped into the water. Carpenters tore up the deck of the *Franklin*, a seventy-four-gun ship of the line built in 1815, in order to put an engine in her. Another old frigate, the *Alabama*, lay nearby.

Each morning Wainwright and Poole crossed the frigid river with their commissioned passengers, occasionally dodging dangerous chunks of ice and sharing the way with hundreds of little boats belonging to the workmen. During the day the boat's crew would be called on a couple of times to carry officers to the city and back, but the rest of the time they picked away at the white lead that coated the engines, or scrubbed at the rust that already pitted the polished metal. When the quitting bell rang, the sailors watched and chuckled as the 2,000 workmen dropped their planes, wrenches, and hammers to bolt for their boats like so many islanders fleeing a volcanic eruption.[7]

The rolls of the engineer department stood about half full when December opened, and on the first day of that month Chief Engineer Cushman decided to try the engines. Taking in some bags of coal for the test, he ordered the fires lighted at 9:00 A.M., and in two hours the gauge showed enough steam to engage the cylinders. For three hours the pistons thumped at fifty revolutions per minute, and for the first day since they came aboard the ship the engine-room crew did not suffer from the biting cold. At midafternoon Cushman called for the fires to be "hauled" and the boilers blown down; his remarks left Wainwright satisfied that the new engines had done fairly well, but Cushman managed to find some faults.[8]

With that relatively successful trial the crew began hoping for sailing orders. Their pay was not likely to begin until the ship headed for sea, for traditionally the "dead horse" time between shipping and sailing went unpaid. Then there was the biting wind and bitter cold, which only worsened as the month progressed, and some mornings it blew too hard for the boats to cross. In all but the worst weather the workmen sculled across for what they considered good wages, and the machinists kept tinkering with the *Kearsarge*'s engines under the supervision of a government inspector named Henderson, who—observed Coal Heaver Poole—seemed in no hurry to do anything save go home when the day's work ended. Each time the mechanics reassembled part of the machinery the engine-room crew would polish it back to its original shine, and the monotony and frustration of wasted effort began to take its inevitable toll on the men. They even worked on Christmas Day.[9]

The civilian employees grew dissatisfied, too, especially when the Navy Department dictated some new rules for Captain Pearson to implement. As the year waned, the commandant was authorized to decide what the "average" pay of the various classes of workmen might be, and to pay nothing more than that. He immediately cut the wages of laborers by 25 cents a day, and demanded that they start work at sunrise in order to make up for the shortage of daylight in late December. The 25-cent reduction hit hard for those who earned only $1.25 or $1.50 per day, and laborers under the age of nineteen were cut back to six bits a day. The workmen staged a rally, and when carpenters' wages were pared, those tradesmen struck, with about two dozen showing up for work of the 650 whom the yard employed. That sort of action was easy to handle, though: the commandant fired the leaders, and everyone else returned to work in a couple of days, albeit "under protest."[10]

The labor dispute did little to slow completion of the *Kearsarge*, which was already going slowly enough for those who belonged to that ship. Most of the remaining work, such as mounting the guns, could be done by the crew. While the civilians and the commandant squabbled over quarters, William Wainwright helped the deck hands bring aboard a 28-pounder rifle on January 14 and, over the next two days, four 32-pounder smoothbores (weighing 5,700 pounds apiece) and two immense black Dahlgren guns with 11-inch bores. Dozens of hands at the tackles lowered the ten-ton Dahlgren smoothbores onto pivot carriages amidships.[11]

Though the *Kearsarge* remained short of men, most of the senior officers had already been chosen. For his executive officer, Captain Pickering drew Lieutenant Thomas C. Harris, who had just celebrated the twentieth anniversary of his original appointment as a midshipman—which he had received the same day as Lieutenant Kell, of the *Sumter*. Harris had last sailed aboard the *Powhatan* as it skirted the Mississippi passes looking for Kell's new ship.[12]

In deference to the jealousy with which regular officers viewed the rank it had taken them so long to attain, the U.S. Navy issued volunteer officers special temporary grades with probationary titles. Instead of the rank of lieutenant, for instance, an experienced mariner might enter the service with the title of acting master or acting volunteer lieutenant. The *Kearsarge* was authorized two acting masters and four acting master's mates, but by the time the ship went into commission she had three of each. The chief of these was James R. Wheeler, a burly merchant captain of British birth who had made his home in Massachusetts. Wheeler was a little older than Pickering himself, and his assignment to the sloop predated the captain's by two days. So did that of Acting Master Eben Stoddard, another Bay State merchant sailor. The third of the acting masters, David H. Sumner, quickly earned the nickname "Old Man Sumner" from the crew. Of the three who signed on as master's mates, Pickering specifically asked for William Harper Yeaton, a native of nearby Stratham and a relative of one of the yard's supervisors. Yeaton was twenty-six years old and had been to sea for about four years altogether, coming home as mate of his last vessel. Captain Pearson signed the young man's appointment on December 17; two days later he approved Charles H. Danforth in the same grade, and just before the ship went into commission Pearson assigned Acting Master's Mate Ezra Bartlett—another Stratham native and the great-grandson of a man who had signed the Declaration of Independence.[13]

The sheer number of officers aboard the *Kearsarge* posed a problem for Pickering. There were eight commissioned officers who had to be accommodated with more spacious living quarters and eating facilities in the wardroom, and there were also eight "stateroom," or "steerage" officers.

Pickering had never served aboard a steamer before, with such a profusion of junior officers in the engineer department; while he found room enough for them in the forward cabins, he remained uncertain of what social standing the chief engineer should be accorded. Was he a steerage officer, along with his assistant engineers, or a wardroom officer like the master's mates? The shipboard alignment of social standing ran from the stern forward: the captain occupied the cabin aft, the wardroom sat forward of that, and so on, as far as the lowly sailors who slept beneath the forecastle. Ultimately Secretary Welles assigned the forward port stateroom to Cushman, explaining that that was the custom in steamers of the *Kearsarge* class. The engineers apparently lobbied for more sumptuous culinary arrangements than the regulations allowed, but Welles decreed that they and the other steerage officers all formed one mess on ships of that size, with one cook and three servants, and if Cushman's officers desired to segregate themselves from the others in steerage they would have to bear the cost out of their own pockets.[14]

The enlistments that had initially come day by day petered out as the fourth week of January opened, and Pickering realized fewer than half the complement of 160 that he had envisioned. Taking the initiative, Cushman went right into the streets of Portsmouth looking for recruits for his engine room. Not until January 24 did Secretary Welles telegraph the commandant at Boston with orders to let the *Kearsarge* have a crew, and late that afternoon a tugboat pulled into the harbor with eighty-one recruits from the Charlestown Navy Yard. Once they had clambered aboard the ship, Captain Pickering ordered the colors and the ship's pennant hoisted. These banners slid up the yards, and Pickering declared the ship in commission. That was the extent of the ceremony, and everyone returned to work; the engines never even stopped churning for the occasion.[15]

In part, Pickering blamed the paucity of recruits on the Navy Department, which threatened to renege on its promise to pay the men from the date they had enlisted. Posters pinned to the walls of Boston and Portsmouth recruiting stations announced that those who signed up would be able to draw pay and allotments for family members from the day their names went on the books, but the paymaster received no such authority from Washington. Pickering pleaded with the commandant to sort out the situation with Secretary Welles, in order that he should not be plagued with desertion by men who felt cheated, and Welles finally replied that any who had enlisted after December 23 would be treated as promised.[16]

Wainwright, Poole, and the others who had come aboard in November discovered that they had donated several weeks of their time, however. Most of them wrote the loss off to experience, though, noting in new diaries that they had "shipped for it," for good or ill, but one recruit decided that he had made a mistake and took steps to correct it. On the morning of January 27 the crewmen strode up the gangplank, their seabags on their shoulders, to finally take permanent lodging on the ship: missing from the few dozen who came aboard that day was a nineteen-year-old landsman named John Coalter.[17]

Those who did take to the ship did not like what they found. The *Kearsarge* was still a mess, with lumber and stores strewn about the decks. Half-bent sails hung from the yards. No one had made provisions for a meal, so the crew went hungry on its first night aboard ship. Nor did the landlubbers among them sleep well during their first night in hammocks: Marine Corporal Austin Quinby, a farmboy from landlocked Sandwich, New Hampshire, slung his canvas bed on the berth deck and leaped into it, only to tumble out on the far side. After several repetitions he managed to keep to the hammock and even sleep a little until the clews at his feet gave way, dropping him to the deck again. He rehung the hammock and enjoyed a short but cold sleep until, at midnight, he was called to stand his four-hour watch on deck. The mercury stood at eight degrees below zero, Quinby claimed, but he found some artificial warmth: sailors had worked the bung out of a barrel of whiskey that had been left unstowed near the gangway. By virtue of a dipper hidden in the hammock nettings Quinby enjoyed periodic solace until turning below at 4:00, brazenly sharing his discovery with a grateful officer of the deck, Mr. Sumner.[18]

With the dawn, shivering sailors and Marines jumped into frozen boots and began stowing supplies again, some of them shoveling coal into the bunkers and coating the ship in a thick jacket of black dust. All the while the steam engines ground away, fitting the moving parts to their brass bearings. The first of February brought signs of impending departure, though, as the last of the coal and stores went into the hold. Deck hands bent the last sail to its yard, and the paymaster doled out advance pay while a light snow covered the coal-blackened ship. The pace of preparations accelerated, and on February 3 William Wainwright asked Chief Engineer Cushman for a few hours' liberty so he could walk over to the Portsmouth mill for a final visit with his father and younger brother. Richard Vincent, whose three weeks as a coal heaver had soured him on navy life, took this last opportunity to get away from the ship, and the deck officer noticed that he was missing during the first dog watch.[19]

While crewmen said their goodbyes—either to their families or to their more trustworthy shipmates—Captain Pickering made his own final arrangements. He sent the sick ashore, sought the discharge of a first-class fireman because the surgeon found him to be epileptic, and (as Coal Heaver Wainwright enjoyed his last liberty at home) sought a replacement for the ship's chronometer, which had suddenly stopped. The timepiece had endured the explosion of an ordnance warehouse, and the blast had evidently jarred it worse than anyone supposed. The next day, February 4, Pickering finally ascertained the day from which the enlisted men's pay would accrue. Tying up his paperwork, he asked for another Marine to take the place of one who had come down with measles, and from the barracks ashore came John Batchelder, a Portsmouth boy. At last, at 10:00 on the morning of February 5, a pilot came aboard, and a couple of seamen cast the *Kearsarge*'s mooring hawsers onto the wharf. For the first time the chief engineer engaged the propeller, and the new cruiser began backing away from the dock.[20]

A crowd had gathered on shore to see the maiden voyage of Portsmouth's latest production. By 11:00 the ship had turned around and started down the river, where guns boomed in salute as she approached Fort Constitution. Acting Master Wheeler, who held the deck trumpet, ordered the compliment returned with a few blank cartridges, and he sent the crew into the rigging to offer three cheers. Once outside the harbor he ordered full speed from the engine room, "to see what she could do." What she could do was about ten knots, which seemed a fair enough clip. After this initial sprint Henderson, the yard superintendent who had overseen installation of the engines, gave them a last look while the crew ate a lunch of bean soup and hardtack. He found them satisfactory, and at 2:00 a boat picked up both Henderson and the pilot. For another hour the *Kearsarge* steamed around within sight of Rye Beach before passing five miles south of the Isle of Shoals. By 3:00 the sloop was in the open sea.[21]

James Bulloch had returned to the Confederacy just as Captain Pickering started advertising for men to serve on the *Kearsarge*. He steamed into Savannah, Georgia, aboard the blockade-runner *Fingal*, coming by way of Bermuda. After reporting briefly at Richmond, Bulloch went back to Savannah to see the *Fingal* loaded with cotton to be applied to the Confederate navy's foreign accounts when the ship returned to England. The Union navy hung just off the coast, though, and Christmas passed with no hope of slipping away. At last Navy Secretary Stephen Mallory told Bulloch to make his way to England any way he could and take command of one of the cruisers he was building there; with those instructions Mallory enclosed Bulloch's formal commission as a commander.

Bulloch balked at the promotion, arguing that too many other officers had stood above him in the old service and would feel slighted to find themselves passed over, but he made no complaint whatever about the orders to take one of the cruisers to sea. That had been his fervent wish, and Mallory had already promised him that he might have the first ship, the *Oreto*, which they now called the *Manassas*. Bulloch feared that ship would get to sea before he returned, however, as it nearly did, and he asked for the second, larger vessel known as the 290. Mallory assented, but still Bulloch could not escape Savannah. At last he accepted an offer to sail for England aboard the *Annie Childs*, which then lay at Wilmington, North Carolina, taking on cargo. Bulloch leaped at the chance; while the *Kearsarge* went into commission at its berth in the Piscataqua River, Bulloch took the train north with some officers he had asked for.[22]

Chief among those officers whom Bulloch requested was John Low, a Scottish-born British subject who had come to Savannah before the war. Although he had just turned twenty-six, he was a well-trained mariner, but he had enlisted as a cavalryman at the outbreak of hostilities. The Navy Department secured his discharge from that branch and sent him to England to help Bulloch, who had put him aboard the *Fingal* as second officer when they returned to the South.[23]

Clarence R. Yonge also accompanied Bulloch to Wilmington. Yonge, who was twenty-eight, had done rather well for himself over the past few years as a clerk for the Savannah, Albany, & Gulf Railroad. He left behind a twenty-year-old wife when he departed Savannah, as well as $4,000 in personal property. The couple had buried an infant son only the previous summer; they had had another, but Yonge's attachment to his family had evidently waned. Bulloch had taken him on as his clerk at $500 a year, but he had also given him a tentative commission as an acting assistant paymaster. The sandy-bearded Yonge had proven efficient enough as a clerk at the Savannah naval station in the first months of the war, but his devotion to the Southern cause was not well seated.[24]

Two midshipmen joined these three at Wilmington. Edward Maffitt Anderson of Georgia had only held his commission two months when he arrived, as had his cousin Eugene Anderson Maffitt, who followed on January 30. These two would serve together for more than two years, and their similar names would confuse historians for more than a century. Maffitt had served ashore as a volunteer in coastal forts, but theirs was a naval family; when the *Oreto*-cum-*Manassas* finally took to the sea as the *Florida*, it would sail under Eugene Maffitt's father.[25]

By January 30 the *Annie Childs* lay along the wharf at Wilmington, ready for sea with a hold full of cotton, resin, and tobacco, plus whatever passengers dared risk the run. At the mouth of Cape Fear three Union vessels with a total of a dozen guns among them, the *Mount Vernon*, the *Monticello*, and the *Chippewa*, hovered like low, black vultures, waiting for blockade runners. At high water on February 1 the *Annie Childs* slipped downriver to Orton Point, twelve miles above the cape, where the blockaders could not yet turn a glass upon her, and Bulloch borrowed a boat from the local army commander. Daily he and the captain of the *Annie Childs* rowed down for a glimpse of the three Federal steamers, two of which appeared to sit on duty at any given moment while another cruised the neighboring inlets.[26]

For four nights the skies remained too clear to slip past them, but around noon on February 5 clouds started rolling in. In the afternoon the captain ordered steam, and at 10:00 that night the *Annie Childs* crept toward the main shipping channel, moving slowly enough that she would not round the cape until after the moon set. The moon went down shortly after midnight, and at 12:15 the low, sleek steamer crossed the bar under the cover of low fog, with stars shining overhead. An engine bearing heated up just then, and the captain had to shut down his engine for an anxious half-hour, but no gunboats showed up to nab the prey: later that night, unaware that two of the three Yankee ships had sailed for coal at Hampton Roads, Bulloch remarked in his diary that the blockading fleet "must have been fast asleep." As soon as the bearing had cooled, the *Annie Childs* lost herself in a heavy drizzle; her helmsman turned her confidently toward the Gulf Stream, and England.[27]

At dawn of February 5 Raphael Semmes awoke in the cabin of the *Sumter*, which lay at anchor in the harbor at Gibraltar. Seven months had passed since his escape from the Mississippi Delta, and during those months he had captured eighteen U.S. merchant vessels. Of these, seven had been impounded by Cuban authorities and returned to their owners. Two more had been retaken by the enemy, costing Semmes the prize crews with which he manned them, while he released two more on ransom bond because they carried cargo owned by citizens of neutral nations. Seven of the ships he had burned, beginning with the *Golden Rocket* and ending with the Massachusetts bark *Neapolitan*, which Semmes had fired on January 18 within sight of the lighthouse at Gibraltar.[28]

The *Sumter* had seen hard days between these captures. Storms had played havoc with her fragile frame, and shortly after the first of the year she had limped into the ancient harbor at Cadiz with empty bunkers, wheezing boilers, and dangerous leaks at her propeller sleeve and bowports. Timid Spanish officials had greeted the Confederate vessel tersely, initially ordering her out within twenty-four hours, but, when Semmes testified to the *Sumter*'s unseaworthiness, the queen's ministers had allowed him a few days to make repairs. The normally lackadaisical carpenters of the nearby navy yard outdid themselves, plugging most of the leaks within three days, whereupon the local governor ("a bull-headed, stupid official," thought Semmes) peremptorily ordered the ship out of the port. Semmes objected that his engine also needed repairs, and his ship's frame was badly weakened, but the governor insisted. On the afternoon of January 17 the *Sumter* sailed out of Cadiz, leaving behind a dozen deserters. The Spanish governor's order indirectly consigned the *Neapolitan* to the flames and brought the *Sumter* to the great fortified rock that marked this fragment of the British empire in Andalusia.[29]

British authorities proved more hospitable than the Spanish, who appeared to fear the wrath of the United States. On his first afternoon at the colony Semmes paid a visit to the governor, Lieutenant General Sir William Codrington. Once the captain assured Codrington that he did not intend to use Gibraltar as a base for forays against American vessels, the *Sumter* earned the welcome of the port. If the ship needed repairs, she enjoyed the use of whatever private facilities she could find. Resupply and refitting would take money, though, and Semmes went ashore almost daily thereafter to visit the post office, where he expected to receive funds from England. As each day passed without the desired packet, he would avail himself of late newspapers in the military library for news from home and information about Federal cruisers. A week into his sojourn at this port he received an urgent telegram from Lieutenant James H. North, the Confederate naval agent in London who had taken over during Bulloch's absence. North told him to leave off any repairs to his machinery and to wait there at Gibraltar for further instructions that were coming by mail.

Semmes spent another week waiting for that letter. His remaining crewmen worked on the ship's rigging and made a survey of the boilers and engines, while Semmes made frequent visits ashore, checking the mail and the papers. One Thursday he toured the great citadel overlooking the harbor in company with Lieutenant Colonel Arthur Fremantle of the Coldstream Guards. Fremantle was the governor's secretary and, according to Semmes, "an ardent Confederate." So ardent was this Englishman that, of the two of them, Fremantle would be the next to set foot on Confederate soil.[30]

North's promised instructions reached Semmes on February 2, as he sauntered ashore. Since the *Sumter* was no longer serviceable, the Confederate commissioner in London had decided to send Semmes the first of Commander Bulloch's new ships abuilding on the Mersey. Semmes quickly composed a telegram to North, warning him not to send the ship; he would come for it. He thought better of telegraphing such a message, though, and instead wrote North a letter. The next day drafts worth $16,000 arrived from

England, with which Semmes hoped to buy coal and escape to sea, but he soon found that none of the coal yards at Gibraltar would sell him coal: the American consul, Horatio Sprague, had buzzed around those coal yards, cajoling or intimidating the merchants into refusing the Confederate ship. On February 5 Semmes sent Lieutenant Kell to the governor with a request to buy a few tons from public stockpiles, but the governor doubted his authority to do that. Stymied, the anxious captain cast about desperately, offering bribes of up to $2 a ton.

As the disabled little cruiser bobbed at anchor, the crew grew restless, too. One afternoon Semmes returned from a visit ashore to find that his coxswain had deserted, leaving the boat's crew drunk. In that condition they pulled him back to the ship, and eleven men on liberty failed to come aboard that night. Semmes was ashore discussing the legalities of apprehending the crew with Governor Codrington when Codrington received a telegram that the new U.S. gunboat *Tuscarora* was standing into the harbor. By noontime she had anchored near the *Sumter*, dwarfing the tired little Confederate steamer. Semmes would be going nowhere for a while.[31]

CHAPTER THREE

Into the Tempest

Oh! ye state-room sailors, who make so much ado
about a fourteen days' passage across the Atlantic.
—Melville, *Typee*

N o one aboard the *Kearsarge* except the commander and his first lieutenant knew whither they were bound. Captain Pickering's original orders had directed him to the Gulf of Mexico for blockade duty, but in mid-January the Navy Department learned of the *Sumter*'s presence at Cadiz, so on January 18 Gideon Welles had instructed Pickering to head for that place. Six days later Welles reminded the commandant at Portsmouth to get the *Kearsarge* to sea quickly, and to have Pickering stop in the Azores in case the *Sumter* had slipped back that way. As the new sloop of war left the Isle of Shoals behind, Pickering therefore gave the officer of the deck a bearing of east-southeast, for the Gulf Stream.[1]

That first afternoon out, the deck crew kept busy securing the two big anchors on the bows and laying out spare chain. Though the air still hung chilly at twenty-six degrees, that felt a lot better than the wind-whipped single digits that the recruits had endured at Portsmouth, and the temperature rose steadily: it held right at the freezing point all day on February 6. But while the temperature improved, the weather simultaneously deteriorated: the barometer stood at 31.70 inches at noon on the sixth, falling to 29.90 in the next eight hours; by 8:00 on the morning of the seventh it had dropped to 29.44 inches. Acting Master Eben Stoddard noted in the log at 6:30 that morning that they had entered the Gulf Stream, where he found the weather "very bad."[2]

Stoddard made his observation with typical New England understatement. With nothing but water in sight the *Kearsarge* bounced about like a shuttlecock (said her yeoman), pitching and rolling so that her yardarms dipped into the water. Heavy seas filled the waist boats, buckling their davits and drooping them low against the bulwarks. The ship's cutter swamped as the lee side rolled nearly into the water, and the waves wrenched the cutter away with the dinghy and a good many oars nestled inside it, uprooting iron stanchions in the hammock nettings to which the cutter's straps had been fastened. A dozen or more new hammocks floated out to be swept away as the cutter and dinghy drifted out of reach, and Mr. Stoddard bellowed through the trumpet to save the launch, which hung on the weather side. Sailors wrestled desperately with this boat, dragging it inboard and lashing it down, but not before it was badly stove against the rail. If anything should happen to the ship now, there remained but two smaller quarter boats, and Captain Pickering observed that they were so awkwardly stowed that it would take a perilously long time to float them.[3]

To those aboard the *Kearsarge*, the possibility of the ship going down without hope of rescue loomed all too near. Some said their prayers aloud, but the pious old yeoman, Carsten DeWit, complained that curses echoed the companionways even as they supposed their last sun had set. John Lambert, a middle-aged fireman who had spent a few years in the bowels of a ship, later related to DeWit how an abject terror overcame him during that first gale. Others cared little whether the ship sank or not, though, for even the most experienced hands fell dreadfully seasick. For those on their first voyage the malady was more than they could bear, and more than one remarked that he would just as soon be thrown overboard. Pickering himself was not immune, nor were the majority of his officers. Corporal Quinby of the Marines no sooner ate or drank anything than it came back up: "All you had to do was to open your mouth and let it out," he wrote. Charles Poole could not get that far, for his rations disgusted him so that he could not swallow them.[4]

Seasickness notwithstanding, the ship required that all hands stand their watches. The gale continued through the night, with water gushing over the rail and cascading off the forecastle to the spar deck as though, said Quinby, from a mill dam. Crewmen spent their four-hour shifts in wet clothing, and water washed onto the berth deck over hatch combings that proved far too shallow. The fire-room hatches aft were too low by a foot and a half, and each wave that broke over the waist rail doused the fires, so the chief engineer had that hatch battened even though that left the engine room insufferably hot. Spillover also threatened the magazine and flooded the captain's cabin from two separate leaks. Pickering called for wooden gratings so he could walk about his quarters, but, as violently as the ship rolled, he had to wear rubber boots anyway. Nor did the storm abate on the morning of the eighth, or the ninth; if anything, the wind increased during the night of the ninth, with huge waves hammering the vessel so unmercifully that it shuddered from stem to stern. The next morning one great sea slammed into the starboard bow and carried away the "head"—the sailors' latrine—with all its fixtures, smashing up the hammock nettings at the same moment. Thereafter those who went forward for the calls of nature came away drenched, and everyone serving before the mast slept in wet hammocks. To seal their misery, the galley had been fitted with a stovepipe too small to create enough draft, and the enlisted men suffered through their off-duty hours amid a pall of smoke that filled the berth deck.[5]

Engineer Cushman shut the engines down for a time that day to let them cool, and the next afternoon the deck officer hove the ship to, aiming her head into the seas. Mr. Sumner discovered a sail to the north toward dusk that day; they saw few other ships during the passage, and any one of them may have been the *Annie Childs* with its five Confederate naval officers, who ran into the same storm in that latitude. By now they had escaped the Roaring Forties, and the wind died a little. The lull permitted Captain Pickering to order the daily grog ration served, and most of the crew queued up for a tot of watered rum. Even cabin boys fell into line for their dram, and Ezra Bartlett watched in fascination as "Boys of 12 & 15 years of age" swallowed the warm, bitter draft with no more change of expression than the oldest salts.[6]

Bartlett underestimated the ages of his subjects. Navy officers had no qualms about signing up boys well below the age of consent; no formal minimums applied as they did in the army, so runaway youths of twelve or fifteen had no need to falsify their ages to get a berth, but the three youngest crewmen on the *Kearsarge* were sixteen years old. Only one of them, James O. Stone, served as a "boy." The other two ranked as landsmen, including the smallest sailor on the ship, 4′9″ James F. Hayes, who had grown up near the Charlestown Navy Yard.

Nor were there any maximum age limits in the naval service. Yeoman DeWit was fifty-four, and Quartermaster James Saunders admitted to fifty-three. Unlike DeWit, Saunders served on deck, where he earned no special privileges for his age and his long service: quartermaster warrants were assigned from cruise to cruise, and the captain could have disrated Saunders to seaman, ordinary seaman, or even landsman if he chose, forcing him to climb the rigging in a hurricane alongside sprouts like Hayes.

Saunders looked the part of an old sailor, with his grey hair and beard and the lady's bust tattooed on his right forearm: tattooing was almost exclusively a sailor's habit at that time, and nearly a third of the crew sported at least one, including little Jimmy Hayes. Like many who shipped before the mast, Quartermaster Saunders was rather short—only 5′4½″ tall. Deck hands on the *Kearsarge* tended to be diminutive (at least those for whom descriptive rolls survive); in an age when the average male was about 5′8″ tall, the sailors in this crew averaged only 5′3¾″. The engine-room crew stood 5′6″ on average, and the Marines almost 5′7″. Corporal Quinby, who lacked an inch of 6′, was the tallest enlisted man on the ship. Captain Pickering stood 6′ even, and most of the other officers and petty officers likewise ranged a couple of inches taller than their subordinates.[7]

The navy did not discriminate by race any more than by age. When the *Kearsarge* left Portsmouth, she carried 23 officers and 143 enlisted men, and at least 14 of those 143 bore some measure of African blood in their veins. Two had signed on as cooks and 2 as stewards, but most served as landsmen (the lowest rating for deck hands) or as cabin boys and stewards who had been promoted to the rate of landsmen for pay purposes. Only 1, Joachim Pease, was rated a full seaman. Aside from the 13 crewmen whom the enrolling officers described as Negro, black, mulatto, or colored, a few others aboard the *Kearsarge* betrayed a mixed pedigree. Chief among these were Francis Viannah and Sabine DeSanto, whom Yeoman DeWit characterized as "black Portuguese," and Manuel Lewis, whom the yeoman simply called "a darkey." All 3 probably showed signs of the Moorish influence in their homeland, though at least Viannah was born in the Azores.[8]

Over a couple of days the storm subsided to what Acting Master Wheeler called "pleasant gales." On February 15 the engineer department disconnected the propeller shaft and left it freewheeling as sails alone carried the vessel east-southeastward. The *Kearsarge*'s propeller did not lift out of the water and acted as something of a drag, but the ship still made eleven knots in the fairest winds without the assistance of the engines; under steam alone she could barely exceed eight knots. After a few hours the wind died so low that the officer of the deck ordered the shaft recoupled, and the engines resumed their deep, rhythmic hum.[9]

The next day was Sunday, and the sea remained sufficiently calm that Captain Pickering called for his first inspection at quarters, but he refrained from requiring practice at general quarters because the ship still rolled too precariously to cast the guns loose. Later the wind picked up again, and for the next three days the *Kearsarge* plowed through a stronger storm than the first one. Seas ran "mountain high," Corporal Quinby recorded, and spray blew as high as the yardarm as each wave broke over the bows. Wheeler ordered everyone to stay aft during the evening watch on February 17, lest anyone be washed overboard, and when a Marine started forward in spite of those instructions, Wheeler chased after him, only to be knocked down himself by a great sea that left him struggling in a foot of water.[10]

All the ship's vulnerable appendages had already been dashed into the sea in the first gale, and this storm damaged nothing more topside, but a leak from some unknown source began filling the bilges. On February 17 alone, the pumps disgorged eleven inches of water. The next morning leaks were discovered in two of the freshwater tanks, too, and the deck officer had their remaining contents pumped into sound tanks. The leaking tanks had absorbed some of the salinated bilgewater, though, spoiling what was left in them; and when the captain of the hold topped off the other tanks with the tainted water, he ruined that, too. The *Kearsarge* had left Portsmouth with 4,000 gallons of fresh water, of which the crew had consumed almost half, but before officers detected their mistake another 1,610 gallons had been contaminated. That left the entire ship with only 300 gallons: that is, less than 2 gallons per man.[11]

The want of water proved especially inconvenient to those on the sick list, which now contained thirty names. Most of those suffering from seasickness had recovered, but diarrhea and respiratory afflictions had swollen the surgeon's list; now, some Marines had come down with measles.

With problems enough of his own, Captain Pickering neglected to even hail—let alone overhaul—a big steamer that passed close by the next evening. It caught him by surprise, bounding along west-by-north under full sail, and it was too dark even to identify her ensign. Those on and off duty crowded onto the forecastle deck in spite of the weather to catch a glimpse of the graceful sight, and with the dawn of February 19 Pickering posted a lookout at the masthead to call out sails as they approached.[12]

By her course, officers judged that the other steamer was bound for the Azores—the Western Islands, as they called them. Pickering was supposed to have stopped there to inquire after the *Sumter*, but the storms had driven him off course and he could not double back now with so little water. The nearest haven lay at Madeira, an island 500 miles off the coast of Africa, and there the captain turned his ship. The ocean struck one last lick on the twentieth, as though determined to drown the *Kearsarge* and all aboard, but February 21 dawned clear and warm. Thirst was the only enemy now, as the sun came out to bake the decks dry. Finally, on the morning of Washington's birthday, the lookout sighted landfall two points off the port bow and cried it out. The helmsman veered in that direction, and by early afternoon the deck hands could see the island from the forecastle, with a vast rainbow arching across it from end to end. It was 5:00 before they passed into the harbor at Funchal, and 6:30 before the anchor clattered into the bay.[13]

The American consul came aboard immediately to brief Captain Pickering on the whereabouts of the *Sumter*, which was still reported to rest at Gibraltar. Chief Engineer Cushman offered a report on the ship's machinery that sounded more alarming than the situation warranted, but the captain dared not continue until Cushman had modified the crankshaft, overhauled the saltwater feed pump and the distilling apparatus, and repaired the starboard blower engine. The engineer reminded Pickering of the low hatch combings that kept the engine room awash, and said he would clean and caulk the boilers and grind the valves while the other work was under way. He judged it would all take five days, and Pickering decided to give him that much time.[14]

The crew, meanwhile, gathered on the forecastle for a look at what, for most of them, was the first foreign soil they had ever seen. Verdant hills, covered in grape vines and speckled here and there with bright white houses, rose high out of the sea. The air was as warm as a New England summer, and homesick Yankees drank deep of the island's green scent. They imbibed nothing else that night, suffering even worse now as the water casks rang empty, and gushing cataracts that washed down the mountainsides right before them only piqued their craving. By morning they had slaked their thirst, though, and the *Kearsarge* was encircled by bumboats full of Portuguese islanders hawking oranges, figs, bananas, loaves of bread, and assortments of nuts. The islanders excelled in the tatting of fine lace, and a dealer offered cuffs, collars, and shawls for the mothers and sweethearts back in the States. Others held up the lap desks, jewelry boxes, and artificial flowers they had made. Some of them spoke English, showing great disappointment when someone explained that few of those aboard the ship owned any money. Tobacco proved a tempting medium, though, and William Wainwright found that he could buy virtually anything he wanted with it; sailors dropped an occasional scrap of plug into the water just to watch the younger bumboatmen dive for it. Charles Poole discovered that his old clothes served as sound currency, too, and he unloaded the more threadbare items in his wardrobe in return for a fat supply of groceries.[15]

Captain Pickering hired some Portuguese carpenters to help Carpenter's Mate Mark Ham repair the head railings and the smashed hammock nettings on the ship's side. The engine-room crew worried the ship's engine apart while deck hands shoveled the coal, but everyone longed to go ashore and sit under the shade of the orange trees—most of the new men little realizing how seldom that privilege would be granted. Orderly Sergeant Charles Young of the Marines did obtain leave to visit the island, where he had stopped sometime before during his long service. The surgeon's steward, George Tittle, accompanied the sergeant, who set out for a few drinks and some feminine companionship, both of which he found forthwith. The two returned to the ship "pretty full," said Corporal Quinby, and the back of the sergeant's coat bore the handprints of his lady friend, whom Tittle described as an old acquaintance.[16]

The captain had said he would give his chief engineer five days, and five days he waited. Hammers clanged in the belly of the ship throughout the night of February 26, and at 6:30 on the twenty-seventh the boatswain called all hands to man the capstan and raise the anchor. The water tanks were full, the coal bunkers were partially replenished, the privy and the bulwarks behind it had been rebuilt, and the *Sumter* lay within reach. At 7:00 the *Kearsarge* put to sea, and almost immediately the ocean turned against them, headwinds buffeting the canvas and heavy seas dashing over the rail, driving everyone below who did not have duty on deck. Landlubbers just recovering from a week or ten days of seasickness quickly found the shallow-keeled ship's rolling annoying, and some of them suffered a relapse.

First, Pickering struck for Cadiz. Now the lookout kept sharp watch, for any sail might be the *Sumter*. On the last day of February the deck officer raised his trumpet and spoke the first vessel hailed by the *Kearsarge*, which turned out to be an English merchantman bound for Brazil. Four sails appeared at once the next day: knowing the prey to be a bark like their own—with square-rigged fore- and mainmasts, and fore-and-aft rigged mizzenmast—the officer on duty went straight to the one that fit that description, but she turned out to be a Spaniard from Cadiz.

Rough seas worsened on March 2. An electrical storm illuminated the masts through the night, and by morning the storm grew strong enough that men new to the sea again remarked that this was "the worst yet." Again the officer with the bullhorn hove the ship to. Mountainous waves lifted her high into the air, then dropped her into chasms fathoms deep. Crewmen one and all endured another drenching, and some of the Catholics took comfort in their rosaries. Coal Heaver Wainwright knew now that he had made a terrible mistake, and fervently wished himself home, underscoring the words "Oh dear" in his journal even before the gale peaked. At the height of it a ship scudded by two miles away on the *Kearsarge*'s weather quarter without an inch of canvas on her yards, but those on deck could only see her when a wave lifted their own craft out of a trough.

It was a happy lookout who sighted land again just before noon on March 4. The sea had calmed now, and the chill ocean air blew away before warm coastal breezes. From the forecastle the deck hands finally spotted it—the long, low shelf of the Iberian Peninsula, lifting into mountains deep in the interior. Then the glaring white city of Cadiz appeared, atop its sheer seawall. The captain signaled for a pilot, who came out in due time, and the first transatlantic voyage of the *Kearsarge* ended when the anchor plunged into Cadiz harbor at 4:00.[17]

Ebenezer Eggleston, the American consul at Cadiz, strutted aboard the next day dressed in the full uniform of a U.S. naval captain, plumes and all. The *Sumter* had been here, he warned, but had passed on to Gibraltar. Pickering already knew that much, and the crewmen learned the same from the bumboats that descended upon this latest ship to arrive. The sailors guessed that "the Rock" would be their next stop, but first their skipper wanted to ship a full load of coal in case it came down to a chase. Coal was short in Cadiz just then, but Pickering waited, using the afternoon to exercise his gun crews for the first time. In slow motion, with copious instruction from the gunner and his mates, men who had never seen such large guns practiced casting them loose, drawing them back to load, and rolling them out the gaps in the bulwarks. Another session ensued the next day, after the ship dropped down to the coaling wharves. With a potential fight only a day or two away, this was a late start, but there was nothing to do for it except to squeeze in every moment's drill that calm seas allowed.[18]

The Spanish coal yard could not satisfy the *Kearsarge* altogether, but Pickering took what he could get and sailed out of the harbor as the sun rose on March 7. The day broke bright and gorgeous on the Gulf of Cadiz. No one aboard the *Kearsarge* knew that events in Virginia would mark this as the last day in the age of wooden warships—they would not even realize it when the news of the ironclad combat at Hampton Roads reached them— but they did sense something in the offing. As they rounded Cape Trafalgar and entered the Straits of Gibraltar, the deck officer called the men to general quarters, and this time when they ran out the guns, live ammunition came up from the magazine. Slowly, carefully, Gunner Franklin Graham and his mates showed the crews how to sponge the tubes of their guns, one man holding the firing vent closed with his thumbstall to prevent a premature discharge. Without targets there was little sense aiming, but this was still basic instruction, and it was enough just to convey the procedure for priming and firing the pieces. Each crew fired a round or two: even the 11-inch Dahlgrens were swung around for an expensive practice shot, the recoil shuddering the deck and deafening the crew, echoing off the steep shores of Morocco and Spain. Today or tomorrow, they supposed, might be the day that would immortalize them.[19]

Neither that day nor the next would offer any opportunity for fame, however. The ship passed through the straits with a tall African peak visible off the starboard quarter, and by late afternoon the Rock of Gibraltar stood off the port rail. At 7:00 that evening the harbor lay in view, and rockets arched up from the deck of the *Kearsarge* as a signal to the *Tuscarora*, which was still supposed to lie at Algeciras. The other vessel's reply soon burned through the sky, and the *Kearsarge* headed in, anchoring quietly on the Spanish side near the *Tuscarora*.[20]

The next afternoon the *Kearsarge* steamed the nine miles over to Gibraltar, passing within pistol range of the sad-looking *Sumter* and anchoring a hundred yards astern of her. Sailors who had been expecting a more worthy opponent seemed disgusted with their first look at the ship they had dreamt about. Her guns looked puny alongside their own big Dahlgrens, and over-all the transformed packet presented a rather seedy sight after seven weeks at anchor. One man aboard the Federal vessel had seen the *Sumter* before, and found her little changed: Charles Fisher, the wardroom officers' black cook and a former crewman on a Mississippi steamboat, had seen the *Habana* in New Orleans in April of 1861, just as the Confederates set to work upon her. Officers and crewmen of the respective vessels glared at one another, but the Federal mariners outnumbered their counterparts by three to one, so deeply had desertion dug into Semmes's manpower: less than half his original crew remained. The Stars and Bars still flew from the mizzen, however, and a grinning Confederate boat's crew passed defiantly back and forth under the bows of the *Kearsarge*. Come nightfall the boisterous strains of "Dixie" broke out on the deck of the *Sumter*, which the *Kearsarge* answered with "The Star Spangled Banner" and "Columbia, the Gem of the Ocean."[21]

Captain Pickering's purpose in visiting Gibraltar probably included intimidation of the *Sumter* crew, in which aim he may have been disappointed, but he also sought to speak with Consul Sprague. In addition to Sprague, the captain found James DeLong, the American consul from Tangier, visiting at the Rock. DeLong came aboard the *Kearsarge* for dinner, where he entertained Pickering with his version of a controversy that he had recently provoked by arresting the paymaster of the *Sumter* and another Confederate citizen when they stepped ashore in Morocco.

Captain Semmes had sent his paymaster, Henry Myers, on a mission to Cadiz to secure a load of coal. Thomas T. Tunstall, an Alabamian who had spent five years as the U.S. consul at that city until his resignation in 1861, volunteered to accompany Myers to offer whatever personal influence he might bring to bear. The French vessel on which they embarked stopped at Tangier, and Myers—a former officer in the U.S. Navy—wandered on shore to visit a friend there who was reported to be ill. Tunstall went with him, and Consul DeLong ordered both of them arrested. Moroccan authorities performed the arrest, and a volunteer lieutenant in charge of the U.S. storeship *Ino* carried the prisoners to sea after braving a mob of outraged British subjects with his armed escort. Trussed in irons the entire time, the two prisoners were transferred to an American bark bound for Boston, where they were eventually lodged in Fort Warren.[22]

The Lincoln administration was just recovering from a diplomatic crisis over the illegal arrest of two Confederate emissaries from a neutral ship at sea, but DeLong defended his actions on the grounds that Morocco, the United States, and other "Christian" powers had signed a treaty allowing foreign consuls jurisdiction over their own citizens. That, he argued, circumvented Moroccan neutrality. Raphael Semmes circulated lengthy letters to the British chargé d'affaires at Tangier, chastising him for his failure to interfere, and to the Confederate commissioners in London and Paris, asking them to pressure the governments there for assistance. Myers and Tunstall were not citizens of the United States but of the Confederate States, he claimed, and they should also have enjoyed the protection of the French flag under which they sailed.[23]

Captain Pickering took DeLong's side, advising the U.S. minister at Madrid that the Tangier consul ought to be supported. In order to offer some backing of his own, Pickering decided to pay Tangier a visit. His ship arrived off the fortified city at 4:00 P.M. March 10, firing a nine-gun salute to the American consul that startled not only the Moors in their boats but the engine-room crew on the *Kearsarge*. Wishing perhaps to impress the natives with the thunder of Yankee ordnance, Pickering followed this with a twenty-one-gun salute to Morocco itself.

The forts responded in kind as the consul led most of the naval officers to his house for wine and victuals. The crewmen teemed at the rails to barter with the inevitable boatmen, whom they found fascinating and mysterious with their topknots and vivid caftans. The rather Puritan Yeoman DeWit noted that Moorish women veiled all but their eyes in deference to modesty, yet bared their calves in baggy knee-pants. Charles Poole could not easily distinguish between the men and the women as he traded with them for fruit, and William Wainwright judged them the "hardest-looking" people he ever saw. Corporal Quinby claimed that some of the Moors came aboard to peddle oranges, one old man bringing along a "Nigger wench" whom he also tried to sell. The old man shuffled away quite dejected, said Quinby, when he learned that the United States was "not in the slave trade."[24]

Though they remained in the harbor overnight, the enlisted men saw nothing more of Tangier than a distant glimpse of the citadel. The following day Captain Pickering and the wardroom officers came back aboard, ordering the anchor up and the ship turned for Algeciras.

That night the *Kearsarge* lost her first crewman. Sabine DeSanto, the Portuguese steward for the ship's steerage officers, had been sick with a "severe cold" since the cruise began. The officers thought him tubercular,

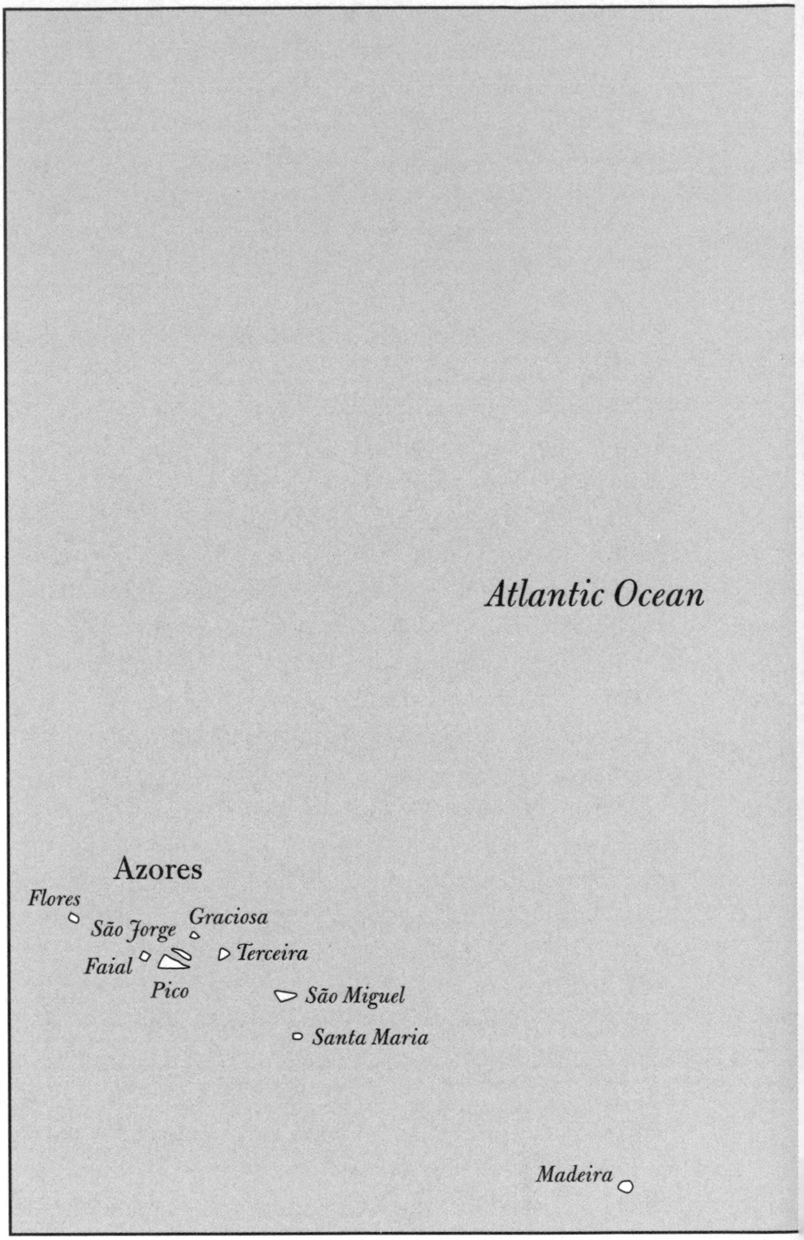

Map 1. Area of Operations, USS *Kearsarge*, February, 1862–September, 1864

Atlantic Ocean

Azores

Flores

São Jorge   Graciosa

Faial   Terceira

Pico   São Miguel

Santa Maria

Madeira

but some of the enlisted men judged him a simple malingerer; a few days earlier, one unsympathetic sailor had elicited a ferocious reprimand from the surgeon by kicking DeSanto in the stomach as he lay on the berth deck— there being no formal sick bay. Pneumonia had apparently set in, and the steward perished that evening, a couple of hours after the ship docked beside the *Tuscarora*. His loss went almost unnoticed by the sailors and engineers, who enjoyed their usual evening of singing and dancing on the forecastle. The thin squawking of a fiddle drifted down to the berth deck even as DeSanto breathed his last.

Surgeon John Mills Browne had had his hands full from the day the *Kearsarge* left Portsmouth. Continuous cold soakings and poor food had put nearly three dozen men under his care within a few days, most of them ailing from respiratory or digestive complaints. Early in the cruise he had performed a tonsillectomy on one man, and the operation proved a complete success; in the course of cleaning the surgical instruments, however, Surgeon's Steward George Tittle punctured his forefinger with the tip of a scalpel. Tittle's hand swelled horribly, and Browne lanced it several times to drain off fluid, but the last joint of the finger turned black and the flesh began dropping away. There was no cure for gangrene short of amputation, and Doctor Browne called for the surgeon of the *Tuscarora* to assist him. On the afternoon of March 12 Ezra Bartlett and a few other officers gathered in the wardroom to hold Tittle down, for the first doses of ether had little effect on him. After two and a half hours the surgeons resorted to chloroform. Tittle inhaled enough anesthetics to kill eight men, said the surgeons, but in the end he felt nothing. This would not be Browne's last amputation on the *Kearsarge*.[25]

CHAPTER FOUR

Iberian Assignation

The yarns of sailors have a direct simplicity, the whole
meaning of which lies within the shell of a cracked nut.
—Conrad, *Heart of Darkness*

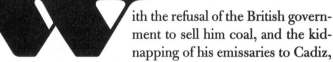ith the refusal of the British govern-
ment to sell him coal, and the kid-
napping of his emissaries to Cadiz,
Raphael Semmes foresaw that his chances of escaping Gibraltar had narrowed nearly to the closing point. Newspapers revealed that six more U.S.
warships, besides the *Tuscarora*, had joined the hunt for his decrepit raider,
and any further delays would seal his ship's fate. Once the confinement of
Paymaster Myers and Mr. Tunstall had been confirmed, Semmes sought
coal personally, and, at about the same moment that the *Kearsarge* anchored
at Funchal, Semmes thought he had secured a source. The captain of an
English merchant steamer offered to sell him coal from his own bunkers, and
the next morning Semmes wasted some more of his remaining fuel to raise
enough steam that he might move the *Sumter* alongside the British vessel.
Just then the English captain came aboard and demanded his price—$12 a
ton. The going rate was $8 a ton, and Semmes sent the profiteer packing.

It was just as well that the deal collapsed, for so did the *Sumter*'s patched
boilers. The engineers had raised only twelve pounds of steam in anticipation of the move before the seams began to part, and Semmes ordered an
immediate survey of the system. His officers condemned the machinery, and
that was the end of any hope the ship might resume its campaign against
Yankee commerce. Gibraltar did not offer adequate repair facilities; with the
Tuscarora hanging so near, Semmes could hardly limp to Cadiz even if

officials there had extended the same welcome to him that they did to Union warships.[1]

Semmes notified the Confederate commissioner in London, John Mason, that he wished to lay up the *Sumter* and do better service elsewhere. Then, while awaiting Mason's opinion, he returned to his postal campaign for the release of Myers and Tunstall. The storeship *Ino* brought them into Gibraltar, and Semmes petitioned Governor Codrington on their behalf. The commander of the *Ino* refused to give them up, instead taking them out to sea as Semmes watched helplessly from the crippled *Sumter*, and a few days later the Yankee captain transferred them to the ship that would carry them to Boston in shackles. Semmes concluded that the British would not involve themselves because they had taken too great a scare from the near-war over the *Trent* affair of recent memory, in which Mason and the commissioner to Paris had been plucked by an arrogant American captain from the deck of an English ship. The United States held onto their prisoners on the excuse of the treaty with Morocco, and eventually the Confederate government conceded sufficiently to exchange Myers for a New York infantry captain who had been captured, fair and square, in battle; Tunstall remained in prison for nearly sixteen months, winning parole only when he promised to reside abroad for the duration.[2]

Mason, who had no direct authority over Captain Semmes, advised him to remain where he was with the *Sumter* and its crew. Even disabled, he argued, the ship distracted Federal cruisers and thus performed a service for the Confederacy. Semmes said he would drag out the bluff, apparently unaware that the little Union squadron at Algeciras knew all about his decrepit engines, and he told Mason that the forty-odd sailors remaining on the ship occupied the Yankees "to the extent of many times our own force."

That was true enough, but the image of that new cruiser on the Mersey may have changed the captain's perspective. He and his officers saw themselves robbed of the chance for distinction while the war ground on without them, and barely a fortnight after his promise to remain idle at Gibraltar Semmes forwarded Mason a memorial from his wardroom officers, who unanimously asked to be relieved for more active duty in some other theater. Contending that the subsistence of the *Sumter* and her crew cost a bare minimum of a thousand dollars a month, Semmes now minimized the effect of his subterfuge, supposing that one Federal ship would remain to guard the Confederate vessel even if it were converted into a hulk, and that the retention of officers and crew would occupy only one additional ship. One enemy ship out of 300 was too little an advantage on which to waste nearly a score of officers, he suggested, asking Mason (in view of the great difficulty of communicating with Richmond) to assume the responsibility of ordering him to lay up the ship and repair to the South with most of the officers under him.[3]

That letter went out by March 31. On April 7 Semmes opened a telegram from Mason directing him to do as he proposed, so he began closing out accounts and deciding who should remain behind or go home. He paid off all but ten of the crewmen, who would serve as shipboard guards and as the boat's crew for the midshipman and master's mate who would stay on in command of the *Sumter*.

Semmes did well to dismiss most of his crew, for his deserters had begun to reinforce the enemy. During March a number of men who had slipped away from the moribund Confederate ship had joined the crew of the *Tuscarora*, whose captain took them aboard with full knowledge of their origin, and on March 26 one of them shipped on the *Kearsarge*. George Augustus Whipple, a twenty-seven-year-old native of Millbury, Massachusetts, had jumped ship a day or two before. Like many Northerners who joined the Southern forces on a lark and then thought better of it, Whipple invented a tale of having been forced into Confederate service when he was caught in New Orleans at the outbreak of hostilities. The Confederate Congress was still eleven days away from passing the South's first conscription law when Whipple appeared before the American consul and swore that he had been forced, nearly a year before, to choose between service in the army or the navy. He chose the navy, he claimed, because it offered a greater opportunity for escape.

U.S. officials perhaps overlooked this fabrication in return for another lie: Whipple also testified under oath that the *Sumter* had received coal in the harbor at Gibraltar on the night of March 19. He witnessed it himself, he said, guessing that she took in about thirty tons. The consul presented a formal complaint to the colonial secretary at Gibraltar, who asked Semmes about the alleged breach of British neutrality. Semmes, who had had no reason to seek coal since late February, shot back a disgusted reply branding Whipple a deliberate perjurer and a double turncoat. That satisfied the colonial secretary, who expressed annoyance upon learning that the consul had disturbed him on no better evidence that the word of a single self-interested deserter.[4]

The last of the supernumerary Confederate crewmen took their final pay and departed on April 9. That evening a number of the *Sumter*'s steerage officers boarded a steamer for Liverpool, while Semmes, Kell, and the rest waited for the Southampton packet boat, which departed several days later. After a six-day passage from Gibraltar to London, Semmes and his brawny executive officer arrived in London, taking rooms on Euston Square, on the northern fringe of Bloomsbury, to await a better opportunity to do service for the Confederacy.[5]

The obvious incapacity of the *Sumter* deprived the *Kearsarge* crewmen of their principal source of excitement. From the outset the dull routine of their existence proved to be their greatest enemy, particularly for those accustomed to a more gregarious life ashore. Coal Heavers Poole and Wainwright complained bitterly of the boredom aboard ship, which irritated Poole and seemed to throw Wainwright into long, deep depressions: Wainwright would abandon his private journal for days at a time after a week of recording the same brief, monotonous entry about the weather and shipboard rumors. The same spiritual malaise struck even the occasional officer, though they enjoyed more comfortable accommodations and the diversion of more frequent trips ashore: by March 13 Master's Mate Ezra Bartlett appears to have abandoned the diary with which he began the cruise so enthusiastically, devoting the rest of its pages to Spanish vocabulary and grammar.[6]

In a letter to his brother, Bartlett described the average day that came to a sailor before the mast. The watches ran four hours each from 8:00 in the evening until 4:00 the following afternoon, when two two-hour "dog watches" broke up the day and alternated the shifts. A man stood one four-hour watch and then had eight to himself, barring special details, so if his sleep was interrupted from midnight until 4:00 A.M. on one night, he would theoretically be able to squeeze in six or seven hours' sleep on each of the next two nights.

On most days the crew was roused at 6:00 A.M. by the shrill boatswain's whistle, which signaled all the activities on ship. Every morning deck hands would plug the scuppers and pump a few inches of seawater onto the decks, which they then scrubbed with brushes and the holystone—a heavy, flat stone with rope handles on either side, by which several men would drag it back and forth across the oak deck, scuffing it almost white. The three dozen men in the engineer department, meanwhile, went below to dust the coal and soot from the engines and clean the burnished iron and brass fittings. On Tuesdays and Fridays the whistle blew at 4:30 in the morning, so the crewmen could wash their clothes and hang them on lines strung from the rigging before cleaning the decks and engine room. Twice a month, usually on the first and fifteenth, the crewmen also rose at 4:30 to scrub their hammocks in the same ankle-deep water used to clean the decks. These ablutions varied little, even in the coldest weather, though everyone came out of them with a good soaking.

From 8:00 until 9:00 each morning breakfast would be served, after which the men shucked their work clothes and dressed in clean mustering uniforms, usually dark blue jumpers and bell-bottomed trousers, but in the hottest weather they wore white, or blue blouses and white trousers. At 9:30 they stood at their quarters—their battle stations—for inspection by officers wearing their epaulettes and swords. In the early days of the cruise the gun crews drilled every day, right after inspection, for half an hour or so; then the boatswain piped down everyone who was not on watch, except for those assigned to special work. At noon the various messes drew their lunches, and at 1:00 they turned out for another hour at the heavy guns. After that, those who were off duty could do as they chose until dinner, which they ate at 4:00. These hours of leisure in the morning and afternoon might be, and frequently were, interrupted by maintenance assignments that almost always proved unpleasant.

At 5:00 came small-arms drill, usually with cutlasses and pistols but sometimes with rifles. In port, when there was little work to do, the captain called a second inspection at 6:00, if only to occupy his crew and assure that ennui did not lead to demoralization. The rest of the evening belonged to the sailors, who were generally piped to their hammocks at 9:00.[7]

Only Sundays differed. The decks had to be scrubbed and the engines cleaned, and the 9:30 inspection still followed breakfast, but at 10:00 A.M. or so the crew gathered on the quarterdeck for general muster. In older ships the quarterdeck, or poop deck, consisted of a raised platform over the after portion of the vessel, comparable to the forecastle that covered the forward end of the *Kearsarge*, but the *Kearsarge* had no raised poop. On such ships the quarterdeck was usually defined as that portion of the spar deck abaft the mainmast, and it was customarily reserved for such functions as the general muster; the enlisted crewmen—those who had shipped "before the mast"— could not loiter there.

At the mustering ceremony the enlisted men fell into ranks parallel to the keel on the port side of the quarterdeck while the officers faced them from the starboard side in dress blue uniforms. The paymaster's clerk, Daniel B. Sargent, would read the ship's muster roll, while each man stepped forward and marched around the engine-room hatch past the officers when his name was called. Once the roll had been called, everyone could pass the day as he chose unless duty interfered.[8]

During those leisure hours the crew had few alternatives for recreation. Some caught up on their sleep, though they had to sleep on the rough deck until hammocks were piped down at evening. Others attended to what little mending their clothes required, or stitched colorful embroidery. Those who could find books or newspapers could pass an hour reading, but the store of literature ran out quickly. Captain Pickering did not allow cards to be played, but he offered no objection to checkers ("draughts") or dominoes. In the evenings the forecastle rang with the music of a pair of violins, a banjo, and a clattering tambourine. Patriotic and nostalgic songs or an impromptu jig started up now and then.[9]

George Williams, the captain's black cook, was the favorite entertainer on the *Kearsarge*. This middle-aged Marylander doubled as the ship's drummer, and he could sing and dance to the satisfaction of all despite his enormous size. He stood only a little taller than average, but he had grown notably stout: Charles Fisher once watched him devour ten men's rations. Williams's shipmates called him "Ham Fat" for the way he constantly hummed a tune of that name, however, and not for his bulk.[10]

When all other amusements had been exhausted, there was always the garrulous sailor with his yarns of long-gone ships and distant places. Sergeant Young of the Marines had spent sixteen years in the service, mostly at sea; he owned an endless repertoire of tales with the requisite leavenings of humor and fantasy, but some of the newcomers to shipboard life seemed not to appreciate their flavor. On their evening at Tangier, with most of the ship's company gathered on deck, he told of an earlier cruise in which none of his messmates got on well together, so he started taking his meals alone, eating only the broken portions of his hardtack allowance and saving the whole pieces. Over the course of three months he accumulated a barrel and a half of crackers, he said, yet he never suffered from hunger. Yeoman DeWit, a pragmatic Yankee, observed that that was remarkable, since he took his meals in the sergeant's mess now, and knew that the sergeant's appetite was "not small." The yeoman asked how much a barrel of crackers weighed, and Young said one would go around 120 pounds. DeWit then asked what the daily ration was per man, which the annoyed Marine admitted was fourteen ounces. DeWit then pointed out to the beet-faced sergeant and the gathered crewmen that he had saved 180 pounds of crackers and eaten well besides, all from what should have been a quarterly allowance of only 84 pounds. The smug yeoman noted that the sailors tittered behind them while the sergeant glared at him.[11]

Francis Viannah, the Faial Portuguese, had one particular story that he liked to tell. Viannah claimed to be clairvoyant. He said that, on a whaling voyage a couple of decades before, he was appointed captain's steward when the original man deserted. He said he was at work in the cabin one day when the boats lowered to chase a whale; just as he heard the lookout call, the cabin around him filled with dense vapors. A vision came to him of a man's hat, head, and blood in the bottom of a stove boat. Just then the captain called him to help lower the boats, which he did. While the boats pulled away, Viannah went back to the cabin, but the mysterious feeling overcame him again and he sat on a chest, convinced that the first mate would be killed. He returned to the deck in obvious distress and approached the captain, who asked Viannah what was wrong with him, whereupon Viannah described the scene that had appeared to him. According to the story the Portuguese told to the *Kearsarge* crew, it was not long before the lookout spotted two of the whaleboats pulling back to the ship, towing the third. The whale's fluke had smashed the bows of the mate's boat (Viannah claimed), lopping off the mate's head and dragging the rest of his body underwater. What remained of the head, and the mate's hat, lay in the bottom of the damaged boat, Viannah declared.

Viannah told his shipmates that since that time he had owned the gift of second sight, and could tell when thieves and other scoundrels had come aboard the ship. Again the skeptical yeoman scoffed at the tale privately, though he said nothing to Viannah.[12]

George Whipple offered a *Kearsarge* audience his own fantasy of life aboard the *Sumter*, which doubtless entranced the men who had sought to sink that vessel. A brawling young Irishman by the name of John Dempsey could also be found of an evening beneath the forecastle, telling stories or singing. Dempsey, who held the position of captain of the afterguard, boisterously proclaimed himself a Douglas Democrat and an opponent of emancipation, to the annoyance of some of the black sailors. The twenty-five-year-old Dempsey was a sailor by trade, as one might have guessed from the tattoo on his right forearm; although he had left a new wife in Boston, he had not outgrown his rowdy disposition.[13]

Dempsey was one of the first aboard the *Kearsarge* to run into trouble, and he found it often. Late in March a coal lighter came alongside to refill the sloop's bunkers, and the lightermen smuggled some rum aboard to sell to the crew. Dempsey apparently procured most of it, with the help of a young Maine man who had shipped under the name Edward Tibbetts. Mr. Stoddard found them drunk and not a little disorderly before noon on March 26, and he ordered both of them thrown into irons, where they stayed for four days. But that did not end the affair: during the second dog watch that evening Stoddard again had the deck when an Irish fireman and a young black landsman started fighting, whereupon Stoddard shackled both of them, too.[14]

The men of the *Kearsarge* missed the chance to see the *Sumter*'s officers leave Gibraltar. A week before Semmes paid off his crew, Captain Pickering ordered his own ship out of the harbor for repairs at Cadiz, which the Confederates had found so inhospitable. The Yankee sailors delighted in this interlude, though the coasts of both Spain and Africa struck them as stark and barren. Enjoying his respite from the engine room with a walk on deck, Charles Poole marveled at centuries-old fortifications that survived from the Moorish occupation. Both he and William Wainwright paid particular attention to Cape Trafalgar, the site of Horatio Nelson's renowned victory over the Spanish fifty-seven years before. Their excursion ended at noon of the next day, though, when a pilot steered the ship into Cadiz.[15]

Situated on the tip of a peninsula that curved like a mother's arm around a bay that Phoenician sailors had coveted as a harbor, Cadiz was the oldest city in Spain. Captain Pickering and Lieutenant Harris lost no time making a visit now that they labored under no urgent schedule, and on Friday afternoon, April 4, they started ashore, leaving the ship to Acting Master Wheeler. Where Mr. Stoddard appeared to maintain control with a firm hand, Wheeler did not fear to let the men have some fun. At 6:00 that evening the boatswain piped the crew to "skylark," which they did with a will, pairing off into couples for dance sets while an orchestra of flutes, fiddles, banjo, and bones began twanging, tooting, and clacking. At 7:00 Wheeler cued the boatswain to line the men up for a cup of grog; when the pipe whistled them to "splice the main brace," they fell in like children at the school bell. Everyone save the infrequent temperance man like Coal Heaver Poole took their turn, even the prudish yeoman, who did so on the excuse of exhaustion after having spent the day looking for his bedding, which had been switched with that of someone too lazy to wash his own. Some of the revelers secretly ducked to the end of the queue for a second, third, or fourth ration. That dulled the judgment of a few, who fell to fighting and discovered that Mr. Wheeler could also order the irons when necessary.[16]

The rest enjoyed themselves all night singing songs, and a few expressed their appreciation by improvising a burlesque horse with a blanket thrown over four stooped men: others climbed on their backs and rode to the wardroom hatch, led by Ham Fat pounding his drum. There they gave three cheers for Mr. Wheeler, who came on deck, mounted the capstan, and thanked them for their show of affection. Some of them suffered the next morning from taking too much liquor too quickly: among them was Captain of the Top Robert Strahan, a stocky little Irish sailor from New Jersey, who offered to strike the officer of the deck and lost his rate for it. Wheeler appears to have released the other miscreants without formally charging them; Strahan's was too dangerous an affront to ignore, however, and he went into confinement to wait for punishment. He was soon joined there by George Andrew, a Chilean sailor who had signed on at Gibraltar less than two weeks before. Andrew burst into a rage over "something" (noted Yeoman DeWit somewhat dryly, after having found his clean bedding), and that "something" prompted him to fling his hammock into the bay. The officer of the deck ordered Andrew to retrieve it, but he refused, swearing mightily until the deck officer arrested him.[17]

Cadiz harbor teemed with ships of all types, from dhows to the latest steamers. Lighter boats with lateen sails darted everywhere, transferring cargoes. The USS *St. Louis* lay at anchor when the *Kearsarge* arrived, as well as an American merchant steamer, the *Oraville*. That ship was headed back to Boston, and Captain Pickering asked her skipper to take four of his sailors as passengers. The four had been sick virtually since the cruise began, and Surgeon Browne saw little hope for their recovery aboard the ship. The merchant captain agreed, taking the invalids and a sack of mail on April 6.[18]

The next day the *Kearsarge* took aboard a pilot and started for the navy yard at La Carraca, nine miles upriver from Cadiz. The *Sumter* had made this same journey less than three months before, keeping to a channel that was only a hundred yards wide although, thanks to constant dredging, it remained deep enough for the heaviest vessels. All around lay marshy plain, but as they neared the yard, the men on deck could see thirty-foot pyramids of densely caked salt—the local industry, aside from shipbuilding. On shore milled thousands of workmen, some barely old enough to lift an axe, and alongside them slaved chain gangs of convicts under the guns of Spanish soldiers in gaudy uniforms of red trousers and yellow coats. This, thought most of the Americans who scanned the scenery, was a terribly desolate place. It was perhaps merciful that they did not know how long they were to spend on "Mud Creek," as Charles Poole called it.[19]

Spanish carpenters came aboard a couple of days later to begin a two-month job that some of the Yankee sailors thought should have been finished in a few days. They were asked to raise the engine-room hatch combings by eighteen inches, as the chief engineer had requested seven weeks before, and to cut new scuppers in the bulwarks, to allow water to drain from the deck more effectively when they shipped heavy seas. Machinists ashore would fashion new plungers for the circulating pump in the condenser while the carpenters hammered away, but the carpenters seemed never to hammer. They would study the job before them for a while, then one of them would begin whittling away while five or six others coached and watched. Every man seemed to have two boys to fetch tools for him; they worked with tools that even the laymen on the *Kearsarge* recognized as outdated and dull, and they complained continually that American oak was too tough. After a few minutes' boring or sawing they would stop to adjust the sashes around their waists, or to roll and smoke a cigarette in so leisurely a fashion that it drove the sailors mad. A coal heaver observed that one yard crew took six days to cut the hole for a single scupper.[20]

Crewmen quickly grew disgusted with Mud Creek, "mud diggers," and what Poole repeatedly called "these lazy drones." Captain Pickering recognized that the tedium might soon induce his men to seek better fortunes elsewhere, and he declined to grant liberty to anyone but officers lest it offer the temptation to desert. He permitted the officers to go virtually when and where they chose, while he instituted the second daily inspection to consume some of the enlisted men's abundant leisure. Some of the men turned footloose in spite of that precaution, or perhaps because of Pickering's undisguised deference to rank: so conscious was he of shipboard status that he sharply reprimanded First Assistant Engineer Whittaker for taking the gangway ahead of some wardroom officers when they all boarded the boat for shore.[21]

Charles Maguire, an Irish immigrant serving as a first-class fireman, developed an elaborate plan to get away. He went to the captain with a sad tale that his father had been dreadfully mangled in an accident aboard the English packet boat of which he was the engineer. Maguire asked for some money to send home, and Pickering directed the paymaster to advance him a few months' pay. Once Maguire had the cash he disappeared with it, and another seaman whom the men called John Taylor—but whom the paymaster knew as John Griffin—went with him. Their absence was not noted until the next morning, April 30, but a Spanish policeman brought them aboard six days later, taking a reward that the captain had advertised. Judging from the pair's appearance, their shipmates guessed the two had had a rough time in the Spaniards' hands. Three weeks later they escaped again, though, leaving great suspicion behind that one of the Marine guards had taken sympathy with them, accepted a bribe, or fallen asleep on watch during the night; no one on the *Kearsarge* ever saw them again.[22]

Another first-class fireman, John Chase of Newburyport, Massachusetts, turned so sick that the surgeon sent him home, too. He departed Cadiz May 13, aboard the Boston-bound *Speedwell*, and the engineer department raised a purse of $140 for him to send to his family until he recovered. These losses through desertion and illness threatened to cut sharply into the handling of the vessel if they were not made up, so Captain Pickering kept constantly on the lookout for recruits. He had already shipped five by the time they arrived at Cadiz, including Whipple, Andrew, and a "supernumerary" whom he discharged as unsatisfactory, but the captain had his choice because Cadiz harbored hundreds of unemployed sailors. Evidently he did not choose well, though, for, of the eight men who joined the crew during this first stay at the royal dockyard, only one finished the cruise. Two men shipped as soon as the *Kearsarge*'s boat touched at Cadiz. Officers returning from leave in Seville early in May brought four more eager prospects with them, three white and one black, of whom the captain took three. Later that month two more deck hands signed on, including a youth from Bucksport, Maine, who had apparently run away to sea in his mid-teens and had not been home since; not until he enlisted in his country's cause did he write his parents for the first time to apprise them of his whereabouts.

Captain Pickering did not find it expedient to ask the origins of his recruits. Thomas Marsh, who claimed American birth, had deserted from the British garrison at Gibraltar and made his way to the navy yard, where Pickering gave him to Engineer Cushman as a coal heaver.[23]

To the delight of everyone aboard, the carpenters finally completed their repairs as June opened. Chief Engineer Cushman fitted the plunger in the freshwater condenser and began distilling two gallons of potable water a minute; on the afternoon of June 7, giddy crewmen manned the capstan and bid what they thought would be a final farewell to La Carraca. They dropped their anchor at Cadiz overnight, but raised it again at 4:00 A.M. June 8 for the short cruise to Algeciras and their old enemy, the *Sumter*; it was perhaps a token of the instant improvement in morale that Coal Heaver Wainwright, who hated to be piped out of his hammock in the dark, was wakened from "a pleasant dream" by the call to weigh anchor. On the trip through the straits the *Kearsarge* boomed a few practice broadsides, and the officers drilled their divisions at small arms, swishing the air with gleaming cutlasses in anticipation of the fight that might come.[24]

The *Kearsarge* sailors learned that the *Sumter* was virtually abandoned as soon as they anchored beside the *Tuscarora*, but, if they experienced any disappointment over it, they were amply compensated by the bag of mail that arrived from home—at least those who received letters. William Wainwright found one, and only one, while his engine-room companion, Poole, did not hear his name called at all. Yeoman DeWit read a letter from his wife dated March 31, but Captain Pickering had later news than that from Portsmouth, and he called DeWit aft to tell him that his mother-in-law had died. The tardiness of his wife's first letter and her failure to send any more troubled the yeoman for months.[25]

The skipper called for a concert to raise the crew's spirits. Musicians from the *Tuscarora* came aboard with part of her crew as audience, and a few sailors were invited from the U.S. storeship *Release*, which lay nearby loading the two sloops with supplies. The *Kearsarge* provided the most and best of the troupe, which featured the officers' cook, Charles Fisher, with seamen William Gowin and Martin Simpson. These three had been allowed to go ashore with the captain at Cadiz to buy some guitars, a cello, an accordion, and a triangle to add to the ship's orchestra, and on the afternoon of June 12 they put them to use. Pickering ordered the awnings spread against the broiling sun, and the signal quartermaster hung every flag in his locker to decorate the ship's rigging. The quarterdeck rang with applause and drumming feet for hours as the players performed burlesque skits, danced, and played minstrel songs. Wainwright thought it better than some shows he had paid two bits to see back in the States.[26]

As much as the performance satisfied everyone, what the men wanted was liberty. The change of scenery helped little to break the monotony, and it grew difficult to distinguish one day from another. Even Captain Pickering lost track of time. On Saturday morning, June 14, he bounded onto the deck and bellowed for Lieutenant Harris to order the men into their mustering clothes, as though for Sunday muster. His executive officer whispered something to him, and he promptly countermanded the order while the sailors snickered from the forecastle. Early the next day a number of homesick landlubbers beat the boatswain's whistle and climbed on deck to watch the sun rise over the Rock of Gibraltar, knowing that that would be their best entertainment of the day.[27]

After muster that morning, Captain Pickering relented and issued five men the first liberty granted in the forecastle. The first lot to go ashore were not well chosen, for they included a notorious rowdy named James Morey and sixteen-year-old Jimmy Hayes, and Pickering had withheld the privilege so long that the liberty men went wild as soon as they encountered one of the abundant cantinas in Algeciras. They started fighting, either among themselves or with the natives, and a Spanish constable threw Morey, Hayes, and Coxswain Thomas Perry into his calaboose, where they spent the night. When they returned to the ship, the officer of the deck clapped them in irons for overstaying their liberty, and the captain declared that that would put an end to liberty ashore for a while.

Pickering tried it again on the next Monday, June 23. Four of that party failed to return, including an Irish quartermaster who would not long hold that rate and Seaman Robert Strahan—the erstwhile captain of the top. Three of them staggered aboard on the twenty-fifth with tales of starvation and squalor in the Spanish jail, where one of them remained until the Fourth of July.[28]

Three days later a more judicious selection of sailors preened themselves for liberty, among them Coal Heaver Poole, who found little of interest in Algeciras because he did not drink. Every other business was a grog shop, he reported, which left him with only the marketplace and its wide variety of fruits to satisfy his tastes. The freedom to stroll unimpeded pleased him no end, though, and he hiked the length of the town, visiting an empty bullring and puzzling out the bizarre sport that the little coliseum hosted. He found the streets dirty and the people "too lazy or indolent to earn a decent living," as he had long ago decided. Algeciras seemed populated mostly with soldiers and beggars, he observed, and—apparently unfamiliar with the custom of siesta in this torrid climate—he clucked disapprovingly at the inhabitants who slept the afternoon away at the doorways of their houses. Like most tourists on foreign soil for the first time, he sought familiar surroundings, buying a meal at the only English hotel in town. After nine hours on the soil of Spain he concluded that he had had enough, and returned to the ship. All of his fellow sojourners likewise came back on time, as did the next day's liberty crew, but on June 28 another row—involving Tom Perry again and Tim Hurley, the ship's cook—broke out between some *Kearsarge* men and sailors from other ships. The Spanish governor told Captain Pickering that that would be that: no more of his men would be allowed to land. When a boatload from the *Kearsarge* tried to defy that order on July 3, they were attacked by guards who beat one fireman senseless with the flats of their swords while a mob of locals stoned liberty men and oarsmen alike back to their boat. Aboard the ship, those who craved to go ashore blamed their own comrades for provoking the inhabitants.[29]

That restricted the crew to the ship again for a time, though a raucous Fourth of July celebration provided a handy diversion. The next morning took everyone back to the routine of swabbing the deck and polishing the brightwork, all of which was done by 8:00 A.M., whereupon the main occupation consisted of finding an occupation. Journals lapsed into the repetitive refrain that there was nothing to do; fights broke out on deck; liquor found its way aboard, and into thirsty sailors' stomachs.

As a garnish to the boredom, the Mediterranean heat sought every compartment in the ship: on July 10 the mercury rose to 114 degrees at 5:30 P.M. On Sunday, July 13, most of the officers left the ship to attend a bullfight at San Roque. Mr. Stoddard, who remained behind as officer of the deck, allowed those who wished to swim to jump over the side, as the crew of a nearby Spanish warship already had. A score or so leapt into the water after booms and ropes had been lowered, including Charles Poole. William Wainwright hung back for some reason that he could not explain to himself. Someone had seen a big fish in the water off the starboard side, and Stoddard ordered the only remaining boat down to investigate. Five men climbed into the boat, one of them taking a harpoon, and they rowed out to look for what they supposed would be their dinner.

The fish was looking for dinner, as well. Off the port side most of the swimmers had climbed onto the booms to watch a race between George Andrew and Seaman Edward Tibbetts when someone on the forecastle screamed that there was a shark in the water. The remaining bathers scurried onto the booms, and voices everywhere called for the boat. The four oarsmen pulled desperately, but the shark turned on his back and raced straight for Tibbetts, passing so close to Andrew that he touched him. Tibbetts, a small man, struck the shark with his fist and deflected him once or twice, but then Tibbetts seemed to leap nearly out of the water, crying that his leg was hurt and begging for someone to throw him a rope. Several shipmates threw them, but they fell just a few feet too short, and finally the shark seized Tibbetts around the ribs and carried him under. The boat arrived just in time for the harpooneer to see the fish three fathoms deep and going deeper with Tibbetts clamped in his jaws: one of the victim's arms was wrapped around the great fin.

Like many who served in the navy during that century, Tibbetts had enlisted under an assumed name, but for a better reason than those who thought they might desert. It was only after he was gone that his mates learned who he really was: Edward H. Sampson, aged nineteen, of Brunswick, Maine. The year before he had shipped with a Maine vessel bound for the Caribbean, and there the *Sumter* had captured it—and him. Paroled on his word not to fight against the Confederacy until exchanged, Sampson thought he might be liable to execution if captured in Federal uniform; hence the nom de guerre.[30] A few miles from the scene of Sampson's death, visible across the bay, that same *Sumter* sat dark and impotent, but still it chained Sampson's shipmates to this harbor.

CHAPTER FIVE

Renaissance

Now would I give a thousand furlongs of sea for an acre
of barren ground—long heath, brown furze, anything.
—Shakespeare, *The Tempest*

Captain Semmes and Lieutenant Kell quickly learned that their navy could offer them no employment in England. The first of the two Confederate cruisers had already slipped out of the country under the name *Oreto*, and everyone in Confederate circles supposed they would soon hear of her as the *Manassas*: the Southern army had retreated from the site of its victory at Manassas at the very moment the *Oreto* escaped, however, so that name would quickly give way to *Florida*. For now British interference and the lack of a crew kept her at Nassau; with her gone from Britain, that left only the unfinished *290* for officers seeking sea duty. Commander Bulloch expected to go out in command of this one, according to his earlier agreement with Mallory, and although Bulloch generously offered to step aside for Semmes, that officer declined to take the ship away from him.

The erstwhile captain of the *Sumter* and his executive officer passed about a month in London, some of it at the home of the Reverend Francis Tremlett, an ardent Confederate sympathizer. Tremlett lived at Belsize Park, near Hampstead, with his mother and sister, and there he played host to an assortment of Southerners, most of them naval officers. News of serial military disasters at the South spurred Semmes and Kell to return home, despite the pleasant interlude at the Tremletts, and opportunity beckoned early in May, when the steamer *Melita* docked in London to load Enfield rifles and uniforms for the Confederacy. During the third week of the month the *Melita* dropped down to Gravesend to take on gunpowder, which—with the other contraband—was destined for transfer to a blockade runner at Nassau. Once assured that the *Melita* was not going to run the blockade herself, which might give Federal warships a legal excuse to take him prisoner, Semmes booked passage. Lieutenant Kell and Francis Galt, the former surgeon of the *Sumter*, went with him.[1]

They sailed May 19. The *Melita*, an iron-hulled, three-masted steamer registered in Hamburg, made the passage to Nassau in twenty days through good weather. The Confederates stepped ashore the morning of June 8, eager to see their homes and families after a year's absence, but within an hour or two their anticipation evaporated. The port bustled with blockade runners and Confederate naval officers, including Lieutenant John Stribling and Marine Lieutenant Becket Howell, who had served on the *Sumter*, as well as the man who had taken command of the *Oreto*, Lieutenant John Maffitt. Semmes fell in with them and found a letter from Mallory enclosing a copy of his May 2 order for Semmes to assume command of the 290. With a mixture of disappointment and glee, he and Kell turned from visions of a visit with loved ones to plans for reaching their new assignment.[2]

Semmes wrote immediately to James North, back in London, telling him of the changes in orders and plans. North, too, had expected to command the 290, and he greeted the news with poor grace.

Originally, Mallory had intended Bulloch to command the *Oreto* and for North to have the 290. When Bulloch pointed out that he might not reach England in time to command the *Oreto*, Mallory had authorized him to take either ship. Bulloch did arrive in good season, though, and he offered the *Oreto* to North, planning on the 290 for himself. Five days after Bulloch posted his letter in Liverpool, however, North wrote from London as though he had not received it; as soon as the *Oreto* had sailed, North complained bitterly to Mallory about Bulloch having been promoted to commander over him, and about the navy secretary giving Bulloch the second vessel, which was now the only one left. Writing from Richmond on March 17, Mallory specifically ordered North to take the *Oreto*, not knowing she had already sailed, but North did not acknowledge receipt of that missive, either. Only when Bulloch informed North that the secretary had changed his mind, directing Bulloch to remain in England and oversee the construction of new vessels and to give the 290 to Semmes, did North respond.

The problem lay partly with the cloak-and-dagger language of the Confederacy's international correspondence. Not wishing to offer Northern representatives any evidence for a diplomatic complaint to the British if his mail should be intercepted, Mallory had remained deliberately vague about the cruisers under construction, avoiding mention of their names until they went to sea. In his orders to North he referred to the *Oreto* as "the vessel built by Captain Bulloch," and the selfish North used that vagueness to full advantage. Though the original orders had been dated March 17, as North knew very well, he gave Bulloch the date on Mallory's repetition of the order—May 2, after the *Oreto* had sailed—quoting the reference to him taking "the vessel built by Captain Bulloch," so as to imply that he was to command the remaining ship, the *290*. Though disappointed to lose the assignment himself, Bulloch expressed willingness to give the ship to North, and he even did so after North came to Liverpool and demanded it, citing again the authority of an order that North seems to have deliberately misinterpreted. By early July North should have received Semmes's letter from Nassau, indicating that Semmes was to command the *290*, but North never let on, perhaps hoping that he could get the ship to sea before official word to that effect had arrived. Bulloch, however, did receive later and more definite instructions to give the *290* to Semmes, and on July 8 he took the ship back from an angry and petulant North.

It is not clear why North failed to assume command of the *Oreto*. Perhaps he suffered last-minute doubts of his own capacity, or possibly he wanted the bigger and better of the two ships. He seemed perfectly willing to distort the record to steal the *290* from his old friend Semmes, but through Bulloch's integrity the vessel went to the man whom both the Navy Department and fate seemed to have designated for her. North, meanwhile, earned a contemptuous rebuke from Mallory and retired to well-deserved obscurity in London.[3]

After sending home letters and gifts, some of which did not make it through the blockade, Semmes and Kell lodged at Nassau's Victoria Hotel to wait for another ship returning to England—where, propitiously enough, Semmes had left most of his other *Sumter* officers to serve aboard the *290* with Bulloch. While they waited, Semmes amused himself by watching the blockade runners through a telescope from their hotel rooms; sometimes he joined Kell, Galt, Stribling, and Maffitt in soirées with Southern ladies whose husbands manned blockade runners, and all of them would read the latest papers from home and sing songs together, including the new "Maryland, My Maryland." On July 13 the British steamer *Bahama*, which had brought Stribling and Howell to Nassau, departed for Liverpool, taking Semmes and his officers. He left Lieutenant Stribling behind, at Maffitt's earnest entreaty, to serve as executive officer on the *Oreto*. In place of Stribling, Semmes took the twenty-five-year-old son of a Confederate navy commander, Arthur Sinclair IV, who had served on the ironclad *Virginia* as the captain's clerk. Sinclair had just been appointed a master—which, in both the Confederate and Union navies, amounted to the grade of lieutenant-in-waiting.[4]

While the party of officers sailed toward England, trouble brewed there over the *290*. Commander Bulloch had carefully adhered to the letter of British neutrality during construction, lest the American consul be able to document his complaints to Her Majesty's authorities, but the builders themselves had urged even greater caution: in a letter that contradicted his later claim that the Lairds knew nothing of the *290*'s warlike destiny, Bulloch informed his navy secretary that the brothers had tried to persuade him to leave out the bolts for the broadside guns. The *290*'s masts would be shipped and her bottom coppered in the Lairds' private drydock, unlike the *Oreto*, so Bulloch resisted his contractors and fitted her out for cruising as closely as he dared. Before the ship left his care, the gun deck bore two swivel sockets for pivot guns, and both bulwarks had been pierced for the broadside muzzles. In so doing he played the gray areas at the fringe of the law, and these final touches prodded the American consul at Liverpool to greater effort.[5]

On June 12, the day of the minstrel show aboard the *Kearsarge*, the *290* steamed out for a trial in the Irish Sea, after which she nosed into the Lairds' Number 4 graving dock. There she remained exactly one month, backing out on July 12 to anchor at the public wharf on Birkenhead's Great Float, where stevedores started toting provisions aboard while a collier filled the new ship's bunkers. Three days previous to this, Consul Thomas Dudley uncorked his inkwell and apprised the collector of customs at Liverpool of his suspicions—bordering on certainty—about the vessel. He included information drawn from the statements of people whose names he declined to reveal, so when the collector passed Dudley's letter on to the customs board, that body rejected it for lack of reliable evidence. Dudley therefore dug into his cashbox and started looking for men who might be willing to sign affidavits. Through a detective he found a shipping master who had seen the *Oreto* dip her colors to the Confederate blockade runner *Annie Childs*, and who said he had seen Commander Bulloch aboard the *Oreto* when she went to sea. Richard Brogan, an apprentice shipwright, swore that Bulloch had asked him to ship as a carpenter's mate on the *290*, of which Brogan supposed Bulloch was to be the captain. A Crimean War veteran of the British navy, William Passmore, testified that the nominal skipper of the *290*, Matthew Butcher, had enlisted him as an able seaman with the promise of a signal quartermaster's berth if one were needed. Both Brogan and Passmore said the ship was built to carry guns, and Brogan repeated shipyard scuttlebutt that the guns would be loaded at the Lairds' facility before she went to sea.[6]

Dudley submitted these and other affidavits to the port collector, who again handed them to his board, and once more that board found no evidence of any violation of the Foreign Enlistment Act or other aspects of British neutrality. Charles Francis Adams, the U.S. ambassador to England, supplemented Dudley's actions with two more affidavits, one from an Englishman who said he had actually engaged as carpenter's mate on the 290, and another from a London native who said he had lived in Mobile since 1847 and had been captured while running the blockade; this fellow alleged that Captain Butcher had verbally accepted him as a deck hand on the new ship. The Liverpool consulate paid cash for at least some of this testimony, which Adams turned over to a barrister and member of Parliament who concluded that the customs collector ought to detain the 290.[7]

The customs officials at Liverpool rejected not only the two additional affidavits but another one that was submitted to them on July 25. They forwarded the entire case to the commissioners of the treasury for routine review, but because of the serious nature of the accusation and the complexities of the law, they took the additional measure of submitting it to the law officers of the Crown. Queen's Advocate Sir John Harding received the papers as the senior law officer, but just then Harding suffered a physical and mental collapse. Sir Austin Layard, undersecretary for foreign affairs, consulted with the prime minister about Harding and suggested to Harding that he ought to resign, but Mrs. Harding interceded with Layard and begged that her husband not be removed from office indelicately, as it would be a severe blow to his pride. The affidavits and Dudley's complaint were therefore delayed a day or two, but before long the documents made their way to the other two law officers, Attorney General William Atherton and Solicitor General Roundell Palmer.[8]

On July 29 these two judged that some of the affidavits provided sufficient excuse to impound the vessel, at least temporarily, but their opinion came too late. On July 26 someone apprised Bulloch that his ship would not be safe on the Mersey two days hence, and he arranged a little melodrama to distract the authorities. Clearly Bulloch could no longer await the arrival of Captain Semmes before putting the 290 (now renamed *Enrica*) to sea. The ship had already ventured out for one trial, and the Lairds had completed their contract, but Bulloch approached them about one last trial run—at least he later insisted that they assumed it would be a trial run. On the morning of July 28 Bulloch, Butcher, and Paymaster Yonge met at the office of the Confederacy's Liverpool financiers—Fraser, Trenholm, & Company. Bulloch told Yonge to put his baggage aboard and advised them both to be ready to leave on the following day. That evening the ship left the Great Float at Birkenhead and eased into the Mersey River, dropping anchor abreast of the Canning Street Dock, off Seacombe.

The next morning a ferry carried Commander Bulloch out to the ship with pilot George Bond, Yonge, and a company of ladies and gentlemen. Among the visitors were two grey-haired Confederate naval officers, Lieutenants North and Arthur Sinclair III, as well as the brothers Laird and their daughters. All of them knew the ship would not be coming back—or so Yonge later claimed. At about 10:00 A.M., with flags fluttering from the rigging and the excursionists milling ostentatiously around the deck, the *Enrica* steamed through the neck and into the open water, followed by the steam tug *Hercules*.

From late morning until midafternoon the ship steamed back and forth between the Liverpool bell buoy and a lightship anchored toward the Isle of Man, making an average 12.8 knots in a light breeze. At 3:00 Bulloch struck an apologetic air and informed his guests that he would have to ask them to return to the city in the tug, for unforeseen circumstances required the *Enrica* to stay out all night before her trials could be completed. He joined his discomfited party on the *Hercules* and, while they steamed back up the Mersey, he engaged the tug for 6:00 the next morning, as well. The *Enrica*, meanwhile, turned for an out-of-the-way anchorage on the coast of Wales.

The ship sailed with some six dozen crewmen, which would have been a fair complement for a merchant vessel of that size. Needing more men for a gunboat, Bulloch had arranged with a shipping agent to provide him with thirty or forty additional sailors, who were to meet the *Hercules* at Woodside landing early on July 30. At 7:00 that morning Bulloch met the tug, which had already loaded an anchor stock, a good-sized timber, and some machine parts intended for the *Enrica*. The agent stood at the dock, too, with about thirty potential recruits, but those men were accompanied by an assortment of waterfront hussies, who clung to their arms with all the feigned affection that the prospect of advance pay could inspire. Holding the firm grip that is so easily fixed on lonely men, the women insisted on accompanying the tug to the mysterious ship where the paymaster dwelt, wherever she might lie.[9]

Early in July Commander Augustus Craven had brought the USS *Tuscarora* to Southampton at the behest of Ambassador Adams, who had warned him that the *290* neared completion. On the day the *Enrica* steamed out of the Mersey, Consul Dudley had telegraphed Craven the news, and the Federal ship left Southampton for Queenstown, on Ireland's southeast coast, from which Craven might post himself to catch the new ship on its way through the customary passage at St. George's Channel. In his pocket Bulloch carried a fresh telegram from a Southampton correspondent, alerting him to the *Tuscarora*'s departure, so while he objected to taking the sailors' women to the *Enrica*, he dared not defy the Liverpool ladies for long. Soon enough he submitted to the demands of the lovesick sailors and their persistent paramours: as the *Hercules* pulled away from Woodside landing, her decks reeked not only with the sharp scents of brandy and body odor but with the unsubtle aroma of an overabundance of face paint and perfume.

They found the *Enrica* in Moelfra Bay, in the Welsh island of Anglesey, where Bulloch had instructed Butcher to take her. Not until 4:00 in the afternoon did they pull alongside the unarmed raider, by which time the noisome couples had grown disagreeably hungry. Bulloch ordered a meal for them, with a prudent amount of grog, and once they had finished their dinner and lighted their pipes, he called the sailors aft to ask if they would sign on for a cruise to—say—Havana, or some port along the way. All but three agreed and signed articles to that effect, taking the month's advance that the ladies so coveted. Sometime after midnight the bevy clambered back aboard the *Hercules* under a pelting rain, with heavy seas impeding the transfer. They were sea-widows all now, save three disgruntled consorts, and they started for Liverpool with the three hesitant mariners, carrying the news that the old 290 was headed for Cuba, probably by way of Nassau.[10]

Guessing that the *Tuscarora* might stop at Queenstown and linger in St. George's Channel, Bulloch decided on slipping out by the more dangerous North Channel, between Scotland and the north of Ireland. At 3:00 the *Enrica* steamed into a frothy Irish Sea under continued heavy rain, bearing to the north and west. Within five hours the skies cleared, the lookout sighted the southwest tip of the Isle of Man, and sailors went out on the yards to set the sails for the first time. With all its canvas spread the *Enrica* made an easy 13½ knots, Bulloch recorded, but then the wind fell. At two that afternoon some islands appeared off the port bow, betokening the Irish coast, and at 4:30 the ship rounded Fair Head, the northeastern tip of Ulster. Squeezing between that promontory and Rathlin Island, Captain Butcher brought the engines to a stop and hailed a fishing smack off the next jut of land, the Giant's Causeway. As the sun settled before them, Pilot Bond and Commander Bulloch started for shore with the fishermen while the *Enrica* turned for the open Atlantic.[11]

Back on the Mersey, a sense of relief reigned. With the *Enrica* gone, the political problem lay with the Foreign Office and the minister to London, rather than with the consul and customs collector at Liverpool. At the request of Lord John Russell, the foreign minister, Undersecretary Layard forwarded the law officers' opinion to the Bahamas and Queenstown, in the hope that the ship could be detained somewhere along its route. Meanwhile Laird Brothers advertised that all four of their docks were now open and ready to build or repair iron or wooden vessels of the largest size. Much to the annoyance of sovereignty-conscious British editors, the *Tuscarora* hovered in St. George's Channel long after any hope of catching the *Enrica* had passed—even after returning steamers reported having witnessed the prey escaping through the other exit.[12]

Commander Bulloch had not only seen the *Enrica* safely to sea, but had equipped and dispatched a tender for her as well. A sympathetic British company—Sinclair, Hamilton, & Company, of London—bought the little bark *Agrippina* for Bulloch, and that nondescript old craft took aboard the prospective raiding ship's two pivot guns and four smaller broadside guns, besides some Enfield rifles, revolvers, and cartridges for those small arms. At her dock south of London, the *Agrippina* also loaded a hundred barrels of powder for the deck guns and enough blue flannel uniforms for 150 sailors. Before the *Enrica* departed the Mersey, Bulloch sent instructions for the *Agrippina* to leave immediately for the Azores, where it would meet an unnamed steamer at Praia bay, on the eastern side of Terceira Island. The registered owners signed Bulloch's directive and forwarded it to the *Agrippina*'s captain, Alexander McQueen.[13]

Bulloch had likewise prepared instructions for Captain Butcher and Paymaster Yonge. Butcher was to sail under canvas as much as possible, both to save coal and to avoid reaching Praia Bay before the engineless *Agrippina*, and once the two had met, he was to begin loading the ship's stores and assembling the carriages for the guns. Before long a Confederate naval officer would arrive to relieve Butcher and finish arming the ship.

The paymaster was instructed to act as the purser of a merchant vessel until the *Enrica* made the open sea, at which time he should mingle with the rated hands and try to inspire their sympathies for the Confederacy. A few words about the South and her cause to the quartermasters and boatswain's mates would spark infectious conversations on the berth deck, Bulloch reasoned, which might attract many of the sailors to their service and give them a sense of loyalty to Captain Semmes when he took over.[14]

The men Yonge was expected to convert were almost exclusively Britons and Irishmen from the Canning Street boardinghouses. Most were unmarried and lacked any compelling connections ashore. James Mair and William Robertson hailed from Glasgow, and John Roberts from Llangawalad, in Anglesey. Frederick Johns lived with his parents on Castle Street, right in Liverpool. These were all bachelors. John Welham, the son of a Sudbury grocer, was a widower. At least one of the recent recruits had gone farther with the dockside doxies than a wiser man might: on Liverpool's Kent Street George Appleby had left behind a bride to spend his half-pay vouchers—something of a professional bride, as it turned out, though Appleby was never to learn of it.[15]

Five Liverpool youths took to sea with the *Enrica*, as did a number of older sailors with much experience. Michael Mars, who had sailed most of his cruises from Bristol, was in his early forties; Englishman George Harwood and Irishman Michael Genshlea both drew pensions from the British government for naval service, and Harwood was a member of the Royal Naval Reserve. William Crawford, Brent Johnson, Henry Fisher, David Roach, Peter Hughes, Mars, Frank Townsend, and Frank Curran belonged to the reserve, too, though some served under aliases. These were the sorts of veterans the ship would need, but for all the decades the crew had collectively spent at sea, these ten old man-of-war's men were the only ones who had ever worked a gun.[16]

The *Enrica*'s officers included John Low, the Scottish-born sailing master who had twice accompanied Commander Bulloch across the Atlantic. As the ship's prow plowed south, Low kept a log that would carry over into the *Enrica*'s new life.

Heavy seas buffeted the vessel as she rounded the western coast of Ireland; the afternoon after Bulloch departed, Low recorded the loss of the port bow post to one violent squall. Three days later, as they entered the same Roaring Forties that had nearly ended the maiden voyage of the *Kearsarge*, stiff gales began rolling the ship dangerously and setting her decks awash. Dawn of August 5 revealed that the foremast stays had been ripped from their mountings, and as Low oversaw the repairs, he noted that they had covered about half the distance to their rendezvous at Terceira.[17]

The *Enrica* had not yet sighted the Azores on August 8 when the *Bahama* sailed up the Mersey and landed Captain Semmes with his subordinates. Other officers, most of whom had served aboard the *Sumter*, joined them at Liverpool. Among these was Richard Armstrong, the midshipman Semmes had left behind at Gibraltar to command the disabled cruiser. Notified that he had been promoted to lieutenant, the nineteen-year-old Georgian rushed to Liverpool to serve again under Semmes, this time second only to Kell.

Armstrong had spent more than three years at the U.S. Naval Academy, where as a mere boy he had rubbed elbows with future admirals, including George Dewey, Alfred Thayer Mahan, Winfield Scott Schley, and Robley Evans. He had entered Annapolis with another plebe from Florida, Joseph Wilson. As Armstrong and Wilson rose to become upperclassmen themselves, they grinned at nervous newcomers like Edward Preble, who would join the *Kearsarge* as a midshipman in 1862, and James Morgan, who resigned the day after Fort Sumter surrendered and lived to record his life as a Confederate midshipman. When their states seceded in January of 1861, Armstrong and Wilson had resigned together. Wilson soon thought better of it, though, and asked to be reinstated a week later—as did Robley Evans, who forsook his Virginia roots and stayed with the Union. But in March

Wilson resigned again for good and went to sea with Semmes and Armstrong in the *Sumter*. Wilson, also a lieutenant now, at twenty, met his old classmate at Liverpool for a new voyage together.[18]

With these two came Miles Freeman, who would serve as chief engineer, and several of the junior engineer officers from the *Sumter*. A ship would usually carry four warrant officers, and Semmes selected three from among the old *Sumter* men who gathered at Liverpool. Boatswain Benjamin Mc-Caskey and Carpenter William Robinson both boasted warrants from the state of Louisiana (though Robinson was a Massachusetts native), and Gunner Thomas Cuddy hailed from South Carolina. For a sailmaker, Semmes took Henry Allcot, of Liverpool, whom Bulloch had recommended. With a total of nearly two dozen Confederate officers, another thirty-seven potential recruits for the *Enrica*'s deck and fire-room crews, and two 32-pounder guns in the hold, Bulloch and Semmes boarded the *Bahama* at the Bramley Moore dock and departed Liverpool on the morning of August 13.

That same day the Provincetown whaling schooner *Rising Sun* sailed into Praia bay, Terceira, where it anchored within sight of a new, bark-rigged ship that identified herself as the *Barcelona*, bound for the war in Mexico. Thanks to a blunder on the part of Paymaster Yonge, the Yankees aboard the *Rising Sun* learned that the ship was not really called the *Barcelona*; when the whaler departed a few days later, the officers of the *Enrica* worried— unnecessarily, as it developed—that the *Rising Sun* would carry news to Federal warships of a suspicious vessel in the Azores.

This Yonge would prove a troublesome devil. Indiscretion appears to have been the more charitable explanation for his volubility: back in Liverpool he had left an "Esteemed Friend" to whom he had promised to write of the cruiser's escapades—a friend who may have been either a lady or, possibly, the American consul.[19]

The *Agrippina* arrived on August 18, and the next day the two ships sidled up to each other, the *Enrica* sailors muttering about the somber old bark that bore only the name of the port of Bristol on her fantail. The big guns and the thirty-twos, made by the British firm of Fawcett, Preston & Co., came out of the old sailing vessel's hold; with the help of block and tackle suspended from spare booms, these were swung across to the deck of the *Enrica*, followed by the shot and shell and the purser's slops. A heavy groundswell inhibited the transfer, and in the evening the *Agrippina* swung away, but by 6:00 A.M. on August 20 they came together again to resume the process. Not long into the day's work another sail appeared in the bay—the *Bahama*, which also pulled alongside. Captain Semmes left the *Bahama* and came aboard the *Enrica* with his wardrobe, leaving Captain Butcher in nominal command for the present.

That afternoon the swells grew so violent that Bulloch decided to relocate the three ships in Angra Bay, on the southern side of the island, where they could complete their transactions in safety and secrecy. With the *Bahama* towing the *Enrica* to save coal, Bulloch directed the procession into a snug, isolated anchorage in West Angra Bay, which was separated from the main harbor of East Angra by a substantial point. The Portuguese customs boat spotted the little flotilla as it came in; before the three ships anchored, the customs officers ordered them around the point with the rest of the ships. Ignoring these officials, Bulloch directed his three captains to drop anchor where they were, and the next morning they all stood off the coast. The sea lay calm that day, and the two tenders unloaded everything meant for the *Enrica* but her coal.

That evening the *Bahama* led the way back to Angra do Heroísmo, but the port authorities suspected something sinister now, and would not permit them to anchor. All three ships then rounded the point again for Bulloch's anchorage at West Angra Bay, and on their passage a sentinel shouted something indistinguishable from shore. A shot rang out when the ships failed to stop, but it did no harm and the vessels proceeded to their anchorage. Late that evening another shot sailed between the *Enrica*'s masts, and it began to look as though the Portuguese wished to detain her.

Dawn of August 22 found the *Enrica* taking on coal from the *Agrippina*, but the work was soon interrupted by a pair of Azorean officials who rowed out with a platoon of soldiers. The two civilians reluctantly boarded the *Enrica* when they were told their soldiers could not come aboard with their arms, but as soon as they landed on deck they spotted the two huge pivot guns and the broadside battery; aft, they saw Gunner Cuddy and his assistants loading rifles and revolvers. The Portuguese grew agitated, and the more plump of the two began babbling wildly in his native tongue. The officers on deck feared they would bound over the side into their boat, and so calmed them with exaggerated bows and soothing words. Once they had settled down enough to enjoy a guided tour of the ship, the officials grew bold again and warned that the coaling would have to stop until the proper paperwork had been entered in the customs office, which the Confederate officers condescended to do. The English consul came aboard in the wake of the flustered functionaries and amused the ship's officers with the story behind the visit of the armed escort: it seemed that the island's leaders feared the little armada had come on a mission of conquest, and the unmistakably warlike cast of the *Enrica*'s deck had naturally confirmed their anxiety. The Portuguese denied having fired a round at the interloper on the previous evening, however, claiming that it was a careless shot from the Lisbon mail packet as it announced its departure for the mainland.[20]

For two more days the crew shoveled coal into the *Enrica*'s bunkers and readied the ship for sea, rigging the guns and caulking the propeller shaft, which had leaked badly on the voyage out. Semmes studied the crew closely as the work progressed. He noted an undesirable here and there, but many of them stretched themselves to impress him, knowing, probably, that they might demand their own prices for service aboard the cruiser.

Deck hands spent the morning of Sunday, August 24, washing the last of the coal dust from the ship. In tandem with the *Bahama*, the *Enrica* stood out to sea at noon, heaving to some five miles off shore. One of the thirty-twos belched the first round that ever flew from the ship's side, and newly appointed Signal Quartermaster Adolphus Marmelstein of Savannah, Georgia, sent the Stars and Bars fluttering up the mizzenmast while the ship's pennant rose at the mainmast. The skeleton crew of the *Bahama* rendered as rousing a cheer as the officers could elicit from so few throats. Officers on the *Enrica* called all hands aft to the quarterdeck, where William Breedlove Smith, Semmes's clerk, read his captain's commission and that of the ship, which would henceforth be known as the Confederate States Steamer *Alabama*. At that Smith fell silent, and Captain Semmes called to the men from amidships, where he stood on a gun carriage beneath the bridge. As the sailors turned to face him, he pointed to the *Bahama* and told them they were free to return to England on that steamer, but if they chose to remain, they would see some adventure.

"Now, my lads," he said, "there is the ship. She is as fine a vessel as ever floated; there is a chance that seldom offers itself to a British seaman, that is to make a little money." He assured them he would not put them "alongside a frigate at first," but promised them "a nice little fight" once they had had some training.

"There is Mr. Kell on the deck," he concluded. "All who wish to sign on see him." Kell and Paymaster Yonge stood by the companion hatch with the ship's articles, and a line formed before them. The pay proved generous: £4 a month for ordinary seamen, £5 and £6 for petty officers, and as much as £7 for firemen, so Yonge kept busy late into the night signing the men to the roll, giving them some advance pay, and making out their allotments. Semmes had primed them for the question through George Harwood, the old Liverpool sailor who collected a pension from the Royal Naval Reserve. Harwood had agreed to serve Semmes for six months as his chief boatswain's mate, and his opinion carried great weight with the younger seamen. Most who had come out on the *Enrica* shipped for the long cruise, as did many who arrived on the *Bahama*, including a fireman named John Latham, from Manchester, who carried with him a certificate as a Royal Naval Coast

Volunteer. He left his allotment in the name of his wife, Martha, who remained behind in Swansea.

Anxious lest he be left like John Maffitt, with too few men to man his yards, Semmes grew satisfied as the enlisted roster swelled to nearly seven dozen names. He would have liked to see another score or more, but within an hour of midnight the line had melted away, and it seemed clear that no one else would take his offer. An exhausted Semmes handed Commander Bulloch a sack of mail from the officers and some of the men, bidding adieu to him and to Captain Butcher as those two returned to the *Bahama*. A quartermaster from Savannah took the great double wheel that stood just forward of the mizzenmast, perhaps wondering at the alien inscription, "Aide toi et Dieu t'aidera." Ordering the officer of the deck to steer for the northeast, the captain of the South's newest warship retired to his cabin and tried to sleep as the *Alabama* rolled and tumbled through the night.[21]

CHAPTER SIX

The Greyhound

Thus to their hopeless eyes the night was shown,
   And grimly darkled o'er the faces pale,
And the dim desolate deep: twelve days had Fear
   Been their familiar, and now Death was here.
—Byron, *Don Juan*

Paymaster Yonge did not sleep well on his first night aboard the *Alabama*. The white oak planks of the upper deck had been fitted and caulked in the dampness of an English winter, and the ensuing spring and summer had remained humid, but a fortnight under the broiling island sun had shrunk the wood and pulled it away from the oakum between the joints. With each roll and pitch the ship took aboard gallons of salt water and spray, most of which ran out the scuppers when the yardarms tilted the other way, but inevitable trickles found their way through the cracks, running into the chambers below. Beneath the mizzenmast lay the wardroom, with the senior officers' staterooms lining either side of the hull, and there much of the seepage drained. Ubiquitous leaks discomfited each of the officers, but Clarence Yonge was the most disposed to complain of his sodden bunk.

Nor did the sailors enjoy better comfort at the forward end of berth deck. With no hammock eyes mounted, they could not yet sling their bedding, and so lay wrapped in blankets on the cold, hard floor, suffering every sway of the ship. Shot boxes that had not yet been bolted down and an assortment of unstowed ship's equipment slid dangerously to and fro, and stomachs grumbled for lack of a hot meal the previous evening; nor would they see cooked rations the next morning, and the constant clanking of the bilge pumps punctuated their night's sleep. When they arose on the morning of August 25, dressed now in the blue uniforms instead of their promiscuous merchant toggery, Lieutenant Kell stirred them into activity with his booming baritone, and for the next four days all hands turned to clearing the decks of clutter. Two ships passed within sight, unchallenged, while the *Alabama* readied its battery. Gunner's Mate Thomas Weir and his quarter gunners, William Crawford and Ralph Masters, supervised the passing of powder and shot down the forward hatch into the magazine, and of shell into the shell room aft, below the steerage officers' quarters. Gunner Cuddy attended to his two big pivot guns, for which the tracks had not been laid.[1]

Captain Semmes appointed as many of his petty officers as he could from among his few American sailors and the Royal Naval Reserve veterans. Four Savannah pilots had come out with him, and of these he appointed James King master at arms, William King and James Dent quartermasters, and Marmelstein signal quartermaster. Charles Godwin, a seaman of no particular skills, became captain of the afterguard; Paymaster Yonge believed Godwin to be an American, but an English shipmate spotted him for a Liverpool man. Harwood agreed to act as chief boatswain's mate until the end of February, when he would be replaced by the second boatswain's mate, Brent Johnson, who also had served in the reserves. So had Quarter Gunner Crawford, who would eventually rise to gunner's mate himself. The only reservist to earn no special rate was Michael Genshlea, an Irishman who signed on as a fireman.

The rest of the petty officers came from the host of Liverpool recruits, with one exception. George Appleby, a native of the Canadian Maritimes who had so recently married a Canning Street widow, assumed the job of yeoman; Paymaster Yonge took Frederick Johns as his steward. Peter Hughes became captain of the foretop, William Morgan captain of the maintop, and James Higgs captain of the hold. The exception was A. G. Bartelli, who was variously described as Italian, Portuguese, French, and American, whom Semmes had encountered on the return from Nassau; Bartelli served as the captain's steward.[2]

One Englishman occupied the wardroom and one lodged in the steerage. Dr. David Herbert Llewelyn, a young but well-trained surgeon from Wiltshire, acted as Surgeon Galt's assistant. George Fullam, whose father conducted a school for navigation in Hull, was himself an accomplished mariner although he was barely a year older than Lieutenant Wilson; Semmes appointed him the senior master's mate. Fullam took his place with the midshipmen in steerage, in the starboard staterooms; the port berths belonged to the engineers.[3]

Lieutenant Kell quickly whipped the crew into good discipline, but one week into the cruise Semmes had to deal directly with a minor revolt among his engineers. Theirs was a relatively new rank in the naval service, and line officers—threatened by the technical changes that rendered their seamanship no more vital than the skill of the engineers—tended to look down on them. Line officers in the Old Navy reserved distinctive perquisites for themselves, some of which were rather petty, and these privileges carried over into the wartime service. The engineers on both sides bridled over it. (Captain Pickering had revealed as much when he passed on the *Kearsarge* engineers' unsuccessful request for their own mess, separate from the steerage officers, and he displayed a line officer's jealousy when he reprimanded his first assistant engineer at Algeciras for the crime of trying to board the liberty boat ahead of the wardroom officers.)

Semmes recognized similar sentiments among his own engineers. Chief Engineer Miles Freeman, a Welshman who had emigrated to Louisiana a while before the war, had served with Semmes and Kell all through the *Sumter*'s cruise: in fact he had been the engineer of that ship when it was the civilian packet *Habana*. Semmes held him in the highest regard, and a brother officer later described him as a cool character, not easily excited; still, when Lieutenant Kell gave Freeman an order that the engineer did not deem appropriate, he ignored it. When Kell rebuked him for it, Freeman lashed back impudently. For that Semmes suspended him, hoping to curb the independent streak in Freeman's department before it crystallized.[4]

With his battery still incomplete, Semmes turned for his first chase with the new ship. A brig appeared off the starboard bow shortly after dawn on August 29, about midway between Terceira and Lisbon. After following her all day, Semmes eased to within six miles of her toward dusk, firing a blank cartridge and running up the Spanish flag. The brig did not respond in any way; since Semmes wanted to turn back to the Azores, he let her sail unmolested into the night.

The next afternoon the lookout spotted a schooner heading in the opposite direction, but Semmes let it go. Later that day the quarter gunners bolted the last of the pivot-gun tracks into place, and Semmes grew more aggressive: before dark he chased after a brig, heaving her to until she ran up French colors. For the rest of that day he watched as Lieutenant Kell assigned men to different gun crews and mustered them at their battle stations. Shorthanded as they were, six of the midshipmen and master's mates had to lend a hand at the eighth gun.[5]

Running mostly under topsail canvas with her fires banked, the *Alabama* overhauled a Portuguese brig on the last day of August and boarded the

French bark *Foi* on the morning of September 2, releasing her once the boarding officer had seen her papers. For nearly seventy-two hours thereafter the lookouts saw no sail, and Lieutenant Kell set the gun crews to practice. Between exercises Gunner Cuddy busied a detail with filling the pivot-gun shells with powder, stowing the job whenever rainclouds drifted overhead. By September 4 they had sailed back into the Azores, and that afternoon Semmes spotted the sharp mountaintop on Pico Island when he turned his glass to the north.

Just after sunrise on September 5 the helmsman veered to chase a brig somewhere near the thirtieth meridian of longitude, but the prey quickly outdistanced the *Alabama*. The deck officer's disappointment did not last long, though, for late that morning the lookout bellowed down the news of another ship. This one had already hove to when the cruiser slunk near, around 2:00 that afternoon, and the reason was obvious: she was a whaler, and a freshly killed sperm whale floated alongside her. The *Alabama* drew up within boarding distance, and Quartermaster Marmelstein raised the British flag at the mizzen. The whaler replied with the Stars and Stripes, and Lieutenant Kell sent Armstrong to her with an armed boat's crew.

The ship proved to be the *Ocmulgee*, of Edgartown, on Martha's Vineyard. Captain Abraham Osborn, whom Semmes described as a long, lean Yankee, may have been fooled by the officers' blue uniforms, and he consented, without much trepidation, to visit the mysterious cruiser with his ship's papers. As the returning boat neared the *Alabama*'s side, the signal quartermaster pulled down the English colors and raised the Confederate flag; the *Alabama* had taken her first prisoner.

During the afternoon Lieutenant Kell appraised the vessel, guessing her to be worth $50,000 with her hold full of whale oil, while details carrying wish lists from the cooks and warrant officers scoured the prize for useful items. They carried off some salt pork and beef, some "small stores," and a good deal of spare rigging, and transferred the thirty-six crewmen to the deck of the *Alabama* to join their captain. On Semmes's order, Master at Arms King manacled Osborn and his officers in retaliation for the treatment accorded to Paymaster Myers by the Federal navy. Marmelstein folded the whaler's flag, after marking it with the date, and stored it away in his signal locker. After dark the captors lay to beside the doomed whaler, rather than burn her and alert any other Americans in the vicinity, but in the morning a boat returned to apply the match. A pair of shots signaled the deaths of two dogs that had lived on the *Ocmulgee*, and soon afterward smoke began rolling out of her hatches. Soaked in sperm oil, the ship blazed furiously. The tied whale, which had died for naught along with all the others the

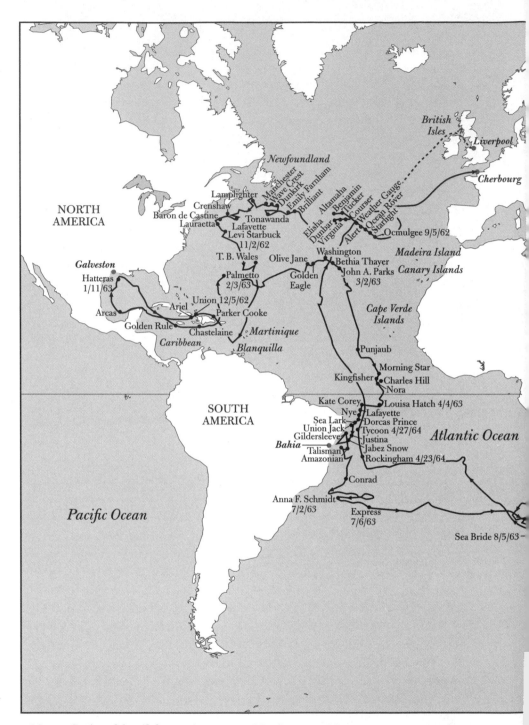

Map 2. Cruise of the *Alabama*, August 24, 1862–June 19, 1864

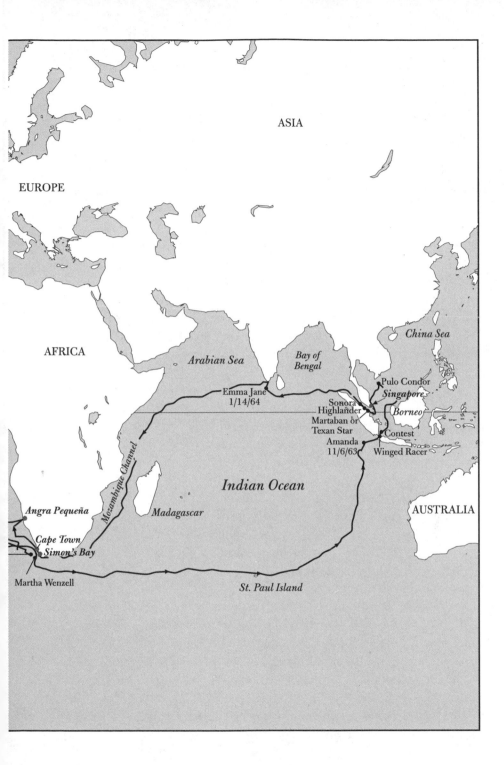

Map labels:

EUROPE

ASIA

AFRICA

Arabian Sea

Bay of Bengal

China Sea

Pulo Condor

Singapore

Borneo

Emma Jane
1/14/64

Sonora
Highlander
Martaban or
Texan Star

Contest

Amanda
11/6/63

Winged Racer

Mozambique Channel

Indian Ocean

AUSTRALIA

Angra Pequeña

Cape Town

Simon's Bay

Madagascar

Martha Wenzell

St. Paul Island

Ocmulgee had killed, contributed to the conflagration as the *Alabama* scudded away in pursuit of what turned out to be a French bark bound for Marseilles.[6]

The island of Flores came into sight that evening, and Semmes spent the night nearby, starting in on the morning of September 7. This being a Sunday morning, he mustered the crew as they headed for the island and had the Articles of War read for them, just as Lieutenant Harris read them on the *Kearsarge*. The thirty-seven whalers watched sullenly from beneath their awnings in the waist of the ship during this ceremony, but a few hours later the ship hove to and sent these Yankees into their own whaleboats, to pull themselves ashore.

As the three whaleboats started for the town of Lajes das Flores, the *Alabama* filled away on the starboard tack to challenge an approaching schooner before she reached territorial waters. At a mile's distance Semmes ran up the British flag again, but the schooner did not reciprocate. A signal from the lee bow gun failed to bring her around, either, so Semmes ordered a shot across her bow. The shot passed between the schooner's masts, but her master ignored even that and strained for port, so the third round sailed within two feet of the mainmast. At that she came around as the U.S. flag went up her halyards. Lieutenant Armstrong discovered her to be the *Starlight*, bound back to Boston from Faial, and she carried mail that included a warning to Secretary of State William Seward about the arming of the *Enrica* at Terceira. Her skipper, a Bostonian in his late twenties, had therefore guessed the intent of the cruiser when he first saw it, but he, like Captain Osborn, noted that the junior officers who boarded the ship wore blue naval apparel—perhaps their old Federal uniforms.

The *Starlight* carried a crew of seven Americans plus a few passengers, with some Azorean ladies among them. Semmes placed Captain Samuel Doane and all his sailors in irons this time, but he left the passengers aboard the schooner, which he occupied with a prize crew for the evening. The next morning the *Alabama* stopped outside Santa Cruz, on the eastern side of Flores, and landed the prisoners and passengers. The island governor came out in a boat with a delegation of his rusticated citizens, and Captain Semmes played the host for an hour or so. Bartelli poured a few glasses of champagne, the captain handed out cigars, and the islanders advertised their plentiful supplies for the marine trade. When Semmes thought he should be on his way, he herded the visitors on deck and saw them down the side, offering apologies for any inconvenience the capture of the *Starlight* might have caused the native passengers.[7]

With the *Starlight* tagging along under the prize crew, the *Alabama* took after a brigantine that raised the Portuguese flag when Semmes hoisted the British ensign. Satisfied with the authenticity of those colors, Semmes turned the ship about and chased down a bark that stood in the opposite direction. This was the *Ocean Rover*, another Massachusetts whaler that had begun its cruise in the spring of 1859. The crew knew little of the war, but had been looking forward to coming home soon to enjoy shares in the sizable profits to be made from the 1,100 barrels of oil they had collected. Instead they spilled into their six whaleboats with what belongings and trade goods they could carry and bent their backs to the oars; the bright yellow light of a near-full moon guided them toward Flores.

The *Ocean Rover* joined the *Starlight* and the *Alabama* for the night, but in the wee hours of the midwatch the deck officer awakened Semmes to warn of a big, bark-rigged ship passing nearby. The *Alabama* gave chase, and with daylight she raised English colors to the prey. The bark did not answer, nor did she slow down for a blank cartridge; but at two miles a shot across her stern brought the U.S. flag to her mast. She was a whaler, too, bound for the Indian Ocean via the Azores and Cape Verde Islands, and she was only sixteen days out of New London. Boarding officers found some tobacco and some needed underclothing aboard, and newspapers of as recent a date as August 18. While the captain and crew of the *Alert* lowered four whaleboats and started for the northern tip of Flores, the prize crews returned from the three whalers and set each of them afire. While the last of them reached full blaze, the lookout called another sail to the northeast, and the cruiser slipped away after the *Weather Gauge*, which had left Provincetown about the same time the *Enrica* had departed Liverpool. Another bark came into sight while the prize crew boarded the *Weather Gauge*, and Semmes took after the new sail as soon as the fifteen crewmen were securely ironed. He chased it through the night, finally overhauling it at 3:00 A.M. only to find that it was a Dutch merchantman bound from Bangkok to Hamburg. On his way back to the prize, Semmes chased a full-rigged ship, but it hoisted English colors and the *Alabama* returned to fire the *Weather Gauge*. The next day, September 11, Semmes hove to off Flores again and disembarked the prisoners from that ship, catching a glimpse of another whaling bark that seemed to cling to shore, as though for the protection of Portuguese sovereignty.[8]

Three days passed without another capture, but on September 13 Semmes overhauled another New Bedford whaler, a little hermaphrodite brig called the *Altamaha*. He took her fifteen crewmen aboard and consigned her to the flames, and late that night he was awakened for the news that a full-rigged ship had passed to windward within a couple of miles. Semmes ordered all sails set, and the *Alabama* soon ate the chase out of the wind, firing a gun to bring her to. Not until the raider came up on her beam and fired a second round from half a mile did the ship heave to, whereupon Semmes sent an officer aboard with a prize crew and orders to raise a light on the mast if she proved to be American. The light rode to the peak, and Semmes retired until daylight, when he learned that he had captured the *Benjamin Tucker*, yet another New Bedford whaler. The captain and his thirty men came aboard the *Alabama* while the boarding officer pilfered some soap and tobacco from the ship and set her ablaze.

Semmes turned back for Flores to rid himself of the prisoners, who now numbered half as many as his whole crew. That night a light rain fell, reminding Lieutenant Kell of the gaping cracks in the upper deck, and the next morning he set the crew to caulking those fissures. In the afternoon he practiced the gun crews, after which the lookout made Flores from the masthead. The prisoners realized that they would soon be landed, and one of them—a Dutchman named Abram Nordhoek—approached Kell to say that he did not wish to go. Ashore on Flores he would have little to show for his eight months aboard the *Benjamin Tucker*; if Kell approved, he would just as soon serve aboard the *Alabama*. With so slim a crew Kell was delighted to have him, and signed him up immediately.

Nordhoek's former shipmates had not even departed the deck when he participated in the capture of his first prize. The whaling schooner *Courser*, of Provincetown, appeared off the starboard bow at dawn as the *Alabama* plowed for Flores, and by 7:30 she hove to at the sound of a blank cartridge and raised the U.S. flag. The fifteen-man crew of this vessel joined the other fifty-three, and all of them spilled into eight whaleboats and started rowing for the island from about five miles out. Meanwhile the prize crew followed the *Alabama* to a distance of ten miles and returned to their ship for gunnery practice. Each of the eight gun crews fired three rounds at the *Courser*, including one shell from the pivot gun, and Semmes described the firing as "pretty fair for green hands for the first time." He made no mention of having hit the target, though, and at dark a detail had to row out and set her afire.[9]

Back in the United States, September 17 would be a bloody day. The Confederate Army of Northern Virginia had crossed into Maryland; while the *Alabama* fired its practice rounds at the *Courser*, that army lay defiantly on the right bank of Antietam Creek, facing twice its numbers on the opposite side. When this day ended, those Southerners would still hold their position—the three-quarters of them who remained under arms, that is—but when they staggered back across the Potomac the war would be dramatically changed.

The men who would die at Antietam still lay wrapped in their blankets under an uncomfortable rain when dawn came to the Azores. Fifty miles west-northwest of Flores, Captain Shadrack Tilton opened the logbook of the whaling bark *Virginia* and recorded his southeasterly course. He had left New Bedford on August 26, the day after the *Elisha Dunbar*. He had spoken the *Dunbar* just six days before, and now he was nearing good hunting grounds, where he saw signs that other ships had taken whales. For all the troubles at home, he saw no reason to doubt that this was the beginning of another long and profitable cruise, but at about 7:30 a strange bark appeared to turn after the *Virginia* as though in chase. At noon it drew alongside and sent a boat's crew over. Captain Tilton may have wondered at the English-accented officer in a grey uniform, but Lieutenant Low informed him that his cruise was over.

Within a few hours Tilton and his crew, which included his son, stood on the deck of the *Alabama* in wrist irons, watching the sizzling wreckage of the *Virginia* as it slid beneath the waves. Low and Lieutenant Kell appraised the ship at $25,000, but four years later the owners would claim damages of $67,500, and the international commission on *Alabama* claims finally awarded them more than $45,000, with nearly $25,000 more in interest.[10]

The next afternoon, following a three-hour chase and one bark from a bow gun, the raider also took in Tilton's friends on the *Elisha Dunbar*. A gale blew up while the prisoners were being transferred, and the *Alabama* turned back to the southeast under reefed topsails and the fore trysail while the flames devoured this tenth victim.

Captain Tilton complained that Semmes ordered him and the rest of his crew into the waist of the *Alabama*—amidships, that is, on the lee side. There they were ironed, save for a pair of ship's boys and the cook and steward, who were allowed to attend to their shipmates. Crewmen raised a weathered sail over their prisoners to keep the rain off them, and gave them some planks to allow them some slumber off the spray-soaked deck, but the gale turned so stiff that these precautions failed to keep the Yankee whalers dry. Worse yet, the storm continued for two days and abated only for a few hours on September 21 before commencing anew for another day and a half. Tilton and his fellows remained soaked most of that time. One man, a German named Gustave Schwalbe, grew so discontented that he threw in his lot with the Confederates, and Lieutenant Kell had his second recruit.[11]

All this weather drove the *Alabama* south, out of the seasonal shipping lanes. Semmes began to suppose that he had lain long enough about the islands; lest a snooping Federal warship find him, he decided to turn westward, toward the coast of the States. On September 20 the helmsman turned away from the Azores and never looked back. Eleven days passed without a single hail from the lookout, and when he did cry "Sail ho," it was a French vessel. Not until the morning of October 3 did another craft come within sight, due south of the Grand Banks of Newfoundland, and Semmes noted that it lay "dead to windward of us," so he did not even try to catch her. Less than two hours later two more ships appeared at once, respectively dead ahead and on the lee bow. Semmes stopped them both, and both were American, just out from New York. The leeward sail was the ship *Brilliant*, bound for London with a cargo of flour and wheat; the other was the *Emily Farnham*, headed for Liverpool. A boat's crew consisting of two officers and four sailors, all armed with revolvers and cutlasses, boarded each ship. For the first time Semmes encountered neutral cargo, for the *Farnham* carried goods owned by Englishmen. He therefore forced the captain to sign a bond for the value of his vessel (to be paid upon Confederate victory), and let her go, but she had to take his prisoners aboard as passengers. After seventeen days under armed guard and raw weather, the former *Virginia* and *Elisha Dunbar* sailors bounded onto the *Emily Farnham* with more glee than the fresh prisoners from the *Brilliant*, or even the captain of the spared ship.

The *Farnham* pulled away for Liverpool with sixty-eight unwilling passengers, leaving behind one of her own crew and three from the *Brilliant*, all Englishmen who had succumbed to Lieutenant Kell's generous pitch. The two-year-old *Brilliant* lived up to her name, for the boarding crew fired her at dark, and she burned within sight all night while the *Alabama* lay becalmed.[12]

They had reentered the trade routes now, about midway between the Azores and New York. Two Prussian ships caught the lookout's attention on October 4, and a French bark on her way to Cherbourg passed surprisingly close in the predawn grey of October 5. While the crew stood to muster and listened to the Articles of War later that day, the lookout spied another sail on its way to the northeast; the helmsman made for her, but Semmes had no heart for a long chase back in the direction where the enemy might be looking for him. He gave up that chance and turned instead for a brig that lay close by, but that one raised a neutral flag as well.

Before dawn on October 7 a bark hove in sight, and the *Alabama* sped alongside, finding her to be the *Wave Crest*, recently from New York with more American grain for England—specifically, Cardiff. The gunners practiced ineffectually on this one, too, before she felt the torch, and late in the afternoon a brigantine came within range to the westward. This chase lasted three hours or more beneath bright moonlight, when the *Dunkirk* gave up the ghost. Her grain would never reach Lisbon. By 11:00 P.M. the crew had been transferred to the *Alabama*, and flames claimed the prize.

The *Dunkirk* afforded Captain Semmes two recruits, one willing and one unwilling. David Leggett volunteered his services; George Forrest, who had deserted from the *Sumter* in Cadiz, had evidently found his way back to New York and shipped on the merchantman, never dreaming that he would see anyone from the little Confederate cruiser again. A junior officer recognized him, and drew up charges that could have sent the turncoat dangling from a yardarm.

Beating back to the east against a strong current, the *Alabama* encountered a packet ship bearing to the westward on the afternoon of October 9. Several hours later she bore down on the prey, finding her to be the *Tonawanda*, on her way to Liverpool with American-owned cargo and some seventy passengers, nearly half of them women. Unable to accommodate so many women aboard, a perplexed Semmes put a prize crew in charge of the packet and told the senior officer to follow him. The returning boat did bring aboard the *Tonawanda*'s black cook, a boy of about seventeen named David Henry White. David hailed from the slave state of Delaware, according to the captain of the passenger vessel; he carried no manumission papers, and in Semmes's eyes that made him contraband of war. The captain assigned him as a wardroom steward, but he directed the paymaster to enter him on the muster roll with the other ship's boys at the rate of £2 sterling per month.[13]

The *Tonawanda* rode the *Alabama*'s wake for four days while the imprisoned captain boarded on the deck of the cruiser to assure against trouble from his own crew. Only one American ship passed in view during that time: the *Manchester*, from New York for Liverpool. Her crew shifted to the *Tonawanda* while the incendiaries prepared her for the torch, and the surviving ships continued their tandem trek westward.

In the idle time between sightings Semmes read the newspapers he took from the prizes—treasuring New York *Heralds* as late as a week old, although they contradicted early reports of Confederate successes in Maryland. He also approved the sentences of George Forrest and Henry Fisher, one of his coxswains, whose courts-martial had been held beneath the wardroom skylight during the chase for the *Tonawanda*. Forrest escaped the noose and was sentenced to serve without pay for the rest of his enlistment, while Fisher, who had twice secured liquor from prizes and fallen hopelessly drunk, was stripped of his rate and reduced to seaman.

In a thick squall October 13 Semmes turned after a ship cruising under topsails only. Such lethargic movement suggested either a whaler that wandered about in search of a spout or a warship looking for enemy sails. Both the chase and the *Tonawanda* disappeared into the rain periodically, but toward dusk the lead narrowed to less than five miles. Semmes saw a pennant flying from the mainmast, and that usually meant a ship of war under commission, so he gave up the chase. To his alarm, though, the ship turned toward the *Alabama* and bore down on her. Kell called the gun crews to quarters, and all the broadside thirty-twos were slung loose. Loaders rammed charges home while the two pivots swung into position, and Marmelstein ran up the English colors. The stranger returned a Spanish flag, and a relieved Semmes watched the guns secured as the helmsman turned back to meet the *Tonawanda*. With a storm threatening, the captain preferred to shed responsibility for his civilian prisoners, and he sent the master of the packet back to her after obtaining his signature on an $80,000 bond. Considering himself lucky despite the enormous inconvenience, the *Tonawanda*'s skipper filled his yards with canvas and hurried away into the night. Two sailors, John Clements and William Halford, remained behind to try their luck with the *Alabama*.[14]

It seemed to be feast or famine for the hunter. Days without a sail would be followed by days of many sails. A ship appeared just before midnight after the *Tonawanda* pulled away, but the gathering gale moved her so swiftly in the opposite direction that the *Alabama* did not even turn about. In the next thirty-two hours the lookouts called four more sightings, but the first three showed Danish, French, and English colors. On the morning of October 15, however, the Boston bark *Lamplighter* ran straight into the trap on its way to Gibraltar with a load of tobacco. The *Alabama* simply lay by and let her come, firing a gun when she reached easy range. The boats lumbered back and forth in heavy seas to transfer the prisoners; when the flames climbed the rigging of this ship, the *Alabama* had destroyed $746,000 in the property of U.S. citizens, by the Confederate officers' own reckoning. That equaled three times the original cost of building and outfitting the *Alabama*, and when the owners of the victim vessels came to represent their claims they would inflate that figure several times.[15]

The weather grew worse the next day, October 16. Early in the morning strong winds increased to one of the worst gales Semmes had experienced in all his years at sea—he who had lost the *Somers* in a storm—and he concluded that he had run into a hurricane. The wind carried away the main yard and tore the maintopsail and fore staysail to shreds. With the maintopsail parted, the foretopmast staysail threatened to pull the ship down into the trough of the sea, but the captain of the forecastle, James Smith, valiantly clambered up and cut that liability away, leaving only the little storm staysail to carry the ship. In almost the same location where the *Kearsarge* had lost her boats on the trip out, heavy seas stove the *Alabama*'s stern and lee quarter boats and dashed in the forward hammock nettings. A strip of the top mainsail wrapped around the nearby clewline and chain sheet. The officer of the deck, Lieutenant Low, ordered all the unoccupied hands and the boys of the watch to gather on the quarterdeck, where he had them lashed against the weather bulwark to avoid losing them over the side to leeward when the ship rolled. And roll she did: cross seas battered the vagabond as the barometer plummeted to 28.64 inches; it had fallen no lower than 29.44 during the tempest that had threatened to sink the *Kearsarge*. Foam and spray blinded everyone on deck.

Then the eye of the storm passed over them, but within half an hour or so the gale resumed with equal force, spinning the ship in all directions as the helmsman struggled to keep headway. By 2:00 the storm had subsided a little, the barometer climbed back up to 29.70, and Lieutenant Kell turned the crew to repairing damages. Topmen climbed into the loosened rigging, sent the broken halves of the main yard down, cut the tangled sail and sheets, and tightened the stays. Captain Semmes looked for another prize from which to replace his boats, and he wondered exactly where he was. For days the sun had hidden behind thick overcast and denied him a sighting, and he had been estimating his position by dead reckoning.

When the sun finally broke out on October 19, Kell ordered the sails loosened to dry, and the crew hung their wet clothing in the rigging. Sunday muster passed off as usual, but afterward details of men attended to the rusting guns while others shipped a makeshift main yard from the remains of the fractured one. Semmes shot the sun at noon, and found that he was south of his estimated latitude by more than a point, and he had thought himself east of his real position by nearly two points of longitude.[16]

The raider overhauled a Dutch brig on October 20 and an English bark the next day. The *Alabama* had nearly reached American waters now, but ten of the last twelve ships had shown neutral flags or papers, and Semmes commented wryly in his journal about such luck. Another heavy storm struck on October 22, and for hours the *Alabama* labored with its weakened yards bare of canvas and only the triangular staysails set. The ship's dinghy was stove beyond repair, and a deck hand just cut it free and let it wash away. The prow plunged deep into the belly of each wave, and water sloshed on deck by tons, no doubt soaking Paymaster Yonge and his fellow wardroom officers.

That gale abated during the night, but the sea remained rough the next morning when the lookout cried of a sail to leeward. This one was English; two more to the east escaped because Semmes wished to tack westward after having been blown sixty miles off course. Late in the afternoon a big bark showed on the horizon heading diagonally across the *Alabama*'s path, and the quartermaster wheeled the rudder a few points to lie across her bearing. The bark answered Semmes's British ensign with the American, and Semmes shifted his colors; at half a mile he brought her around with a bow gun and sent Lieutenant Wilson in a boat for her captain and papers.

This was the *Lafayette*, of New Haven, bound from New York with more Yankee grain for Belfast. The owners had tried to mask their property as that of the Irish receivers, but Semmes declared their paperwork fraudulent and took the merchant crew aboard. By 10:00 P.M. the *Alabama* had left the *Lafayette* burning in her wake.[17]

From newspapers taken off the *Lafayette*, Semmes learned that the Federals already knew of his captures along the Grand Banks. In fact Captain George Hagar, of the *Brilliant*, had carried the word back to the mainland, and Gideon Welles warned the commander of his North Atlantic Blockading Squadron on October 19. Even more recent papers came into Semmes's hands on October 26, when he gathered in the schooner *Crenshaw*, three days out from New York. According to these journals Secretary Welles had sent several ships after the *Alabama*, which he still called the *290*, and one report incorrectly named the *Vanderbilt* as one of the chase vessels. This mammoth sidewheeler, capable of fourteen knots despite carrying fourteen huge deck guns, all of them larger than the *Alabama*'s pivots, was the one ship Semmes feared above all others. Nevertheless he kept his course for New York while the reported flotilla approached him.

The crews of the *Lafayette* and the *Crenshaw* supplied the *Alabama* with three more ordinary seamen, all Germans or Dutchmen, and a sailor named Alfred Morris shipped from the doomed Boston bark *Lauraetta* on October 28. Some forty-five other prisoners from the last three captures declined to engage for the raiding business, and when Semmes ran down the decrepit Bangor brig *Baron de Castine* the next day, he let her go with the prisoners as passengers. He gave her enough provisions to return to Boston, which she did by November 2.[18]

Semmes had hoped to run into New York and make a few captures off that city—he was now barely 200 miles away—but Engineer Freeman guessed that only four days' supply of coal remained, so Semmes turned south, for his preplanned rendezvous with the *Agrippina*. On November 2 he encountered the *Levi Starbuck*, a New Bedford whaler that had left home five days before, bound for the Pacific. With a militia draft going into effect in New England, the twenty-nine whaling crewmen may have hoped to avoid service, for by the end of the *Starbuck*'s planned thirty-month cruise the war would have been virtually over. Certainly none of them offered to sign on with the *Alabama*. Semmes therefore ordered the prize's hold rifled for supplies (the cooks found a welcome store of cabbages and turnips), and he took from her cabin newspapers as new as four days old before applying the torch.

For some days the hunter found no prey, having drifted out of the shipping corridor on its beeline course for the Caribbean, but on the morning of

November 8 the *Alabama* overhauled the ship *T. B. Wales*, returning to Boston from Calcutta. The *Wales* carried linseed oil and saltpeter, with which gunpowder is produced, and Semmes decided to burn her even though the passengers included two women and some children; the husband of one of the women apparently failed, albeit judiciously so, to identify himself as the homeward-bound former U.S. consul to Mauritius. Semmes took these innocents aboard and rousted some officers from their staterooms to accommodate the ladies and the youngsters. The officer who oversaw the kindling of the *T. B. Wales* destroyed a ship and cargo worth almost exactly the same as the *Alabama*.

This last prize supplied the raider with a new main yard to replace the one lost in the hurricane, but she also provided a more valuable asset. That day and the next, eleven different members of the captured crew came forward—Englishmen, Irishmen, one Frenchman, and a Portuguese—to put their names on the *Alabama*'s roll. Semmes welcomed them all, for they brought him almost up to full strength, and at the Sunday morning muster on November 9 he counted 110 enlisted men. As the voices of children rose from belowdecks and the sailors enjoyed their Sunday afternoon siesta, the cruiser sped south, for Martinique.[19]

CHAPTER SEVEN

Interlude

Bluish 'mid the burning water, full in face Trafalgar lay.
—Browning, "Home Thoughts from the Sea"

The tedium of watching the *Sumter* only worsened as the hot Mediterranean summer progressed. Ten days after the shark attack, John Dempsey, the newlywed captain of the afterguard, sought liberty ashore, where he consoled himself again with local distillates. When he returned the next morning, he let fly at the officer of the deck in loud and mutinous terms. Two other staggering revelers went into irons with him, but Dempsey earned the first full-blown court-martial aboard the *Kearsarge*. On July 28 Lieutenant Harris, Surgeon Browne, and the three acting masters convened their court on the quarterdeck with a sail draped from a spar to impose the illusion of privacy. When the curtain came away, Dempsey had been stripped of his rate and the additional $2 a month it brought him, and he drew a month of extra duty besides losing a month's pay. Francis Viannah, the clairvoyant Portuguese, took over as captain of the top.[1]

Coal Heavers Poole and Wainwright complained constantly of their boredom in late July, describing the same off-duty amusements that seemed no longer to amuse: those who could find books or newspapers read them; those not yet tired of draughts and dominoes began new games, yearning to deal the cards that Captain Pickering forbade; those who had fallen into true depression simply slept. Wainwright said at the end of the month that he was "getting the blues" from the monotony, and Poole found the duty so dull that he hoped the *Sumter* would go to sea just so they could enjoy some excitement. A few men had not even stepped ashore since the cruise began, but most of these took their first liberty on August 4 and 5. Eleven of them remained at Algeciras at 2:00 on the afternoon of August 6 when the *Kearsarge* suddenly lifted its anchor and stood out to sea, in search of a brig reportedly bound from Barcelona to the Confederacy.

The American consul at Gibraltar, Horatio Sprague, had learned from his counterpart in Barcelona that the *Mary Scaife* had arrived there on July 27 from Charleston, bearing Carolina cotton and resin. The Barcelona representative wired Gibraltar on August 6 that the brig had departed under the British flag with a cargo of soap, coffee, lead, shoe leather, silk, olive oil, and red wine, and she had to pass through the Straits of Gibraltar. Sprague warned Captain Pickering that the brig would claim to be headed for Cadiz.

Pickering spent all day in the straits, not daring to stray beyond sight of the Rock lest the *Sumter* leap to life, but at dark the *Kearsarge* turned back for the stranded liberty men. They all returned in the one boat that came for them, but with no great enthusiasm: a few extra days in the city would have saddened none of them. The next day, and for ten days thereafter, Pickering resumed cruising the "gut" between the continents, keeping always within twenty or thirty miles of Gibraltar. Each day he hailed numerous vessels, mostly brigs, chasing them down when they failed to respond, but they all proved to be neutrals or American. One Spanish brig answered the challenge with "No entiendo," and Pickering let her go.

Most evenings Pickering brought his ship back to its anchorage at Algeciras, but the night of August 12 shone bright with moonlight so he set the watches and stayed out, to the pleasure of the crew. Around 10:00 that night someone saw a school of porpoises gamboling about the ship—exercising their legendary but misplaced trust in human beings—and Captain Pickering tried his hand at harpooning one. He made no strike, and offered a ration of grog to anyone who could. One of the boatswain's mates took the weapon and skewered three successive dolphins, which Acting Master Wheeler dispatched messily on deck with a knife while the cooks gathered up the meat for a feast.

When he anchored on August 15, Pickering found a letter from Consul Sprague warning him of an informal grievance lodged by the acting governor of Gibraltar, who resented the daily excursions around Her Majesty's colony. The *Kearsarge* had scouted the entire perimeter of the Rock, and had halted or "reconnoitered" too many ships within sight of the governor's mansion, and Sir Robert Walpole considered it a violation of British neutrality. Any further such affronts, he hinted, would bring a formal complaint.

The threat apparently meant less to Pickering than the hope of capturing a blockade runner after more than six months of undistinguished service, and at dawn he prepared to sail for the straits again, but a messenger from

Sprague stopped him. Sprague sent along a Cadiz newspaper that reported the arrival of a brig called the *Good Luck*: this was the new name of the *Mary Scaife*, which had been sold, at least nominally, to Spanish owners. She had slipped through during one of the *Kearsarge*'s nights in port, or had sailed right by under the foreign flag; perhaps her deck officer had called out "No entiendo." That was one prize Charles Pickering would not claim, and twenty weeks later a volunteer acting master's mate in charge of a one-gun tender would catch the elusive brig—altered to a schooner rig—in the Florida Keys.[2]

With the escape of that ship the excitement ended, and the dull shipboard routine resumed. August 17 was a Sunday, and by dawn the engine-room crew "drew" the fires, emptying the fireboxes. At 10:00 A.M. Pickering called for muster, for the first time in white summer uniforms; when the ceremony ended, he bestowed liberty on a handful, including Coal Heaver Wainwright, who had not ventured on shore since the *Kearsarge* left Portsmouth.

"I felt like a young colt when I got ashore," Wainwright wrote that night. He found Algeciras a dirty city with narrow streets and unimpressive citizens, but he saw one redeeming quality in the form of the numerous bars. There was plenty of good wine in the place, he said, and he drank a good deal of it. Still, when the liberty boat ran ashore that night, he felt no regrets.

While alcohol could be had anywhere in Algeciras, water came at a premium, and purveyors brought it in from the countryside on their donkeys to sell it by the gallon. Charles Poole scorned the ubiquitous liquor distributors, but he shared Wainwright's contempt for the people and their towns, echoing the jibes at the close, littered streets of Algeciras. The bright gleam of low, whitewashed buildings with their terra-cotta tile roofs elicited no appreciation from that son of the New England shore. Nor did he care for the smaller town just down the coast that the sailors called Orange Grove. There the inhabitants could afford no whitewash to defy the broiling sun, or tiles for their roofs, and Poole sneered at the "mud" hovels covered in thatch, which he pronounced "very dirty looking." He recoiled, too, at the apparent irreverence of the citizens: on one tramp ashore he stumbled into the funeral procession of a young child, and the tail of the column echoed with laughter as the mourners ambled along, smoking nonchalantly. When Poole ventured ashore, he usually sought a room in town and struck out for the surrounding countryside, wandering among the fruit trees, the empty bullfighting rings, and the cemeteries.[3]

Neither Wainwright nor Poole took notice of the women in Algeciras and San Roque, but Captain Pickering and the officers' cook, Charles Fisher, both found them enchanting. The captain seemed to prefer the Spanish beauties to the English women of Gibraltar, advising one invited guest to "keep to the *port* side where the dark eyed Señoritas dwell." Pickering's friendship with one lady drew snide comments from a Spanish lieutenant and a U.S. consular agent, who relayed the Spaniard's complaint that "Gentlemen of your ship are in the habit of bringing on shore goods for some of the 'Ladays' of this place"; the agent's observation drew an indignant reply from the captain.

Fisher fell briefly under the spell of a milkman's daughter whom he encountered while buying provisions. She was "the loveliest girl I've seen in Spain," he thought, with her "Melting black eyes and beautiful glossy black hair." For some the allure of exotic women proved too strong to resist, and more than one of those aboard the *Kearsarge* came to regret it before the cruise ended.

With such attractions in town some must have found it difficult to remain aboard ship, where so many confined men grew unsociable and downright antagonistic. Fisher himself developed a dislike for several men besides the "Boston Rowdy" Dempsey, and he thought the captain of the forecastle, Jimmy Haley, was "decidedly the ugliest man on the ship." By that he meant to say that Haley, "an old *Mick*" from Ringaskiddy, in Cork, was disagreeable—regardless of how handsome or homely he may have been. Admitting to thirty-eight years of age, Haley had spent about twenty of them at sea, beginning with a stint aboard Her Majesty's gunboat *Shamrock*. Fisher claimed the old salt did little but swear and bicker all day, characterizing him as the "porcupine" of the crew for his continual cursing and quarreling.

Fireman George Remick, a machinist from Newburyport, earned Fisher's recognition as the "wickedest" man in the ship's company. Like Haley, he swore constantly at everyone—even at his food, said Fisher—but in the black cook's eyes the worst of Remick's traits was his politics, for he sympathized with the slave South. The fireman had said that Lincoln was no better than Jefferson Davis, and he especially railed at the president's oppression of Democrats in the border states, which he perceived as the creation of a "slave country" in the remaining United States. Joel Sanborn, another fireman who had also been a machinist in civilian life, found Remick good fodder for a satirical rhyme; when the crew began repeating Sanborn's verses, his subject raced around the ship in a frenzy, demanding to know who had written them.

Occasionally patience failed the test of such prolonged proximity, and words turned to blows. At least four fights warranting the captain's attention broke out in one August fortnight. Five men who proved troublesome time and again—Fireman Henry Jamison, Coal Heaver Robert Motley, seamen Benedict Drury and Thomas Buckley, and Ham Fat, the captain's cook—landed in irons for these brawls.[4]

Even the officers grew testy with one another. Sydney Smith, one of the third assistant engineers, disobeyed some minor ship's order in mid-August and drew a week's suspension from Lieutenant Harris. Demonstrating the same hostility toward line officers that had surfaced among the engineers on the *Alabama*, an aggravated Chief Engineer Cushman made snide reference to the suspension in his engineer log, and Captain Pickering reprimanded him for that, calling his written remarks "*erroneous, insubordinate, & disrespectful.*"[5]

One Saturday in late August the wardroom steward, Robert Scott, decided that he had suffered such company and monotony as long as he could. He went ashore to buy delicacies for the officers on August 23, carrying $75 of their common mess fund, and with that money he treated the boat's crew to a drink. With a handshake he told the captain's steward, Edward Williams, that he had no intention of returning to the ship. He would go to the British governor and report himself "a runaway nigger," and ask for asylum. Williams, who was also black, took the secret back to the *Kearsarge* with him, and later Scott's friends learned that he had succeeded.[6]

The storeship *Release* arrived alongside on the day after Scott deserted, bringing mail and announcing that it would head home for Boston the next day. Surgeon Browne took the opportunity to send three wretchedly ill men home with her—a Marine and two sailors, one of whom had come aboard in Spain. For weeks now they had suffered from what some of their shipmates learned was cholera morbus, and they seemed not to improve in the stale air of the ship: the *Kearsarge* provided no formal sick bay, and Browne's patients had to lie in a corner of the berth deck. A fortnight later Captain Pickering also boarded his first assistant engineer, James Whittaker, on a steamer for home: Whittaker thought he had invented a means of sinking ironclad warships, and the Navy Department wanted to have a word with him.[7]

The sack of mail left by the *Release* disappointed Yeoman DeWit, who grew frantic now about his family. His last letter from home had been dated March 31, and with each delivery he lined up eagerly, only to fall deeper into dejection when the last letter was handed out. The August 25 shipment left him scribbling "The Lord help me" in his journal, and a week later he recorded another disappointment. Nor was he alone. Charles Poole fell into a funk barely four months into the cruise for lack of mail, but he rebounded instantly when a letter finally reached him, remarking that the news of his family's good health took a "big load" from his mind. William Wainwright frequently commiserated with himself over his family's failure to send news ("No letters for Bill," he noted on September 7), and Charles Fisher complained as late as April of 1864 that the mail bag had contained "No letters for me, as usual." For most single sailors the lack of mail merely contributed to their boredom, but for family men like DeWit it was torture; his wife was not young, and his children were numerous, so anything might have gone wrong. For all his raucous, devil-may-care antics under the influence of liquor, even John Dempsey fretted over the more common concern of the younger, married sailor, for he had left a young bride in port, and she had recently borne him a son. When many months had passed without word from her, he sent a letter to his sister, asking her to take it to his wife and "ask her if she ever intends to write to me again."[8]

The saving grace of naval service, for many aboard the *Kearsarge*, was the daily ration of grog. That quarter-gill of watered rum offered something to look forward to: it was issued on the assumption that it warded off disease, but perhaps the only illness it prevented was depression. Many an old salt viewed the afternoon dram as the principal attraction of life at sea. The growing temperance movement eventually took a toll on the practice, though, and Congress voted to abolish the regular spirit ration in the navy after September 1, 1862. The order arrived late in the Mediterranean, but it was read to the *Kearsarge*'s assembled crewmen at Sunday muster on September 14, and a few took it with poor grace. Teetotaler Poole rejoiced at the decision, which would yield him an additional 5 cents in pay each day, but he acknowledged that the announcement "cast a Gloom over the Liquor loving ones." William Wainwright, who would take a drink when he could get it, did not seem particularly saddened by the order, but he, too, observed that "some of the old soakers don't like it." The order called for the prohibition of distilled liquor aboard U.S. vessels of war except as medical stores, but sympathetic captains like Charles Pickering allotted generous space in their holds for several barrels of such medicine.[9]

The hold of the *Kearsarge* contained another liquid that was not supposed to be there: on that same Sunday, September 14, the captain of the hold reported four inches of water in the starboard midship shell room. Because of persistent leaks since the voyage began, it became a habit to inspect the belly of the ship, but for many weeks it had proven dry. Presumably with the assistance of one of the engineers, the deck officer concluded that the water escaped from a leak in the feed pipe that led straight through the shell rooms; this pipe fed the pump that the ship used for washing the deck and fighting fires.[10]

As if to test that hose for firefighting capacity, Pickering called for a surprise exercise at general quarters. The crew did this frequently, but this time the captain waited until everyone was fast asleep. Around midnight Landsman William Bastine rolled the drum, and sailors began spilling out of their hammocks. They lashed their bedding together, pounded up the dark companionways to store the bedrolls in the nettings, and raced for their battle stations. A new man who had come aboard to try out as wardroom steward in place of Robert Scott had not yet been issued a hammock, and he lay asleep on the berth deck beneath his shipmates when the alarm sounded. A big black sailor—perhaps George "Ham Fat" Williams, who would have been the one to beat the drum had he not been off duty—landed on top of him, and the novice sprang to his feet, only to be knocked into one corner as someone swung a hammock. He tumbled into another corner as someone else ran into him. At last, to the amusement of all who had witnessed his terror, he sang out, "I don't belong to the ship!"

Confusion reigned in the darkness. Ham Fat lost his shoes but continued to his station in the magazine, and although the exercise was supposed to be carried on in silence, he came pounding barefoot down the ladder bellowing "General Quarters." Up on deck the guns were cast loose and rolled back as though for loading while assigned firemen unreeled the hoses and attached them to the pump head. For an hour every man stood at his post, the gunners pretending to load and the firemen aiming brass nozzles at imaginary fires. William Wainwright manned a hose in the steerage, where he occasionally contemplated the powder magazine right beneath him. Charles Poole stood by with Armorer George Russell to hand out rifles, then scrambled for the shell room to bring up 11-inch projectiles for the Dahlgren guns.

At last the boatswain's whistle piped the hammocks back down, and everyone slung them and crawled in for what sleep they might find; an anxious George Williams stomped straight for the head. Within twenty-four hours the probationary wardroom steward had departed the ship, carrying off his belongings and his bruises.[11]

The weather cooled slightly in late September, and the berth deck turned more bearable. From the anchorage near Orange Grove the men also enjoyed a more pleasant vista, and sometimes riding parties of English officers and their ladies ranged along the beach within easy sight. Sometimes the sailors themselves rented horses on liberty, and galloped along the shore or rode over to Algeciras if they sought more metropolitan pleasures.

In honor of the season Captain Pickering called for a mixed uniform of blue trousers, white jumpers, and blue caps with white covers. The Sunday muster in these clothes offered "a very neat appearance" on deck, thought one of the coal heavers. As far as Pickering and the crew knew, this pleasant interlude would conclude their sojourn in southern Europe, for Secretary Welles had promised to send out a ship to relieve them. Next they would go to the Gulf of Mexico, near the mouth of the Mississippi, just as the Navy Department had planned from the start, where at last their ennui might be allayed with a little action.

Any visions of home were shattered at the end of the month, but the prospects for excitement improved. Late on the night of September 28 a telegram arrived at Algeciras from the U.S. minister at Lisbon, warning of the *Alabama*'s depredations in the Azores. The American consul at Algeciras delivered that message to Captain Pickering the next morning. With the coal bunkers just filled a couple of days before, Pickering needed only to replenish his food and supplies, and he steamed the ship over to Gibraltar to spend the last day of the month boarding provisions. At 7:00 that evening he turned his ship for the straits.

At 10:00 the next morning Pickering encountered the *Tuscarora* just off the port of Cadiz. The two ships hove to off that port while Captain Craven and some of his officers came aboard to confer: Craven had also just heard the news. The skippers decided to strike straight for the Azores; while they talked, the *Tuscarora* circled twice around the *Kearsarge*, as though in challenge, and when Craven returned to his ship, at noon, the race was on. In the afternoon the *Kearsarge*'s crankshaft sleeves heated up a bit, and the chief engineer advised the deck officer to slow down. By dark the *Tuscarora* was hull down and well ahead, and the next day she was nowhere in sight. Pickering made twelve knots by setting every sail and straining the engines as much as he dared, and that afternoon the *Tuscarora* appeared briefly off the lee beam, but then she disappeared permanently.[12]

For three more days the *Kearsarge* plowed open sea, to the delight of most of her crew. The fresh breezes and the interruption of their monotony stirred some of diarists among them to the verge of poetry, or what passed for poetry with them. The sun had not yet risen behind them on October 5 when the lookout called land off the port bow, and the quartermaster steered wide of the islands of Santa Maria and São Miguel. A school of whales played nearby, leaping and diving within easy sight of the ship as though specifically for the amusement of the off-duty men.

That evening the ship nosed into the harbor at Terceira, where Pickering understood the *Alabama* had been sighted first. Finding no strange sails there, he backed his vessel out and turned to the southwest, for Faial. As the steamer pulled away, the lights of Angra do Heroísmo twinkled as prettily for the Union sailors as they had for Raphael Semmes's men six weeks before. Surely this was business, thought Poole, Wainwright, and a good many of their shipmates: it was for romantic views and the excitement of the chase that they had enlisted.

At dawn the next day the ship squeezed between São Jorge and the island of Pico, where loungers noted the curious prominence that gave the island its name. A conical mountain appeared to have another hill sitting on top of it like a great wart, the peak rising some 7,500 feet above the surrounding land. Like others of their generation who were confronted with mountains of that shape, the *Kearsarge* men were reminded of a sugar loaf. A couple of hours later the ship put in at Horta, on Faial, and the crewmen climbed the forecastle to admire the checkerboard farm lots on the slopes, and the windmills that seemed to grace every hilltop. The New Englanders who had marveled at the greenery of Madeira on Washington's birthday remained impressed with the lush vegetation of the Azores in October, when their own hometowns would gleam with the brilliance of dying leaves.

Captain Pickering may have been surprised to learn that the *Tuscarora* had not yet arrived. Nor had the *Alabama* been seen since dropping her last prisoners at Flores on September 16, and that news discouraged Pickering and his crew alike. For all of the raider's disappearance, though, some fifteen American vessels huddled in the harbor under the thin guise of foreign flags; when the nationality of the *Kearsarge* had been confirmed, all those alien banners came fluttering down and that many U.S. flags took their places. Six of the captains whose ships Semmes had burned came aboard the next day to make their laments. That same morning the *Tuscarora* steamed sheepishly into the bay, a full twenty-four hours behind the vessel she had seemed to outstrip so easily. Twice, now, had Captain Craven missed the *Alabama*.[13]

Captain Pickering reported briefly to Gideon Welles via the American consul's packet, sending along a bag of mail from the crew. While deck hands topped off the coal bunkers, Mr. Cushman worked on the engines. The brass sleeves around the crankshaft had worn down a sixteenth of an inch already, just on the trip out from Gibraltar, and some 400 pounds of filings had washed out with the water that lubricated the shaft casing. Pickering asked some officers from the *Tuscarora* to sit on an independent survey board to evaluate the problem, and they advised leaving the sleeve water faucet wide open, to keep fresh water circulating around the shaft. That might not prevent the sleeves from grinding away altogether, but it might cool them sufficiently that the ship could continue its search for the *Alabama* a while longer.[14]

In the first minutes of October 8 the *Kearsarge* headed out to sea. At first light three bells rang—5:30 A.M.—and the lookout shouted "Sail ho!" from the foretop crosstrees: he had spotted a steamer to the east that seemed to be harrying a small brig. The *Kearsarge* turned to have a look. When the steamer saw this, she seemed to speed away, and Captain Pickering took greater interest in her. He ordered full steam, and the engine room quickly turned out seventy revolutions per minute, though Coal Heaver Wainwright supposed they should have been able to make eighty. At 9:00 the crankpins heated up again and they had to stop the engines; after fifteen minutes Mr. Cushman engaged them once more, and the shaft ground deeper into its brass mounts, yielding thirteen knots despite pitching against a heavy head sea.

Through the glass the chase proved to be a big sidewheel steamer, eliminating any hope that she might be the *Alabama*, but the *Kearsarge* kept after her on the chance that she carried contraband from, or for, the Confederacy. On his part, the captain of the sidewheeler probably feared it was the *Alabama* in his wake, and he threw everything he could into his boilers. His crew tossed barrels of oil over the side to lighten the ship, and the *Kearsarge* steamed straight through the jetsam. At 2:00 that afternoon they passed Terceira, bound northeast, and the *Kearsarge* seemed to gain slowly. The afternoon watch took down the fore and main yards and dragged all the spare chain aft to shift weight in that direction and raise the bow, in hopes of reducing resistance from those head seas.

At 4:00 and again at 7:00 the engines had to cool, and during each respite they lost all that they had gained. The chase evidently ran out of coal and started burning wood, and although she doused her lights, the *Kearsarge* managed to follow her into the night by the sparks pouring from her smokestack. Pickering brought the entire crew on deck save the watch in the engine room, partly to keep them ready for an encounter and partly to shift their collective weight back from the berth deck. During the evening watch Pickering directed Surgeon Browne to issue the fire-room crew grog because they seemed so exhausted, and Browne obliged the captain with the professional opinion that they indeed needed some stimulants.

Coal Heaver Poole's watch took over at midnight. The lookout still claimed he could see the sidewheeler's sparks when the captain asked, so Pickering changed course two points and inquired again. After a time the lookout insisted that she lay in sight, but no one on deck could make her out, and in the morning she was gone. After a pursuit of more than 200 miles, Pickering gave up. He ordered the propeller disconnected, the sails set, and the wheel turned back for Terceira. When Poole left the fire room that morning, he thought the engines looked as though they had just been dragged up from the ocean floor, and both he and Wainwright wrote of them as "played out." At daylight the engineers started dragging spare parts out of the forehold, and they banged away at the machinery all that day and into the next as the *Kearsarge* lumbered slowly back the way she had come, their hammers preventing sleepy sailors like Charles Poole from finding a few moments' nap.[15]

The ship made Angra do Heroísmo just after noon on October 11 and started the next morning for Horta, where the *Tuscarora* still lay. The old sailing sloop USS *St. Louis*, eighteen guns, had also stopped by to tell of seeing one steamer in chase of another—the *Kearsarge*, probably, after the sidewheeler. While they lay at Horta, Cushman brought Pickering the bad news that the ship's engines could not safely top forty-five revolutions without five days' worth of repairs, and Pickering reluctantly determined to start back for Spain.

For three days the *Kearsarge* lay at her anchor in the harbor while bumboats swarmed about the little American flotilla. The crewmen stocked up on soft bread, milk, eggs, and butter, and William Wainwright feasted on melons.

The *Kearsarge* minstrels made their way ashore during the layover and performed a benefit for the island's poor, whoever and wherever they might be. Charles Fisher, William Gowin, Martin Hoyt, Martin Simpson, William Bastine, and Ham Fat secured the town theater and ordered some handbills from a printer. Simpson's uncle served as postmaster of Horta; when they visited him, he warned them that the governor had prohibited the performance because of a brawl the night before, in which some *Kearsarge* sailors had taken a prominent part. They rushed in a body to Consul Charles Dabney, who smoothed it over with the governor, and that night they played to a packed house; Fisher recorded that the crowd cheered Hoyt and Gowin, and gave Simpson deafening applause, but it was Ham Fat who stole the show. After he sang "Round de House" and "Essence of Old Virginny," Williams had only to walk on stage to throw the audience into fits.

Finally the ship raised the anchor on October 15, cruising through the islands at a leisurely pace and stopping at São Miguel the next day so Pickering could speak with the vice-consul at Ponta Delgada. As the captain chatted with the diplomat, his cutter crew absconded to find some wine, which they did. Two of the oarsmen, Thomas Jones and Daniel Lahey, did not return at all, and Pickering shoved off without them. Andrew Rowley lay dead drunk in the bottom of the boat as the shorthanded crew pulled back to the ship, and when they landed on deck Pickering directed Lieutenant Harris to convene a court-martial for him.[16]

On the way out from the harbor Pickering thought to practice the gun crews, and deck hands threw together three empty barrels, tacking some makeshift flagpoles on them. Once that had been cast overboard, the ship sailed away and the drummer beat the crew to quarters. First the thirty-twos fired off a few rounds without much effect, but when the target had drifted too far away for those guns, the Dahlgrens opened up with shell. Acting Master Stoddard commanded the aft pivot, and he threw a few shots perceptibly close. At 3:55 P.M., however, Mr. Wheeler aimed the forward pivot and struck the barrels squarely, splintering them. Leaving their litter to float ashore somewhere, the *Kearsarge* headed south for Santa Maria, rounding that island before veering toward Madeira. Yeoman DeWit—who, barely one month before, had marched his fifty-five-year-old frame all the way from Algeciras to San Roque and then to Gibraltar and back to avoid paying $3 for a pair of spectacles—could not help wondering how much the hour's gunnery had cost his government.[17]

Three mornings later, not far from Madeira, the lookout sighted a steamer to windward. When the *Kearsarge* had drawn close enough, Wheeler ordered a blank cartridge fired to signal a halt. The steamer hove to, the *Kearsarge* sent a boat, and in a light drizzle the captain of the *Eddystone*, of Bucksport, Maine, crawled up the side of the sloop. He had left port recently enough that he knew of the *Alabama* and her antics in these seas, and he supposed even as he boarded this ship that her American flag was a hoax. Only when Wheeler identified himself did the merchant captain relax, laughing at himself and admitting that he had already packed his clothes in anticipation as soon as he heard the *Kearsarge* fire its gun. When the *Kearsarge*'s cutter ferried him back to his ship, the grateful skipper insisted on sending back a barrel of bread and some good Madeira wine.[18]

The *Kearsarge* stopped at Madeira itself the next day. Captain Pickering put in at Funchal, taking advantage of the Portuguese officials' disinclination to curtail the resupply of belligerent vessels. Where no Union vessel could coal more than once every three months in British or French waters (or, supposedly, in Spanish territory), he had no trouble taking on enough to fill his bunkers only two weeks after he had done so at Horta. Authorities so distant from one another, even from provinces of the same government, would not be likely to compare notes on such details. If he was bound for the more careful kingdom of Spain, which observed its neutrality more conscientiously, Pickering would want to arrive as fully provisioned as he could.

The enlisted men stocked up as well when the inevitable bumboats came to greet them, and one island entrepreneur even brought some ice cream to the ship: Charles Poole noted that this fellow's stock sold out fast. For all the vigilance of the deck officer some of Madeira's most famous product came aboard, perhaps under the coat of an officer returning from shore, and the *Kearsarge* had hardly continued on its way the next evening when Captain Pickering suspended Gunner Graham for being drunk. Seaman Rowley had just come out of irons for his liquid indiscretion, and he would lose three months' pay for it, but Graham's punishment consisted of retiring to his stateroom for a week.[19]

The *Kearsarge* beat back to Algeciras, taking four days and passing within sight of an old Moorish town on the coast of Africa. The ship entered the Straits of Gibraltar late on October 24, and the captain kept all hands awake until the ship arrived at Gibraltar bay, lest some technical miracle had put the crippled *Sumter* back in commission during the past month. Not until 3:00 A.M. did the ship drop anchor at Algeciras, and bleary-eyed crewmen groped for their hammocks only to awaken at 6:30 the next morning. When they stumbled up on the forecastle, those who cared to look could still see the dark, dingy hull of the little Confederate warship under the shadow of the Rock as the sun rose red and bright behind it.[20]

CHAPTER EIGHT

Doldrums

Of all the Spanish towns is none more pretty,
  Cadiz perhaps—
—Byron, *Don Juan*

A small steamer hove into sight on October 30. From the quarterdeck of the *Kearsarge*, at Algeciras, the officer of the deck made out the Stars and Stripes with his glass and ordered the signal quartermaster to raise the ship's number, 491. The stranger hoisted number 150 in return, and consultation with the naval register proved her to be the *Chippewa*, fresh from Hampton Roads. The four-gun screw steamer, slightly smaller than the *Sumter*, anchored near the *Kearsarge* to assist in watching over the crippled Confederate raider.

At that moment the *Sumter* lay nude of sails and virtually empty of coal. A marine sergeant commanded her, for, while the *Kearsarge* had steamed after the *Alabama*, the two senior officers of the Confederate hulk had quarreled, and the acting master's mate had shot the midshipman dead. British authorities arrested the murderer, returning him to the Confederacy (where he went free and commenced running the blockade in his own vessel), and Lieutenant Robert Chapman returned to his old ship from Paris to take charge of the eight remaining crewmen. Chapman, the *Sumter*'s former third officer, arrived in Gibraltar on the Southampton mail packet the evening of November 1.[1]

That same day, Gideon Welles wrote to Captain Pickering, formally rescinding his orders to bring the *Kearsarge* back to the Gulf Squadron. In light of the *Alabama*'s depredations, the navy secretary told Pickering to remain in Europe, protecting Atlantic commerce and visiting the Azores and Madeira as frequently as possible. By the time this message reached Pickering, the *Alabama* had entered the Caribbean, but that made little difference to the commander of the *Kearsarge*. On November 2 the engineers examined the propeller as the ship lay at anchor off Orange Grove, and they found that the shaft had worn so badly that the flukes of the screw were cutting dangerously into the heel of the ship's keel. The sloop could hardly take to sea again without extensive repairs in drydock. The next day Pickering steamed over to Gibraltar for another glance at the *Sumter*; then he left the *Chippewa* to guard her, turning for Cadiz.

General quarters sounded aboard the ship one last time in 1862 at 1:00 on the morning of November 4. Just as the *Kearsarge* passed Trafalgar Bay, a ship appeared on the horizon. The drum beat, and men bounded out of their hammocks in the darkness, tying up their bedding and tossing it into the hammock nettings when they reached the spar deck. The guns were cast loose, and the Marine crew of the 28-pounder rifle loaded their piece, standing by on the forecastle for the word to loose a warning shot. The sail came close enough to hail, answering that she was the British mail packet on her way to Gibraltar. That sent the *Kearsarge* sailors back to bed for a few hours, except for the men at the rifled gun, who could not draw the shot they had rammed down the muzzle. The walls of Cadiz shone bright in the early morning light, and the deck officer solved the difficulty by firing off the bow gun to signal for a pilot. By nine that morning the ailing sloop lay anchored in the ancient harbor.[2]

The *Kearsarge* had to wait nearly four weeks for a drydock to come open, riding out the time in the teeming harbor. Cadiz had no wharves; lateen-rigged lighters instead hurried about between ship and shore, loading and unloading. Bumboats surrounded the Federal warship daily, selling soft bread and fruit. The sailors pestered Paymaster Smith for advances of cash for these delicacies, disgusted as they quickly became with the yellow Spanish beef that appeared in their vegetable soup: it fell apart as soon as it was boiled, complained Charles Poole. When they had money to buy from the boats, the crewmen usually tossed their regular rations overboard. Once, they even petitioned for salt beef in lieu of the crumbling yellow variety, but navy regulations called for fresh beef whenever the ship lay in port—to prevent scurvy, according to Yeoman DeWit.

Ordinarily, a *Kearsarge* sailor drew a pound of salt pork each day, as well as a gill of beans, fourteen ounces of bread, a couple of ounces of pickles, half an ounce of coffee, and a quarter-ounce of tea. Three times each week he drew a pound of salt beef and half a pound of flour; on Sundays he was treated to rice.

Except for the captain, the entire crew divided into messes for meals. Captain Pickering merited his own personal cook and a steward—big, black George Williams and his brother, Edward—while the wardroom officers shared a pair of such attendants. Charles Fisher served loyally as their cook, but the wardroom did not fare well in stewards: Scott, the original, deserted in August, and his successor decamped after the crew trampled him during the general quarters drill. Less than a week after returning to Cadiz the senior officers shipped Henry Adams as their steward, but he did not last long, either. The engineers and steerage officers were authorized a cook and three servants, but they never seem to have enjoyed the luxury of an officially designated cook. Their steward, Sabine de Santo, perished from consumption just five weeks out from home, and they evidently selected alternate servants from among the enlisted "boys."

The rest of the ship's company, from the boatswain on down, split into groups of a dozen or fifteen. Master at Arms Jason Watrus, Yeoman DeWit, and Surgeon's Steward Tittle messed with the Marines, for instance, and the remaining warrant officers gravitated to other enlisted groups. Each mess designated one of its number to draw the rations and prepare them for the kitchen before giving them over to Ship's Cook Tim Hurley. When Hurley had finished his boiling, baking, or frying, the mess cooks retrieved the rations from him and distributed them to their messmates. Sometimes a mess would ask the paymaster to stop the regular rations and pay out their equivalent in cash, with which the mess caterer would buy potatoes, or extra coffee and sugar. Charles Poole assumed the role of caterer to his mess for nearly three months, meanwhile avoiding his shift in the engine room except to spell some exhausted coal heaver in the heat of a chase, but by the time the ship arrived at Cadiz, he had given up his culinary post and resumed his shovel. His mates were so pleased with his tenure, though, that they nominated him again during the winter.[3]

The *Kearsarge* suffered the buffeting of a severe gale the second night after its arrival at Cadiz, the wind whipping out of the south with enough force to drag some of the ships and foul their anchor cables. Sometime during the darkness the captain's gig was ripped from its davits and blown away, but two days later another ship's boat towed it back.

The morning that the gig was retrieved, the *Chippewa* steamed into the harbor, bearing word that Semmes was reported on his way back to the Azores. The story may have arisen from a corrupted account of the *Agrippina*'s journey from London with coal for the raider, some weeks before; by the time the rumor reached Spain, it insisted that Semmes's old transport, the *Bahama*, was steaming there with more recruits and munitions for the *Alabama*. For a touch of exotic distortion, a Turkish ship was said to have carried dispatches to those islands for him. Captain Pickering ordered the *Chippewa* to continue on for the Azores without him, meanwhile addressing his regrets to the secretary of the navy for "the unfortunate condition of the *Kearsarge* at the present time." When the engineless *St. Louis* came in from Lisbon the next day, Pickering ordered her out to sea, too.[4]

The "unfortunate condition" of the *Kearsarge*, though more the fault of her builders than her captain, appears to have undone that officer in the eyes of his superiors, who saw only that their senior line officer in Europe spent a great deal of time in port, and that the most troublesome Confederate raider of all had surfaced in his bailiwick and slipped away. Pickering's November 8 letter to Washington would have taken no more than four weeks to deliver; it was four weeks and one day later that Gideon Welles ordered the commander of the USS *Vanderbilt* to leave New York for Faial with a pair of officers to replace Pickering and Lieutenant Harris.[5]

As yet Pickering knew none of this. He occupied himself with shipboard discipline, which began to fall apart almost as soon as the anchor dropped. The first problem developed with one of the officers, Third Assistant Engineer Frederick Miller, who thought he might take the night air during the middle watch, which he was standing in the engine room. With fires banked he saw no harm, leaving things in the hands of a fireman. Midshipman Preble had the deck, and he caught the engineer away from his post; the next morning Pickering suspended him from duty. Miller did not take his punishment well, and less than a month later Pickering had to suspend him for another ten days for "gross insubordination and disrespect" to the officer of the deck.

Officers' discipline always consisted of these suspensions, for the disgrace and embarrassment was thought to take greater effect on them than on the enlisted men. Gunner Graham had earned only a week's vacation from his duties for coming to duty drunk, but two days after Graham returned to duty, George Bailey, a "first class boy," was court-martialed for insolence to the officer of the deck and drew thirty days' confinement in irons, on bread and water, with a fine of three months' pay and three months of extra duty. He had already spent sixty days in the ship's "sweatbox" since the September 2 offense, so the court-martial called the account square and returned him to duty. A couple of weeks after the ship arrived at Cadiz, Landsman Thomas Buckley was clapped in irons for a week after he, too, grew flip with the deck officer.[6]

Pickering found it even more difficult to maintain control when a drydock berth finally opened for his ship. A Spanish pilot guided the *Kearsarge* up the river to La Carraca on November 29—getting her grounded in the mud for several hours along the way—and the crew began to misbehave almost from the moment the ship docked. Liquor found its way aboard from the shipyard, and the very next morning William Fisher was locked in the hold for getting drunk. George Bailey joined him there three days later, after repeating the drunken rantings that had put him in irons for most of the autumn. On December 4 the master at arms threw Coal Heaver Timothy Lynch in with the two black youths (liquor having loosened Lynch's tongue, too), and the cell door opened for an intoxicated John Dempsey on December 5.

The next victim of Spanish wine was the duty officer himself. William H. Yeaton, whom Captain Pickering had particularly wanted for a master's mate, stood his weekend watch on the dock, holding onto a post to keep upright and babbling nonsense to himself. The enlisted men cared little for him (Charles Fisher called him "the *butt* of the ship's crew"), and as they passed him on their way to liberty they would shout that "the Gunboat Yeaton is disabled by having a brick in his hat." At last Lieutenant Harris sent Gunner Graham and Boatswain James Walton to drag Yeaton aboard and put him to bed. He remained drunk at evening muster, though, and early Monday morning he drew the predictable suspension.

Over the next week three of the more troublesome sailors returned from liberty under the influence, and all three were court-martialed for it. Quartermaster William Smith and First-Class Fireman Joseph Dugan overstayed their liberty a few days later, and came back drunk as well. The double standard prevailed, however, and their entire punishment appears to have consisted of having their names noted on the log. This quartermaster was one of three men aboard the *Kearsarge* named William Smith, and he had been a sailor several years; except for his weakness for the bottle the officers prized him, and before the ship returned to the United States he would be the only noncommissioned man on board to win an officer's berth.[7]

Those who remained sober and on duty—a majority of the crew, despite the lengthy list of delinquents—worked for two straight days and nights unloading the magazines and shell rooms, for which they, too, were rewarded with a ration of whiskey. The engineer department disconnected the propeller the first week in December and wrestled it off the end of the shaft. The second week passed in removing the shaft itself from the ship by working it out the stern. That was finally accomplished on December 15. Crewmen plugged the resulting hole that afternoon, and the next day they watched as the dock filled again. A tug dragged the *Kearsarge* to the opposite side of the creek, where it anchored in the mud for what the American sailors correctly feared would be a long stay.

The captain authorized liberty for as many as eighteen men at a time through most of December, starting with the deck crew since their services were not needed during the removal of the propeller shaft. As Christmas neared, the engineers felt trapped aboard the ship, with nothing to read or do and only the bleak landscape to gaze upon.

"I think this is very pleasant," wrote a sarcastic Charles Poole, "lying in Mud Creek with salt heaps on one side and a Navy yard on the other where they cannot speak a word of English and surrounded by Mud Scows and Mud Diggers with nothing but mud to look at day after Day."[8]

The monotony wore more quickly on some than on others. Robert Motley and Richard Benson took liberty on the morning of December 22 and never returned. Quarter Gunner Christian Smith departed for liberty on New Year's Eve, and that was the last anyone ever saw of him. James Mellus, a first-class fireman, deserted on January 4, and his departure left his comrades even more dissatisfied than before. William Wainwright called Mellus "a tip-top fellow," and expressed great regret that he would no longer enjoy his company. "He and I were great chums," wrote Wainwright. When Poole recorded the fireman's desertion, he confessed that he wished he had joined him. Only honor and patriotism prevented him from taking French leave, too.[9]

Christmas left dejected sailors even more homesick. Poole and his comrades dwelt upon the miserable lot they had so injudiciously traded for a warm hearth and family, and a special holiday meal did little to raise their spirits. At noon the boatswain piped all hands to eat on deck, with mess cloths spread before them as they sat cross-legged. For once the cook served them their preferred salt beef and hardtack, with a dessert of plum duff. The attraction of the duff, an old navy dish approximating a thick raisin dumpling, lay mostly in tasting different from the usual rations. Poole recorded that the *Kearsarge* duff had been boiled until it was hard enough to kick, but he saw the futility of complaining about it. The ever-resourceful William Fisher procured a liquid dessert to liven his meal, and so spent Christmas Day back in irons.[10]

Both Poole and William Wainwright won a coveted two-day liberty on December 30. They were working in the cramped shaft alley in the bowels of the ship when Chief Engineer Cushman told them they could go. Poole dropped his tools instantly, raced to his duffel bag to drag out some clean blue mustering clothes, and pounded up the ladder to the spar deck with the others right behind him. On New Year's Day Poole returned to the ship with his mates at the appointed hour, but Wainwright's party lagged behind. Wainwright kept rowdy company this liberty, and his name was jotted down alongside those of Fireman Henry Jamison, Jimmy Haley, and John Dempsey. Even after Wainwright returned, he seemed to kick himself for doing so, remarking that the pleasure of a jaunt ashore left him all the more disgusted with life on a U.S. warship.[11]

Reflecting the same sort of thinking that moved Gideon Welles to replace Captain Pickering, Poole spent the first anniversary of his enlistment musing on the boredom. He intended to stick out his three years come what may, but he wished it could be a more active life. "I am in hopes that something will turn up to make us feel as though we had done something to serve our country in this its hour of need," he lamented. He agreed lustily with the lyrics of one shipmate's shanty that ended, "a Man of War's life is a very good life, for all those who like it but not for me."[12]

Surliness and despair prevailed as 1863 opened. Desertions increased, and in some cases Captain Pickering counted these losses good fortune. One Dutch recruit who went by the name Daniel Clark was brought before the skipper after someone caught him stealing from a shipmate, and Pickering simply put him out of the ship, writing him down a couple of days later as a deserter.

Affairs took an ugly turn on January 21. Coxswain Thomas Igo and William Spencer, an ordinary seaman who had shipped at Algeciras late in June, took the boat ashore for some errand that morning. They ran afoul of the bottle, though, and did not return soon enough to satisfy the officer of the deck, who had to signal vigorously to bring them back. They eventually returned, but so obviously drunk were they that the deck officer called for Mr. Watrus, the master at arms. That burly functionary arrived and started to lead Igo away, as the senior and more responsible offender, when Spencer picked up a spit box and struck Watrus with it. The boatswain and Sergeant Young leaped into the fray, and either Young or Watrus drew his sword, slashing Spencer on the arm. The three officers finally subdued the mutineers and dragged them down to the sweatbox, where they manacled them for over a week before bringing them up for another quarterdeck court-martial. Igo, who seems not to have done more than struggle against confinement, lost two months' pay and was reduced to seaman. Spencer's offense was the most grievous conceivable on board a naval vessel short of outright mutiny, and he was sentenced to a month in double irons in addition to the fine and demotion that Igo suffered. Wainwright noted that, had there been a fleet present with a commodore aboard, the two would have been sent back to the States wearing a ball and chain, for a prison sentence.[13]

To many aboard the *Kearsarge*, the long weeks on the mud flats seemed like a prison sentence, too, despite the occasional diversion of a musical performance like the one held right after the courts-martial. The consul from Cadiz came aboard with some ladies, the *Kearsarge* minstrels put on their blackface—at least those who needed it—and the signal quartermaster decked the ship in international colors. Fun-loving seamen like William Gowin and William Fisher, whose antics usually led to trouble, put their talents to work for the entertainment of their fellows that evening, and their comrades probably enjoyed it better than the officers, for whom such amusements were less uncommon. The festivities continued until midnight, but the next morning the sun rose again on Mud Creek, the salt pyramids, and the indolent Spanish workmen.[14]

Those Spaniards were "slower than dead men," wrote Wainwright, and his captain had long before passed a similar complaint on to a subordinate. "I can not hurry these Andalusians," Pickering told the commander of the *Tuscarora*; "their holidays exceed their working days."

The enforced lassitude proved all the harder to take when word reached La Carraca, late on February 7, that the *Sumter* had escaped from Gibraltar despite the presence of the *Chippewa*. The former raider had been sold to a British concern and had been renamed the *Gibraltar*, but Federal authorities refused to recognize the transferred title. Supposing that the Confederates meant only to set the precedent of selling Confederate vessels in British ports, American officials feared little from the decrepit steamer save the precedent itself, but *Kearsarge* sailors swore in frustration at the image of their old rival sliding by only a dozen or fifteen miles away while their sloop lay fast in the mud with its machinery on the dock. In light of this news Captain Pickering may not have suffered any great surprise when he learned, within the week, that his replacement had arrived in the Azores.[15]

CHAPTER NINE

Caribbean Passage

Where the remote Bermudas ride
In th' ocean's bosom unespied.
—Marvell, "Bermudas"

Regulations allowed Confederate naval officers to wear lightweight frock coats in summer, or in the tropics, but even if Semmes and his subordinates had kept such extensive wardrobes, they still would have had to button on vests over their shirts. Though authorized by those same regulations to change from grey wool into white duck frocks and trousers in warm weather, the *Alabama*'s enlisted men had never been issued anything but the heavy blue uniforms that their U.S. Navy counterparts wore. By November 16 the cruiser had sailed far enough south that their apparel grew uncomfortable, as Semmes noted when he mustered the crew that balmy Sunday. Aside from that, the mustachioed commander would probably never find himself more satisfied with the appearance of his men and his ship, littered though it was with prisoners: guns, deck, and bulwarks all shone brilliantly, and after twelve weeks at sea the crew seemed to have reached peak discipline. "They have come very kindly into the traces," Semmes noted that day. Forty-eight hours later he might have revised that observation.[1]

The next afternoon, from his perch above white canvas billows as the ship ran under full sail, the lookout sighted Dominica off the starboard bow. Semmes directed the quartermaster to turn a few points to the west, so as to slip into the Caribbean through the Dominica Passage, between that island and Guadaloupe. Turning south once the channel lay behind, the

Alabama struck for Martinique, which bore into view just before the sun rose. Though the captain always played stingy with his coal, he ordered steam up and the propeller lowered now, and the flukes began to turn as the sun peaked over the equator.

Here had Semmes lain in the frail *Sumter* just one year before, blockaded in the harbor of St. Pierre by the USS *Iroquois*. St. Pierre appeared in his glass a few hours later, but he passed it by for the bigger port of Fort Royal, the little island's capital. The *Alabama* steamed in with the blue English ensign and pennant flying. At 9:30 the anchor rattled to the bottom, and men lined the landward side to have their first close look at civilization in months. From the shore came boatloads of entrepreneurs, just like those who swarmed about the *Kearsarge* in the Atlantic ports.

Soon the junior officers understood why they had come: here lay the *Agrippina*, laden with Cardiff coal. Once the health officers had passed the ship, Semmes sent an emissary ashore to ask permission for the prisoners to land, and to look for fresh provisions. Almost immediately the paintbrushes came out of their lockers, and sailors climbed the ratlines to repair month-old storm damage. The island governor remembered the captain from his 1861 visit, and welcomed his ship, but Semmes decided not to coal here. The *Agrippina* had been at anchor for more than a week now, and her skipper, Alexander McQueen, had spent much of that time in the wharfside grog shops, boasting, when the liquor struck him right, of his dingy bark's famous consort. Instead of the stealthy arrival he had wished, Semmes found that he was expected—at least by those who had believed McQueen—and he looked nervously to sea. He ordered the Scotsman to leave the harbor immediately and proceed to another rendezvous on the Venezuelan island of La Blanquilla. By dusk the *Agrippina* was gone.

From the *Agrippina* came a bag of mail, and from the bumboats a stream of fruit and vegetables. The prisoners shuffled gratefully ashore, all (save the Mauritius consul and his family) wringing their wrists where the irons had been clamped. A dozen men had recently asked for advances, most for £5 apiece, and George Forrest convinced them to give him much of it on the promise that he would buy rum. Slipping down the anchor chain, he swam to one of the boats and bought all the liquor he could, arranging to pull it aboard when the officers could be distracted. By nightfall the watch had warmed itself with Forrest's groceries to such an extent that a brawl erupted, and one man was stabbed in the arm. The officers who tried to quell it found the drunks on the verge of mutiny, one man hurling a belaying pin at the deck officer who tried to break up the fight. Lieutenant Kell rushed down to warn the captain. Semmes ran on deck and ordered the drummer to beat general quarters.

Drunk and sober alike, the sailors responded to their training and raced to their battle stations. The officers appeared with sidearms and cutlasses, which Semmes ordered them to use on anyone who failed to jump when he spoke. The gun crews stood to their pieces, some of the gunners reeling wildly, as the master at arms followed Semmes and Kell around the ship, arresting the most obviously inebriated and locking double irons on their wrists, gagging most of them to keep them quiet. When nearly a score of the culprits had been restrained, Semmes gathered them at the gangway and equipped his Savannah quartermasters with buckets and lines. These petty officers, whom he trusted more because of their Southern birth, began sloshing the mutineers in the face with salt water, and though they laughed off the punishment at first, the buckets hit them so quickly, one after another, that they soon lost the breath for laughter, choking on a mouthful now and then until they came near drowning. One by one they begged the captain's mercy until the mutiny had deteriorated into a gaggle of drenched penitents. George Forrest stood aloof, perfectly sober; Semmes discovered his role in the riot and had him tied, spread-eagled, in the rigging of the mizzenmast, meanwhile locking up the worst of the mutineers.

The next morning, before the *Alabama* could sail, a warship appeared off the port flying the U.S. flag. Semmes, who had doubtless feared this eventuality since hearing of McQueen's yammering, directed the decks cleared for action, and he sought some reputable merchant ashore who would take his ship's money for safekeeping. When the potential caretakers demanded 5 percent of the funds for their services, Semmes indignantly ordered the cash back aboard. Once he learned that the Federal ship was the *San Jacinto*, half again the size of his with eleven big guns, he decided there was no sense fighting her, and that he could more easily run for it. After dark that cloudy night Semmes took a pilot aboard and started for sea in a light rain, dropping the pilot less than an hour later and running out all his guns, loaded and primed. The *San Jacinto* missed the prey in the darkness, and by 9:30 Semmes had secured his guns and piped his crew down.[2]

The *Alabama* scudded down the Grenada Basin inside the Windward Islands until the *Agrippina* appeared off the port bow at midmorning of November 21. Together the two barks rounded the spits of land known as Los Hermanos and made La Blanquilla early in the afternoon. The cruiser led the way to the western face of the island, seeking an anchorage in the lee of the trade wind. In the harbor there lay a schooner that raised the Stars and Stripes in greeting, and Quartermaster Marmelstein reciprocated with the same flag; the Yankee ship soon dropped a boat with her captain, who came to pay his respects.

The schooner was the *Clara L. Sparks*, a Provincetown whaler. The deck officer met her boat at the gangway, mentioned that the cruiser was looking for the "pirate Steamer 'Alabama,'" and asked if the whaling captain would pilot him into the harbor. The Cape Cod skipper agreed, remarking that he hoped they would catch the raider, but his tone changed when the *Alabama* came to anchor and the Confederate ensign went up the mizzen. The astounded whaling master begged to be spared, but, as much as Semmes wished to burn the Yankee schooner, he dared not. Venezuela claimed the nearly uninhabited island, but Semmes might have disputed that ownership and taken the whaler had it not been for three or four goatherds who lent that claim a touch of legitimacy. Instead he determined merely to detain the ship until he had finished coaling, and to keep the captain and first mate aboard during the night to insure against any escape attempt.

It was 4:30 that afternoon when the raider let go its anchor in seventeen fathoms of clear water, with a bright, sandy beach before the bow. An hour later the *Agrippina* dropped anchor nearby. At dawn Semmes brought her alongside, lashed the two ships together, and the enlisted men began transferring the black, dusty cargo, sweating copiously under the hot South American sun. A light sea rubbed the hulls against each other until dusk, the ships bonking and squeaking monotonously as paint and splinters peeled off the strakes. The job continued the next day, Sunday, and by noon Monday the bunkers lay mounded full.

With that Semmes gave some of the crew permission to go ashore, resting fairly certain that they could find none of the liquor that had caused so much trouble at Martinique. The men occupied themselves with bathing on the beach, and a few officers went ashore, too, to fish or hunt. Pelicans glided overhead in their graceful little squadrons; the shore abounded with flamingoes and plover, and some of these birds came aboard the ship for dinner, or merely as colorful trophies. A number of the enlisted men were allowed to take rifles ashore, too, but when they found no satisfactory game, they began shooting wild jackasses and some of the herdsmen's goats for pure sport. "We all thought it was very good fun," a midshipman told his mother, "but it was good for all hands that Captain Semmes knew nothing of it."[3]

For all the *Alabama*'s bulging bunkers, the *Agrippina* still bore plenty of coal for another load, so Semmes directed Captain McQueen to meet him again a few weeks later at another desolate island in the Bay of Campeche, off the Yucatan Peninsula. Three of the *Alabama*'s seamen and one fireman had fallen ill, lingering without improvement for so long that Semmes decided to discharge them and send them home on the *Agrippina*. When three of that ship's crew volunteered to sail with the raider, Semmes signed them on in a twinkling.

That Wednesday the second court-martial in seven weeks convened to try

George Forrest. He had already escaped a noose for desertion, and he might have met the same fate for his part in the mutiny, which the officers believed he had deliberately organized. Probably to the eventual detriment of discipline on the ship, the court spared his life again, sentencing him instead to immediate discharge, "in disgrace," with nothing but the clothing he had owned when they found him on the *Dunkirk*. At 7:30 that evening Semmes addressed the assembled crew in hopes of impressing other potential troublemakers with the significance of Forrest's sentence—a significance that was doubtless lost on Forrest himself, who was only too happy to get away. Master at Arms James King escorted the prisoner ashore, after which someone slipped him the equivalent of four months' pay, which his friends had raised for him. His plight might have been more serious, marooned as he would have been, but for the *Clara L. Sparks*, which took him aboard as a crewman. As soon as the boat returned, the *Alabama* hoisted its anchor and put to sea, Semmes first releasing the whaling captain, whose gushing gratitude he silenced with a promise to burn his ship if he ever caught him in open water.[4]

Now Semmes sought a "California steamer." These ships, which passed regularly between the Isthmus of Panama and New York, usually carried large quantities of bullion from the gold fields. Cornelius Vanderbilt had made his fortune in the trade from the town of Aspinwall, on the Caribbean coast of Panama, to which a railroad shuttled goods and passengers that had been landed on the Pacific side. Anticipating that he might run afoul of a Union warship in these waters, Semmes instructed Gunner Thomas Cuddy to look to his armament and bring up some grapeshot—hot work, with the temperature hovering in the upper eighties. Cuddy shifted one of his 32-pounders across the deck to a porthole near the bridge that spanned the *Alabama* amidships, arranging tackles there so it could be fired from that position, thus giving a broadside of six guns to a side instead of five if the occasion should call for it. Assisted by a gunner's mate and two quarter gunners, one of whom belonged to the Royal Naval Reserve, Cuddy also modified the cartridges for the forward pivot: the amount of powder that it took to throw a hundred-pound shell a satisfactory distance caused too strong a recoil for this rifle, which seemed too lightweight for the size of its bore. Cuddy redistributed the charges, sewing them into smaller cartridges, lest the gun be thrown from its carriage or uproot the carriage from its track. Lack of sufficient ammunition prevented him from experimenting with the new charges, and discouraged Semmes from offering the target practice he would have liked; instead, the periodic exercises at general quarters consisted mostly of one dry run after another.[5]

On the second day out from La Blanquilla Semmes released the last pair of prisoners from the Fort Royal mutiny. The worst of the rebellious element appeared to have been quelled, and the captain observed that the ship's boys now posed the worst disciplinary problems aboard the ship. Six of them served the ship, including the erstwhile slave David White, who, considering his background, probably behaved himself. The rest were all Liverpool street urchins—orphans or runaways too young and inexperienced to manage a berth before the mast. For £2 each month they served the officers, assisted the cooks, carried messages, and, in their abundant leisure, played pranks and acted like the children they really were. Arthur Sinclair later told a story about one rapscallion named Robert Egan, a Castle Street lad, who did not wait more than a few days after the *Alabama* was commissioned before he stuffed the ship's pet cat into the muzzle of one of the pivot guns and screwed in the tampion, hoping to see poor Puss fired out of the gun the first time it was loaded. According to Sinclair, the cat was ultimately found and Egan, the principal suspect, was suspended sullenly from the mizzen rigging by his wrists and ankles.[6]

While Cuddy saw to the battery and Semmes to shipboard discipline, Lieutenant Kell attended to appearances, overseeing a general sprucing-up of coal dust and grime. As the helmsman worked his way through busy Mona Passage, between Santo Domingo and Puerto Rico, through which Semmes had felt certain they would have to fight their way, Kell and the boatswain put the off-duty men to work sanding and holystoning the deck.

With Mona Passage safely behind, the *Alabama* turned west, skirting north of Hispaniola, where the lookout spotted the little bark *Parker Cook*, of Boston. Marmelstein ran up the U.S. flag, the bark replied in kind, and the Confederate showed his true colors. The boarding officers found generous quantities of provisions, of which the cruiser's storerooms had grown dangerously empty, and the crew worked until well after dark taking aboard casks of salt pork, cheese, and hard bread. The decks were again littered with prisoners, one of whom signed on under Semmes, and at 10:00 flames began to climb the masts of the unfortunate merchantman. After a respite of more than three weeks, the *Alabama* was back in the raiding business.[7]

Semmes jolted out of his bed before dawn the next morning when the deck officer's voice shouted from outside his door that a large vessel was running directly toward the *Alabama*. With the moon already down, Semmes knew that it would be pitch dark, and that a ship would have to be fairly on top of them before anyone could see it; worse yet, his own ship lay hove to, with no steam up and not a sail set. Dressing hastily, he bounded on deck with visions of 11-inch Dahlgren guns aimed at point-blank range, and he ordered the duty officer to loose the sails and fill away. The stranger had already begun to pass without paying any notice, though, and the startled captain returned to his cabin.

The same thing happened two nights later. Hove to again to avoid grounding in these treacherous waters, Semmes was just turning in when a nervous lieutenant warned him of a big ship, apparently a steamer, bearing right down on them. Again Semmes ran up the companionway, calling for the lieutenant to fill away, but when he saw a small brig passing well clear, he knew that it was another false alarm. Near midnight that same evening he rose yet again, albeit with less apprehension, for a Spanish schooner.[8]

Cruising toward the Windward Passage, between Cuba and Haiti, Semmes wondered where all the U.S. warships were, supposing that perhaps they had swept down to the Lesser Antilles, where he had last been seen. As it happened, only the commander and crew of the *San Jacinto* yet knew of the *Alabama*'s presence in the Caribbean. The Federal captain had dropped word of his fruitless encounter with the raider when he stopped at St. Thomas on November 26, and had turned back for Guadaloupe and Martinique just as Semmes veered north, 300 miles to the west. A few other Union gunboats patroled in the Bahamas, and one lay near Key West. At that moment the commander of the West India Squadron, Charles Wilkes, was cruising the northern coast of Cuba, several hundred miles west of the Windward Passage, while Semmes slipped through that channel. Even when he heard news of a ship in the passage resembling the dreaded *Alabama*, he discredited the report, though he sailed belatedly in his flagship *Wachusett* to investigate.[9]

By then the Confederate vessel had taken another prize, the Baltimore schooner *Union*, fifty miles southeast of Guantanamo Bay. Native Marylander that he was, Semmes may have been gratified to find the little ship carrying a neutral cargo, and the *Union* certainly served as a handy cartel for the *Parker Cook* prisoners. The schooner's captain apprised Semmes that the California steamers were no longer using the Windward Passage, but Semmes doubted his sincerity and hove to again that night, determined to wait another day.

Judging by the New York newspapers he had gleaned from various prizes, Semmes expected the regular steamer to come through from New York on December 6. He cruised north and east, back into the passage, toward which Commodore Wilkes was also steaming from Matanzas. The *Alabama* lay in wait south of Cape Maisi all day, but no sail of any kind appeared. There Semmes kept her the next day as well, close into the land so that ships bound south could not spot him until they came within range. He mustered the crew as usual that morning, and Lieutenant Kell read the Articles of War—

just as Lieutenant Harris read them each Sunday on the *Kearsarge*. About an hour after lunch the lookout spied a sidewheel steamer, and Semmes called for the engineer to spread his fires as the propeller dropped into the water.

The drum beat the crew to quarters as though the steamer were an enemy sloop, which she might well have been, and the gunners loaded with shell. The *Alabama* cut away from the cape and fell in behind the stranger, hoisting the U.S. flag. The same colors appeared on the chase, which Semmes now supposed was the California steamer he had sought. A blank cartridge failed to bring the big passenger vessel around, and for a time she seemed to pull away.

The *Ariel*, owned by Cornelius Vanderbilt himself, carried more than 700 passengers, 140 of whom were U.S. Marines under a major. Captain Albert Jones rang the engine room for full steam ahead, but the *Alabama* raised her own steam rapidly and soon started gaining. The Marine major formed his men in the waist of the *Ariel*, but a Federal navy commander traveling to his Pacific Coast assignment took one look at the six-gun broadside that faced him and knew that the riflemen did not have a chance. Semmes ordered a second shot fired, this one directly at the *Ariel*'s rigging, and someone yanked a third lanyard without orders, bringing down more than half of the transport's foremast. At that the Union naval officer and the Marine major both advised Captain Jones to heave to, and the *Alabama* had the biggest prize she would ever take.[10]

Lieutenant Armstrong led the well-armed boat's crew that boarded the steamer, and this vastly outnumbered squad, a dozen strong, found the leathernecks drawn up in a little line of battle on deck. Their officers surrendered them, though, and the dozen Confederates disarmed the Marine battalion. The first boat back to the *Alabama* took 124 muskets and 16 swords, while Lieutenant Low later turned up a rifled 12-pounder cannon with plenty of ammunition. The Marines and their naval officer all signed paroles, and Captain Jones went back to the raider with Low.

Once the *Ariel* had been stripped of weapons, just under $10,000 in cash, and the latest newspapers—some less than a week old—Semmes sent a prize crew of ten sailors, two engineers, and two officers aboard her under Lieutenant Low. The two vessels then stood back in to the cape, where Semmes intended to lie in wait for the *Ariel*'s homeward-bound counterpart, which the newspapers indicated had left Aspinwall on December 5.

That should have brought the gold-laden steamer through the passage the next day, and in anticipation of a race Semmes ordered Engineer Freeman to temporarily cripple the *Ariel*'s boilers and throw her sails overboard, lest the Marines overpower his prize crew and escape while the *Alabama* chased the better prey. After nightfall, however, he ordered the machinery reassembled, steaming to the southwest, for Jamaica (and, unknown to Semmes, away from Charles Wilkes and the *Wachusett*), with the big prize following. The New York ship would use the same route, he supposed, and in the darkness he expected her to run right into range. Barring that good luck, Semmes intended to escort the *Ariel* into Kingston to see whether the British governor would let him land his prisoners.

During the night of December 8 the *Alabama* boarded a Dutch bark, and the next morning the deck officer spoke an English schooner near Navassa Island. That evening Semmes neared Morant Point Light, off the eastern tip of Jamaica, when the lookout spotted a hermaphrodite brig. The raider turned after it, fired a blank round to bring it to, and, just as one of his boats began creaking into the water, Semmes learned that a valve casting had given way in his own engine, leaving it perfectly useless. Semmes watched helplessly while his boat disappeared into the night after the brig, which had suddenly taken flight again, and he dared not even fire a live round at the chase, for fear of striking his own boat. For an hour the anxious captain glanced alternately at his valuable prize, catching up to Morant Point, and into the blackness where his boat had disappeared.

Eventually the boat returned, having run down the brig under a failing wind. It had been a German vessel, just out from Kingston, where its captain said the yellow fever was raging at that very moment. With that news Semmes gave up the notion of landing his passengers there, but with Captain Jones pacing the *Alabama*'s deck Semmes adjured everyone to make no mention of their disabled engine. By midnight Jones was ferried back to his ship, for which he signed a ransom bond greater than the cost of building the *Alabama*, and the *Ariel* resumed its journey, bearing hundreds of discomfited pilgrims on a quest that had been difficult enough without this exciting interlude.

Sick with worry, fatigue, and a touch of fever, Semmes took to his cabin while his ship ran close along the verdant northern coast of Jamaica under topsails, laying to at night and avoiding all other vessels. Miles Freeman worked his engineers relentlessly, day and night, to repair the broken valve, knocking off at midnight on December 11. The next morning their hammers rang again, and that evening Freeman reported to his relieved commander that the repair was complete.[11]

Semmes occupied his time during the repairs by reading the New York newspapers taken from the *Ariel*. Those indiscreet journals had speculated on the destination of an impromptu army forming in New York and at Fort Monroe under Nathaniel Banks, a political general from Massachusetts who was best known for the thrashing Stonewall Jackson had given his army the previous spring. That expedition was bound for Galveston, Texas, according to newspaper sources. Raphael Semmes supposed that the troops would travel without much naval support, for the Confederate navy posed no great threat and the *Alabama*'s presence remained unknown in the United States. Calculating that the transports bearing Banks's army should reach Galveston early in January, Semmes preferred to let word leak out that the *Alabama* had departed these waters, and he avoided even a stop for fresh fruit and vegetables at the Cayman Islands. He lay in the track of any California gold steamers that might take the Yucatan Channel, between that peninsula and the western tip of Cuba, thinking that such a prize might be worth revealing his presence, but strong gales dashed his ship about while clouds obscured the sun and prevented him from shooting his position. Uncertain of his location, Semmes fretted up the Bay of Honduras while seas washed the decks and leaked through, drenching the wardroom compartments. The officers all called on Paymaster Yonge for new bedding when salt water soaked their mattresses, and (as usual) Yonge himself complained bitterly of the discomfort.[12]

With the passage of the winter solstice the *Alabama* began skirting along the flat northern coast of the Yucatan Peninsula, Semmes finally abandoning the prospects of a gold steamer in order to keep his prearranged rendezvous with Captain McQueen and the *Agrippina*. At 9:00 on the morning of December 23 all hands manned the capstan to hoist the anchors that Semmes had dropped to avoid drifting aground in the shallow waters of Campeche Bank. Early that afternoon the Arcas keys loomed on the horizon to the south, tiny and forsaken on the light-green sea, and at sunset Semmes ordered the anchors down again in eleven fathoms. Within minutes the *Agrippina* anchored alongside.

In the morning Semmes himself supervised an expedition of the *Alabama*'s cutter, whaleboat, and gig, which scouted the three little coral spits for the safest and least windblown anchorage. Just after noon the boats returned, and the mother ship eased into the center of the triangle formed by the islands. The reefs all showed clearly from beneath the pristine waters. The coal tender followed along, and by midafternoon the two lay cozily at anchor in nine safe fathoms.[13]

At this season the Arcas lay uninhabited by any living thing save gulls. A fisherman's hut sat on the big island at the northern tip of the triangle, and a boat lay unused on shore. On Christmas Day Semmes allowed his crew ashore for a frolic, and they put the fisherman's nets to use, catching a few small turtles. Midshipmen Anderson and Maffitt took a boat out, joined by Master at Arms James King, a fellow Savannah native whom Anderson referred to as "Jimmy," and these three brought in a thirty-pound turtle for their own soup bowls. The lagoon teemed with tropical fish, some of which also livened the drab shipboard diet. A few sailors feasted on some injudiciously brazen gulls and their eggs, though Anderson found the fowl "too fishy."[14]

The captain himself stepped ashore for a holiday jaunt, taking his noontime bearing from the door of the hut. Not since Liverpool had he felt land beneath his feet, nineteen weeks before. The anniversary reminded him of how long he had been away from his family, which naturally turned him to reflections on the war and on the abolitionist Northerners whom he blamed for the conflict. That afternoon he returned to his cabin and scribbled ferociously against that "Puritan population."

Semmes might also have credited Puritan influence with the sudden temperance exercised aboard Union naval vessels. Sailors on the *Alabama* still took their daily grog, however—excluding the officers—and on Christmas evening Semmes allowed an extra ration. The hands lined up to splice the main brace, but a few of them remained unsatisfied even with the second gill. When they started ballasting the *Agrippina* the next day, carrying stone from ashore in the cutter, someone managed to smuggle some rum aboard from that vessel, which had stopped in port more recently.

For a couple of days more the liquor remained a secret, but on Sunday evening a few corks were pulled in the forecastle. Their tongues thus loosened, some of the crew expressed their boredom openly, and Chief Boatswain's Mate George Harwood asked if he might not return to England in the *Agrippina*. Harwood had enlisted for only six months, and his term would expire in barely eight weeks; so infrequently did the *Alabama* put into port that he thought it reasonable to demand an early release. Naval custom dictated the opposite, however, and men who had signed on for a specified period habitually served longer than they had agreed, going home only when the cruise ended or when it proved convenient to the ship's commander to put them ashore. Semmes therefore refused the old Liverpool mariner, who continued on duty cheerfully enough, but the next day one of the deck hands imbibed enough of the smuggled spirits that he packed his duffel and started for the *Agrippina* without orders. While the rest of the crew coaled from the older bark, this hapless fellow sat locked in double irons.[15]

The two ships remained in the little archipelago for a fortnight. As the new year opened, Semmes kept a small team of caulkers busy plugging the gaps between the deck planking, while others painted the hull and tarred the masts. Even Midshipman Anderson rolled up his sleeves and dipped his hands in the tar pot to relieve the monotony. Another crewman found himself tied to the mizzen rigging when he answered an officer rather too smartly, and Semmes noted that "my men will rebel a little yet." According to his calculations, the Banks expedition was due about then off Galveston harbor, and with his men turning so restless he yearned to put to sea. While a tardy Captain Wilkes and the *Wachusett* searched for him on the other side of the Yucatan, Semmes lay between the Arcas reefs in hopes of missing a norther that the barometer seemed to promise, but instead he had to ride out a southeasterly gale that dragged the *Alabama* into six fathoms and dangerously near one of the reefs reaching down from the northern island.

The weather cleared on January 4. With her water casks replenished from the *Alabama*'s condenser, the *Agrippina* prepared for the journey back to England, where Semmes had directed Captain McQueen to pick up more coal and a couple of deck guns for his empty ports. The enlisted men spent the day with Paymaster Yonge, assigning their allotments in order that parents and families—including wharf brides like Yeoman Appleby's Elizabeth—might collect the fruits of Confederate service from the office of Fraser, Trenholm, & Company. The *Agrippina* would also take a bag of mail back with her, including any that might be bound back through the blockade to the Confederacy, so officers and men alike bent over tables and casks to give the latest news from the famous raider.[16]

Knowing that Lincoln's Emancipation Proclamation was scheduled for implementation on the first day of 1863, the steerage officers conspired to leave behind a practical joke in the form of a wooden headboard for Father Abraham's mock grave. The four-by-two-foot plank was carved with the inscription "In memory of Abraham Lincoln, President of the late United States, who died of Nigger on the brain, 1st January, 1863." Signing themselves simply as "290," the number by which the *Alabama* was still widely known, they planted the board on the morning of January 5, locating it on the highest dune of the island where the hut sat. Captain Semmes probably assisted them in their deviltry through his fluency in Spanish, for they left a note in that language with the marker, asking that it be delivered to the nearest U.S. consul.

At 10:40 A.M. the propeller began to turn and sailors climbed into the rigging to make sail, leaving Captain McQueen and his old bark still at anchor in the open roadstead south of the fishing hut. With little opportunity for anyone to betray their destination, Semmes had no qualms about letting it out that he hoped to attack a squadron of transports off the Texas city. Beginning that very afternoon, he instituted an ominous daily exercise at the guns.[17]

CHAPTER TEN

Baptism

Off shot the specter bark
—Coleridge, "Rime of the Ancient Mariner"

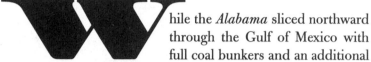hile the *Alabama* sliced northward through the Gulf of Mexico with full coal bunkers and an additional supply of bagged coal on deck, the Banks expedition that Captain Semmes had hoped to disperse was already ashore in Louisiana, and General Banks had no plans to use his troops anywhere near Galveston. The Confederates had recaptured that city on New Year's Day, and Banks was sufficiently occupied with affairs on the Mississippi. Instead of a fleet of troop-laden transports ripe for sinking, six well-armed Federal vessels sat off the port to prevent any blockade runners from slipping supplies in. The little armada could bring fifty-one guns to bear against the *Alabama*'s eight original guns and the little rifle taken from the *Ariel*, and nearly half the Union guns sat aboard the USS *Brooklyn*, which had chased fruitlessly after the fragile *Sumter* eighteen months before.

The *Alabama* approached within range of this unexpected flotilla as the sun rose on Sunday, January 11. The weekly muster proceeded as usual, and Lieutenant Kell read the Articles of War. At noon Semmes shot the sun, finding that he lay within thirty miles of the city. He wished to sight the vessels before they saw him, so he could lay to all day and run in at night to wreak havoc among the transports, but the man in the maintop proved a little sleepy, and the *Alabama* sailed over the horizon straight into the glasses of three of the Union lookouts. That bit of negligence worked to Semmes's benefit, though, for not only did it allow him to recognize the fleet as warships, it also drew one of them after him when he spun his own wheel away. To the Confederate's even greater fortune, it was the weakest of the three Yankee steamers that turned after him.

Anticipating another lucrative blockade runner like several his vessel had caught already, Lieutenant Commander Homer C. Blake responded to a signal from the *Brooklyn* to chase the strange sail that had come into view to the southeast. At 3:30 he ordered the anchor hoisted on the sidewheel steamer *Hatteras*; the engineers stoked the boiler, and the converted passenger ferry churned after the suspected blockade runner.[1]

Spoiling for a fight after reading Northern newspaper stories that characterized them as pirates, the *Alabama*'s officers buckled on their sidearms while the off-duty watch came on deck to ready the guns for action. The *Hatteras* could not reach full speed until about 4:00, and Semmes deliberately slowed his pace to keep Blake interested, sending men into the rigging to shorten sails. The propeller came down, and once in a while Semmes would call for a few turns of the screw to pull away from the blockader. The horizon obscured the other Union ships as the sun settled, but Semmes wanted to move beyond the sound of gunfire, so as not to be disturbed in his little ambush. At last, about 6:00 P.M., Semmes deemed it dark enough to take in all his sails without alerting the Union commander. He called the crew to quarters, loaded the starboard battery with five-second shells, and came about to await the sidewheeler.

Somewhat alarmed to see his prey suddenly lying in wait, Commander Blake suspected that this might be the elusive *Alabama*, which had been reported in the Caribbean, and he trained the only four guns that bore from his own starboard battery. Those four consisted of two 32-pounder carronades and a couple of small rifles, each throwing less than half the weight of the *Alabama*'s smaller pivot. When the *Hatteras* pulled within shouting range, Blake likewise turned broadside and identified his vessel, demanding the stranger's name.

"Her Majesty's Steamer *Petrel*," shouted the *Alabama*'s duty officer from the quarterdeck. Paying little attention to the pseudonym, the skeptical Blake warned that he was sending a boat aboard, and he lowered a cutter with four seamen, an acting master, and a first-class boy to investigate the craft. While the boat pulled away, the Confederate deck officer tried several times to hear the reply to his own demands, but neither he nor anyone else aboard could make out the Federal vessel's name. The words "United States Steamer" came crisply enough across the water, however, and Lieutenant Kell finally grabbed the speaking horn and bellowed, "We are the Confederate steamer *Alabama*," which Commander Blake heard clearly despite the rapid rattle of artillery that followed it.

The *Alabama* emptied a full broadside into the iron hull of the *Hatteras* at a range of less than a hundred yards. Blake returned fire, trying—he said later—to ease alongside and board what he finally realized was the dreaded raider. The two ships pulled away from the forgotten cutter, drifting as close as 25 or 30 yards from each other, then drawing as far apart as 200 yards.

The *Alabama* fired furiously. Chief Boatswain's Mate Harwood, who only two weeks before had begged to be sent home, shouted taunts after each round his gun fired, urging his crew to sponge, load, run their piece out, and fire again. Brent Johnson, the other boatswain's mate, had obviously taken offense at newspaper references to the origins of the *Alabama*'s crew, and with each discharge of his gun he howled, "That's from the scum of England." While the gun crews sweated in the darkness, the opposing ships wandered so near that unassigned men fired rifles and revolvers over the quarterdeck rail.

The *Hatteras* returned her four-gun broadside to the *Alabama*'s six, and after several volleys the raider suffered some thirteen pockmarks in her hull, most of the rounds striking amidships and none doing serious damage. A couple of shots flew through Semmes's cabin, and one passed over the quarterdeck near the horseblock where Semmes stood. Not a single projectile struck low enough to open a leak. The *Hatteras* took one shell amidships that set her hold on fire, while another passed through the sick bay and ignited an adjacent room. A third pierced the boiler, killing a couple of Irish firemen and filling the engine room with steam. Helpless now, the outgunned blockader continued to fire as the rest of the fleet watched the flashes and listened to the *Alabama*'s big pivots from the bar off Galveston, twenty miles away. In a little over thirteen minutes from the first salvo, Blake ordered lee guns fired in token of surrender and sent another boat to ask for help.

Cheers went up from the *Alabama*'s deck as the officers called for "three times three for Dixie." Boats from the victor and from the sinking *Hatteras* splashed into the shallow sea to look for survivors, and when the shouting stopped, 17 Union officers and 101 sailors stood on the raider's deck, 5 of them wounded. With the pair of firemen who were supposed killed, and the six men pulling for land now in the boat, that accounted for the entire crew of the vanquished vessel. Carpenter's Mate William Rinton complained of a flesh wound in the cheek, and Captain Semmes noted that someone else had been slightly wounded, but no one aboard the *Alabama* went off duty because of injuries the Yankees had inflicted.

Once the boats and battery had been secured on deck, Boatswain Mecaskey's pipe called all hands for another splice of the main brace before Lieutenant Kell sent the off-duty watch to their hammocks. The master at arms manacled all the enlisted prisoners, while the captured officers were distributed among the steerage and wardroom compartments—Commander Blake sharing the captain's cabin. Then, still unaware of the missing boat's crew, Semmes ordered his ship away from the settled *Hatteras*, whose main truck stuck out of the water. There the *Brooklyn* found her late the next morning, her pennant still fluttering a few feet above the waves.[2]

The Gulf of Mexico offered only two narrow escape routes, one by the Straits of Florida and the other through the Yucatan Channel, and Semmes made for the channel with all speed now that his presence was known. At noon of the second day after the battle, the lookout called a sail dead ahead, and with nothing to lose Semmes gave chase, hoisting American colors. The quarry lifted the British ensign, and a knowing eye on the *Alabama* recognized her as the homeward-bound *Agrippina*. Fearful that Captain Mc-Queen might throw their incriminating mailbag overboard, Semmes told Quartermaster Marmelstein to quickly exchange his Yankee flag for the Confederate emblem; when the Stars and Bars went up the mizzen, the *Agrippina* dipped her own colors in salute. Semmes plowed on past his tender, expecting to meet her next off the eastern tip of Brazil, but this would be the last time he ever saw Captain McQueen or his vessel.

Bucking wind and current, Semmes passed unopposed through the Yucatan Channel, where the commodore of the Galveston blockade had advised sending a few gunboats. At that very moment Charles Wilkes lay two dozen leagues away, at Mujeres Island, with the *Wachusett* and the *Sonoma*, each of which carried ten guns. While the *Alabama* slipped through just beyond his sight, the self-important Wilkes wrote Gideon Welles to announce the capture of a blockade runner, which would add considerably to the prize money he had already accumulated during this war. Welles had already recorded his disgust with Wilkes, remarking that he "has more zeal for and finds it more profitable to capture blockade-runners than to hunt for the Alabama," and within a few weeks he would offer the old sailor the permanent rank of commodore if only he would retire.[3]

Just before dawn on January 20 Semmes spotted the coast of Jamaica. It took all day to cruise the length of the island, and that evening the *Alabama* hove around off Plum Point lighthouse and fired a gun to signal for a pilot, showing the French tricolor at the masthead. The British signalman at Port Royal harbor therefore notified his superiors that a French man-of-war was on its way in, but the deck officer on the English warship *Greyhound* detected the true nature of the *Alabama* and instructed his ship's bandmaster to strike up "Dixie." The *Greyhound*'s executive officer made no objection to the air, but the *Greyhound*'s commander, having his dinner aboard the flagship *Aboukir*, hurried back to his own ship as soon as he learned that the newcomer was the Confederate raider. Such a salute constituted a partisan display; rather than breach Her Majesty's neutrality, he scolded his duty officer and directed the band to play an assortment of national anthems, including some from the United States.

Port Royal, on the peninsula outside Kingston, hosted several British frigates, and the next morning officers from three of them came aboard to visit the now-famous Captain Semmes—before they learned of Commodore Hugh Dunlop's orders against such social calls on the belligerent vessel. Semmes asked Dunlop's permission to repair his damages, land his prisoners, replenish his provisions, and load his coal bunkers: once the hammers had begun to pound, he left the ship in Kell's custody and proceeded into the mountains for a few days' holiday at the invitation of an admiring English minister.[4]

The lieutenant governor of the island forwarded permission that evening for the prisoners to land, and the following morning Lieutenant Kell saw them paroled and ferried them to the dock, from which they went in search of the U.S. consul. A number of the *Alabama* crewmen followed them on their first liberty in a populated port, including Paymaster Yonge, who carried a letter to his "esteemed friend" back in Liverpool.

Only a few hours sufficed to bring enough coal and food aboard, but the ruptures in the hull proved troublesome. William Robinson, the ship's Boston-bred carpenter, managed to repair most of the damage, but he needed the help of the shipyard workmen to patch the six most serious holes near the waterline. These repairs were not complete when Captain Semmes returned aboard on the afternoon of January 24.[5]

After satisfying a crowd's demand for a speech ashore at Kingston, Semmes climbed into his gig, and four broad backs pulled him back to the ship. When he climbed on deck, he found that he had been wise to avoid ports of call, for half his crew still remained ashore, refusing to return to duty. The other half sulked aboard, perfectly nettled that they would have no chance at liberty because of their shipmates' perfidy. Worst of all, one of the officers had joined the revelers ashore. Paymaster Yonge had apparently carried the professional courtesies toward the enemy sailors to an unseemly extreme, cavorting with Union seamen and drinking to their health so much as to impair his own. Perhaps he had succumbed to the blandishments of the officer who had shared his stateroom the ten days since the battle, or he may have held cryptic communication with enemy agents since the ship departed Liverpool. Standing orders prevented any of the *Alabama*'s officers from staying on shore overnight without the commander's permission, so Yonge would have been in hot water even if he had come back on his own, but he did not have that opportunity. When Kell heard of Yonge's indiscretion, he had sent a guard into town to bring him aboard, suspending him from his duties until Semmes returned.[6]

Yonge had composed an undated letter of resignation, working through several drafts, but if it had any effect on Semmes, it only enraged him at the weakling's poor example and flagging devotion. Semmes immediately stripped him of his sword and discharged him like Forrest, but without trial. He offered the miscreant the option of remaining under arrest in his room until the ship might stop at a Confederate port, but Yonge apparently had no immediate interest in returning to the Deep South. He turned his accounts over to Surgeon Galt at Semmes's direction, and, with what gold he could salvage from any pay due him, the disgraced Georgian stepped off the deck of the *Alabama* on the morning of January 25. His wife remained at Savannah, but Yonge secured lodging with a young widow in Kingston. After a few weeks he married her, too, and in March he took passage back to Liverpool with her, paying their way with money gained from the sale of everything she owned but one slave boy.

The police had to help Semmes gather his dissipated liberty men, but even after they had wrestled most of them back aboard, three daredevils leaped from the ship and tried to catch a ride to shore on a passing boat. Even the police failed to find all the deserters, and at least one of them claimed the protection of the Crown. Fireman John Latham left the ship with that first contingent on January 21, touring the town with Thomas Potter. When a patrol from the *Alabama* collared him at a hotel on January 25, he appealed to the superintendent of police; when Latham reached into his shirt and produced his certificate as a Royal Naval Coast volunteer, the superintendent demanded that they set him free. The *Alabama* sailed that evening without Latham—and without another fireman, an ordinary seaman, and one of the Liverpool "boys," as well as four of the autumn recruits. The chief petty officer of the ship, Master at Arms James King, sat in manacles for his spree ashore, and he had the company of several shipmates who protested too loudly when Semmes refused their requests for liberty.[7]

After returning the visits of the English captains, paying his port bills, and surreptitiously shipping one lone British navy deserter for the engine room, Semmes bid Jamaica and his misfits goodbye. With the helm set almost due east, the *Alabama* skirted the southern coast of Hispaniola for Mona Passage. The first morning out a sail came within range, and the raider ran down the bark *Golden Rule*, bound for Aspinwall. While James King stood for his court-martial in the wardroom, the boat's crew rifled the prize for some rigging and a trove of fresh newspapers, which excited the Southerners aboard with news of the sinking of the Federal ironclad *Monitor* and the repulse of an early assault on Vicksburg. By nightfall a crew of nine merchantmen stood on the *Alabama*'s deck, and their former ship sat blazing in their wake. Late the next evening the Boston brig *Chastelaine* fell across the raider's path, and her timbers lighted the horizon that midnight. The following afternoon Semmes stopped off at the city of Santo Domingo to drop his passengers, finding that the pilot was an old acquaintance from his visit there during the Mexican War.[8]

Anxious to escape from the Caribbean before the Union navy finally came awake, Semmes lingered in port only one night. The morning of January 29 the *Alabama* started east again after taking on some fresh fruit and salt provisions, the court-martial all the while winnowing through the cases of the errant starboard watch. That evening the ship slipped into Mona Passage, but ninety minutes into that dangerous channel Engineer Freeman had to shut down the engines to make some repairs. For three hours the vulnerable fugitive lay hove to under trysails in one of the principal corridors where the Yankees should have posted a gunboat. After midnight Freeman signaled that the repairs were complete, and the helmsman steered on through the passage and northward, toward Bermuda. Once through, Semmes ordered the propeller up and the fires banked. On the last day of January the court-martial finally dissolved, squaring the last of the Kingston offenses, and a number of penitent petty officers took their places on the yards alongside the seamen, among them Carpenter's Mate Rinton of the scarred cheek, Gunner's Mate Thomas Weir, and the senior enlisted man, James King—one of the Savannah pilots on whom Semmes depended so much. The gloom of such solemn proceedings quickly faded, though. By noon of that day the *Alabama* sailed once more over the North American Basin, and Semmes could see nothing but the pale blue of water a mile deep.[9]

With no danger from without, the raider nearly succumbed to carelessness within on February 2. The captain of the hold, an old Liverpool sailor named Jimmy Higgs, slipped into the spirit room, just beneath the captain's cabin, to run off some liquor. He carried a lighted candle with him, contrary to regulations and common sense, and the fumes quickly exploded. One of his assistants shouted that there was a fire, while Higgs and the others ran for some blankets to beat out the flames. Captain Semmes heard the alarm as he paced the quarterdeck, and he called the ship to quarters to fight the fire, but the blankets did the job before anyone could run a hose that far. Semmes suffered Higgs to don the flat iron bracelets that night.

The following day the Maine schooner *Palmetto* fell prey to the *Alabama* on its way to San Juan with provisions that the Confederate captain was happy to take aboard. With the skipper and his little crew on deck, Semmes turned east again, toward Madeira, and for the next eighteen days the lookout sighted nothing that Semmes cared to chase save one schooner from Nova Scotia, which he hove to in the seaweed-laden Sargasso Sea. Rather than reveal himself to any Federal vessels, like the *Vanderbilt*, which he knew was after him in the Caribbean, Semmes told the Yarmouth captain that his ship was the USS *Dacotah*.[10]

The hulking *Vanderbilt* lay at St. Thomas just then, after cruising fruitlessly in the *Alabama*'s abandoned hunting ground. Semmes sailed with little to worry about at mid-ocean, and with the *Kearsarge* disabled at La Carraca, the nearest U.S. warships were the sloop *Mohican* (a veritable duplicate of the *Kearsarge*) and the old fifty-one-gun frigate *Sabine*, both of which lurked in the Cape Verde Islands, a couple of thousand miles to the southeast.

For eighteen days the hunter encountered only three small sails, all neutral, but when the lookout cried, "Sail ho!" on the morning of February 21, he saw four ships nearly at once. The *Alabama* leaped after the first one, but it had the wind of her, and Semmes turned toward two others. He called for steam as the pair appeared to signal each other and part, each taking a different tack. Two hours into the chase a blank cartridge failed to slow the bigger of them, and a second blank, calling attention to the Confederate flag at the mizzen, merely impelled the prey to greater effort. The crew of the rifled pivot fired a round overhead, and the gun captain stood with his lanyard taut when the ship *Golden Eagle* hove to. Semmes put a prize crew aboard her and took after the second sail, which pulled up about 3:30 P.M. after the first warning shot. This was the *Olive Jane* of Boston, a port whose ships the Puritan-hating Semmes certainly loved to burn, and since the *Olive Jane* carried a cargo of liquor, he made haste to do just that. By dusk the *Golden Eagle* also danced with flames.

Now the *Alabama* had cruised back into a popular trade route, and sails popped into sight every few hours. A French bark took two French citizens who had been passengers on the *Olive Jane*, but for two days Semmes failed to find similar passage to England for the boatswain's mate, Harwood, and Fireman James McFadden, whose contract had also expired. Not until the night of February 27, an hour after sending all his prisoners (save two recruits) away on a ransomed New York ship, did Semmes manage to persuade the captain of a London-bound China trader to carry the pair of discharged veterans home.[11]

Turning back toward the south for his meeting with the *Agrippina*, Semmes ran across the *Bethiah Thayer*, of Rockland, Maine, early on the first of March. He quickly ransomed the guano-laden ship for its neutral cargo, sailing after yet another vessel even before holding the regular Sunday muster. The second chase was a British bark, but right after dawn the next morning the helmsman wore the *Alabama* completely around to run down another Maine ship, the *John A. Parks*, which provided New York newspapers less than three weeks old. The newspapers cheered Semmes with confirmation of the *Florida*'s escape from Mobile, and the hold full of lumber made a brilliant bonfire after Semmes concluded that the paper claim of neutral cargo was a hoax. Before the day ended, Semmes found a British bark willing to take the captain of the *Parks*, his wife, and his two nephews to England, but the score of crewmen had to ride the waist of the *Alabama* for a fortnight, until she captured the *Punjaub*, midway between the coasts of Africa and Brazil. The *Punjaub* escaped on a ransom bond. So did the *Morning Star*, taken under a lowering sky on March 23, just north of the equator. With neutral cargo on its way to London from Calcutta, the *Morning Star* was allowed to proceed, disappearing into the occasional lightning and thunder of a soaking rainstorm. The Massachusetts whaling schooner *Kingfisher* was not so lucky. Stopped by the raider on the same afternoon that the *Morning Star* was allowed to continue, the little whaler went up in flames. So did the *Nora* and the *Charles Hill*, both from Boston and sailing from Liverpool; the *Alabama* captured them together on March 25. The *Hill*'s paperwork included a letter from the previous October, when the *Alabama*'s fame had only begun to spread, advising the master to certify all cargo as British property. Semmes noted the letter with a wry comment in his journal even as the twin plumes of smoke rose high into the sky above the sea. He also recorded another bout with some smuggled whiskey, under the influence of which some of his best hands turned unruly, and the acquisition of some new volunteers from the prizes. Eventually these three vessels provided the *Alabama* with ten sailors.[12]

Ten more days passed before another victim fell within view of the *Alabama*'s lookout. On April 4 Master's Mate James Evans, a bushy-bearded Charleston pilot, boarded the *Louisa Hatch*, which turned out to be full of smokeless Cardiff coal. This prize would be spared the torch until Semmes could transfer the cargo to his own hold, and the next morning Semmes relieved Evans with Master's Mate Fullam and a prize crew.

Semmes intended to take the *Hatch* into the harbor at Fernando de Noronha, the island off Brazil where he expected to meet the *Agrippina*. Fullam followed in the prize for two days before the weather turned ugly, with a rain squall preventing calculation of their location at noon of April 7 and rain driving down in torrents that evening, only to continue into the next day. Semmes consulted with Fullam on his destination that day, giving him the captain of the *Kingfisher* for a pilot, but they lost sight of each other during the storm that night. The next day, with the rigging draped in drenched clothing, Semmes took the *Louisa Hatch* in tow and tried coaling at sea by running boats back and forth. The ships had to maintain headway, though, and they moved too fast for the boats to tie alongside; they attempted to stop the engines to accommodate these impromptu lighters, but the jerking motion of reengaging the propeller snapped the towline. After two days with little progress, Semmes just towed the prize into the harbor at the island on the evening of April 10 and tied it alongside the *Alabama*. Swells came up during the night, though, and the tethered vessels began slamming against each other, smashing the shroud channels on the *Alabama*'s bow and snapping off the topsail yard on the mainmast. The next morning the two ships anchored separately, and the boats began to ply between them again despite oppressively warm and humid air.[13]

Semmes sent his new acting paymaster, Dr. Galt, to ask the island's governor about provisions. The governor returned a letter in Portuguese with a pair of emissaries, one of whom was a German who served as interpreter. Captain Semmes greeted them as state visitors, advising Bartelli the steward to open a bottle of champagne, and while Bartelli popped the cork, the German revealed that he was no official whatever, but rather a prisoner of the penal colony on the island, serving the last eighteen months of his sentence for forgery. The disgusted Bartelli nonetheless poured the bubbly, and they took a glass all around while the forger explained what delicacies the governor would gladly trade for fresh beef, pork, and fowl. Semmes listened carefully for the hint that he had violated Brazilian neutrality—which he had, by bringing his prize into one of that country's ports—but he heard no complaint. He, like Captain Pickering of the *Kearsarge*, profited from either the carelessness or the political ignorance of Portuguese-speaking islanders, and the illegal transfer of coal continued.

During the night the sight of a steamer nearing the island alarmed the watch officer. Semmes called general quarters, but the stranger never veered toward the harbor, and the exhausted crewmen returned to their hammocks. The dirty, dusty work went on through Sunday, April 12, while Semmes and Dr. Galt went ashore to see the governor, who sent horses for them. The governor's "mansion" was a house in the village, a mile from shore. He proved to be a major in the Brazilian army, and the Confederates found him eating breakfast with his wife, whom Semmes found "a sprightly, bright mulatto." With them sat "a pretty girl, quite white, of about 16," and the local priest.

During his sojourn with the governor and some visiting farmers, Semmes made it clear that the *Louisa Hatch* was a captured ship, and not a tender, but he recorded that the governor remained silent on that point. After trotting around the island with his host and inspecting the agricultural enterprises, Semmes and his paymaster made their way back to the *Alabama* late in the afternoon.[14]

Heavy rain and rising seas convinced Semmes to put off coaling on April 13 and bring everyone, prisoners and prize crew alike, back aboard the *Alabama*. All that night the ship lay with steam up and the anchor cable ready to slip, lest they all be dashed ashore, but the dawn found the raider still at her anchorage. Islanders brought the provisions aboard, charging dearly for them, but Semmes felt the crew needed fresh meat so badly that he paid their prices. To compensate for the expense, he arranged to sell some of the *Louisa Hatch*'s coal to a Brazilian schooner that shared the harbor with him, and he entertained an offer to buy the prize itself, but even at half the value of the vessel the prospective buyers cringed.[15]

The prize crew returned to the *Louisa Hatch*, and coaling resumed throughout April 14. The last shovelful went into the bunkers the next morning, and a few moments later a pair of whaling vessels appeared off the island. A boat cast away from each of them and started in, reaching the *Louisa Hatch* first. Mr. Fullam came to the rail as master of the ship, chatting with the captains of the whalers until suddenly they realized their mistake. Later Semmes deduced that one of the Yankees had seen a Confederate boat's ensign draped over the spanker boom to dry, which put the lie to the story Fullam had given them. The boats pulled for shore, while the *Alabama* got up steam and raced out to nab the two prizes before they ran in for the three-mile limit.[16]

The smaller victim was the brigantine *Kate Cory*, of Westport, Connecticut, and the other was the bark *Lafayette*, of New Bedford. The boarding officer torched the *Lafayette* immediately (she was the second of that name burned by the *Alabama*), but Semmes ordered the brigantine towed into the harbor, planning to use it as a cartel to send his growing phalanx of prisoners home.

Most of that night the flames from the *Lafayette* lit the sky. In the morning Semmes learned, to his surprise and satisfaction, that the governor would allow him to land prisoners on shore. With that he paroled about 110 men and landed them with plenty of provisions. Many of them asked to stay, but with the ten recruits from the *Kingfisher*, the *Charles Hill*, and the *Nora*, the *Alabama*'s crew stood nearly complete. Semmes took only four hands from the *Louisa Hatch*.[17]

That night Fullam captained the *Louisa Hatch* to her final anchorage, five miles off shore, and James Evans piloted the *Kate Cory* in his wake. The master's mates then abandoned and burned the two oaken vessels, each of which was named for a New England lady who may have lived to read about it in the newspapers.

For four more days Captain Semmes awaited the *Agrippina*, which should have left Cardiff on March 16, eleven days after the *Louisa Hatch*. A Brazilian schooner took some of the *Alabama*'s prisoners to Pernambuco on the evening of April 21, and the next morning Semmes decided he could wait no longer. With his damaged spars replaced from captured stock, he steamed out of the island harbor on an easterly course, reverting to sail power that afternoon and sending the lookout back into the maintop. Two days later the *Alabama* ran down the whaling bark *Nye*, which had left New Bedford even before Abraham Lincoln's election sparked the Southern states to secede. The *Nye* had not visited a port since the previous May, so her captain knew little or nothing about Confederate cruisers.

The *Dorcas Prince*, forty-four days from New York on a voyage to Shanghai, hove to at the sound of a blank from the bow gun on April 26 and supplied the *Alabama* with some useful stores before going up in flames near midnight. Her cargo of American coal, which Semmes suspected was bound for U.S. warships in the Pacific, offered no attraction to the captain of a vessel filled with the Cornish variety.[18]

On May 3 the raider chased down two American ships in quick succession. Just after noon that day a boat's crew boarded the *Union Jack*, a bark from Boston also on its way to Shanghai, and the *Alabama* immediately filled away to pursue a clipper. In another hour the *Sea Lark*'s journey to San Francisco was brought to an abrupt end. Her hold yielded the richest cargo the *Alabama* ever recorded, and that evening fire consumed what Lieutenant Kell had estimated at $627,000 worth of ships and cargo. Among the prisoners from the *Union Jack* stood the new U.S. consul at Foo Chow.

From newspapers no more recent than March 27, Semmes learned that David Farragut had passed the batteries at Port Hudson, on the Mississippi, construing it as an unsuccessful attack on that stronghold when Farragut had, actually, succeeded in his main aim of going upriver with some naval firepower. Twirling the waxed ends of his trademark mustache as he scanned the papers for useful information, Semmes seemed to seek the most optimistic interpretation of reported setbacks. Now and then he revealed that ominous news had affected him in spite of his active denial, but he disguised such hints even from himself, recording them in savage remarks on the enemy's moral degradation. Anniversaries frequently stirred him to vituperation. He had entered the U.S. Navy as a midshipman on April 1, 1826, and on that date in 1863 he observed that during the intervening years "the U.S. grew from weakness to strength, and they have been destroyed," adding the word "they" with a caret to emphasize the Southern preference for independent states and a weak central government. On his wedding anniversary, May 2, he mourned the third passage of that date without having seen his family, cursing "this Yankee war." On May 5 he scoffed at the unchristian remarks of an Indiana politician to a Philadelphia gathering, noting that the Yankees appeared jubilant at the prospect of starving the South. He clipped the speech from the paper and pasted it in his journal, adding another two days later.

On May 10, at about the same time that the embalmers began their work on the body of "Stonewall" Jackson, the *Alabama* stopped a Scandinavian bark that had left Bahia the day before. That was the alternate meeting place Semmes had offered Captain McQueen, and the bark's master reported no American warships in that harbor. The next afternoon the *Alabama* steamed into the harbor at Bahia, with her captain on the quarterdeck, sweeping his glass for a glimpse of his ship's consort. The *Agrippina* had not arrived, after eight weeks, and Captain Semmes would never see her again.[19]

Lieutenant John McIntosh Kell, CSN, wearing his old U.S. Navy uniform, on the day before the CSS *Sumter* sailed from New Orleans (Naval Historical Center, Washington Navy Yard, Washington, D.C.)

USS *Kearsarge* (Library of Congress)

Thomas C. Harris, USN. As a lieutenant and lieutenant commander he was the *Kearsarge*'s first executive officer (U.S. Army Military History Institute, Carlisle Barracks, Pa.)

William M. Cushman,
the tubercular chief
engineer of the *Kearsarge*
(Library of Congress)

Sketch of the CSS *Alabama* sent to Mrs. John McIntosh Kell from England in 1862 by Lieutenant Robert Minor, CSN (John McIntosh Kell Papers, Duke University)

Scale model of the CSS *Alabama* by P. L. Dunman (William S. Hoole Special Collections, University of Alabama)

Lieutenant John McIntosh Kell (*left*) and Commander Raphael Semmes at the after pivot gun of the CSS *Alabama*, coast of South Africa, 1863 (Naval Historical Center, Washington Navy Yard, Washington, D.C.)

Lieutenants Arthur Sinclair (*left*) and Richard F. Armstrong leaning on one of the CSS *Alabama*'s 32-pounder carronades, coast of South Africa, 1863 (Old Dartmouth Historical Society Whaling Museum, New Bedford, Mass.)

Lieutenant Joseph D. Wilson, CSS *Alabama* (William S. Hoole Special Collections, University of Alabama)

Master's Mate George T. Fullam, CSS *Alabama* (William S. Hoole Special Collections, University of Alabama)

Master's Mate James Evans, CSS *Alabama* (William S. Hoole Special Collections, University of Alabama)

Acting Chief Engineer Miles Freeman, CSS *Alabama* (William S. Hoole Special Collections, University of Alabama)

Third Assistant Engineer John M. Pundt, CSS *Alabama* (William S. Hoole Special Collections, University of Alabama)

Midshipman Eugene Anderson Maffitt, CSS *Alabama* (William S. Hoole Special Collections, University of Alabama)

Midshipman Edward Maffitt Anderson, CSS *Alabama* (William S. Hoole Special Collections, University of Alabama)

Gunner Thomas Cuddy, CSS *Alabama* (William S. Hoole Special Collections, University of Alabama)

Cherbourg Harbor, June 30, 1864. Most of the officers of the *Kearsarge* before the mizzenmast. *Left to right:* Chief Engineer William H. Cushman; Surgeon John M. Browne; Captain John A. Winslow; Master's Mate Ezra Bartlett; Paymaster's Steward Daniel B. Sargent; Lieutenant Commander James S. Thornton; Second Assistant Engineer William H. Badlam; Third Assistant Engineer Henry McConnell; Acting Master James R. Wheeler; Boatswain James C. Walton; Third Assistant Engineer Sidney L. Smith; Master's Mate William Smith; Master's Mate Charles H. Danforth; Acting Master Eben M. Stoddard; Acting Master David H. Sumner; Paymaster Joseph Adams Smith. Master's Mate William Smith is misidentified in the original as Gunner Franklin A. Graham, but he bears no resemblance to Graham. Smith fought the battle as a quartermaster, but he was promoted to master's mate about the time of this photo; his promotion is entered in the log of July 8, 1864. (U.S. Army Military History Institute, Carlisle Barracks, Pa.)

Cherbourg harbor, June 30, 1864. Acting Master James R. Wheeler (*left*) and Third Assistant Engineer Sidney L. Smith at the *Kearsarge*'s forward 11-inch pivot gun, camera looking aft (U.S. Army Military History Institute, Carlisle Barracks, Pa.)

Cherbourg harbor, June 30, 1864. Acting Master Eben M. Stoddard (*left*) and Chief Engineer William H. Cushman at the aft pivot gun of the *Kearsarge*, the camera facing forward (U.S. Army Military History Institute, Carlisle Barracks, Pa.)

Cherbourg harbor, June 30, 1864. Most of the engineer department of the *Kearsarge*, with Third Assistant Engineer Sidney L. Smith at right (U.S. Army Military History Institute, Carlisle Barracks, Pa.)

Cherbourg harbor, June 30, 1864. Officers and men behind a 32-pounder carronade on the quarterdeck of the *Kearsarge*. The officers, *left to right,* are Acting Master's Mate Charles H. Danforth; Gunner Franklin A. Graham; Midshipman Edward E. Preble; Acting Master's Mate Ezra Bartlett. The boy in the middle is Second Class Boy Manuel José Gallardo, age twelve, who enlisted in Spain a few months before the battle (U.S. Army Military History Institute, Carlisle Barracks, Pa.)

Right. Oriental Hotel, Southampton, England, where Semmes and Kell lodged after the sinking of the *Alabama* (photo by the author, 1993)

Below. Cimitière ancien, Cherbourg: graves (*left to right*) of George Appleby (CSS *Alabama*), William Gowin (USS *Kearsarge*), and James King (*Alabama*). Grave at far right is that of Assistant Surgeon J. J. Allingham, USS *Frolic*, who died October 13, 1865. (photo by the author, 1993)

Mount Kearsarge, in Bartlett and Chatham, N.H. Officially known as Kearsarge North, this is the mountain after which assistant navy secretary Gustavus Fox insisted that his wife named the USS *Kearsarge*. (photo by the author, 1985)

1915 reunion of the *Kearsarge* survivors who participated in the fight with the *Alabama*. *Front, left to right:* John C. Woodbury; Henry S. Hobson; William M. Smith; William H. Giles; Martin Hoyt; Patrick McKeever. *Rear, left to right:* George H. Russell; William I. Evans; John J. McAllen; Austin M. Quinby; Peter M. Ludy; John T. Bickford. Hobson, McAllen, and Quinby were Marines. (U.S. Army Military History Institute, Carlisle Barracks, Pa.)

Idle at last. The drydock in which the CSS *Alabama* was constructed at the Laird shipyard in Birkenhead. Photo taken by the author from a nearby church belfry, August 6, 1993, just one week after the 165-year-old shipyard ceased operations.

CHAPTER ELEVEN

The Succession

As idle as a painted ship upon a painted ocean
—Coleridge, "Rime of the Ancient Mariner"

T hanks to the lassitude of Spanish machinists and their British supervisors, the *Kearsarge* lay at La Carraca more than four
months. If Mud Creek had wearied the crew before, it drove them nearly
crazy this time. The usual proportion of intemperates used their liberty to
patronize the wine shops just outside the yard, and some of them had to be
brought back by force, but even the steadier hands grew restless. Once the
ship had moved back into the drydock, within spitting distance of the wharf,
the temptation grew irresistible. After spending one Sunday confined to the
deck of the ship, gazing longingly at the dock and the dry land beyond it, a
delegation approached the first lieutenant and asked if they might not spend
their mealtimes just off the ship. The lieutenant yielded, and for days afterward the dock was crowded with noontime and evening athletics. Some
inventive soul borrowed cannonballs from the shot racks and challenged all
comers in the shotput, while others pitched quoits or played "Base Ball"
with improvised equipment. Coal Heaver Charles Poole favored the latter
game, because it reminded him of when he was a boy.[1]

The executive officer to whom the sailors appealed was Acting Master
James Wheeler, who had taken up the duties temporarily in the middle of
February. Lieutenant Commander Harris had been ordered back to the
United States to take command of the USS *Chippewa*, and the crew bid him
goodbye at Sunday muster, February 15. Those who mentioned his depar-
ture in their journals had little to say about Harris, although a Marine

corporal who appears to have embellished his journal years later praised him as a bright, lively fellow who made his men toe the mark and never touched a dram. The *Kearsarge*'s paymaster, Joseph Adams Smith, seemed to think less of the old "luff" at the time, and when Harris's successor boarded the ship in April, Smith remarked that he was "a sailor, a gentleman, an officer & a man, which is more than I can venture to say belonged to the officer whose place he took."[2]

Thomas Harris was thirty-seven years old when he left the deck of the *Kearsarge*, and he would live less than a dozen years longer. The surgeon at the Philadelphia Naval Asylum would record him as a victim of typho-malarial fever, with congestion and inflammation of the lungs, but the final illness may have been a mere complication of tuberculosis, which felled an unusual number of men who served on the maiden cruise of the *Kearsarge*. The officers fared the worst of any aboard, and they may have contracted it from William Cushman, the chief engineer. Cushman had served in dusty engine rooms for six years before coming aboard, and aside from Yeoman DeWit, who was in his upper fifties, Cushman would be the first to perish. He died less than a year after leaving the ship, and the examining surgeon attributed the disease to a bout of pneumonia on the *Kearsarge*; like the attack that killed Harris, Cushman's pneumonia may have been more of a symptom than a cause.

Consumption likewise killed Gunner Franklin Graham. In 1869 Graham ended a second cruise on the *Kearsarge* when he was ordered home as an invalid, and after six months of rest he returned to duty at Mare Island, California. He survived three years of shore duty there, but died just five weeks after boarding his next ship. Seth Hartwell, who arrived on the *Kearsarge* as the captain's clerk in 1863, served at Mare Island with Graham in 1873, but his health was deteriorating rapidly then, and he died in the naval hospital there in the spring of 1876. The ship's carpenter, Mark Ham, first saw Surgeon Browne about a severe cough in June of 1863, and Browne kept him in his improvised sick bay for nearly a week before sending him back to duty. Respiratory trouble brought Ham back to the doctor once more before the cruise ended, and a shipmate on the *Vandalia* later said that Ham started coughing up blood in 1867. Early in 1869 Ham died in his Portsmouth home, where a final hemorrhage left the walls spattered with his blood.

Several other commissioned, warranted, or rated officers complained of lingering coughs and throat infections before the *Kearsarge* put back to the United States, and they may have carried the disease in their lungs even though they eventually succumbed to other afflictions. Enlisted men fell victim to the century's worst killer, too, but the causes of their deaths are more difficult to determine, at least among the deck hands. Seaman James Lee, who became a captain of the top, survived until the summer of 1877, when he would have been thirty-seven, and shipmates testified that he suffered from a persistent cough from March of 1864. The Portuguese captain of the afterguard, Francis Viannah, died in 1868 of ailments that the doctors never seemed able to identify accurately, and his fiftyish body may simply have been worn out after a life at sea. The lifelong sailors who composed most of the deck crews either did not live long enough to apply for the disability pensions that would detail their illnesses, or they did not leave widows to collect them. Their fates remain mostly a mystery, but the cold, damp berth deck and the constant soakings provided an environment where the tuberculosis bacillus could flourish, if only a carrier should introduce it. The coal heavers and firemen, most of whom returned to their lives on land when the cruise ended, did not die so young, nor do they appear to have picked up the pulmonary maladies so readily.[3]

The first lieutenant's departure offered a little amusement at Sunday muster on the first day of March. Captain Pickering's clerk, Charles Muzzey, stepped up to read the Articles of War that Harris had virtually memorized, but neither Muzzey's voice nor his wind could do the job. He broke down once, then twice, and by the third time the gathered sailors had begun snickering in spite of themselves, smothering outright laughter as Captain Pickering scowled upon them. Muzzey had not reached the halfway point when Surgeon Browne stepped forward and took the papers from him.

According to the scuttlebutt in the Marines' mess, early in March Captain Pickering confronted the Spanish yard superintendents, whom he suspected of lollygagging on his ship's repairs. If they did not have the *Kearsarge* ready for sea in a certain amount of time—the story did not specify how long—he would take the propeller shaft on deck and sail for home. Whatever truth there might have been to this rumor, the shaft did come alongside on March 3, and the engineer department began working it into "shaft alley" the next day. By March 8 gangs were struggling with block and tackle and huge ropes to mount the propeller on the tail of the shaft, and the ship floated out of the dock two days later.

After a trial run down to the harbor, the *Kearsarge* returned to La Carraca for a little more work. For their extra efforts in the reassembly, many of the engineers were allowed an afternoon ashore on March 12, but with so little time they dared not pass beyond San Fernando, where Coal Heaver Poole feasted on figs while his compatriot Wainwright would have sampled the wine shops. They both remarked on the thousands of Spanish laborers in the yard, half of whom seemed younger than fifteen. The employees flocked to eight gates at quitting time each day, where soldiers searched them all for government tools before they could leave.

Back at the ship, work never ceased. Except for the morning muster, even Sunday passed unnoticed as Pickering prepared to deliver the *Kearsarge* to her next commander ("Uncle Sam does not have any Sundays in Wartimes," Poole observed). After hearing the president's Emancipation Proclamation read on the quarterdeck, Wainwright began the Sabbath by chipping away at the new brass bearings in shaft alley. A brass sliver lodged in his right eye, and rubbing it with his dirty fingers only worsened the pain. Surgeon Browne removed the fragment, fitted a patch over the eye, and put Wainwright on the sick list. The patient began complaining of his inactivity before the day ended.[4]

The *Tuscarora* had arrived at Cadiz from the Azores, bringing word of a Confederate ship coaling at Tenerife, in the Canary Islands. Everyone aboard the *Kearsarge* supposed that this was another cruiser, but she proved to be the blockade runner *Georgiana*, which would be wrecked a few weeks hence while trying to enter Charleston harbor. With their spirits lifted by the hope of a little excitement, officers and crew alike bid good riddance to Mud Creek on March 17 and started downriver to Cadiz, where they began loading stores from the *Release*.

Two Algeciras recruits failed to answer that morning's roll call, though, and remained behind as the salt pyramids and the teeming dockyard disappeared. William Spencer had taken part in the brawl of January 21, which culminated in the attack on Sergeant Young and the master at arms, and no one would miss him. Frank Wilson, on the other hand, had won two promotions in his year aboard the ship, but the same court-martial that tried Spencer had reduced him to seaman, and he evidently took the demotion badly. The next morning Captain Pickering released another offending recruit from confinement and assigned him to the crew of the second cutter, only to lose this fellow, too, when the cutter landed at Cadiz that afternoon.[5]

Gunner Graham and Master's Mate Bartlett spent two days supervising the return of the *Kearsarge*'s powder and projectiles from the Cadiz powder house, which sat on a hill high above the wharf. Bartlett found it a harrowing job, for the older sailors would not hesitate to sit on an upturned powder keg and light their pipes. Graham himself barely avoided serious injury when the outside wheel of a cart carrying 11-inch shells slipped off the narrow wharf. The shells bounced out and bowled Graham off the wharf onto the rocks below, but none of the shells landed on him and he broke no bones. He came out of it badly bruised, but he stayed on duty.[6]

With the exception of a seaman who slipped ashore for an unauthorized holiday on March 22, the enlisted men remained confined to their ship for the entire week the *Kearsarge* spent in Cadiz harbor. The officers, meanwhile, enjoyed evenings ashore. Most of the wardroom denizens attended the latest opera, featuring a tenor by the name of Don Zoncarde, and one of them brought along a recruit when he returned. Captain Pickering bid adieu to the Cadiz consul March 23, advising him that he was off to deliver his command over to her new skipper, but he made one final jaunt into the city on March 24. A gale kicked up almost as soon as he landed, preventing him from returning to the ship; the storm continued throughout the next day, and Pickering could not reach the ship until the morning of March 26, when he immediately gave the order to raise the anchors. By 11:20 the pilot left the deck, and the deck officer set the sea watches. A lookout climbed to the crosstrees while exhausted birds, blown to sea in the two days' gale, alighted all over the ship.[7]

Commander Craven, of the *Tuscarora*, had found no evidence of any armed Southern cruisers in European waters, and he had expressed the opinion that none could operate in that region because of the difficulty in obtaining fuel. Yet, even as Captain Pickering made his last cruise in the *Kearsarge*, he watched for suspicious craft. One appeared on the second morning, after the tip of Portugal's Cape Vincent passed out of view: at 7:00 the ship came out of the northeast with all sails set and no steam up—just as a Confederate raiding vessel might move if coal were hard to come by. At Pickering's signal big George Willams beat the drum, and the gun crews cast their pieces loose. The quartermaster turned his wheel straight for the stranger, and, when Old Glory went up the mizzen, the other ship hoisted an odd flag, with a green field, a white cross, and a piece of vegetation in the center of the cross. The two ships passed within shouting distance, and Pickering satisfied himself that he had found no cruiser, but neither did he recognize the flag. Equivocating long enough that the other steamer disappeared over the horizon, Pickering finally determined to chase her, hoping perhaps for one prize before he yielded his warship. A little after noon he directed the officer of the deck to wear ship and take after the steamer with the mysterious flag.

Deck hands bet they would never catch the stranger now, but with the repaired propeller churning madly the *Kearsarge* bounded over the waves like a greyhound. "She carries a bone in her mouth," remarked Paymaster Smith of this chase. Within an hour the lookout called out that he saw the prey. By 3:00 they had come alongside her again, sending a trumpeted demand for the vessel's name. Some heard the name *Pekin*, but others understood it as the *Sea King*. Registered in Trieste, the ship had just departed Liverpool on its way to China, with a stop at Madeira, and the curious flag represented no country at all, but the China Tea Company. With that Pickering turned the *Kearsarge* back about and resumed his course.[8]

The next day Pickering tested the crew that he would soon turn over to another officer. When the drum beat everyone to quarters, the captain passed from one man to another, interrogating each on his duties in action. Never before had Pickering held so detailed an inspection, and the men stood for two and a half hours at their stations. Ham Fat beat retreat for the noon meal, but at 1:00 the fire bell rang, and each sailor ran back to his fire station, most supposing that the ship was actually ablaze, for none expected another drill so soon after the morning's ordeal. This was Pickering's final examination of his crew, though, and they worked well into the afternoon against the imaginary flames. That night the berth deck did not echo with the unauthorized chatter that might bring a reproof from the master at arms; when the boatswain piped the hammocks down, only the sound of snoring broke the stillness of the ocean night.[9]

Pickering might well have kept an eye turned for worthwhile prizes. Even as the *Kearsarge* bounded through high seas on April 1, the ship that would be known as the *Georgia* slipped out the Firth of Clyde and through the North Channel, headed for a rocky, isolated harbor in the island of Ushant, off the northwestern tip of France. Had Pickering sailed as far to the north as he had to the west, he would have arrived just in time to nab that fledgling cruiser. Orders took him to the Azores instead, and after the diversion of the tea ship Pickering brooked no delay. He plowed through rough seas that rolled the ship mercilessly, bringing on another bout of nausea for the weaker stomachs, and in a cold rain on the first afternoon of April the cry of "Land ho" fell from the masthead when little Santa Maria Island rose out of the cloudy distance.

Waiting for the gale to abate before trying the islands, Pickering lay off São Miguel while porpoises leaped around the ship. He finally moored in the harbor of Ponta Delgada. Leaving there the morning of April 4, the *Kearsarge* sailed toward Terceira and hove to off that island for the night, within sight of the harbor where the *Enrica*, the *Bahama*, and the *Agrippina* had made their illicit rendezvous seven months previously. In the morning Pickering guided the ship around Terceira and through the familiar strait between Pico (whose mountain wore its customary sombrero of clouds) and São Jorge, anchoring off Horta before noon. In the afternoon the American consul came aboard to introduce the ship's new commander and first lieutenant.[10]

Both of the new officers wore chinstrap beards—one black and one grey. Captain John A. Winslow, who claimed Massachusetts as his home although he was a native of North Carolina, had arrived on Faial aboard the great armed sidewheel steamer *Vanderbilt* on Christmas Eve, and so had waited nearly fifteen weeks for his new command. He used the time to recuperate from the inflamed lungs and infected eye that had been troubling him since his departure from a gunboat on the Mississippi River, and he made observations of the shipping traffic in the islands. Among those observations lay the rumor that the *Alabama* had shown up off Flores on March 22, and Winslow gave the story enough credit that he planned to linger among the islands for a few weeks. Catching up with Captain Semmes would offer him great personal satisfaction, for they had known each other in the old navy: Winslow had shared his stateroom with Semmes, after the foundering of the brig *Somers*.

At thirty-six, James S. Thornton had spent twenty-two years in the navy, and the previous summer he had finally been bumped up from lieutenant. As the commander of a little gunboat he had participated in the blockade of Mobile, and his had been one of the ships that the *Florida* had slipped past in early September. Like many of the crew, Thornton was a native of New Hampshire; like Master's Mate Ezra Bartlett, Thornton was also the direct, lineal descendant of a Granite Stater who had signed the Declaration of Independence.[11]

With handshakes all around, the officers agreed to put off the formal transition until Wednesday, April 8. In the interim the crew loaded more coal and scrubbed up the deck with a vengeance afterward, scraping the planks white again with the holystone; in leisure moments the fruit-famished sailors and Marines bartered greedily with the inevitable bumboats that crowded alongside. Remarkably, no one seems to have smuggled enough liquor aboard to mar the assumption of command, and at 10:30 Wednesday morning the crew mustered on the quarterdeck in their cleanest blue uniforms. Winslow and Thornton climbed ostentatiously over the side, Pickering introduced them, and together they inspected the men. At last Captain Pickering offered his final salute and climbed down into the gig, and, as the oarsmen rowed him ashore, Thornton ordered the men into the rigging to cheer him. By all accounts it was a sad scene: Coal Heaver William Wainwright expressed sorrow at Pickering's departure, and Yeoman DeWit recorded that everyone had become attached to their old skipper. Charles Fisher, the cook, echoed DeWit's accolade, repeating that the regard for "this fine officer" was universal, and Paymaster Smith rejected the criticism of those who thought Pickering had not shown sufficient energy in the use of his ship; if anything, thought Smith, the *Tuscarora* had done a good deal less, and had used up a lot more public resources in doing it. Ten months later, on a moonlit night off Charleston, South Carolina, Charles Pickering would win a dubious place in history as the commander of the first warship ever sunk by a submarine.[12]

A quartermaster aboard the Confederate States Steamer *Georgia* raised her pennant as the ship emerged from the rocky horseshoe harbor at Ushant Island on April 9. That same day, while Lieutenant Thornton signed on a black islander as a coal heaver, the crew lined the forecastle rail to wave goodbye to Captain Pickering's clerk, Muzzey, as he departed for Boston on a little brig. Muzzey fluttered his handkerchief at his homesick former shipmates. Between the summerlike aroma of orange trees that drifted from the land, and the knowledge that the clerk would stand on New England soil before the month was out, this farewell stung the homesick sailors with a particular pang. They had little time to dwell upon it, though, for John Winslow soon had them scampering about to ready the ship for sea.

The boatswain piped the entire crew to their feet at 4:30 the next morning. Winslow stood on deck at 8:00 when the ship turned to sea in a fair breeze with all sails set, and his appearance caused some of the diarists to mention it, for captains rarely spent much time out of their cabins. Their wishes usually reached the deck through the first lieutenant, who passed them on to the duty officer. As far as the crew might be concerned, the first lieutenant was the senior officer, to whom special requests were directed, and complaints made; the captain remained aloof, unapproachable, and almost godlike. Secure in his chamber below the quarterdeck, he was the source of all the first lieutenant's authority, and his whim decided whether frantic sailors could visit the shore after a long cruise, or whether a misbehaving petty officer would retain his rate or spend a month in the sweatbox, on bread and water; not many years had passed since he might also sign the order to hang a man from the yardarm. For all his prominence on the quarterdeck, Winslow had no intention of allowing any familiarity from the enlisted men, and on that first night at sea he confined his own cook, Ham Fat, for a delayed binge with some Horta Bay wine.

The first lieutenant, meanwhile, performed most of the ceremonial functions, and intervened whenever the officer of the deck ran into trouble. Until relatively recently, the U.S. Navy had recognized only three permanent ranks: lieutenant, commander, and captain, with the honorary rank of commodore for a captain who had charge of a fleet. Only on the larger American warships did the commanding officer himself rank higher than lieutenant, and it was even less often that the executive officer was not of that grade. The man who held that position was therefore habitually known as the "first lieutenant"—or the "first luff" in the British navy (and, consequently, on the British-manned *Alabama*). With the expansion of the naval branch at the outbreak of the Civil War, though, the Navy Department soon found it expedient to add some grades. In 1862 the rank of lieutenant commander began to appear under the signature of some officers (usually lieutenants who had command of a vessel), and on the upper end of the scale the rank of admiral was created to reward the accomplishments of men like David Farragut. James Thornton had profited from that development, for he rose almost instantly to lieutenant commander. Tradition dies hard in the armed services, however, so Lieutenant Commander Thornton felt no slight when the crew referred to him as the first lieutenant, or simply as "Lieutenant Thornton," even though both he and Captain Winslow wore an unusual amount of gold braid on their sleeves for the senior officers of so small a gunboat.[13]

It was Thornton, therefore, who inspected the crew at quarters that first Sunday, as the ship still tossed about among the Azores. The vessel rolled so violently during his circuit of the gun crews that some had to leave their stations and pay their tribute to Neptune through the gun ports.

Winslow stopped at Angra do Heroísmo, to see for himself where the *Alabama* had shipped her guns, then he directed a course around the little island of Graciosa on the way to Flores, the westernmost of the archipelago. The *Kearsarge* anchored off Lajes das Flores, from which hordes of Portuguese rowed out to visit. With them came a Massachusetts man who had spent the winter on Flores after the *Alabama* landed him. His story interested the crew, but their captain apparently found nothing concrete about the rumored sighting of the Confederate raider, and he turned back for the main islands the next day.

The cruise back to Terceira offered the calmest day that anyone aboard the ship ever saw at sea, and on April 14 both Charles Poole and William Wainwright described the ocean as "a vast mirror," unbroken by the peak of a single wave. Beautiful as it was when he stood off duty on the forecastle, Wainwright found it unpleasant when he started his watch in the fire room, for the calm required more steam and deprived the engine room of any draft to relieve the resulting heat.

That placid surface assumed a slight swell a couple of days later, when Winslow anchored the ship at Angra to repair the engines, and even that gentle motion sickened some visiting parties of Portuguese who crowded the deck. For days they continued to clamber aboard, though, and the rolling deck pitched them about like so many drunks, to the everlasting amusement of the sailors. The ship passed Sunday in the harbor—Captain Winslow preaching the first sermon ever heard on the quarterdeck, and after their own services ended ashore, the islanders again flocked to the mysterious vessel, which they had dubbed "the Black Spirit of the islands." As many as 500 hopped onto the deck during the course of the day, from the governor of the island to the lowly tenant farmers, some wearing lace and some wearing rags.[14]

Not wishing to offend these civilians, whose conviviality and hospitality so raised the spirits of these lonely sailors, the officers found it difficult to hustle them ashore late on the afternoon of April 20, when Captain Winslow wanted to weigh anchor for a visit with the commander of the *St. Louis* at Faial. After an hour's coaxing and bowing the last guest departed, however, and toward evening the *Kearsarge* stood out to sea.

On the way over to Horta, Winslow practiced the crew at both the big guns and small arms, making some fair shots at a target with the pivots. Musket drill with fourteen-pound Sharps breechloading rifles did not include practice shots that day, or almost any day, but it tended to wear the men out after an hour or so, especially when the mercury rose, and the early Azorean summer was already about to begin. The next morning Winslow returned to Angra after a chat with his counterpart, and he directed more target practice on the way back. The guns were run back in just before noon, whereupon the anchors were dropped again and Chief Engineer Cushman prepared to work on the crank pin bearings, which were so soft they overheated whenever the propeller had to be engaged. The coal heavers banked their fires, looking forward to some liberty in an exotic location, but within an hour someone on deck spotted a steamer ten miles off shore. Three boat crews that had started ashore returned, and within twenty-two minutes the *Kearsarge* followed in pursuit.

Winslow suspected that Confederate blockade runners would start using Terceira as a coal and supply depot again, now that Federal suspicions had cooled, and he supposed that this low, fast steamer had been looking for the harbor when the *Kearsarge* loomed into view. Because of the overheated bearings and a thick coat of algae that clung to the fresh linseed oil on the *Kearsarge*'s belly, Winslow found that his new ship could not overtake the chase. After three hours he relayed a message to fire a round from the rifle on the forecastle and raised Portuguese colors, but the steamer ignored it. By 6:00 that evening the *Kearsarge* had fired two more shots with no effect. Surgeon Browne and the captain conspired to recommend a gallon of whiskey for distribution to the coal heavers and firemen, but their best efforts availed nothing. At 7:15 the anonymous steamer disappeared into the growing darkness. The next morning, anchored off Angra once more, Winslow learned that he had been chasing the British mail steamer.[15]

That night the citizens of Angra organized a ball in honor of the *Kearsarge* and her officers. The enlisted men spent the day sprucing up the ship for the event, but only the officers enjoyed the dinner and dance itself, donning full dress uniforms with braided epaulettes, sword belts, and white kid gloves. Exhausted from the fruitless chase of the day before and his cleaning duties that day, William Wainwright scorned the ball that he was not invited to attend, claiming that he would rather sleep, but he might have decided otherwise had he seen what he missed. These lonesome sailors prized the sight of a woman more than anything, and the paymaster judged that some of the beauties who attended the ball would have rivaled any in Paris. Wainwright saw them for himself the next morning, when the officers finally returned aboard, bringing some of their dance partners with them.[16]

The following Sunday found the ship at Horta once again, where the captain granted afternoon liberty to twenty-three lucky sailors after divine services. The *St. Louis* still lay in the harbor, and some of her crew came aboard to visit while others encountered the *Kearsarge* sailors ashore. After a few drinks the natural rivalry of the respective liberty men got the better of them, and they began fighting in a Horta bar. All but one of the *Kearsarge* men returned at sundown, as the captain had specified: Jimmy Saunders, that short, grey-haired, fifty-four-year-old quartermaster with the bust of a woman tattooed on his forearm, allowed either the wine or the women to lure him away overnight.

Lieutenant Thornton had served aboard the USS *Hartford* when it ran the gantlet past Fort Jackson and Fort St. Phillip just a year before, and that ship had worn her spare chains draped over the sides to protect the boilers and the engines from penetrating shells. Thornton apparently proposed the idea for his new ship—at least his family later claimed that for him—and on April 27 the first length of chain was bolted to the hull of the *Kearsarge*. Sitting in seats slung from the yards, deck hands screwed eyebolts into the New Hampshire oak and fastened the chains to them, starting about midway between the foremast and the mainmast and working backward, stopping between the mainmast and the mizzen. This enormous chain mail ran from the level of the main deck to the waterline, affording no extra protection to the gun crews, but as far as propulsion was concerned, the *Kearsarge* was an ironclad. Carpenter's Mate Mark Ham planned to veneer the ironwork in boards, beveling the fore and aft ends of the addition as well as the bottom so the boxing would offer less resistance to the sea. Once painted black like the rest of the hull, the raised surface would blend inconspicuously under all but the closest inspections. By May 4 the last length of chain had been fastened to the ship's waist.[17]

Just prior to leaving Horta on May 8, Lieutenant Thornton recruited a wardroom boy in the form of a young islander who could not speak the first word of English. He took the name José Dabney—the American consul at Horta was Charles Dabney—but the crew called him "Pico," because that was his native island. He bore the most forlorn expression as his home fell farther and farther behind, but English would come to him and he would see the cruise finished.

Arriving at Angra in a steady drizzle the next noon, Captain Winslow learned that two blockade runners had stopped there for coal, just as he had supposed they would. The crewmen cursed their luck, wondering if they would ever experience the excitement and profit of taking a prize, but Winslow reasoned that the steamers would have carried no recognizable contraband until they arrived in the Bahamas. Nonetheless, he decided to put to sea that night for Ponta Delgada, on São Miguel. After Sunday muster the next morning a likely ship came into view, but it proved to be a Portuguese man-of-war.

That afternoon the *Kearsarge* anchored near a brig commanded by a Maine man who offered news from home. At dawn a British gunboat alarmed the lookout again, and the crew raced to quarters, but the sloop turned into the harbor in a friendly fashion. Later in the day Winslow ordered the ship around to a primitive hamlet on the coast, where he and most of his officers climbed into one of the cutters and made for shore: hot sulphur springs lay a few miles inland there. The officers rode donkeys in and spent the night, the older ones soaking their aching joints while incredulous islanders gaped at the steamship.

Late on the night of May 13 the *Kearsarge* veered back to Horta, where another American ship had reportedly been burned. Sending a boat ashore at Terceira and Santa Cruz, on Graciosa, Winslow could learn nothing, nor did anyone at Horta know of the burned vessel. "We are neatly Hoaxed," thought Charles Poole, who suspected that someone had seen a whaler trying oil.[18]

Satisfied that the Azores would yield no prizes now, Winslow turned his ship for Madeira, disconnecting the propeller to save the delicate crankshaft bearings. Only when the lookout called a ship in sight did the captain call for steam and the engines, lapsing back to sail alone when the chase showed the British ensign.

One lookout, whom Poole described as an Irishman with a talent for blundering, sat in the crosstrees on this cruise. He called "Sail ho" at one point, and Boatswain Walton yelled back "Where away?" Instead of responding with the direction, the lookout replied that there were two ships.

"Can you make them out?" Walton asked, referring to their type of rig.

"No, sir," said the Irishman, to the intense amusement of all those within earshot. "One I can see and the other I can't."

Stopping at Funchal, where six men won liberty and two took it without permission, Winslow picked up the launch that the *Kearsarge* had left, much damaged, on its first port call of the cruise, fifteen months before. The two absentees returned three days later, just before their sloop sailed for the Straits of Gibraltar.

A steamer bearing on a course for Gibraltar lured the *Kearsarge* into a chase on the morning of May 26. With the coast of Africa off the starboard beam, the warship pulled abreast of the prey near the straits themselves and discovered that it was a French transport, bound for Toulon with wounded soldiers from the war in Mexico. Two hours later the *Kearsarge* sailed into Gibraltar at full speed, but the helmsman had to veer abruptly when a bumbling Spanish steamer crossed his path. Instead of colliding bows-on with the culprit, the *Kearsarge* tore the steering gear off two hulks and carried away the jib boom and bowsprit of a full-rigged brig, smashing her own dinghy and rail and sheering off the top of the steam vent pipe. The smokestack took quite a dent, and with a little more momentum it, too, might have toppled. An hour or so of work with hawsers brought the ship clear of the luckless brig, and the *Kearsarge* steamed sheepishly over to Algeciras as the dusk began to settle.[19]

Except for the great dent in the smokestack, the damage was almost entirely repaired by the second day after the accident. As soon as the last shroud had been secured, the ship headed back into the straits and out into the Atlantic, past Cape Trafalgar. Before sunrise of May 29 the city of Cadiz bore off the lee bow, and a pilot guided the *Kearsarge* into the anchorage it had left just two months before. The white stucco buildings gleamed bright and beautiful under a scorching sun, but for the hands on this ship Cadiz served only as a reminder of the bleak shipyard on Mud Creek, and indeed that is where Captain Winslow meant to take his vessel. "I shall be a Spaniard myself if we stay in Spain much longer," lamented William Wainwright.[20]

CHAPTER TWELVE

Consigned to the Sea

The navy is the asylum for the perverse, the home of
the unfortunate. Here the sons of adversity meet the
children of calamity, and here the children of calamity
meet the offspring of sin.
—Melville, *White Jacket*

oal Heaver Wainwright did not suffer alone.
His comrade Poole expressed disdain for
Spain and Spaniards, judging them indolent
and unduly proud compared with the "honest and industrious" Portuguese
whom he preferred. Either in words or in actions, nearly everyone showed
the ennui of sixteen months' shuttling between the Iberian Peninsula and the
island territories. One seaman from the original crew could bear no more as
the cruise reached its midpoint and, when the *Kearsarge* prepared to depart
for La Carraca, he absconded from the third cutter on the last landing at
Algeciras. The ship had not lain at anchor two days in Cadiz harbor before
Charles Poole remarked that he felt like a convict who had already spent
long years in prison.

Captain Winslow probably sensed the crew's frustration, and he loosed a
score or so of his more restless sailors on the city as he waited for a vacant
dock at the shipyard on Mud Creek. Poole was one of those allowed ashore,
and that Puritan soul treated himself to a jaunt around the streets, where he
witnessed a Catholic funeral procession—removing his hat for this Papist
ceremony only when asked to. He stopped at a museum to see the paintings
and statuary, and scanned the preserved stonework of a Roman coliseum,

160

all of which momentarily quenched his thirst for Spanish culture. Deck hands, most of them old salts, struck for their customary haunts to satisfy different tastes, indulging themselves so intently that many of them missed the next morning's liberty launch back to the ship. Ranking petty officers stood prominently among the missing, including boatswain's mates Thomas Burns and Charles Butts, John Dempsey (who had been promoted to quarter gunner since his court-martial), and stocky little Robert Strahan, the captain of the maintop. First Class Boy James Stone and seamen James Morey and William Giles—three Massachusetts sailors whose names would frequently grace the log for their drunken liberty celebrations—also failed to return, but the captain of the port sent Morey, dead drunk, back to his ship late on the morning of June 5. The rest remained in jail on shore while another contingent took their turn, William Wainwright among them.[1]

Because they might wish to flee from the legendary discipline of the navy, or for other reasons, recruits frequently shipped under assumed names, as had Edward "Tibbetts." Even Gunner Franklin Graham had enlisted under an alias as a fourteen-year-old cabin boy aboard the *Constitution* in 1844. William Giles may have done the same when he signed the *Kearsarge* muster roll, for his left arm bore the initials "WH." Whatever his real name, he and his fellow prisoners were delivered to a boat from the warship on the third day after their arrests.[2]

As these crestfallen few trudged down to the landing, they may have seen a horde of their shipmates flocking ashore. It was a Sunday morning, and Cadiz would have a bullfight; Winslow freed more than a third of the enlisted men and all but two of the officers to amuse themselves in the ancient city. Most of the officers probably sought the bullring, while the bluejackets disappeared into the alleys and bordellos. Back at the ship, others who had enjoyed liberty too recently to go ashore again paddled about the harbor in the launch during their off-duty hours, but those on watch worked away the Sabbath, hammering on the plank covering Mark Ham had contrived for the *Kearsarge*'s chain armor.

Toward the end of the second week at Cadiz Winslow steamed his vessel up to the coal yard and began filling his bunkers. The job took all of Friday and Saturday. "I should like to [see] some of you fancy ducks in the coal bunkers today," wrote a grimy William Wainwright, who helped clean up the deck just in time to receive some mail from home.

The following day the captain held another of his Sunday services on the quarterdeck. His congregation grew smaller by the week: Winslow was "a dry old preacher," Wainwright noted, predicting "he will be alone soon."[3]

Monday morning the crew woke up to the thumping of a loose coal barge that broke out one of the *Kearsarge*'s side lights. Once the runaway barge had been tethered, the ship proceeded to the rocky wharf where Gunner Graham had nearly been killed. Though Winslow expected to be only a day or two in the drydock, the Spanish officials would not allow him to bring in his powder, so Graham oversaw the drudgery as the kegs, cartridges, and loaded shells came out of the hold. On Tuesday the ship steamed into the drydock; as soon as it was drained, the crew started down the sides in boatswain's chairs, scraping off the festoons of seaweed that had accumulated in the three months since the *Kearsarge* had left this place. Winslow blamed the rapid fouling of his ship's bottom on the thick coat of linseed oil that had been applied when she was last in this same dock.

The carpenter's mate took the opportunity to repair the cutwater, which had suffered in the collision at Gibraltar, and the engineers installed more durable crankshaft bearings. With his own men wielding the tools instead of the Spaniards, Winslow found that the work went much faster, for none of them wished to spend another hour longer on Mud Creek than they had to. By noon of Wednesday the copper below the ship's waterline gleamed in the summer sunlight, and she floated away that afternoon, docking at the powder house wharf again. After landing two ailing crewmen so they could be sent home, and picking up the third recruit gained during this sojourn in Cadiz, Winslow ordered the ship out to sea on Thursday evening.

To the dismay of those who sought new sights, the helmsman turned for Gibraltar again. This, however, would be another brief stop. Arriving on the morning of June 19, the *Kearsarge* anchored near a storeship and took an assortment of supplies aboard before steaming back into the straits that night. Though none aboard knew it, they would never again set eyes on the great rock.[4]

For a week or more Captain Winslow had known of the departure from England of a blockade runner called the *Lord Clyde*. As the story reached Winslow's ears, the ship was "a new *Alabama*," and the captain meant to strike straight for Madeira and the Azores to intercept it. At Funchal the lookout did spot a suspicious British steamer that was about to sail, but she was obviously not the rumored commerce raider. Small and loaded dangerously deep with coal, the *Smoker* nevertheless piqued Winslow's curiosity, especially after he learned that her destination was Tampico, on the Mexican coast, from which blockade runners ran regularly into Texas. The *Kearsarge* lay quietly at anchor until the little vessel started to sea, the same evening that the Federal sloop arrived. Hoisting his own anchor half an hour later, Winslow caught up with the ungainly steamer some ten miles off the port and brought her to.[5]

For the first time since the *Kearsarge* had been launched, one of her boats boarded a vessel to search for contraband. Flailing at the loose coal for hours with shovels, the Yankee sailors uncovered nothing but more coal, and Winslow ultimately decided to let her go. The *Smoker* pulled away with her crew smirking a little too contentedly, thought Corporal Quinby of the Marines, but from his perspective on the forecastle Charles Poole vowed that he would never go to sea on such a "Rat Trap as that." If they ever heard the news, the *Kearsarge* sailors would have had the last laugh, for less than three months later the *Smoker* ended her career on a Mexican beach, her hold filled with Confederate cotton.[6]

Suspecting that Confederate ships might use Madeira as a coaling station, Winslow anchored off the tiny island of Porto Santo, northeast of Madeira, to lie in wait. Porto Santo seemed nearly desolate, with little vegetation and few inhabitants, and those who did live there mistrusted this curious visitor. Ships found little reason to frequent their shores, and although the islanders rowed out for a closer look, they kept their distance, declining the gestures of invitation from the *Kearsarge* forecastle: someone deduced that they feared the blue-clad sailors would not let them leave the ship once they boarded it. After long entreaty one brave soul ventured on deck, and his fellow villagers soon followed, but no amount of coaxing could bring any of them below the spar deck that day. They were a filthy bunch, Poole observed, with sand in their hair and dirt caked on their bodies as though they had never been introduced to soap and water. The next day the islanders returned, staring in astonishment through the skylights at the ship's huge engines, but none of them dared go below for the grand tour. Like the day before, though, one of them screwed up his courage at last and followed an engineer into the engine room, where a playful coal heaver lifted a gauge lock: a plume of steam came screaming out of it, and the native bounded up the ladder "as though he had been shot."[7]

With the potential for a scrap looming, Captain Winslow spent the better part of June 29 training his crew at their weapons. For an hour or more the various crews worked the big guns, firing a few practice rounds, and after that six divisions armed themselves with rifles and performed the manual of arms. Even the officers' cook, Charles Fisher, came on deck to learn the drill, complaining of how heavy the fourteen-pound Sharps grew after two hours of exercise. George Russell, the ship's armorer, doled out 320 rounds of ammunition, and everyone took a few shots; Charles Poole observed that this was the first time he had fired a rifle in his nineteen months of service.

The marksmen turned in their weapons to break for lunch, but at 2:00 in the afternoon the boatswain whistled "arm and away." With Midshipman Preble in charge, a score of sailors wrestled the ship's 12-pounder boat howitzer into the launch while the Marines piled into a cutter under the eye of Sergeant Young. All pulled for shore as the islanders looked on, alarmed at all the shooting. Preble directed a couple of shots right from the launch, then he piloted the boat as close to the land as it could reach. The oarsmen lifted the howitzer out to drag it ashore. The Marines splashed into the shallows nearby, and the two parties marched off down the beach for an imaginary skirmish. Preble saw an inviting rock half a mile out in the surf, and the novice artillerymen expended five loads of powder and solid shot in the effort to shatter it. The rock survived, but one of the spectators on the *Kearsarge*'s forecastle credited the gunners with some fair shots, considering that they had never before fired the gun.

Drained by their day's exertions, the crews of the two boats answered readily when the ship raised the signal for them to return, and by 5:30 that evening they were straining to lift the howitzer back on deck. At midnight all hands raised the anchor and started for Madeira, leaving the confused and nervous inhabitants of Porto Santo behind. With the propeller disconnected, a grateful watch sat idly in the engine room, lighting their pipes and exchanging stories.[8]

At Funchal the consul bustled aboard to warn Winslow of a Confederate "privateer" spotted recently in the Canary Islands. The *Kearsarge* almost immediately put to sea with all sails set and the engine cranking at sixty revolutions a minute. Coal Heaver Poole lighted up at the prospect of seeing a new island, but his comrade Wainwright, who had so enjoyed the effortless sail into Madeira, grumbled now at having to bend his back to the coal bunkers for what he fully suspected to be "another wild goose chase." Indeed, the consul at Tenerife (yet another member of the diplomatic Dabney family) had witnessed the visit of a British steamer bound for China, rather than a commerce raider.

Poole had plenty of time to enjoy his new vista, for the *Kearsarge* lay off Tenerife three days. During those three days that the crew gazed on the lush, towering mountains of this volcanic isle, events that started their war toward its end were unraveling in Pennsylvania and Mississippi, but these sailors would hear nothing of it for weeks; with their distant perspective, they would not grasp the significance of the news for many months.

After transporting Consul Dabney's family to a holiday spa on the other side of the main island, the *Kearsarge* turned once more for the Azores on the afternoon of July 3. Independence Day passed without any kind of notice save the jottings of certain patriotic diarists, but, when the ship stopped briefly at Madeira, Lieutenant Thornton bought some chickens and enough pale ale to serve each man a bottle apiece. Charles Fisher and the ship's cook, Tim Hurley, made chicken pies, and the noon meal of July 6 made up for the lost Fourth.[9]

In the interest of adding potential speed, Winslow ordered the gaff top-sail bent as the ship bounded northward without steam; never before had that boom carried canvas. Winslow did much that his predecessor had not tried, and he seemed to pursue strange vessels more diligently. A sidewheel steamer that he ordered overhauled on July 5 turned out to be a French man-of-war, and the *Kearsarge* had just finished coaling at Horta, on Faial, when Winslow demanded steam to chase a ship that appeared off the coast; that one veered into the harbor, though, and proved to be a British transport on its way home from the coast of Africa. The crew chafed at Winslow's aggression, especially the firemen and coal heavers, on whom the most work fell when the ship went in chase of anything, but their captain based his suspicions on good grounds. While his ship had lain at Tenerife, he had narrowly missed the *Phantom*, which had stopped for coal at Funchal on its way to Nassau and Wilmington, and about the same time another Wilmington-bound blockade runner had coaled at São Miguel, in the Azores. Those before the mast cursed their perpetual tardiness no less than their captain did, for whenever a contraband ship eluded them, they missed out on some prize money, though much less than Winslow would have received; Winslow, of course, also lost the professional acclaim that he cherished even more.[10]

An iron sidewheel steamer flying the British flag appeared off Horta on the morning of July 17 and turned into the port, anchoring just astern of the *Kearsarge*. Her skipper refused to present his papers to the port authority, who therefore quarantined the ship, allowing no one to come ashore. Winslow warned his engine room to raise steam and be ready to follow the newcomer, and after lunch the stranger bolted for open water. Up on the quarterdeck Winslow called for all hands to man the capstan bars and heave the ship around to follow, but, before the anchor could be brought up, the engine room heard a call for "go ahead strong." The propeller started churning, thrusting the ship ahead and locking the anchor under the lee bow. Heave as they might, six dozen men could do nothing more than bite the anchor's flukes deeper into the hull, and with her first real prize in sight the *Kearsarge* limped along like a hobbled horse, dragging forty feet of chain and the burdensome anchor.

The chase fled between Pico and São Jorge, with the warship following at nine knots. Had it not been for the anchor, the race would have ended there, but the unarmed steamer slipped slowly away. Lieutenant Thornton ordered the crew of the forecastle rifle to clear their gun away and fire a shell, but it fell short. Officers and men alike looked to Winslow for permission to cut the tackle and let the fouled anchor go, but he shook his head. Finally the chase steamed out of sight in the direction of Terceira, where the *Kearsarge* arrived after dark. Dousing all lights, Winslow cruised past Angra, but he could see nothing until he eased into the roadstead himself, where he found his prey at anchor. He ordered the capstan unlocked, and with a frustratingly easy rattle his own jammed anchor plunged to the bottom.

The next morning the captain of the sidewheeler, John Taylor, came aboard the *Kearsarge* and informed Winslow that his ship was the *Juno*, of Bristol, bound for Bermuda. He demanded indignantly why Winslow had fired the shot at him.

"To bring you to, of course," Captain Winslow replied. Taylor invited Winslow to inspect the *Juno*'s cargo then and there, if he so wished, but the Federal officer reasoned that Taylor must have put his contraband ashore, with the expectation of taking it back when the examination was complete. Taylor offered his word that his ship carried no prohibited cargo, but Winslow replied that he would find out for himself when he put to sea. While taking his departure, Taylor reminded the naval officer that he had run away from the *Kearsarge* once, and could do so again.[11]

The *Juno* spent July 19 and part of July 20 taking in coal. In the evenings her crew lined the forecastle, singing "Dixie," "Off to Charleston," and a strange ballad called "Root, Hog, or Die." Winslow allowed his men to reciprocate with their own national airs, and for two days afterward the two ships lay like lion and antelope, the one waiting for the other to flee before leaping into pursuit. Augustus Johnson, a short, sturdy Swede who had shipped at Cadiz the previous autumn, stood at the tackle with an axe, ready to drop the anchor: the boatswain's mates had attached a buoy by which they might find it later. Observing this from the *Juno*, Captain Taylor tried to trick the *Kearsarge* into letting the anchor go prematurely, hoping perhaps that Winslow would not then risk slipping his second anchor. Backing away from his own anchor as though he were about to slip it himself, Taylor lunged his ship forward but then backed his engines. Winslow did not fall for the ruse, though, and the *Juno* remained another night.

Just before noon on July 22, the *Juno* backed away again and lurched ahead, this time heading out to sea. Seaman Johnson swung his axe, and the *Kearsarge* followed quickly. As crowds of islanders lined the nearby hills to watch the race, the sidewheeler turned sharply to the east, along the coast, and squeezed through a passage no more than twenty yards wide between Terceira and Cabras Island. Winslow dared not try that route with his bulkier sloop; instead he rounded the island, sighting the chase a mile and a half away. In half an hour he overtook the *Juno*, and his counterpart offered to let him come aboard there. Winslow declined, noting that they lay in Portuguese territorial waters, but he promised to have a look when the *Juno* passed the three-mile limit. Eventually Taylor did strike for open water, and when cross-bearings indicated that they had left Portuguese jurisdiction, Winslow sent a boat aboard to examine that portion of the *Juno*'s papers that Taylor had not burned.

Finding nothing to suggest any port but Bermuda as an alternate destination, Winslow used Taylor's eastward course—away from Bermuda—as an excuse to detain his ship. He sent Chief Engineer Cushman, Boatswain Walton, and a couple of first-class firemen aboard, all armed with revolvers and cutlasses, to prevent any sabotage to the prize's engines while the boat's crew began rummaging through the hold and shoveling down into the coal bunkers. With the U.S. flag at their mizzens, both ships turned on a course for Taylor's reported destination, keeping company during the night. By morning they made Horta, and Winslow relieved the prize crew with a second gang, William Wainwright among them. The *Juno* remained off shore (for Winslow did not dare bring a prize into a neutral port, as Raphael Semmes sometimes did), but the *Kearsarge* anchored in the bay.

Captain Taylor took word to the British consul on Faial, who confronted Winslow with a demand for the release of the *Juno*. The Federal captain resisted as long as he dared, but by 4:00 in the afternoon his prize crew had uncovered no flagrantly contraband goods. The drugs and cotton-processing equipment that did turn up may well have found willing markets in the South, but no munitions emerged from beneath the coal. Corporal Quinby heard that some heavy boxes had just been discovered when the order came to replace everything and restore the ship to Captain Taylor; but Winslow understood that his men could not reach the bottom of the bunker without throwing much of the coal overboard, and that he hesitated to do. The crew gossiped that their captain should have left the *Juno*'s hatches unopened and sent her back to Boston under a prize crew, for adjudication in a prize court, where the cargo could have been completely overhauled. Faced with a protest from the British consul, however, Winslow returned Taylor to the deck of his ship, where the brazen Briton raised his national colors and proceeded to "Bermuda." At the vernal equinox he and his ship would be captured (by the same blockader that would chase the *Phantom* aground one day later) while trying to dash into Wilmington, and the *Juno* would wind up going to Boston, anyway.[12]

The *Kearsarge* returned to Terceira, anchoring this time off the rockier village of Praia, on the northeast coast. Captain Winslow permitted his frustrated crew liberty here in contingents of forty a day, and he took advantage of this more unpopulated location to order another rifle drill ashore. The villagers proved more old-fashioned than those of Angra, and they marveled at the practicing riflemen like the natives of Porto Santo; the captain's cook went ashore for groceries and chuckled at the big bonnets ("like flour scoops") worn by the women.

On July 29, one week after the ship slipped its cable, Winslow returned to the roadstead at Angra to retrieve the lost anchor. The buoy bobbed where the ship had rested. A boat's crew rowed over to fasten the chain to the buoy and raise the anchor, but once the windlass took its strain the rope snapped, letting the anchor and its own length of chain sink to the bottom. The end of the rope appeared to have been cut with a knife, and everyone suspected Southern sympathizers among the passing British ships: *Kearsarge* crewmen habitually blamed the English for taking the Confederates' side. The rest of that day the boats plied across the spot, trolling with grappling hooks, but it was not until noon the next day that Quartermaster William Poole—no kinsman of Charles Poole—snagged the chain and brought it up. In celebration, Captain Winslow invited a brass band to play on the quarterdeck that evening.[13]

Such diversion only temporarily alleviated a growing fatigue with the Azores and the monotonous duty that kept the *Kearsarge* there. Indications of unusual irritability surfaced in diaries and on the ship's log. William Wainwright confessed that he never wished to see the islands again, and his less reflective shipmates expressed their disgust through insolence and combativeness. James Morey spent a few days in confinement for impudence to an officer, while both Petty Officer Robert Strahan and William Alsdorf, a recruit, were court-martialed. A new flurry of fighting gripped the crew, and not a week passed without some of the younger sailors thrown into irons for assaulting their comrades. The arrest of Henry Jamison surprised no one, for that fireman had earned a reputation with his vile temper, but even the jovial William Gowin—the ship's minstrel and clown—fell into a scuffle. Little Jimmy Hayes, a cabin boy less than five feet tall, spent a couple of days in solitary confinement on bread and water for a brawl ashore in which he stabbed one of his own crew with a knife—perhaps a natural enough reaction for a lad who had given his civilian occupation as "carver."

Under his authority as surgeon, Dr. Browne stopped all liberty twice in the first half of August because the men were coming back so badly injured from their barroom battles. Many returned late from their liberty, and some did not come back at all: three of the original crew deserted at Ponta Delgada, on São Miguel Island. Old shellbacks like Quartermaster Saunders simply took every opportunity to get roaring drunk, recuperating in the ship's sweat box and somehow consoling themselves with the reflection that they had relieved their boredom.[14]

There is little doubt that Saunders was probably the quartermaster of whom Charles Poole recorded a story the following fall. For his legendary offenses ashore Saunders was not allowed liberty while the ship lay in a French port, so he begged Lieutenant Thornton for a bottle of brandy to drink aboard. Thornton granted the request, so long as the quartermaster agreed to be locked in a compartment while he drank it, and until he sobered up. He started forward with the precious bottle, but the surgeon learned of it. Worried that the quartermaster might drain the liquor with toxic effect or otherwise injure himself, Dr. Browne sent a cabin boy after him with the tale that Thornton had accidentally given him a bottle of poison; if he would surrender it to the boy, the doctor would send his messenger back with the real thing. He did give up the bottle, but no brandy ever returned, though the quartermaster cursed high and low over the treachery.[15]

The surgeon may have stopped liberty to avoid more than the cuts and bruises of cantina fights: he may also have had fever on his mind. The *Kearsarge* pulled out of Ponta Delgada on the evening of August 15 (wrapping the anchor chain of a brig around the propeller in the process, but finally backing out of it), and by the next afternoon Landsman Mark Emery lay writhing on the berth deck, babbling deliriously.

Emery had shipped in Cadiz nearly fifteen months before, having apparently run away to sea from his home in Bucksport, Maine, four years earlier. His shipmates found him friendly, even "much beloved," and he was one of the minority of crewmen who never suffered any disciplinary action. He endured three days of delirium, ranting that he wished to see the mother he had left in Maine. As his fever heightened, he mistook all who approached him for his mother. At last, as the watches changed on the morning of August 19, he fell silent and passed away. His messmates sewed his body inside his hammock with a pair of 32-pound solid shot at his feet, and lay him on the quarterdeck, covering him with the American flag. At 1:00 the boatswain piped all hands on deck to bury the dead. The crew gathered, a detail of Emery's closest friends holding the body horizontally on a plank with the feet and cannonballs propped on the port gangway. Captain Winslow read the burial service, and when he uttered the words "as we commit this body to the deep," the pallbearers raised the head of the board. The weighted white shroud slipped from beneath the flag, hitting the water with "a dull splash" and sinking instantly. A solemn crowd turned back to duty, more than one of them shocked at the suddenness of death and burial at sea.[16]

Bad luck seemed to taunt the ship that day. An hour after the funeral service, the island of Flores bore on the horizon, and the *Kearsarge* anchored in the harbor of Santa Cruz. Just as a gale picked up, Winslow sent a provision boat to shore, where it secured some vegetables and crated chickens; as the craft returned that evening, a ringbolt tore from its stern while it was being lifted to the davits. Vegetables, fowl, and crew plunged together into the turbulent water in the darkness, and for a time William Gowin and another oarsman appeared to be lost, but both kept themselves afloat until another boat rescued them.

Winslow turned back to Faial the next day, but as the topmen set the sails and the engineers emptied their furnaces for a general cleaning, fifteen other men fell ill, some with the same symptoms that Emery had exhibited. The worst case was that of Clement Boener, a Prussian teenager who had signed with the engineer department at La Carraca; Boener raved in German while the ship stopped at Horta and entertained a party of ladies and gentlemen, carrying them on an excursion to Terceira. To the intense disgust of his shipmates, the civilians sang and danced on the quarterdeck while Boener's condition deteriorated steadily. The ship turned back for Faial in the evening, the guests retiring to borrowed wardroom compartments until they docked at Horta at dawn. Friends of the stricken coal heaver had watched over him in shifts during the night, William Wainwright taking over sometime after midnight. With the arrival off Horta, Boener grew suddenly worse, sinking fast until just before the breakfast call, when he fell perfectly quiet. Dr. Browne held a mirror to his mouth, pronounced him dead, and directed his assistants to wash the body and dress it in summer whites. Augustus Johnson threw a coffin together and stained it with gun blacking. One of the firemen fashioned a brass nameplate and screwed it to the lid.

At 5:00 that evening the launch came alongside. With the flags of both the ship and the launch flying at half staff, the box was lowered for transport to shore. Master's Mate Charles Danforth and Third Assistant Engineer Sidney Smith led a delegation from the engineer department, including William Wainwright and Charles Poole, and when the boat reached the pier, it was met by a Catholic priest. Following the priest, the detail took turns carrying the dead Westphalian to the church, a mile from shore. After a ceremony that seemed to trouble the suspicious Protestant attendants, they carried their shipmate to a pleasant little cemetery behind the church, filled his grave, raised a simple marker acknowledging Boener's name, ship, and date of death, and returned to their somber vessel.[17]

CHAPTER THIRTEEN

Cape of Good Hope

The death-fires danced at night
—Coleridge, "Rime of the Ancient Mariner"

A s the dawn of May 13, 1863, broadened over Bahia, Brazil, the deck officer of the *Alabama* turned his glass on a strange, brig-rigged, steam warship that had anchored half a mile off the port sometime after midnight. No Federal gunboats had been seen in Bahia for months, port officials had said, so perhaps one was due. The chance of another fight stirred the watch on duty until, at the customary hour of 8:00 A.M., both vessels raised their colors. The stranger hoisted the Stars and Bars at the precise moment that the same Confederate emblem slid up the mizzen of the *Alabama.* She was the *Georgia*, bought last March and armed at the island of Ushant, off the Brittany coast, just five weeks before. Once the commander of the *Georgia* recognized his counterpart, he moved his ship into the harbor and anchored nearby. Though no one at Bahia knew of it until the next day, the CSS *Florida* had just left the port of Pernambuco the day before, and the Confederacy had unwittingly formed a South Atlantic squadron.[1]

From Brazilian newspapers, Captain Semmes learned that his visit at Fernando de Noronha had caused some political trouble once his prisoners landed at Pernambuco. That flap troubled the president of the state of Bahia, who expressed hope that the *Alabama* would soon depart the capital's port. Shifting the blame for any neutrality violations onto the governor of the island, who had given him leave to coal and to land his prisoners, Semmes again won permission from the president to send his nine dozen new prisoners—including some women and a couple of infants—ashore at Bahia. He was also told that he could buy provisions, but the president refused to allow him to coal from the British bark *Castor*, which had come to supply the *Georgia*. The refusal appeared to stem from the American consul's claim that the *Castor* carried weapons meant for the Confederate vessels.

The *Agrippina* had shown up at Fernando de Noronha on April 30, eight days after the *Alabama* had left. Semmes remained ignorant of her arrival, even though the *Florida* boarded the *Agrippina* there, for his path never crossed that of the *Florida*. Supposing his tender had met with meteorological or political disaster, or that Captain McQueen had broken faith with him, Semmes gave the *Agrippina* up as lost.[2]

On the day after the *Georgia*'s arrival, Semmes, the ranking officer, led a holiday party of officers from both ships into the interior. At the invitation of an English railroad superintendent they boarded a train at the river's edge just after noon on May 14, riding the length of Bahia and climbing the crescent of bluff that cradled the city against the sea. Rattling two dozen miles inland, Semmes and the Louisiana officers with him must have felt homesick, passing bayous and lagoons interspersed with fields of sugar cane and cotton. The road lay unfinished, and at the inland terminus the officers debarked for a sumptuous lunch, complete with champagne. Lieutenant Kell strolled the edge of the forest, his big red hands incongruously decorated with the blossoms of bright, dainty flowers that he intended to press for the ladies at home and his London hostess, Louisa Tremlett. Returning to the cars late in the afternoon, the excursionists turned back for the city, where glittering white houses shone bright against the lush green foliage. With Semmes and Dr. Galt, Kell scoured the beach for some unique shells to send with the flowers, and by dusk the Confederates had all boarded their ships.

The next evening the officers came ashore with their distinguished commander once again, for a festive ball in their own honor at the home of another admiring subject of Her Majesty. The endless entertainment wore out some of the Confederates: a seventeen-year-old midshipman from the *Georgia* recalled, more than half a century later, that Midshipman Anderson fell asleep in the captain's gig and nestled against Captain Semmes's shoulder with greater familiarity than any waking person would have dared.[3]

The admiring attentions of British expatriates were matched neither by the Brazilian population nor by the authorities. The state president sent an envoy to the *Alabama* asking Semmes to show his commission, but Semmes responded coldly that he would hardly do so on the mere verbal request of a man in civilian clothing who bore no letter of authority himself. The retreating emissary heard Semmes say that he would be glad to present his commission to the president in person, however, and that afternoon Semmes and the president passed an hour in conversation about belligerent rights and the subject of coaling the *Georgia* and *Alabama*.

The *Georgia* began taking fuel from the *Castor* on May 15, but that operation ceased the next morning when the port authorities ordered the two ships parted. Several days passed as Semmes corresponded with the president and his subordinates, offering to coal from launches so no arms or munitions could be secretly transferred, but finally they came to the expedient of selling the *Castor*'s cargo to a merchant ashore, who then sold it back to the two Confederate cruisers at a substantial premium.[4]

The president complained directly to Semmes of the conduct of his crewmen on liberty in Bahia. Their antics were no secret to Semmes, who asked the president to clap them in prison as a favor to him, in hopes of recovering more of his lost lambs than he had at Kingston. The police obliged, and as a result only two men were missing when the crew was called aboard on May 20. Both were original members of the crew, but one of the desertions surprised everyone aboard the *Alabama*. James King, the Savannah pilot who had served as master at arms until his binge at Kingston, had quietly disappeared. These Savannah quartermasters had stood as their captain's stalwarts among the petty officers, and Semmes depended on them to help the officers keep the crew under control. King had taken a hand in subduing the November mutiny at Martinique, and the captain had evidently either restored him to his rank or intended to do so, for only after he deserted did someone take his place. This was the second native-born Confederate to abandon his comrades in four months, and both had left families in Savannah.

Semmes also spent at least one night fretting over the absence of a commissioned officer. The third lieutenant, Joseph Wilson, did not return from liberty one evening, and when he appeared on deck the next morning, Lieutenant Kell demanded his excuse. In a flippant tone Wilson replied that he had no excuse; he had simply not wished to come back that night. Semmes suspended him and confined him to his stateroom, where the unrepentant Wilson sulked for a solid week.[5]

George Appleby, the Liverpool bridegroom, may have taken the opportunity of a layover in port to celebrate the impending first anniversary of his marriage, which would fall on May 24. He must have returned to the ship a bit more reluctantly than the rest, and the morning after he was brought back, the captain peremptorily stripped him of his yeoman's rate and put him before the mast as a seaman.

With a gift of 528 pounds of gunpowder from the *Georgia*, to replace the cartridges expended in the fight with the *Hatteras*, Semmes ordered the gangplank pulled in and the fires spread on the morning of May 21. At noon the *Alabama* steamed out of Bahia, and the world's only rendezvous of major Confederate cruisers was over.[6]

Overpowering homesickness clouded Semmes's brow as he began the next leg of his cruise. It was not two years since he had opened the log of the *Sumter*, and all the news he could gather indicated no withering of Federal determination. He reasoned that the Northern will to fight would succumb only to the destruction of their commerce by cruisers like his own, or by an invasion of the North itself. He doubted the strength of the few Confederate raiders to strangle enemy trade, and he knew nothing yet of Robert E. Lee's victory at Chancellorsville, or of that general's contemplated incursion into Pennsylvania; in his seaborne reverie he hoped instead that his counterparts on land would wrest Kentucky from Union forces.[7]

For a month the *Alabama* tacked up and down on the coast of Brazil. Within eleven days commencing May 25, the lookout made out ten vessels, half of which carried American papers. The ship *Gildersleeve* and the bark *Justina* both hove to on the twenty-fifth, and Semmes decided to transfer his prisoners to the smaller craft, ransoming it while the *Gildersleeve* burned. On May 29 the *Jabez Snow*, of Rockport, Maine, became the fortieth ship burned by the *Alabama*; she carried Cardiff coal, but the bunkers of the *Alabama* still bulged with the coal loaded at Bahia. Four days later the Boston bark *Amazonian* hove to at a distance of nearly five miles when the *Alabama*'s pivot rifle let fly at her, and the fires were kindled in her cabin by nightfall. After a fruitless all-day chase on June 4, the lookout sighted a ship ablaze in the distance; the helmsman turned for it, but the light flickered out suddenly. Semmes continued toward the spot where the ship might have gone down, heaving to until the sun rose again on June 5 in order to pick up any survivors. The dawn showed nothing but calm water, though, and Semmes concluded that the light he had seen was the wreckage of the *Amazonian*, which must have drifted a dozen leagues in two days.[8]

Even as the *Alabama* lay by the grave of its last victim, another one appeared in the form of the full-rigged ship *Talisman*, speeding south on its way to Shanghai. Deck hands scampered into the tops to loosen the top-gallants, and the cruiser filled away to intercept this big prize, which hove around at the first blank cartridge. The clipper's crew and four passengers— including one woman—came aboard the *Alabama*, and Captain Semmes's eyes brightened when his boarding officer reported finding four brass 12-pounder cannon aboard, on naval carriages, with plenty of powder and shot. He ordered all the ammunition and two of the guns brought over to his own ship before anyone applied the match to the doomed merchantman.[9]

The following afternoon a boat from the *Alabama* boarded a ship that flew the British flag, but which looked suspiciously American. Her papers documented that she was another product of a Maine shipyard, but had been sold to Englishmen within the past couple of years. The captain and crew were all Britons, so Semmes concluded that he would not fire the ship, though he suspected that a prize court ashore might find the transfer fraudulent and condemn the vessel. With a barrel each of bread and beef to pay their way, he convinced the English captain to take the lady prisoner and her husband, who were bound for Calcutta, and as the sun dipped toward the horizon, he watched the would-be prize resume its journey.

Fifteen days passed between captures this time. Semmes found that his cruiser grew sluggish under sail alone, probably from a fouled bottom, and he could only intercept those ships on a course that intersected his own: "a stern chase has become a forlorn hope with us," he recorded on June 15. For all that the *Alabama*'s notorious speed had deteriorated, though, her effectiveness had improved, as the dearth of Federal sails reflected. Within twenty-four hours on June 16 and 17, the raider overhauled four ships, two of which proved foreign in both origin and ownership, but two others bore telltale signs of American build. The English bark *G. Azzopadi*, bound from Boston, had been the American *Joseph Hale* until the previous October, when the *Alabama*'s reputation reached New England. The big Australian packet *Queen of Beauty* had recently roved the seas as the *Challenger*, but now she flew British colors. In his journal, Semmes remarked wryly that Yankee shipping houses seemed to hide beneath the English ensign, which they professed to hate so much "except in the way of trade."[10]

The morning of June 20 began with two sails visible from the maintop. One bore an unmistakably American rig, and Semmes chose that one, following her all day. By now the *Alabama* had ranged deep into the South Atlantic, and the crew made this chase in their woolen pea jackets, for what would have been the eve of summer north of the equator was the beginning of winter here. At last Semmes had to order steam up and the propeller dropped to catch the bark, which finally hove to in the darkness of early evening. Master's Mate George Fullam commanded the boat that boarded the vessel, which he found to be the *Conrad*, sailing from Buenos Aires to New York with Argentinian wool. Her papers showed Philadelphia ownership, and Semmes condemned her immediately.

The *Conrad* operated with a small crew, and one woman accompanied them. She "claimed" to be a passenger, noted a disgusted Semmes, who evidently pegged her for a prostitute, and he scribbled a remark about "the indecent scoundrels" at the end of his entry that day.

With the two naval guns taken from the *Talisman* (he had long since jettisoned the unseaworthy howitzer from the *Ariel*), Semmes determined to transform the *Conrad* into a miniature Confederate cruiser. He outfitted the little bark with the pair of 12-pounders, with a score of rifles and half a dozen revolvers from the *Ariel* booty, and with fifteen of his own crew.[11]

To command this new ship, Semmes chose his most experienced but lowest-ranking lieutenant, John Low, who had safely piloted the *Alabama* through the October hurricane. He gave him three officers—Midshipman William Sinclair, Signal Quartermaster Adolphus Marmelstein, and Seaman John F. Minor—whom Semmes respectively promoted to master and master's mates. Sinclair hailed from the same Southern family as Arthur Sinclair, whom Semmes appointed fourth lieutenant to replace Low, and Marmelstein was one of the four Savannah pilots who served as the *Alabama*'s first quartermasters. Minor was also a Southerner, born to a prominent Virginia family, but he had shipped less than three months before from a Boston-owned ship out of Liverpool; Semmes depended on Minor's family connections to assure his fealty, and indeed Minor would continue to serve the Confederacy at sea for months after that nation ceased to exist.[12]

Ten of the eleven enlisted men who would serve the new cruiser came from the unrated seamen on the mother ship. Seven had sailed from Terceira with the *Alabama*, and two of them became quartermasters. The senior boatswain's mate, Martin Molk, had shipped from the *Agrippina* at Blanquilla, while his assistant, Robert Owens, had volunteered in the spring from the *Louisa Hatch*. Samuel Brewer, who had come from the *T. B. Wales*, boarded the new ship as a simple seaman. An eleventh hand, Steward Thomas Allman, was one of the *Conrad*'s original crew, and elected to stay with the vessel.

By sunset of June 21 the transfer of arms and supplies had been completed, and the two crews climbed into the rigging of their ships. The Stars and Bars skidded up both mizzenmasts, Lieutenant Low fired one of his little guns in salute, and Semmes celebrated the equinox with formal recognition of the CSS *Tuscaloosa*. As cheers echoed over the chill waters of the South Atlantic, the ships drifted apart, Low remembering his former commander's secret instructions to rendezvous on the coast of Africa.[13]

The *Tuscaloosa* had hardly sailed from view when the *Alabama* hove a bigger bark to. This one would be no prize, having English registry, but it had already seen enough bad luck, with severe leaks sprung below and a crewman badly injured after a fall from aloft. With Dr. Galt attending to the paymaster's duties, David Llewelyn acted as the ship's surgeon, and he boarded the British vessel long enough to minister to the maimed boy. The unfortunate bark had turned back for Rio de Janeiro, her crew having refused to proceed farther without repairs, and the skipper agreed to transport all the prisoners from the last few prizes. Semmes offered a chronometer and a week's provisions in return, and he realized half a dozen recruits from the thirty-six sailors who cluttered the waist of his ship. The other thirty, plus the female "passenger," boarded the *Mary Kendall* for Rio.[14]

With the departure of Lieutenant Low, Arthur Sinclair became the *Alabama*'s third watch officer. Midshipman Irvine Bulloch, the younger brother of Commander Bulloch, stepped up to Sinclair's vacant sailing master's office, standing watches himself. Sinclair had just turned twenty-six, making him five years older than the two lieutenants next above him, but, despite his family's naval heritage, Sinclair owned little deck experience of any kind. He claimed to have spent four years' apprenticeship under his father in the Pacific Squadron, but he had served as his father's clerk. He also alleged, years later, that he had been commissioned a master's mate at the outbreak of the war, and that he acted as an aide to the commander of the CSS *Virginia* during that ironclad's battles at Hampton Roads. In fact, Sinclair was also only the captain's clerk aboard the *Virginia*, and he had probably received the position through his father's acquaintance with the commander of that ship. After he grew old, Sinclair boasted of his nautical prowess, apparently claiming that Semmes had had great confidence in his ability. Thirty years after the *Alabama* met her end, Sinclair told an interviewer that Semmes had remarked he could "sleep contentedly" knowing that Sinclair was on duty. When an amused Lieutenant Armstrong heard this story, he wrote John Kell's wife to suggest otherwise.

" 'Pears to me somehow," Armstrong told her, "that when S. was on deck your husband was up & dressed in his room." Nor does Captain Semmes's own journal reveal any great regard for Lieutenant Sinclair, who later imagined that he had been promoted to commander for gallantry in action.[15]

"This young man seems to be disposed to insubordination," noted the mustachioed master of the *Alabama*. The tradition of linear promotion dissuaded Semmes from passing anyone over Sinclair, though, regardless of however unsuited he may have been for his original commission.[16]

Neither was Joseph Wilson earning his captain's undying respect just now. In squally weather on June 26 the *Alabama* chased after a ship sometime after dark, and a blank cartridge failed to bring her around. Lieutenant Kell called all hands to quarters in the rainy darkness, and every gun was cast loose by its crew. A second round, this time with a projectile in it, convinced the captain of the chase to clew up his sails and haul around. It turned out to be a French vessel on its way to Le Havre, so the guns were quickly secured and the off-watch retired to the berth deck. Sometime during the exercise Kell had not been satisfied with Lieutenant Wilson's performance, however, and he had evidently barked at the young Floridian, who responded with more of the sauce that had led him to trouble at Bahia. Semmes put Wilson under stateroom arrest for another week, criticizing him for his tendency to "sulk, be obstinate & wrong-headed, and to give trouble."[17]

Of all the remaining junior lieutenants, therefore, the youngest offered the least difficulty. Six-footer Richard Armstrong was now just twenty years old, and his name never adorned Semmes's private journal entries, either in criticism or in commendation. Armstrong nevertheless believed that Semmes treated him more harshly than he did the other officers, though perhaps he only felt that Semmes did not sufficiently appreciate Armstrong's maturity, in light of the transgressions of Wilson and Sinclair.[18]

The petty officers of the ship collectively informed Semmes on June 27 that much of the men's bread ration was infested with weevils, and examination of the remaining cartons demonstrated that all of it had been invaded. With only a thirty-day supply anyway, Semmes reversed his course for Rio de Janeiro rather than risk continuing on to South Africa. Providence supplied him with bread along the way—or, rather, Boston did—when the *Anna F. Schmidt* stumbled across his path near midnight of July 1. The chase carried through the night, and after daybreak the *Alabama* fired a blank from three miles away. That brought the Stars and Stripes to the *Anna Schmidt*'s masthead, and a second shot ended the pursuit.

This ship had also experienced ill fortune since casting off from Boston on January 17. Her upper works loosened in a heavy sea, she had put in at St. Thomas from February until May, and now this. The cruiser's boat crews spent the entire day loading all the food, medicine, clothing, shoes, and sundries that had been meant for the dandies of San Francisco, continuing their work even as the *Alabama* slipped away to run down another American ship that had been sold to British owners, to avoid just such an occurrence.[19]

At the dinner hour the boarding party fired the prize, and the *Alabama* stood away. That evening the helmsman turned for a big ship that answered the first blank cartridge with one of her own, never slowing. Semmes called all hands, lowered the propeller to give chase, and ordered the port battery loaded with shells on five-second fuses. Down in his stateroom, Lieutenant Wilson collared a messenger and sent him on deck to ask for release from his week-long arrest, which Semmes allowed. The chase lasted for hours in a stiff breeze, but by midnight the *Alabama* had pulled close enough to discover that the game was not so helpless this time: ten guns peered from as many ports on each side. Still Semmes insisted on drawing close enough to hail, and Lieutenant Kell offered his own ship's name first. The frigate's first officer responded with "Her British Majesty's Ship *Clio*," and a relieved

Semmes turned away. The *Clio* had swung toward the burning *Anna F. Schmidt* in the hope of rescuing survivors, only to deduce from the *Alabama*'s presence that the fire was an act of war in which a British warship had no part.[20]

Now back on course for Cape Horn, the *Alabama* scooped up the *Express*, another Boston ship plying between Peru and Belgium with guano. The master of the *Express* had brought both his wife and her maidservant along on the voyage, and once these two were ensconced in one of the officers' staterooms, Lieutenant Kell made his usual pitch to the prisoners. Five men from the last two captures signed on with the raider, bringing Semmes near to a full complement again. With these, he could muster 120 hands, and with 23 officers he had enough to serve the ship well and fight efficiently, if it came to that.

The rest of July availed nothing. Baffling headwinds and buffeting seas slowed eastward progress, worrying Semmes—who still fretted over his thirty-day supply of bread, since he had thrown the weevily rations overboard. The barometer began to plunge, and he reluctantly realized that he was back in the middle of winter. His course lay outside the usual trade routes, so for sixteen days he saw no ship whatever, but on the afternoon of July 22 the lookout called "Sail ho!" By then the *Alabama* had ranged within five degrees of longitude from Cape Town, and Semmes's anxiety abated.

The sail was an English ship homeward bound, and for the price of a chronometer Semmes relieved himself of the captains of his last two prizes, plus the women. Four days later the boats boarded three different neutrals, one of which reported a strange steamer hovering in the vicinity; that drew Semmes's attention, for it might be a Federal warship. A Cape Town schooner corroborated the report the next day. Before night fell on July 27, the lookout spotted the Lion's Rump, on the Cape of Good Hope.[21]

Semmes turned up the coast, for Saldanha Bay. The night of July 28 he tried to shoot between Dassen Island and the mainland, but dark fell too quickly and he dared not try that dangerous passage in the dark. Late the next morning the *Alabama* steamed through the rocky strait and made the bay, anchoring in just over five fathoms there shortly after noon, thanks to the piloting services of a helpful local schooner captain.

Semmes found Saldanha relatively desolate, with only some distant farmhouses visible from the sandy, treeless shore. With few of the more pernicious influences of a civilized port, he dared to put his men ashore in small contingents, and he landed on the beach himself early on the morning of July 30. A party of officers followed soon thereafter, carrying rifles, and they brought back a springbok in time for breakfast. The enlisted men who took liberty behaved as sailors usually do, finding liquor where one might never have expected it. Three of them—all recruits who had shipped since the sojourn at Kingston—failed to come back on the morning of August 1, as agreed. Instead, they made their way to Cape Town, where they filled the taverns with tales of good pay and prize money.[22]

When Semmes came back from a stroll that afternoon, he regretted most of all to hear that his chief boatswain's mate, Brent Johnson, had drawn a knife against Master's Mate James Evans in the course of his own punctual—but drunken—return from shore. Johnson, an old, bearded salt from Barnstable, in Devon, had been one of those Royal Naval Reserve veterans whom Semmes relied on so heavily, with a record that included the Crimean War and service in support of Garibaldi, but the captain could ill afford to ignore anyone who offered violence to an officer. A couple of short decades before, the mere attempt would have led to the gallows, but Semmes had to make do with what punishment he could mete out aboard ship. In the end, a court-martial sentenced the venerable seaman to three months of solitary confinement, after which he was to be disrated and discharged with none of the regular pay or prize money that had accumulated over the past year. It seemed hard to treat so valuable a man as Johnson even more harshly than the deserter Forrest had suffered, but with shipboard discipline flagging, Semmes dared do no less.

"I have a precious set of rascals on board," he wrote that night. That was the end of liberty at Saldanha Bay for all but the officers.[23]

A boatload of junior officers pulled for shore to hunt on August 3, while scores of Boer settlers visited the *Alabama*. Few of them spoke English, despite England's long sovereignty over South Africa, and Semmes even found many of the newspapers printed in Dutch. One bright young man had never been aboard a ship before, Semmes deduced, and the female visitors all seemed primitively innocent. He remarked on the "plump, ruddy Dutch girls, whose large, rough hands and awkward bows, or courtesies [*sic*] showed them to be honest lasses from the neighboring farms, accustomed to milking the cows and churning the butter."

After lunch the captain made for shore again to enjoy the flora, finding geraniums growing wild. As the sun sank, he climbed back into his gig to return for evening quarters, but on his way to the ship he encountered the officers who had gone gunning. In the bottom of their dinghy lay the body of Simeon Cummings, one of the third assistant engineers. Cummings had accidentally shot himself as he pulled his rifle from the boat, catching the hammer on a thwart and sending the bullet through his lungs. Semmes had first met Cummings aboard the *Sumter*, finding him a loyal Confederate for all of his Northern birth, and the engineer's death saddened the entire ship's company.[24]

The body lay on the quarterdeck that night, and the next morning the boatswain's whistle sang the same call to "Bury the Dead" that rang aboard the USS *Kearsarge* a couple of weeks later, on the far side of the equator. Lieutenant Kell led a funeral procession of six boats ashore with an honor guard and four pallbearers—Master's Mate Fullam, the chief engineer, and two of his surviving third assistant engineers. The officers all mounted horses on shore, loaded the body in a wagon, and carried it to a private cemetery a mile and a half inland. There they covered their dead comrade and posted a temporary headboard, already composing the epitaph for a permanent stone, and returned to the *Alabama*.[25]

At dawn the crew weighed anchor and stood out for Cape Town, but a few miles out to sea the lookout called a sail off the starboard bow. Recognizing his own *Tuscaloosa*, Semmes sent a boat to retrieve Lieutenant Low, who reported having captured and bonded just one American ship. Semmes directed Low to make for Simon's Bay, just down the coast from Cape Town, and the little cruiser turned that way while Semmes steamed for Table Bay and Cape Town itself.[26]

Outside his destination right after noon, Semmes saw a bark with an American look to her. Taking chase, he approached under the British ensign, finding the bark with U.S. colors flying. A blank round had no effect, so the *Alabama* pulled alongside, and the deck officer threatened to shoot into the bark if it did not stop. The merchant captain still kept right on for Green Point, the entrance to Table Bay, which lay only six miles away. A musket shot whistling over his deck also seemed not to convince the Yankee, but finally he clewed up his sails some five miles outside British territorial waters. James Evans went aboard the vessel, the *Sea Bride* of Boston, which had completed all but the last five miles of its transatlantic journey. Evans returned with the master and his papers. Convinced that he had a legitimate prize, Semmes transferred the *Sea Bride*'s sailors to his ship and placed Mr. Fullam in charge of her with a crew of eight men. He ordered Fullam to stand off and on Table Bay, not daring to bring a prize into this neutral port as he had at Fernando de Noronha, and he instructed the master's mate to meet him at Saldanha Bay on August 15 if he should be blown out to sea by a gale.[27]

Such a gale blew up that evening, with thunder and lightning, and it continued for two days. The *Alabama* rode it out in the anchorage, not far from the British frigate *Valorous*, which arrived in response to the Confederate cruiser's appearance, to insure the respect of British neutrality. After a change of prize masters, the *Sea Bride* disappeared in the storm, which threw two brigs against the rocky points off the bay and wrecked them.

Lieutenant Wilson went ashore with his captain's compliments for the governor, and visitors mobbed the ship, at least one boatload running along-side as soon as the anchor dropped. The steamer *Lady Jocelyn* arrived from London that afternoon, her crew raising three cheers for the *Alabama*, and the Confederates returned the honor.

The *Cape Argus* reported that Cape Town's inhabitants, "rich and poor, halt, maimed, lame and blind . . . went off to see the Alabama, her captain, and her officers." When he was not besieged with the proffered hands of prominent inhabitants, Captain Semmes spent his time corresponding with the British authorities, who passed on objections from the American consul that the *Sea Bride* had lain within British waters when she was taken. The British seemed to believe Semmes's version of events, though, when he presented cross-bearings that demonstrated a distance of five miles.[28]

When the wind abated on August 9, the *Alabama* steamed peacefully around to Simon's Bay, where the British naval station and the *Tuscaloosa* both lay. On the way, Semmes took the time to overhaul another American bark, the *Martha Wenzell*, which also hailed from Boston. While the morose master of that rice-laden vessel rode a boat back to the cruiser, Semmes double-checked his bearings and found that, this time, he had run inside British waters. Incredulous at his luck, the Yankee skipper learned from the legendary "pirate" that he was free to go.

At Simon's Bay the *Alabama* found as warm a greeting from official South Africa as it had from the hoi polloi in Table Bay, if the expression did fall short of the delirium of Cape Town itself. On the following morning Semmes visited the admiral of the port at his home, to explain his accidental capture of the *Martha Wenzell* inside British territory, and the admiral invited him to a half-hour's conversation with his family. Semmes dined aboard the *Kwan-Tung*, another of the Chinese gunboats, and on August 11 he called on the admiral again aboard his flagship.

The *Alabama*'s hands gave her the customary caulking, scraping, and painting that marked every stay in port, but they worked around more crowds of visitors. The ship had found Cape Town suffering from a long-standing bout of economic depression, and fever had recently ravaged the population, so the appearance of this famous raider offered new gossip and excitement that captivated the population. "Alabama fever" raged now, as artists and photographers raced to capture the ship before it departed. One painter reportedly even considered naming his new infant Alabama. On August 12 a photographer named Green carried his equipment to the quarterdeck of the ship and began immortalizing the officers, snapping Captain Semmes seated, Lieutenant Kell standing, and the pair standing by the rear pivot gun. Semmes posed, binoculars in hand, while Kell leaned on the rail that protected the gun room skylight; others of the crew occupied themselves in the background, and someone, probably the steward Bartelli, poked his head from the cabin hatchway. When he had finished with the senior officers, Green made at least one study of Lieutenants Armstrong and Sinclair leaning on a 32-pounder while a warrant officer paced behind them and a turbaned African visitor huddled against the bulwarks. Most of the junior officers also sat for portraits, though probably in the comfort of the artist's studio ashore.

A reporter for the *South African Advertiser and Mail* stood close enough to the renowned "pirate," Semmes, to observe that his face was "care-worn and sunburnt." The captain's hair matched the grey of his uniform, as did his eyes, "now mild and dreamy." Both his face and his clothing showed the wear of his year aboard the cruiser: the correspondent noted that Semmes wore "an old grey stained uniform . . . with battered shoulder straps and faded gold trimmings. . . . He is 53 years old but looks somewhat older."[29]

Lieutenant Kell enjoyed no leisure to visit ashore. He oversaw maintenance and repairs while his captain vacationed; the hirsute Georgian barely found enough time to finish a weeks-old letter to his wife, from whom he had not heard in over a year. After another lunch with the admiral and the colonial governor on August 13, Semmes ordered the *Tuscaloosa* out on another cruise, and he determined to put to sea himself the next day. Fog delayed his departure until near noon. Three more old hands stayed behind— two seamen who had shipped from prizes in the autumn, and Thomas Weir, an original crewman whom Semmes had appointed quartermaster. Two of the cabin boys and a pair from a boat's crew tried to run away, too, but they were all retrieved. To replace the three latest deserters and the three who decamped at Saldanha Bay, Semmes shipped nine likely candidates from ashore, who all went to sea as "stowaways" to skirt the prohibition of shipping hands or munitions in a neutral port. Once the *Alabama* had passed into international waters, Lieutenant Kell signed them all to their articles; Semmes immediately appointed one of them—Russell Hobbs, an experienced Delaware sailor in his mid-fifties—to the vacant quartermaster's berth. In addition to these nine enlisted men, Semmes himself had appointed a pair of new master's mates, both of whom had been stranded in Cape Town while on leave from the Prussian navy.[30]

Somewhere to the north, Semmes expected to find the *Sea Bride*, to which the *Tuscaloosa* had carried word of a new rendezvous site. For the first time since the *Alabama* took to the seas, Semmes intended to sell one of his prizes for cash.

CHAPTER FOURTEEN

East by West

One ship is very much like another,
and the sea is always the same.
—Conrad, *Heart of Darkness*

lthough their enthusiastic reception by the civilian
and naval populations had cheered the *Alabama*'s officers no end, they might have
traced part of their Cape Town giddiness to the optimistic reports of the war
at home. In Virginia, Robert E. Lee had repulsed an enormous Federal army
under Joe Hooker at Chancellorsville, and in the West the Vicksburg and
Port Hudson garrisons seemed to hold their own against repeated Union
threats. While the ship plowed northward, Captain Semmes savored the
most recent newspaper articles, detailing Lee's invasion of Pennsylvania.
The news came early enough to inspire Confederate confidence—especially
for Semmes, who believed the South's only hope now lay in taking the war
to Northern dooryards—but during the six weeks it had taken the account
to reach London, and then Cape Town, Lee's army had retired to Virginia,
beaten and battered.

But if those bad tidings had not yet reached the tip of Africa, other
journals did carry ominous news. In late June the *Times* of London re-
counted testimony given before the Court of the Exchequer about certain
seizures of ships and goods by Confederate vessels, and Semmes quickly
recognized the star witness: his own former paymaster, Clarence Yonge.
After a month ashore at Kingston, Yonge had returned to Liverpool with his
landlady as his bride; he told the court that she was "a young widow," deftly
skirting the question of whether he had abandoned his Savannah wife. By

now he had forsaken the second wife as well, leaving her a fraction of the money remaining from the liquidation of her property. Now Yonge worked for the U.S. government, and in affidavits and courtroom testimony he related his entire career as a Confederate officer, implicating Commander Bulloch and the Laird yard as well as detailing the exploits of the British subjects among the officers and crew. Edward Fitzmaurice, one of the ailing *Alabama* seamen discharged at Blanquilla, followed Yonge to the stand in an effort to cash in on the Yankees' consular generosity, but his recollections offered nothing worthy of reimbursement.

While he remained in England, Yonge lived on the money passed to him by the American consul at Liverpool, Thomas Dudley, who pursued his case against the Confederacy with the word of turncoats such as Yonge, Fitzmaurice, and John Latham. Yonge shifted around Lancashire, Yorkshire, and London, complaining of minor inconveniences and the boredom of the more pastoral locations where Dudley lodged him; after the June court appearance Dudley housed his songbird in Dublin. Revealing almost adolescent immaturity, the renegade Confederate looked to Dudley for pocket money, friendship, and finally for paternal advice, meanwhile offering whatever information he could about the Lairds' ships and Confederate naval officers—even suggesting a prospective recruit for the Union army from among his British acquaintances. Dudley kept his new servant poor but comfortable, lest he flee the country before the United States had extracted all the testimony he could provide, and the truckling Yonge lingered as long as he was required.[1]

Yonge's testimony revealed the degree of complicity between British citizens and the Confederate navy's representatives, as well as some obvious violations of the Foreign Enlistment Act. As England's responsibility for the *Alabama*'s depredations emerged, more conservative Britons reassessed their support for that seagoing champion of Southern independence. Editors and politicians curtailed their praise and began to offer criticism, though indirectly at first. After a lag of several weeks, London heard of the delirious reception of the *Alabama* at Cape Town. Soon thereafter *The English News*, published in Britain for the South African colonies, repeated a translation of an article from the *Journal des Debats* that offered an unsympathetic interpretation of the *Alabama*'s career: Captain Semmes burned his prizes because the Confederacy lacked open ports to which they might be taken for admiralty adjudication, explained the excerpt. Implying agreement with the French newspaper, the *News* quoted the *Journal*'s contention that such a circumstance offered no excuse for the destruction of potentially neutral property at sea: if the South wanted a legitimate tribunal, let it break the blockade.[2]

The intended sale of the *Sea Bride* required Semmes to kill a few more days before reaching her, in order to allow the buyers to reach the rendezvous and complete the transaction, for it would not do to leave the *Alabama* sitting long in a port unprotected by British warships. His caution was well advised, for at that moment the Union navy's big *Vanderbilt* lay at St. Helena, taking on enough coal to cruise around the Cape of Good Hope and back. Semmes had arranged to make the transfer at the harbor of Angra Pequeña, more than 500 miles up the western coast of Africa from Cape Town. There, on the edge of the Namibian desert, they would violate the territorial claims of no known power.[3]

For a dozen days the *Alabama* tacked up the coast, stopping a few English and Dutch ships but permitting most strange sails to pass unmolested: the cruiser had grown too slow to catch anything without full steam, and Semmes viewed his coal as too precious to waste in a sea from which the American flag seemed to have disappeared. The coast appeared uninhabited here, without a tree or a bush and with only some island guano collectors and a neighboring colony of penguins as tokens of animal life. Fog and clouds foiled Semmes when he finally tried to shoot his position and turn for the land, but at last he came up with a schooner bound for the same harbor and followed her in, anchoring near the *Sea Bride* and the *Tuscaloosa*. He arrived just in time, for the *Alabama*'s condensing apparatus had begun to malfunction, producing drinking water that ranged from brackish to briny. Not long after the anchor dropped into the seven fathoms of Shearwater Bay, a number of the officers shoved off for Low's little cruiser, looking for a fresh drink. Semmes sent his own pitcher over with them.

Lieutenant Low brought aboard the £3,500 proceeds from the *Sea Bride* that afternoon, August 28. Merchants had also agreed to accept the cargo of wool from the hold of the *Tuscaloosa*, which they intended to send to England for sale, depositing most of the profits in the Bank of Liverpool on Semmes's account. The next morning Semmes began loading his own storerooms with bread and flour from the *Sea Bride*, and he took a dozen big casks of water from the buyer's schooner, to last until the engineers could repair the condenser. In the evening everyone feasted on fish netted in the bay. On Sunday morning he mustered his crew and landed one of the recaptured Simons Town deserters, whose court-martial had sentenced him to dismissal from the ship. With the following dawn the *Alabama* shook out its sails and turned south again. The *Tuscaloosa*, meanwhile, sailed for the coast of Brazil, Lieutenant Low carrying instructions to meet the *Alabama* again at Cape Town in four months or so.[4]

No sooner had they left Angra Pequeña than Semmes found cause to reprimand another of his officers. He ordered Lieutenant Kell to see that the lieutenants all learned how to drill their divisions at the manual of arms and in the usual exercises of small arms. To accomplish that, he wanted them to attend the drills conducted by Lieutenant Becket Howell, the Marine officer. Sinclair, the newest lieutenant, failed to appear at the first session, and Kell demanded a reason. Sinclair pointed out that his predecessor, Lieutenant Low, had never been required to attend such drills, and that the Marine officer was paid precisely to drill the men. Kell, who had once been dismissed from the U.S. Navy for refusing to obey an order that he considered beneath the dignity of his rank, nevertheless took the petulant Sinclair's impudence to "Old Beeswax," who administered one of his renowned rebukes.[5]

On the second morning of September the lookout descried a ship with an unmistakably American cut; when the boarding officer asked for the captain's papers, he discovered that they had overhauled the same vessel less than six months before. On March 15 the *Punjaub* had been owned by a Boston firm, but because of neutral cargo Semmes had let her continue on to London, under bond, with the prisoners from the *John A. Parks*. Now the ship represented another facet of the *Alabama*'s success, for she had been sold to English owners on reaching that port.

A contrary gale kept the cruiser from its course for a couple of days, throwing even Semmes about in his cabin and dampening him with new leaks from the quarterdeck. The delay worried him somewhat, for when the engineers tried the condenser again, they found that it would not work at all. Cutting the crew's daily ration of water to half a gallon, Semmes hoped for a fair wind, meanwhile damning life aboard ship. "The fact is," he wrote, "I am past the age when men ought to be subjected to the hardships and discomforts of the sea."[6]

When the *Alabama* finally did reach the anchorage at Simons Town on September 16, the captain soon swallowed his glee. He had just missed the two-week layover of the *Georgia*, and so had the *Vanderbilt*, which had departed that very port just five days previously, lingering off shore a day or two after that. For the *Alabama*, the gales had done more good than harm, but Semmes harbored no illusions that the steamer would not be back, along with its fourteen huge guns. To worsen his despair, he learned from late papers that the entire Mississippi now lay in Federal hands, that Lee had been whipped in Pennsylvania, and that another Union army was marching for Georgia and his own home state of Alabama.

After the customary respects to port authorities, Semmes began looking for coal. The ravenous *Vanderbilt* had taken the last ton from Simons Town, so he sent around to Cape Town for a load and treated himself to a leisurely jaunt in the hills beyond town. Before departing the ship he authorized liberty for different divisions, and his thirsty sailors thundered into the barrooms. Hardly anyone returned within the specified hour at morning muster, and several failed to return at all. Semmes suspected the U.S. consul at Cape Town of bribing his men to stay away from the ship, and in turn he offered the police a reward for bringing them back. Each night three or four more of the crew disappeared, and Semmes noted that everyone returned late, and usually drunk, except one or two men—petty officers included.[7]

All the officers also trooped ashore, many of them picking up their August portraits at the office of the *Cape Argus* or at Green's photographic studio. Some read of their own experiences in George Fullam's journal, published as a supplement to the *South African Advertiser and Mail* three days after they returned from Angra Pequeña. Leaving Lieutenant Kell in charge of the ship, Semmes himself spent part of every day ashore, dining with the admiral or wandering in his extensive gardens. The remaining crew repaired the ship's worn blowpipe and foretopmast, and started filling the bunkers when a coalship pulled alongside on September 21.[8]

Semmes wished to leave South Africa as soon as he could, rather than allow the *Vanderbilt* to trap him there and blockade him as he had been at Gibraltar in the *Sumter*. He also wanted as much of his crew as he could find, though, and he stopped all liberty with that of September 21. Over the next two days the police dragged a few of his delinquents back aboard, but diplomatic squabbles over the sale of the *Sea Bride* had so badly strained relations with colonial authorities that finally even the rewards ceased to bring back his crewmen. On September 24 Semmes heard a mistaken report that the *Vanderbilt* had been spotted nearby; despite a brewing gale, he put to sea near midnight, under a full moon, leaving fourteen of his hands in the brothels and pubs of the Cape colony. Only two original crewmen numbered among the fourteen deserters—one was the troublesome cabin boy, Robert Egan—and three had only shipped forty days before, in that same port. Of them all, the captain missed only the old Irishman who had served as the ship's fiddler. To bolster the watches, Semmes shipped thirteen replacements as nominal stowaways. None of the thirteen seemed a likely prospect.

"Vagabonds," Semmes called them, "hungry and nearly shirtless." Paying perfunctory tribute to British neutrality, he recorded their names (or aliases) in the log only the next morning, after the ship made the open sea and after Paymaster Galt had dressed the derelicts in new uniforms. With this fresh infusion of green hands, Semmes could ill afford to waste a good one, and he released Brent Johnson from his confinement, commuting the rest of his sentence and promising to appeal to the Confederate Congress for his pay and prize money. The old salt took his place before the mast as a full seaman, but without his former rate. James Brosnan, another of the original Terceira crew, had taken over as chief boatswain's mate.[9]

At that moment the *Vanderbilt* actually lay in the harbor of Port-Louis, on the island of Mauritius, hundreds of miles to the northeast. Semmes gave the customary lanes a wide berth, veering south and then due east, passing well below the route his nemesis would likely take. That took him out of the trade routes, as well, and during the four weeks of his Indian Ocean crossing the *Alabama* stopped only one British steamer making its way to Singapore. Venturing not quite far enough south to risk icebergs, he also skirted a series of cyclones, the edges of which propelled his vessel eastward at speeds up to ten knots for hours at a time. While Semmes appreciated the speed, he worried about the effect of constant heavy gales on the hull, which began to "complain and work in every timber."[10]

Indian Ocean storms gathered quickly as well as frequently, Semmes noticed. One evening, as the *Alabama* fairly flew like a clipper, with studdingsails billowing from booms at the tips of her yards, a squall swept in and a gale kicked up that lasted all night. Ordinarily the deck officer would have hauled in sail gradually, over the course of the night, but this blow so strained the yards that within two hours the ship had been reduced to no more canvas than single-reefed topsails. Frequent rain and perpetual overcast dampened every plank, hammock, and scrap of clothing on the ship, including Semmes's own bed and bookcases, and without fires in the engine room there was no hope of drying anything.

Within a fortnight of leaving the cape, the *Alabama* had made 2,400 miles, for an average speed of more than seven knots. Not until October 12 did the lookout cry land, and then only the tiny island of St. Paul; Semmes had hoped to cruise there for a couple of days, but the winds blew him onward. On October 16, the first anniversary of the dreadful hurricane that nearly sank his ship, a cyclone overtook the *Alabama* and hurled it before the vortex for seven long hours, at better than eleven knots. One sea filled the gig, dragging the ship so dangerously that the boat had to be cut away. When the danger passed, Semmes reflected that the storm had thrown his cruiser about "like a mere cockboat."[11]

During the long intervals between action and shore visits, the tired captain amused himself with observations on geography, meteorology, and natural history. He watched the barometer closely, and the marine thermometer, to avoid icebergs, faithfully jotting the results into his journal. On his birthday, two days out from Simons Town, he lamented at length the enforced separation from his family and the war that caused it. As his course carried him into and out of various marine habitats, he recorded the appearance and disappearance of the cape pigeon, the petrel, and strange birds such as the big, brown gull of these waters, which reminded him of the ubiquitous albatross. The day after the cyclone he remarked that he had reached the point of earth that sat directly opposite his home in Mobile, reasoning that at least from that longitude he would be moving nearer home with every mile, whichever direction he followed.

From St. Paul Island the helmsman turned slowly northward, toward the Strait of Sunda, between Java and Sumatra. Just before dawn of October 21 the keel crossed the Tropic of Capricorn at the one-hundredth meridian, and the weather abated almost immediately. For the first time since the Cape of Good Hope, the *Alabama*'s deck lay still enough that Semmes dared hold gun exercises with the broadside thirty-twos and the pivots.[12]

While the quartermaster at the *Alabama*'s wheel held his course for the strait, the USS *Wyoming* waited at that gateway to the Java Sea. The commander of the *Wyoming*, David McDougal, doubted the presence of any Confederate cruisers in Eastern waters. He knew that the *Alabama* and the *Tuscaloosa* had visited Cape Town, but nothing suspicious had since been reported from vessels bound to the East Indies. Commander McDougal worried more about Malay pirates and renegade Japanese princes: his six-gun steamer had engaged three hostile Japanese vessels and several land batteries barely three months previously, losing eleven men killed and wounded. Early in November McDougal spoke the British steamer *Mona* as it passed through the Sunda Strait, learning that it had been boarded well east of Cape Town on October 3 by a cruiser calling itself the USS *Dacotah*, but he brushed off the news. The *Mona* had actually been boarded by Master's Mate George Fullam, of the *Alabama*.

On the basis of some vague reports that he did not especially credit, McDougal started for Christmas Island, where stockpiles of coal ostensibly awaited Southern ships. He steamed south from the strait on the morning of November 10; had a heavy rain not set in before dawn, he might have seen the *Alabama* steaming into the strait from the west.[13]

Semmes had already made his first capture in the Far East, running down the bark *Amanda*, of Bangor, Maine, on November 6. The *Amanda* burned barely a hundred miles from the Strait of Sunda, and the *Wyoming* passed within sight of her watery grave when Commander McDougal steamed for Christmas Island. Raphael Semmes already knew of the *Wyoming*'s presence in the strait, and he half expected to fight her when he passed through, but to keep McDougal off his guard he identified his own ship as the USS *Mohican* whenever he hailed neutral vessels.

Semmes also sought the clipper *Winged Racer*, which a British captain had named as one U.S. ship that lay in the vicinity. The *Alabama* had no sooner exited the northern end of the strait, without meeting the *Wyoming*, when the lookout spotted a sail that fit the description of the *Winged Racer*. That she proved to be, and that afternoon captor and captive anchored near an island off the coast of Java. For weeks the Confederate crew had done without coffee, butter, and other treasured comforts because of inexplicable shortages in the supplies bought at Simons Town, and details worked until well after midnight to strip the clipper of everything edible or desirable, including a shipment of cigars. While they lightered goods from the prize to the cruiser, the paymaster bartered with Malay bumboatmen for fresh fruit, birds, and some vegetables. The prisoners from both the *Amanda* and the *Winged Racer* elected to row ashore in the *Racer*'s boats, and Semmes was glad to see them go. Before dawn the *Alabama* weighed anchor and turned north, toward Borneo, leaving the blazing hulk for the curiosity of any insomniacs in nearby Batavia.[14]

A few hours later, just as the engineers proceeded to drop steam and lift the propeller, another sleek clipper appeared, looking every inch American. When the *Alabama* came close enough, a quartermaster ran up the Stars and Stripes, and the clipper showed the same colors. At that Semmes ordered a blank round while his U.S. flag came fluttering down to be replaced by the Confederate banner—not the Stars and Bars, which the *Alabama* had always flown heretofore, but the new flag that Semmes had learned about at Cape Town, with the Confederate battle flag as the union of a white field. Instead of heaving to, the clipper spread more canvas and took to her heels, and the *Alabama* made all sail herself. On Semmes's orders the fires had been allowed to go out altogether, but, when they seemed to make no headway against the chase, the engineers lighted the boilers once more. With her fouled bottom and peeling copper sheathing, the cruiser stood little chance against so fleet a vessel, but a light breeze offered no encouragement to the prey. A rifle shot fell short of the clipper, whose captain took no notice; while steam built in his boilers, Semmes ordered the broadside guns dragged aft and the crew to stand on the quarterdeck to lift the bows. After more than an hour's race, the *Alabama*'s steam propulsion told, and she gained enough for the crew of one of the broadside guns to throw a shot between the chase's masts. That was enough for her master, who brought the well-known New York clipper *Contest* around to await the inevitable boarding party. By midnight he and his crew lodged aboard the deck of the *Alabama*, which sailed away from the burning wreckage of their magnificent clipper, the engineer department having finally completed the job of hoisting the cruiser's propeller.[15]

Those prisoners remained on the spar deck two days later, when Semmes called for the cigars taken from the *Winged Racer*. The captain of the hold broke the box open, and under the captain's eye the contents were doled out equally among the officers and men. Some of the older hands took the occasion to express their annoyance at long cruising without seeing any of the vaunted prize money; shortages of virtual essentials like coffee had not improved the growing dissatisfaction, either, and a handful of cigars hardly made up for the privation. Formerly dependable sailors, including Seamen Michael Mars and Frank Townsend, turned sullen at what they perceived as an insulting substitute for the gold they had been promised, and they conspired with their fellows to demonstrate their contempt, convincing most of them to toss their cigars overboard. Semmes arrested Townsend, Fireman John Riley, and Albert Hyer, a March recruit who had only been promoted to seaman twelve days before. A general court-martial sat the next day, charging the trio with mutinous conduct, and all three were dropped back a rate. Townsend, whom Semmes viewed as the ringleader, also drew thirty days in irons, on bread and water, with three month's loss of pay—this for the man who had composed the *Alabama*'s victory poem after the fight with the *Hatteras*. The captain apparently declined to try Mars, one of his best deck hands, though he did offer him summary punishment in the form of extra duty, a small fine, and a brief tricing in the mizzen rigging.[16]

The first mate of the *Contest* took careful note of the crew's behavior. He reported witnessing capital offenses go unreported to the captain, claiming that one man struck a master's mate, for which the culprit might have expected to be shot on an American ship. The seamen regularly defied or abused the petty officers, he observed. When Semmes did learn of misbehavior he might punish it, said the Yankee, but he seemed "afraid to push too far." The rigging hung loose, the ship was dirty, and neither the officers nor the men wore uniforms except during formal musters. The deck officers came to duty with revolvers and cutlasses, according to that witness, but small arms drill had been suspended—for fear of what the men might do if they were armed, he supposed. Only once during their nine days on the *Alabama* did the prisoners see their conquerors even practice at the heavy guns, and that seemed to go badly, with much profanity in place of proficiency.[17]

Easing up the western coast of Borneo, Semmes fell in with a British ship called the *Avalanche*. He asked to board her, running up the Dutch flag so common in those islands, and to further the disguise he sent Max von Meulnier, one of the Prussian master's mates, to make the visit. Meulnier introduced himself as an officer of such-and-such a Netherlands warship, but the English captain smirked and shook his head.

"That won't do," he said. "I was on board of her in Liverpool when she was launched." The ruse exploded, Meulnier asked if the *Avalanche* would consent to take the prisoners from the *Contest* in return for the gift of a chronometer, to which the captain acceded. He also offered Semmes some

British newspapers as late as October 10, with news from America less than two months old, and through the boarding officers he relayed the information that American ships were laying up at Singapore in fear of the raider. Commander McDougal, of the *Wyoming*, had noticed as much nearly a month earlier, before the *Alabama*'s presence in the East was even known. "Nearly all of the American vessels in the China seas have changed flags," McDougal had written Gideon Welles on October 22, "otherwise [they] get no employment."[18]

The day after the *Avalanche* took the *Alabama*'s prisoners, the deck officer spoke Siamese and French barks that reported more American vessels hiding in Bangkok and Manila. Gratified by this evidence of his ship's effectiveness, Semmes continued north amid uncharted shoals, crossing the equator under faint, sometimes nonexistent breezes. Even with all canvas spread, the ship could hardly make headway against a stubborn current, and coal had run so low that Semmes dared not use it save in an emergency. For two days boats' crews ran a kedge anchor out ahead of the ship, whereupon all hands manned the capstan and dragged the sluggish cruiser ahead by main strength. When headwinds added their strength, Semmes nodded to the engineers to fire up the boilers, but even then they could muster little more than six knots. All the while, the *Wyoming* might be right on their trail.

The *Wyoming* steamed for Singapore just then, keeping to the coast of Sumatra, so Semmes need not have worried about it as much as he did. Eventually the wind picked up—into a perfect gale, for in these waters it seemed to be either feast or famine—and the *Alabama* scudded rapidly across the South China Sea toward the mouth of the Mekong River. Just before noon on December 2 the lookout saw a bark flying south before the wind, but Semmes did not deign even to turn for it, knowing he would never catch it. Perhaps an hour later the same lookout called land ahead, and Semmes fixed his binoculars on a cluster of little islands. Near dusk the *Alabama* skirted the western face of the largest one, consisting mostly of a lush, precipitous, 1,800-foot mountain. This was Pulo Condore, fifteen leagues off the coast of Cochin China. Semmes guided his ship to an anchorage in the lee of another island, facing the harbor of Pulo Condore, where in the darkness he made out a light.[19]

Eighteen months previously, in Saigon, Emperor Tu Duc had ceded Pulo Condore and three mainland provinces to the French as the first step in a colonial process that would come to bitter fruition just a century later. The light that Raphael Semmes saw from the deck of the *Alabama* illuminated the thatched hut that served as mansion for the island's governor, a French naval ensign by the name of Bizot. In the harbor sat a lightly armed junk under the command of a midshipman, representing the power of France.[20]

With the permission of the young governor, the *Alabama* anchored in the bay at Pulo Condore the next day, turning her broadside to the entrance in case the *Wyoming* came snooping. Paymaster Galt went ashore seeking more fruit and vegetables, but he returned empty-handed in the evening. At first the French seemed unfriendly, believing the rumors that the cruiser sent every vessel it captured to the bottom, with all hands, but even after that myth had been dispelled, the governor could offer little in the way of roughage. The islanders had all fled to the interior to escape the conqueror's lash, save a few slaves who built huts for the fifty or sixty troops who garrisoned the outpost. Baboons and flying foxes had devastated the fruit trees, and the island offered too little level land for aggressive cultivation, even if the labor could have been found.

Once the *Alabama* left its graving yard on the Mersey, it never saw another drydock. Yet the peeling copper plates beneath its waterline needed scraping and patching, so by heeling the ship over and improvising a partially submersible compartment that the pumps could keep clear, Lieutenant Kell managed to scour the ship's belly one section at a time. As usual, he remained aboard and tended to the repairs while his subordinates fled to shore in small parties. The enlisted men were allowed the use of the boats for both fishing and pleasure sailing, and each expedition to the island returned with the carcass of some strange, unfortunate creature. More than once the hunting parties killed flying foxes for nothing more than to bring their shipmates such a curiosity, disdaining to eat the meat of a bat. Other squads returned with the bodies of Komodo dragons, one of them six feet long. For no purpose except to see him die, one officer shot a baboon that wandered to the beach, remarking how the beast clapped its hands over the wound like a man and screamed as though for help. Captain Semmes even took an interest in the killing of that baboon when the other primates gathered about and dug a grave for their brother in the sand. The curiosity diverted the fatigued wayfarer from his growing homesickness, which the strange sights of the Orient merely heightened.

The mail packet from Saigon stopped by on December 10, and when that vessel carried word of the *Alabama*'s location to Singapore, it would require only a couple of days for any U.S. gunboat that happened to lie there to steam out to Pulo Condore. Semmes dared not remain much longer, and on December 14 he readied the ship for sea. With no liquor or women to distract them, his crew offered no trouble, and all hands stood on deck to lift the anchor at 4:00 the next morning. Rested and a little more content, thanks to the fresh meat and coconuts given them by the French ensign, they looked to the southwest, to Singapore.[21]

Once more Commander McDougal missed his chance at maritime immortality, leaving the vicinity of Singapore for Manila on December 10; three days later the mail packet that might have pointed the *Wyoming* in the right direction brought the news of its exciting discovery at Pulo Condore. The *Alabama* took six leisurely days to reach Singapore, anchoring off the island on the evening of December 21. The next morning, exactly three months after the last shovelful of coal was loaded at Simons Town, a Malay pilot led them into the coaling depot at New Harbor, where in ten short hours the bunkers were completely replenished. That done, the paymaster began counting boxes of provisions as they went into the storerooms.[22]

On December 22 nearly ninety ships, eighteen of which were skulking Americans, crowded the harbor at Singapore. Two of those U.S. merchant-men, the *Oriental* and the *Sonora*, slipped out while the *Alabama* was coaling, hoping to put enough water between themselves and the raider before it put to sea again. Either Semmes did not see the pair escape, or he wished to let them go so as to have some game when he returned to the hunt. That evening the *Alabama* took its place in the bay as one watch scurried ashore for liberty. The next morning the ship accepted visitors from the dock, as it did at every British port, but this time the welcome seemed less overwhelming: in a month local editors would refer to the *Alabama*'s visit as "unfortunate." Once again leaving his long-suffering first luff to care for the ship, Captain Semmes wandered into the teeming city, whose Chinese and Malay residents huddled on the edge of a jungle dominated by the Bengal tiger.[23]

CHAPTER FIFTEEN

Subterfuge

An emerald set in the ring of the sea.

—Joyce, *Ulysses*

On the night of August 17, 1863, the CSS *Florida* appeared off the coast of Ireland, landing an officer whose duty it was to proceed to Paris, where he would ask permission for his ship to seek engine repairs at a French navy yard. Captain John Maffitt then turned his sleek cruiser for Brest, at the tip of Brittany, almost incidentally overtaking and burning the American clipper *Anglo Saxon* on the way. The *Florida* anchored at Brest on August 23, going into quarantine for a few days before gaining admission to the national dock.

On September 7 the news of the *Florida*'s Irish visit reached Captain John Winslow aboard the *Kearsarge*, at the island of Madeira. Winslow put to sea that same evening, running into a strong northeast headwind that forced him to burn coal rapidly. Heavy seas rolled and pitched the sloop ferociously, showering the spar deck so steadily that it lay constantly awash. Those coming on deck had to gauge the roll of the ship to avoid leaping straight into a descending wave, and everyone, above deck or below, remained soaked with the spray. The weather grew so miserable that Thomas Buckley deliberately abandoned his post in the crosstrees, leaving the ship without a lookout until an officer noticed his absence. Despite the weather, the duty officers practiced the gun crews at general quarters in anticipation of a looming fight, and in one alarm on September 9 Acting Master Stoddard had the decks cleared for action within six minutes.

After a week of such weather the coal bunkers grew dangerously empty, and Winslow headed for another supply at El Ferrol, on the northwestern tip of Spain. While the crew dickered with bumboat traders, Winslow communicated with shore and learned that his prey had docked at Brest, so the moment the last shovel of coal slid down the scuttle the crew manned the capstan bars. By now dusk had begun to settle, and the paranoid Spaniards had drawn a boom across the narrow neck of their harbor; after some shouting back and forth between quarterdecks, a harbor tug opened the obstruction long enough for the *Kearsarge* to hurry northward.[1]

Before breakfast of September 17 the lookout sighted land. Acting Master Sumner brought the ship to the mouth of the harbor at Brest and signaled for a pilot, asking him if the *Florida* were still there. The reply came back that she was, and the deck began to buzz. Sailors craned for a glimpse of their first active "rebel pirate," and officers trained telescopes and binoculars on the array of masts at anchor, but none matched the description of their enemy. The crippled cruiser had entered the drydock already, and lay beyond sight of the mercantile anchorage.

That afternoon, once Captain Winslow had determined that the *Florida* would not be going to sea anytime soon, the *Kearsarge* dropped its anchor in the harbor. All hands lined the forecastle rails to gape at their first new country in more than a year. The scenery pleased them almost as much as the bumboat vendors who spilled onto the deck the next morning, for these merchants were mostly women. They brought bread, butter, sausages, fruit, baked goods, chocolate, and—for the liberty-bound mariner—scented oil and pomades. They also smuggled aboard a good deal of beer, which sold with predictable speed.

"Jack likes anything that comes in bottles," wrote a disapproving Charles Poole.[2]

Between the beer, the perfumed goods, and the female entrepreneurs, George Whipple found himself unable to wait for the captain to grant liberty. By the second evening at Brest he had slipped ashore, where he stayed for three days. Two more men deserted the third cutter on the morning of the twenty-first, but the police sent them back as prisoners that same evening.

The *Florida* backed out of the drydock on September 22, and the next morning a pilot guided her to anchor alongside a hulk, near the entrance to the harbor. With such ominous movements, Winslow dared not release anyone on liberty yet, and not until the twenty-fifth did he even send the ship's cook ashore for provisions, landing him with Quartermaster William Smith, whom Winslow valued as one of his best petty officers. Smith was also a fair drinker, however; when the boat went ashore for them that evening, neither Smith nor the cook had come back to the dock. They showed up later that night, but the next day two more men absconded, including the cantankerous Henry Jamison. Some of the *Kearsarge* boats that docked on September 25 encountered men from the *Florida*, most of whom resided ashore, and after some shouted taunts the antagonists fell to fighting. Winslow ordered his coxswains to keep their oarsmen in the boats thereafter, but two days later men from the Confederate vessel assailed some of the *Kearsarge*'s crewmen anyway.

Others from the *Florida* lingered in friendly conversation with the *Kearsarge* sailors. Yeoman DeWit enjoyed a pleasant half-hour with three of Captain Maffitt's American hands, all three of whom hailed from Boston. A Frenchman representing himself as one of the *Florida*'s crew appeared on the deck of the Federal ship with the bumboat women, asking if he might not join that ship's company. Surgeon Browne examined him, pronouncing him fit, and the paymaster advanced him $8 the following morning. That was the last anyone ever saw of him.[3]

Even with the possibility of a naval engagement, shipboard maintenance never ended. One of the first tasks in Brest consisted of cleaning the bilges—a filthy job hated by all, but all took part in order to finish it within a single day. Then the engineer department painted the engines, while deck hands tarred the masts and bent new sails.

Brittany proved cold and rainy in September, and the masts and yards grew slippery while the topmen's fingers lost their grip in the chill, damp air, all of which nearly led to tragedy when Winslow ordered the sails furled and cased on September 28. At eight bells (4:00 P.M.), Zaran Phillips, a Massachusetts shoemaker who had just passed his thirty-ninth birthday, climbed up the mizzenmast to gather in the gaff spanker sail. He was a big man as *Kearsarge* sailors went, standing some 5'10", with a sturdy frame; when his hands and feet both slipped, he came hurtling to the deck head downward, slamming into the horse block on the quarterdeck. Discussing the evening meal in the cabin, Captain Winslow and Charles Fisher, the officers' cook, heard the dull, sickening thud as Phillips landed immediately overhead. Shipmates rushing to hear the dying man's last words found, to their intense surprise, that he had merely broken his collarbone and scraped himself about the face and neck.

The dreary autumn climate soon doused everyone's enthusiasm for this new scenery. The port was pretty enough, with the heights rising majestically all about, massive bridges spanning the river gorge, and the nightly display of gaslights ashore; counting gaslights offered fresh amusement to these Victorian vagabonds. With no regular shore leave, though, and nearly perpetual rainfall, claustrophobia settled in again. Information gleaned through the French authorities indicated that the *Florida* would not be leaving anytime soon, and to add to the gloom, a French troop transport lay under long quarantine near the mouth of the harbor, having brought yellow fever back from the campaign in Mexico; periodically the ship would weigh anchor and put to sea, to cast overboard the bodies of those who had died.[4]

Amid such general boredom, a good story would fly through the ship like a trapped starling, and no less a personage than Captain Winslow provided such a story early in October. With little business on Saturday afternoon, Winslow fell asleep in his cabin and began dreaming. In the dream his black cabin boy, Jim Henson (who ranked as a landsman, but served as a steward), committed some dastardly transgression. Winslow awoke in a rage, calling for Henson to be slapped in irons and locked in solitary confinement. Jason Watrus, the master at arms, obliged the captain's wishes, and the puzzled teenager followed Watrus to his undeserved punishment. Meanwhile the captain returned to his slumber and forgot the incident, waking later in the evening and wondering aloud, rather vigorously, where his servant had gone. When told that Watrus had confined the boy, Winslow called indignantly for the master at arms, who, with infinitely poor timing, had taken unauthorized leave of the ship. When told that he, himself, had ordered Henson put into irons, Winslow denied any such thing, but ultimately it all came back to him. Perhaps in his desire to forget the fiasco, he appears to have overlooked Watrus's absence.[5]

While most of the *Florida*'s crewmen remained in portside boardinghouses, one watch kept to the ship, passing the *Kearsarge* occasionally in their launch with the Confederate flag flying. Captain Maffitt had asked to be relieved because of ill health, and his successor appeared to retain little control over his crew, especially those who dwelt ashore. The attacks on isolated *Kearsarge* sailors continued despite the ban on liberty, some of the Confederates assaulting Federal officers, and Captain Winslow conveyed messages to the admiral of the port as well as to his counterpart on the *Florida*. The new commander of the Confederate raider refused to accept the letter, returning it unopened by the hand of a junior officer. With the Stars and Bars flying from the stern, the *Florida*'s boat pulled beneath the quarterdeck of the *Kearsarge* on October 9, while curious Yankee sailors peered over the side. The Confederate officer stood upright in his grey uniform, complete with gold trim, while his oarsmen lounged in motley civilian dress, but neither officer nor men attempted to board. With the unwelcome letter returned, they began pulling back to their own ship. Winslow's complaint to Admiral Gueydon reaped better results, though, and two knife-wielding assailants from the *Florida* went to trial in Brest.[6]

For the Union sailors, bound to their forecastle and berth decks as they were, dominoes and checkers relieved the monotony somewhat, and Captain Winslow appeared less hostile to card games than had his predecessor;

still, many preserved their sanity through the exchange of ship scuttlebutt. Someone heard that the suspected blockade runner *Juno* had been captured off Mobile, while the *Smoker* had wrecked in the Bahamas. Both had passed within grasp of the *Kearsarge*, and they would have meant much prize money to officers and crew alike. A certain resentment welled up in the breasts of some who passed the information on, and William Alsdorf apparently conveyed the story with a touch of sarcasm toward Captain Winslow, for letting the prizes slip away. For that indiscretion, Winslow put him in solitary for five full days. Alsdorf, who had only joined the ship nine months before and had already endured one court-martial, was not endearing himself to his new commander.

The rumors turned out to be wrong in detail only, however. The USS *Connecticut* took the *Juno* off Cape Fear, as it tried to enter Wilmington, and the *Smoker* had grounded and broken apart on a Mexican beach while loading Texas cotton for the run back to England.[7]

The weather deteriorated with each succeeding day of October, yet the unpleasant routine continued. The paymaster served out pea coats, woolen socks, and new boots for cold-weather work, but still the men griped as the barometer worsened every unpleasant chore. Coal Heavers Poole and Wainwright complained of having to clean the bilges again at the middle of the month, and during foggy, "disagreeable" weather they spent one day daubing coal tar on the smokestack with a tiny scrap of rag. At dawn on a chilly Saturday they wallowed barefoot on the flooded deck to wash their hammocks, warming themselves as well as they could at 8:00 A.M. with a breakfast of coffee, a pan of potato scouse, and some hardtack. Their big meal came at noon, with fresh beef and some vegetable soup, and here in France they at least found the meat more palatable than the yellow, decayed material of Spain. That yielded small consolation for the miserable, depressing weather, but spirits picked up on October 23 when Captain Winslow announced that everyone would enjoy a day's liberty in increments of sixteen or twenty men apiece. He had deduced that the engine parts needed by the *Florida* would not arrive for some time, and with the arrest of the *Florida* men he apparently doubted there would be any more serious encounters.[8]

Poole and Wainwright took their jaunt ashore in the same contingent, on October 26. On their way up the river to the dock they passed the *Florida*, examining her rig and battery while the liberty boat glided by. The great iron drawbridge hovered overhead for a few minutes, then the boat docked at a stone pier. A seemingly endless stairway led up to the city itself, which impressed both Poole and Wainwright. The houses and streets alike were all constructed of stone, and these New Englanders marveled at the women's wooden clogs, which set the paving stones aclatter, and their tall lace caps that looked, Poole thought, like "a Bank of Snow in Motion."

Once in the hills of Brest, Poole and Wainwright parted company, each pursuing his preferred entertainment. Poole strolled aimlessly until the steep thoroughfares wore him out, then he sought a photographer to take his portrait for the folks at home. Wainwright rented a room at the English Hotel, where people could understand him, and indulged in the region's cheap brandy. He seemed to appreciate the city's handsome women better than his more restrained companion of the fire room, but (if his journal can be believed) he stuck to his refreshments at two cents a glass. Others of their party doubtless found their way to the port's inevitable brothels, where some would encounter immediate pleasure and eventual regret. Perhaps some carried their own afflictions to the ladies of France, like Third Assistant Engineer Henry McConnell: McConnell had only recently been discharged from the *Kearsarge*'s sick bay with an eruption of primary syphilis that he had picked up in the Azores.

In the morning Poole, Wainwright, and the rest (save one, who had sought different diversion) rose early to make their way to the pier. Wainwright downed a dawn splash of brandy, dropped his two sous, and resigned himself to the drudgery of his lot aboard ship. Poole, on the other hand, savored his liberty to the last moment, noting the soldiers, sailors, and farmers who milled about the streets in the early morning, and the amazing poise of the common women who went about their business with jars on top of their heads and knitting in their hands. At last they all came to the precipitous stairwell, at the bottom of which boats flocked from every ship in the harbor, and by breakfast they had resumed their duties in the engine room.

That afternoon another boatload headed for the pier, among them the perennially difficult Boatswain's Mate Thomas Burns, Quarter Gunner John Dempsey, and George Whipple, none of whom would come back with the next morning's boat. For men like these, every liberty had to be spent as though it were the last.[9]

While Charles Poole and William Wainwright enjoyed their different pursuits ashore, the Confederate steamer *Georgia* passed within easy reach of Brest, rounding Brittany on her way to Cherbourg. John Winslow knew nothing of the lost opportunity, though, until October 29, when a British ship anchored in the harbor and its skipper told him that his vessel had been boarded by the *Georgia*. With a gale blowing, supplies short, and his first lieutenant ashore, Winslow waited for two days before starting after the raider. He even contemplated turning south, for Cadiz, to replenish his supply of food, small stores, and clothing, but that would look like running away from a confrontation; in the end he chose to make a couple of passes by the English Channel. The *Florida* still needed more parts that Paris machinists could not supply within less than a month or two, so even the slim chance of finding the *Georgia* seemed more tempting than waiting at Brest.[10]

The gale still blew on the morning of October 31, and the pilot's boat tossed so violently that some doubted he would ever make it to the quarterdeck. At last he clambered aboard, early in the afternoon, and at 1:00 the *Kearsarge* stood to sea. This passage equaled the cruise from Madeira in turbulence, and once again the off-watch could only keep dry by avoiding the companionways to the spar deck; often someone would pop out on deck for some errand and return in a few minutes, drenched literally to the skin. For two days the ship rolled so violently that the sailing master could not have shot the sun had it been visible, and Captain Winslow could not ascertain exactly where his ship lay. The rocky, spray-blown Isles of Scilly finally appeared on the second afternoon, identifying the southwestern extremity of England, and the helmsman guided the *Kearsarge* seaward of them, curving into the Celtic Sea. Winslow lost his way again the next day, and had to hail a brig to determine his location; only the comforting glow of numerous lighthouses warned him away from the shoals. Late on November 2 he hove the ship to off Kinsale Head, on the southern coast of Ireland.

The next morning the *Kearsarge* steamed into Queenstown harbor, anchoring just east of the Spit Light. Giddy enlisted men crowded the forecastle again, stretching for a glimpse of something new and hoping their captain might grant them liberty in this verdant land. Charles Poole judged Queenstown small for so busy a port, with scattered old houses giving the place an "antique" look. The docks teemed with emigrants for America, and with ships from all over the world. Poole discovered one vessel from Newburyport, where his sister lived, and for some of his shipmates Queenstown itself was as good as home. With the splash of the anchor the customary flock of hawkers and spectators rowed out to the ship, speaking English with a fluency that gratified the homesick sailors, and among them Quarter Gunner Dempsey encountered people who knew his family. The parents of a few crewmen lived within walking distance of the dock; two sailors found the temptation irresistible, and deserted the cutter that landed Captain Winslow, who was bound for Cork. Jimmy Haley, the captain of the forecastle, was allowed ashore to visit his sister, who still lived in nearby Ringaskiddy.[11]

Winslow had come looking for coal, and for potential recruits to flesh out his dwindling roster. The admiral of the port sent a lieutenant to the *Kearsarge* on the second morning of its sojourn, demanding that the ship leave within twenty-four hours, according to the British laws regarding belligerent craft. With Winslow absent on an official visit ashore, James Thornton replied that he would leave when his captain ordered him to. Naval officials and British-owned Irish newspapers took that as defiance, and there followed a little boasting about what the Queenstown fleet might do to bring the arrogant Yankee officers into compliance. The British navy kept two old sixty-gun frigates in the harbor, as well as half a dozen smaller wooden gunboats and an armed training brig, but the *Cork Examiner* reminded its readers that those ancient tubs presented toothless broadsides with an exaggerated strength that existed only on paper: the *Kearsarge*'s "iron sides" and eight guns might be a match for the entire fleet, the editor warned.[12]

While the captain remained in Cork, Lieutenant Thornton kept his back conspicuously turned. With the collusion of petty officers such as Haley (who collected five boys in their late teens), sixteen men applied for service on the sloop, hoping for what they considered the good pay of $12 a month or for ultimate passage to the United States, or both. Their questions led them to Boatswain James Walton, who sent them to the forecastle, where conspiratorial enlisted men guided them below, to Surgeon Browne's quarters. There the doctor examined them, directing those who were fit for service to the berth deck, where they were cautioned to remain until the ship returned to sea, lest Her Majesty's officials invoke the Foreign Enlistment Act. Captain Winslow finished his business ashore on November 5, having learned that the *Georgia* was docked at Cherbourg, on France's Cotentin Peninsula. He returned to his ship late that afternoon, turning back for Brest that evening. By dawn the next day the sixteen "stowaways" had been "discovered," for most of them were leaning over the rail in heavy seas, "paying their respects to Neptune," as Coal Heaver Wainwright put it. They were all native lads from Queenstown, Ringaskiddy, and Whitepoint, bearing names like Sullivan, Murphy, Patterson, Leary, and O'Connell, and few of them had ever been to sea. A Queenstown clerk named Martin Ahern, who had just been fired by Messrs. Scott & Company, bent over the rail with the others. One of the recruits was assigned to Wainwright's watch, and when that landlubber grew green about the gills, Wainwright asked whether he were turning seasick; the new man tried to answer, but lost his lunch as he opened his mouth.[13]

Six weeks before, Raphael Semmes had circumvented the Foreign Enlistment Act by simply waiting until he had departed British colonial waters before shipping his Simons Town recruits, but Captain Winslow concocted an even more elaborate charade. As soon as his ship reached Brest, he sent an officer ashore in the launch with all sixteen destitute Irishmen, offering to land them, penniless, on that foreign soil. As anticipated, they all declined to land, instead officially appealing to the captain's mercy. Their names were accordingly entered on the ship's roster, "for the purpose of their support and comfort," and they donned U.S. Navy uniforms.[14]

Winslow made no mention of this incident when he wrote to the secretary of the navy that day. Never suspecting that anyone would learn of his illegal recruits, he promised to go after the *Georgia* if she tried to leave Cherbourg—provided he should learn of it in time. Otherwise, he said he would lie there at Brest and keep watch over the *Florida*, which had done far more damage to American shipping than had the unlucky *Georgia*. Hoping his government would send at least one ship to help him, Winslow reminded Washington that Brest offered three different channels by which the raider might escape: he suspected that that was why Maffitt had decided to seek the drydock there. By standing toward the island of Ushant the *Kearsarge* could watch all three exits, but that was a full twenty miles away. Only good luck could bring Winslow reliable news of the *Georgia*'s departure, and his duties became even more complicated late in November when the newly purchased CSS *Rappahannock* escaped down the Thames River, crossed the English Channel, and put into Calais for emergency repairs.[15]

Only Thanksgiving provided the crew of the *Kearsarge* any memorable diversion from the endless and dreadfully bleak Breton days. The cooks prepared roast goose and mince pie, but some missed the old-navy treat of an extra grog ration; nowadays there was not even the daily ration, and William Wainwright yearned for a drink. Ham Fat had managed to smuggle some rum aboard, but with his usual poor restraint he could not wait for the holiday and drained his bottle the evening before, so he spent Thanksgiving in irons.

The morning after the feast the captain announced another day of leisure, and the crew of the captain's gig challenged the third cutter to a race. Officers placed their bets (they could not allow the enlisted men to gamble, unless through the same pretended blindness that had brought the Queenstown recruits aboard), and the gig won by a full length. After the race, cards came from beneath dozens of blue blouses, and the deck rang with the shouts and groans of players who won or lost at "forty-five," euchre, "four up," "old sledge," and "cribbage." Neither did Winslow let on that he saw the cards, and the men kept up the pretense by substituting tokens for their money. A few hours of fun made poor compensation for months of inactivity and bad weather, though. "France may do very well for a frenchman," wrote Wainwright on the last day of November, "but it don't suit me."[16]

Within a fortnight English authorities had learned of the sixteen "stowaways" the *Kearsarge* took from Queenstown, and the U.S. minister to France, William Dayton, advised Captain Winslow to return them if their services were not essential to the ship's operation. Dayton feared repercussions not only from the British, whose subjects these men were, but from the French officials, in whose territory the enlistments had been consummated. After all, if American diplomats were to protest the shipping of hands for the *Florida* at Brest, as they planned to do when that raider readied for sea, it would hardly help their argument to have done the same thing on one of their own ships.

Winslow dutifully departed Brest on December 5 with his unsuspecting Irish recruits still working their watches. In the wee hours of December 7 the ship hove to off Queenstown, just missing another famous prize. The blockade runner *Gibraltar* had spent the weekend in Queenstown after a run from Wilmington, by way of Bermuda, but she slipped out for Liverpool and another cargo of contraband late Sunday night. The wardroom officers and enlisted men of the *Kearsarge* could readily have recognized this ship, for she was none other than the former Confederate cruiser *Sumter*. The two vessels churned through the same water only a few hours apart.[17]

Off Queenstown the *Kearsarge* signaled for a pilot, but when the boat came out, the captain declined his services, asking only that he ferry the disconsolate refugees ashore and carry a letter to the admiral of the port. The pilot took the passengers, whom the harbor authorities confined in the customs house, pending an investigation. Both Winslow and his executive officer prepared statements disavowing any complicity in the shipping of those men, but they carefully avoided any mention of the number of Irishmen who had come aboard, referring only to "several men" who had concealed themselves on the waiting ship. Nor did they admit having planned to enlist them, instead asserting that they only meant to care for them so long as it might take to return them to their own shores.

The *Kearsarge* steamed away from Queenstown late that afternoon, without putting into the harbor, and the officer of the deck entered a notation in the log that sixteen "stowaways" had been landed—the same number that had been "discovered" on board. Admiral Lewis Jones and Irish newspapers all reported that only fifteen men came ashore from the Yankee cruiser, though, and one of the disappointed recruits told authorities that the former clerk of Messrs. Scott & Company, Michael Ahern, had remained aboard as an assistant to Paymaster Smith: on his earlier visit, Captain Winslow had admitted to the admiral that he particularly wanted a clerk. The fifteen were all quickly released by the British authorities under the promise to give testimony, and they began milling around Queenstown in their Federal uniforms, telling their stories at the local grog shops. Admiral Jones was later told that a sixteenth man did land, but he appears to have been duped on that point.[18]

Since he had been forced to interrupt his watch over the *Florida* anyway, an embarrassed and angry Winslow decided to drop in on some other Confederate vessels. He rounded the Scilly Isles again, appearing off the western end of the long, fortified breakwater at Cherbourg two days after disembarking the Irishmen. With a spyglass he could have seen the *Georgia* as it rested in the inner harbor, awaiting fresh water and coal, but she evidently had no intention of coming out for battle. Winslow therefore turned the *Kearsarge* about and steamed for Portsmouth, England, where the *Agrippina* was said to lie waiting with coal or other supplies for one of the three Confederate cruisers now in France. That old bark had already sailed, however, so—after one night's layover to let some officers watch a prizefight in the city—the *Kearsarge* went back to Brest, finding the *Florida* still lying at anchor, idle.[19]

With the end of the little excursion the tedious toil resumed, sixteen hands short now (or fifteen, at least), so each man's burden seemed greater. The first full day back, a Saturday, the engineer set his department to the filthy chore of cleaning the flues, and on Monday a worse job began when a coal brig pulled alongside. The captain of this vessel insisted on weighing his cargo so carefully that it took three days to fill the bunkers, even with the crew shoveling late into the night on Wednesday. And as if the regular ship's duties were not sufficiently annoying, Captain Winslow sometimes seemed to create additional work for no evident reason. One Sunday he ordered steam up and called for a pilot, causing the stokers to shovel and sweat for more than two hours before he discharged the pilot and ordered the engine room to stand down. Cleaning the gritty boilers for the usual Sunday inspection after they had cooled down, some of the coal heavers wondered if Winslow had lost his mind.[20]

To ameliorate the crew's growing disgust for this station, Winslow again offered periodic liberty, but with each day's leave he risked losing more men whose absence he could ill afford. Men who held responsible rates on the ship seemed to forget themselves in Brest. At different times a quartermaster, the carpenter's mate, the armorer, and the ship's cook joined such incorrigible debauchees as James Morey, Jimmy Hayes, William Fisher, and Benedict Drury in overstaying their allotted time ashore. Zaran Phillips, whose shoulder had not yet completely healed from his tumble out of the mizzenmast, came back three days late with a great gash in his forehead that he had suffered during another fall in the course of his binge. Aboard ship the frustration manifested itself in insolence, quarrels, fights, drunkenness, and occasional desertions. Even Midshipman Preble incurred the captain's wrath, drawing the usual suspension and confinement to his steerage compartment. The *Florida* thugs still posed a threat, too: a week before Christmas they jumped the master at arms while he sauntered the streets of Brest, and several of them pummeled the boatswain's mate, Thomas Burns, whom they caught in a bordello. French police arrested one of the *Florida*'s sailors on December 21 when he assaulted yet another man from the *Kearsarge*, and the victim was summoned to testify before the magistrate, who sentenced the prisoner to six months at hard labor.[21]

Christmas came with roast goose and assorted condiments, offering one more interlude in what was becoming a dreadfully tedious and uncomfortable existence. This was the first real winter the *Kearsarge* had endured since leaving Portsmouth, and the intervening months in Spain and the warm Atlantic islands had spoiled the crew. Those in the engineer department had the luxury of hot water for their laundry, and the warm engine room for drying their clothes, but even they had to slosh about on deck for the biweekly washing of hammocks in frigid seawater. Rain and clouds kept the ship damp and chilly, and William Wainwright lamented having left his cozy New Hampshire home. Both he and his engine-room companion, Poole, tried to console themselves by reasoning that they fared far better than soldiers in the Army of the Potomac who ate nothing but beans and slept in the mud, but Wainwright noticed that he was not the only one who had grown chronically sick of the navy.[22]

CHAPTER SIXTEEN

Crossings

"Farewell, my Spain! a long farewell!" he cried,

   "Perhaps I may revisit thee no more."

—Byron, *Don Juan*

---

few of the *Kearsarge* crewmen still lounged on the forecastle after their noon meal on December 26 when someone shouted that the *Florida* was moving. A tug had the raider in tow, dragging it from its anchorage beside the hulk in the basin. The Confederate steamer's twin stacks belched no smoke, so excitement aboard the Federal sloop remained somewhat less than uncontrollable, but, when the *Florida* anchored in the roadstead, everyone understood that her engines were thought to be ready.

Two days later the *Florida* began taking powder and shells back aboard, and loading provisions. Nervous about Captain Winslow's ambition to sink the cruiser, the port admiral sent a line-of-battle ship to anchor between the two, but after the scandal that his Queenstown venture had raised, Winslow had no intention of defying another neutral nation's laws. If he could not leave the port for twenty-four hours after the *Florida*, he would leave before she sailed. On the afternoon of December 29 the *Kearsarge* steamed out to sea to wait.

With her went a mysterious character who told the crew he had deserted from the *Georgia* as that ship lay in Cherbourg harbor. He had been captured near the Canary Islands aboard the Boston collier *Bold Hunter*, early in October, and when the Confederates landed their prisoners at Tenerife, he had opted to ship with his captors, ostensibly because he preferred not to land at Tenerife. The *Georgia* had put into Cherbourg two months before, raising the question of why he had waited so long to desert, but as desperate as Captain Winslow had grown for manpower, he did not question the stranger's story. The crew assumed the newcomer had been "shipped," but, like the autumn recruit who absconded with his advance pay, his name never appeared on the log; he seems to have disappeared before anyone came to know him.

For two days Winslow cruised back and forth, trying to remain continually in sight of at least two of the three channels, but at last he turned for Ushant, the rocky island where the *Georgia* had taken her guns aboard the previous spring. The master of a fishing boat agreed to pilot the steamer into the dangerous, horseshoe-shaped harbor at Lampaul, from which Winslow smiled to see that his lookout would have a clear view of the mouth of Brest harbor. He offered $10 and twenty-four hours' liberty to the first man who spotted the *Florida* coming out, and the wardroom officers collected pledges of another $100. Inspired by profitable patriotism, numerous hands remained awake long after their watches had ended, gazing toward the coast as late as midnight while two lighthouses twinkled nearby.[1]

Dawn showed the island to be even less inviting than Brest. A couple of houses, the homes of shepherds, sat on the hillsides, while rangy, hungry sheep roamed the thin grass that grew on the rocks. The little harbor hosted a hundred-foot-high megalith that rose out of the water like a giant ship, moored forever, taking up much of the limited space. The wind picked up on New Year's Day, tossing the *Kearsarge* uncomfortably within its granite-lined basin, so the captain directed the duty officer to drop the second anchor. When breakers began lifting the seas higher, near midnight, Winslow decided he had better leave while he still could. Despite the darkness and the lack of a pilot, he ordered the off-duty men out of their hammocks to hoist the slipping anchors; William Wainwright could not believe his ears, and declined to budge until the master at arms came through and upbraided him. Wainwright dressed and trudged up on deck, where everyone strained at the capstan. It took an hour to lift both anchors. The captain stood on the forecastle while his ship steamed for the open sea, picking his way carefully back through the channel the fisherman had shown him. All hands carried their hearts in their mouths, momentarily expecting the fatal jolt of a rock ripping through the bottom, but the helmsman brought them through safely.

That afternoon the lookout saw two steamers off the lee bow, and the deck officer, James Wheeler, ordered up the fore-and-aft sails to chase them, notifying Winslow. Supposing this might be the *Florida* heading out, with a French warship to escort her beyond territorial waters, Winslow called for full steam and bade the drummer to beat general quarters. After a chase of an hour and a half, telescopes distinguished the French flag fluttering from both ships' mastheads.[2]

A passing British steamer spoke of an American man-of-war in Brest harbor, and Captain Winslow grew curious. For weeks he had begged and hinted for another vessel to help him guard the three Confederate ships and their numerous escape routes; could it be that his appeals had borne fruit? More confident of his usual channel now, he guided his steamer into Brest himself. The *Florida* lay at the anchorage where he had last seen her, but no "American" cruiser appeared anywhere in the roadstead. Some of the officers understood they would go ashore to communicate with the consul (and incidentally enjoy themselves for a couple of hours), but Winslow must have feared the *Florida* would take advantage of his return to bolt from the harbor and force him to remain behind for the requisite twenty-four hours. Even as the officers' boat rattled down the davit pulleys, he ordered it back up and pointed out to sea again, prompting some of the enlisted men to wonder once more about his sanity.

Returning to Ushant the next morning, Winslow signaled in vain for a pilot. Not until he began to repeat his feat in reverse did a pilot boat start out to meet him, but the captain had already negotiated the worst of the channel; he waved the tardy islander away, anchoring in the shadow of the big rock. Here the *Kearsarge* remained for twelve days, her crew keeping watch and practicing for a scrap at close quarters. The armorer handed out the Sharps rifles and a few hundred rounds of ammunition, and everyone took a few shots at 400 yards. Charles Poole "astonished" himself with his good aim, and some of his shipmates did fairly well, too, he noted. At general quarters Poole's first task consisted of handing out those rifles in the armory, after which it was his duty to lift 11-inch shells up from the shell room to the main deck. During such exercises his fellow coal heaver, Wainwright, was stationed with a fire hose in the steerage, right over the magazine, though he seemed to think the gun deck might be less dangerous. In general quarters not everyone took arms, but everyone had to fight—"man and boy," observed the officers' cook. Firemen held hoses fed by scalding water from the boilers, to repel boarders, while others carried axes to cut away damaged rigging or masts. By the end of the second year of their cruise the original hands knew their duties thoroughly, and now Captain Winslow wished to be certain of the recruits.[3]

Fresh provisions had long ago disappeared on the *Kearsarge*, at least from the enlisted men's diet, and some of the men began to experiment. Islanders came out to sell soft bread, potatoes, and dried fish, finding so willing a market that one shepherd carried aboard a live, if somewhat undernourished, sheep. At the ridiculous price of $5 the sheep was reprieved and went back with his master, but the other articles circulated widely. Both Poole and Wainwright used the dried fish to brew a coagulated sort of chowder, finding it tasty after the salted meat and hardtack they had subsisted on for weeks. Occasionally officers went ashore to hunt birds, and one day the chief engineer invited Wainwright to accompany him. Cushman downed a small plover after missing his first shot, then he offered the coal heaver the gun. The birds flew at the slightest alarm, so Wainwright had to crawl carefully toward them before squeezing off a shot. When he did, the weapon misfired, and he had to return to ask Cushman for another percussion cap. The second cap snapped, too, and the frustrated nimrod scoured the treeless shore for a splinter of wood to clear the nipple of his gun. Nothing came to hand, and as the inevitable rain commenced, he and Cushman returned to the ship, the officer carrying the gun and Wainwright packing the forlorn fruits of their hunt in one cupped palm. His shipmates chided him for a human retriever—growling, barking, and whistling for him until he regretted the little adventure.[4]

By the middle of January even the salted provisions had dwindled to less than a fortnight's supply, leaving Captain Winslow no choice but to sail whither beef and pork might be had. His ship needed fresh water especially, for the condenser tubes had broken down. Of all that he needed, Brest could provide him only with water, so he steamed back into that port to fill his casks. From sources there he learned that the *Florida* had engaged in a trial run that revealed certain deficiencies in one of her engines, so the raider would have to linger for a few days or weeks longer. With that information, Winslow determined to proceed to Cadiz on the morning of January 17.[5]

Winslow sought not only provisions in Cadiz, but sailors. The ship had remained shorthanded since the Irishmen departed at Queenstown, and if there were going to be a broadside duel, the *Kearsarge* would need more hands. Had the captain not wielded such peremptory authority aboard a man-of-war, the crew would have dwindled even more, for a substantial number of those deck hands who were recruited in Boston had signed on for only two years, instead of three. Their enlistments had begun to expire, beginning with that of Seaman James Magee, on Christmas Eve. Over the next four weeks at least seventeen key sailors came to the ends of their contracts, including the two quarter gunners, John Dempsey and Andrew Rowley; Sailmaker's Mate Joshua Carey; Boatswain's Mate William Bond; the captains of the maintop, the hold, and the afterguard; and dependable seamen such as William Gowin, William Morgan, James Bradley, and William Giles. Winslow allowed none of them to think of going home. "The captain deems it necessary to retain them on board," read the log in each instance, and their enlistments were extended to the end of the cruise with the consolation of a 25 percent increase in their pay.[6]

Three days out of Brest the weather turned pleasant enough that Charles Poole sat out on top of the forecastle to absorb the sunlight when his watch ended; all winter the cold and wind had driven him and his shipmates below, where they had huddled on the crowded berth deck as long as their duty prevented them from going out. As the *Kearsarge* sailed the rugged coast of Portugal, to rest the engines and hoard the little remaining coal, the masts cut through a low-flying flock of brant geese that served to mark the northward-creeping boundary of European spring. When the anchor dropped in Cadiz harbor on January 23, an appreciative William Wainwright remarked that the afternoon had turned warm enough to walk the decks in bare feet.

The engineer department went to work cleaning valves and replacing leaky boiler tubes, through which the salt water had eaten. When they had finished with that, a coal barge moved alongside, and a plume of black dust rose as the shovels began to ring. In one day the crew transferred ninety-five tons, Poole observed, but the shovelers came away looking like the cast of an enormous minstrel show. While the coal rattled down the scuttles, machinists repaired the condenser tubing, permitting the captain to raise the daily allowance of water to two gallons and a quarter per man. Details started toting small stores below on January 29, but Spanish merchants tried to foist some of their contaminated inventory on the ship. Paymaster Smith detected at least some of it, condemning 600 pounds of insect-ridden flour, a barrel of weevily beans, more than 100 pounds of moldy sugar, and two tins of meat that had outlived its preservation expectations. The survey crew that rejected the goods disposed of it in the usual manner of an era in which the earth's resources seemed limitless: they threw it overboard, right there in the harbor.

Once the provisions had all been loaded and the malfunctioning equipment was back in order, the boatswain and chief engineer turned their respective departments back to regular maintenance, slushing the rigging, painting the boilers and the hull, and tarring the smokestack. Poole philosophized that the deck of a man-of-war was one of the world's greatest workshops, where superiors seemed willing to take anything apart and reassemble it, "merely to keep you at work."[7]

Neither did the officers neglect their duty. Remembering the continuing journalistic furor over his Queenstown caper, Captain Winslow consulted with the American consul about shipping recruits in Cadiz, but he began accepting applicants before the official reply arrived. Even as the crew coaled ship, he enlisted seven stranded British subjects—a mix of English and Irish seamen, most of whom soon showed their faithlessness. A Welshman calling himself John Briset came aboard as a coal heaver on February 2, eliciting Poole's opinion that recruits flocked to the American warships because they offered better pay, more humane discipline, and lighter duty than the foreign merchantmen; Poole only hoped that Briset would not pursue the "drinking and fighting" that seemed instinctive among Celtic mariners.

With their captain's permission, many of the crew enjoyed an opportunity to exercise those pastimes during the sunny stayover in Spain. Nearly everyone took a turn at liberty. Such teetotalers as Poole attended the opera (an Italian presentation, "La Favarita"), where even a few tipplers (William Wainwright among them) sat through a performance, but the true sailors struck for the cantinas. Of the earliest boatload to go ashore, more of those whom the captain had "retained on board" defied their curfews than anyone. William Gowin, the jovial musician, failed to make the morning launch, as did James Bradley, William Giles, and Robert Strahan, the stocky little captain of the maintop.[8]

On February 4 the American consul apprised Winslow of a report that had just missed him as he left Brest. The U.S. consul in Le Havre had passed on a rumor that Confederate naval officers planned to mobilize their French flotilla for a concerted attack on the *Kearsarge*. The *Georgia* and the *Rappahannock* would rendezvous with the *Florida* for the blow, according to stories that reached newspapers on both sides of the English Channel, and the *Florida* would choose the location by sending Winslow a challenge to fight. William Dayton, the minister at Paris, assured Winslow that the French would not allow the unarmed *Rappahannock* to board its guns or ammunition before leaving Calais, which reduced the odds considerably, but when the tale reached Cadiz on February 4, it spurred Winslow to ask whether he might borrow a couple of extra guns from the *St. Louis*, if he should fall in with that old frigate. This news, and the accompanying advice to augment his force, encouraged Winslow to enlist every man he could find, to form a couple of extra gun crews. He directed James Wheeler ashore to recruit, and the acting master sent back a steady stream of prospective hands. Winslow took them all, overfilling all his departments and mystifying his sailors, who did not understand why he might wish to crowd the roster while he could.

The new men hailed from all over the world. Two Prussians joined, one as a deck hand and one as a coal heaver; ironically, both said they had fled their native country to avoid conscription in its impending war with Denmark. The deck officer logged the name of Van Burn François, a fifteen-year-old Belgian, as accurately as he could, giving him the rank of landsman instead of cabin boy. Landsman "John" Netto, a Spaniard who had come aboard at Algeciras as a steward a year and half before, ran away as soon as the *Kearsarge* returned to his native soil, and the officers replaced him with a tiny twelve-year-old, Manuel José Gallardo, who stood barely four feet tall. William Burns, a Newfoundlander, joined the deck watch on February 12. Nearly two dozen men put their names on the roll during this visit at Cadiz, and some of them claimed American citizenship—they said they were natives of Boston, New Bedford, New York, and Baltimore—but foreigners composed the majority. A few emerged from the city prison, Poole suspected. With these recruits, a crewman could point to representatives of more than a score of nationalities, from Down East to the Far East, with Russians, Dutch, Portuguese, an Italian, a Chilean, and one lone Polynesian from the distant island of Guam.[9]

With all these men, Winslow might still have wondered whether he could prevail against the combined Confederate ships. Only six days after his first assurances against the possibility, Minister Dayton warned that the *Rappahannock* might already have been armed, and that she was ready to leave port with her 60 crewmen and another contingent to be picked up elsewhere. Some 150 men had allegedly departed England to strengthen the *Florida*'s skeleton crew, while the *Georgia* would carry a fair complement herself. The expected challenge had already been issued by January 21, according to the London newspapers, for an engagement six miles outside Brest, early in February. Winslow knew of no such challenge, dismissing the need for publicizing it so dramatically when all he wished for was a meeting with the enemy; just as dramatically, he told the Le Havre consul that he feared no junction of the *Georgia* and the *Florida*, and wanted no such combination thwarted. He qualified such bravado in a postscript to the London legation, though, suggesting that if the *Florida*'s battery and company had been increased, "it would be no longer prudent to permit her to join the *Georgia*." He added that some final tinkering with the engines would delay him at Cadiz, and he could not expect to reach Brest until perhaps February 18.

Gideon Welles reviewed this correspondence a few weeks later when it reached his office at the Navy Department. By then any danger of a fleet action against the *Kearsarge* had passed, if it ever existed, and the old man considered only the political ramifications of holding communications with the enemy on such matters. At the bottom of Winslow's reference to the putative challenge, Welles scribbled a note: "To accept or send a challenge would be to recognize the pirates on terms of equality, elevating them and degrading our own." He repeated the essence of that endorsement in a letter to Winslow early in March.[10]

While the last recruit swaggered aboard on February 12, the powder division lined up at the gangway to bid goodbye to Master's Mate Yeaton (he of the "brick in his hat"), who had been sent ashore for an unspecified illness. Captain Winslow departed Cadiz the next morning, with two fiddlers squawking away while the crew manned the capstan bars. Running under steam most of the way, the *Kearsarge* reached Brest on the day Winslow had predicted. So anxiously did the captain charge into the channel that he barely missed some rocks, ringing a single bell to slow the engines and veering clear only when whitecaps betrayed the reef, which trailed for miles out of the port. Inside the harbor, sweeping binoculars turned up no sign of the *Florida*. She had slipped away in the night, over a week before. Winslow groaned his apology to Washington, but the news brought little melancholy to the forecastle, for the deck hands and engine-room watches reasoned that, with the prey gone from this port, the hunter could leave, also. The sailors before the mast understood that the government would blame the *Kearsarge*—that it would be a "slur" on the ship and her crew, as one of them put it—but they consoled themselves by reflecting on the simple mathematics of a single ship guarding three separate ports.

The *Georgia* had already left Cherbourg, too, as Winslow learned with deepening regret. He need not have frowned so broadly at that, though, for both ships had left French territory under pressure from Paris. The presence of his own ship and the persistent complaints of his country's diplomats had taken their toll on the Confederate welcome in France. The marine minister formally reaffirmed the emperor's 1861 neutrality proclamation, illustrating that the imperial government's sympathy for the waning Southern nation had finally begun to give way to irritation over the international difficulties the cruisers had brought to her ports.[11]

To enforce that proclamation, a French naval officer notified Winslow on February 19 that, unless he needed provisions or emergency repairs, he would have to depart Brest within twenty-four hours. Once he had gleaned all the available information about the fugitive cruisers, therefore, Winslow steamed for the English Channel and Cherbourg. The forenoon watch awoke to snow-covered decks on the morning of February 21, sweeping it aside and pressing on through bitter cold, rounding Cap de la Hague early on Washington's birthday. A steamer loomed in the vicinity of Cherbourg, but when the *Kearsarge* raced ahead to intercept it, it turned out to be an ironclad belonging to the French navy. Winslow hove to outside the Cherbourg breakwater; shortly afterward another steamer started from behind that barrier, but she wheeled about and headed back once the *Kearsarge* filled away to chase her. Winslow sent a boat into the harbor to learn the nature of this craft, hardly daring to hope it might be the *Georgia*, and indeed he found it to be an American merchantman whose captain had taken him for a Confederate commerce raider. Two such vessels huddled in the shadow of Cherbourg's seventeenth- and eighteenth-century waterfront buildings. Winslow offered to escort them into the open sea, but their masters declined when they saw how quickly the Federal captain abandoned them at a report of the *Georgia* off Pointe de Barfleur.

Pointe de Barfleur lay less than twenty miles east of the Cherbourg breakwater. It marked the opening to the broad bay fed by the Seine, and as the *Kearsarge* cruised around the little cape, her crewmen might have glimpsed the distant beaches where, eighty years later, thousands of ships would disgorge the greatest invasion force that ever put to sea. No Southern steamer lingered there now, however, so Winslow sheered away for England, to search for coal.[12]

The English Channel's infamous weather battered the sloop all the way to Dover, where the roads stood crowded with ships seeking haven against the gale. Winslow had to wait for high tide to steam into the harbor, anchoring there on February 25. While junior officers sought a supply of coal, the off-duty men scanned the towering chalk cliffs and the dark stone houses of the town, which assumed all the more dreary an atmosphere with its rain-slickened slate roofs. The castle loomed atop the cliffs, centuries old, and alongside it rose an ancient church fashioned from the same ubiquitous grey slate. Visitors came aboard as always, though, including a gaggle of whispering women who brightened the port's dismal image.[13]

Between the twenty-four-hour regulation and the three-month limit on refilling his bunkers within British waters, Captain Winslow decided to arrange for a coal brig to meet him in the channel, outside territorial jurisdiction. Once the deal was struck, Winslow dashed across the Straits of Dover to Boulogne, where the *Kearsarge* bobbed at anchor in dense fog to await the fuel. As the ship waited, a mysterious character came aboard, claiming to have been an engineer on the *Florida*; he said he would soon learn the whereabouts of that craft, and offered to relay the information. The man purported to act on the orders of the American legation in London, and the consulate confirmed this. Winslow suspected the turncoat as a double agent who merely meant to divert the *Kearsarge* from blockading the *Rappahannock* at Calais.

Winslow's visitor may have been William Hutchison Jackson, a Marylander and former second assistant engineer on the *Florida*, of whom Captain Maffitt had said "a more unfortunate appointment could not have been made." Jackson had left the *Florida* at Brest, and with Maffitt's poor opinion he did not receive an assignment when she left that harbor. Ultimately Jackson drew a spot on the *Rappahannock*, which never left Calais during the remainder of the war.[14]

When the brig arrived, on the last afternoon in February, her crew harbored a quantity of rum to sell to the frustrated man-of-war's men, and the liquor found a willing market. No one had been allowed ashore save Charles Fisher, who was filling in as Captain Winslow's personal cook while Ham Fat stood ready to beat the drum if they should fall upon any of the three Southern cruisers. The coaling consumed the rest of that night, carrying into the first two days of March, and toward the end of the load a rising swell brought the two ships together abruptly enough to smash some of the *Kearsarge*'s sheet chains. The greatest difficulty came from the dipsomaniacs among the crew, who cavorted wildly with their illicit bottles. Dempsey the quarter gunner, Boatswain's Mate Thomas Burns, and an assortment of deck hands brought the master at arms running with the noise of their brawling and their mutinous, belligerent cursing. Robert Strahan took his periodic turn in double irons again, as did William Gowin, who had evidently exhausted his abundant good humor after twenty-five months on the same ship.

The deck still wore its coating of coal dust when a group of French naval officers came aboard to visit, bringing with them another cluster of visitors, including some women. David Sumner had the duty, and he pleaded with the women not to come aboard because the crew was about to hose down the ship, but the ladies insisted on having a look. Considering their exalted escorts, Acting Master Sumner dared not refuse them, but as the men washed off the dust, they made certain to send little floods flowing toward the women, who would shriek playfully and trot away with ankles and calves flashing from beneath their lifted skirts.[15]

The *Kearsarge* lingered another couple of days off Boulogne after the coal brig sailed, but on the second night the officer of the deck observed an unusual number of fishing boats that seemed to swing closer than he liked to the sides of the sloop as they beat into and out of the harbor. He began to suspect a Confederate effort to board the vessel, so he alerted the armorer, who laid by a number of loaded revolvers. The engineers attached a hose to the boilers, ready to scald anyone who tried to climb the sides, but, for all the preparations, the offending boats held only curious or reckless fishermen.

Running up the Danish flag late the following morning, Captain Winslow turned up the coast for Calais and the stranded *Rappahannock*. The *Kearsarge* lay off that city for several hours, but Winslow could neither see nor learn anything of the crippled cruiser, so he sent a boat ashore that evening. Darkness had already fallen, and the French would not allow the boat to land at night, but Winslow decided not to wait until dawn. Instead, he made for England again, dropping off Paymaster Smith and Acting Master

Wheeler at Deal, directing them to proceed to London with a request to repair the *Kearsarge* in the government drydock on the Thames. To allow enough time for the pair to complete their mission, the captain turned back to France for another glimpse of the *Rappahannock*, the presence of which at Calais he finally confirmed.[16]

In celebration of the discovery, Winslow scheduled an exercise at general quarters for midnight, and Ham Fat awakened the entire crew with his pounding drum at the appointed hour. Sleepy sailors tumbled out of their hammocks, thinking that the *Rappahannock* was coming out of the harbor. The realism of the drill inspired the veterans and the newcomers alike, and they stumbled into one another all the more, lashing their bedding to fill the hammock nettings and chanting their duties to themselves by way of reminder. More than one of the recruits fell in a heap as he encountered a sprinting salt, and the babel of foreign tongues heightened the confusion. Nervous, cold, and more or less bruised, the crewmen reached their battle stations and found it was all for practice. After an hour's shivering at the guns or down in the magazine, the boatswain's whistle sent them all back to bed, stiff and grumbling. Old hands like William Wainwright and Charles Poole had begun to suppose that this would be the closest they would ever come to combat on the open water.[17]

CHAPTER SEVENTEEN

Homecoming

To Cherbourg port she sailed one day,

Roll, *Alabama*, roll,

To take her count of prize money,

Oh, roll, *Alabama*, roll.

—Old sea shanty

The mutinous atmosphere of an overtaxed crew and the resulting imposition of harsh discipline had taken its toll aboard the *Alabama*. Seven men ran away into the crowded alleys of Singapore the evening of December 22 alone. An armed detail brought back two the next day, but five more had absconded by the time Semmes ordered the ship to sea on Christmas Eve. The deserters consisted of two cabin boys and five seamen, four of them recruits, but Semmes also lost three petty officers, two of whom had been with him since Terceira. The greatest loss was probably Quartermaster William King, whose departure left only one of the four Savannah pilots who had begun the cruise. Semmes promoted the rehabilitated Brent Johnson to fill King's shoes, and he signed on four more recruits who slipped out of port with the ship, including Henry Higgins, whose father had been emigration officer at Liverpool. Coincidentally, one of the four was named James King, but this wandering Liverpudlian bore no relation to the two Savannah Kings.[1]

At midmorning on December 24 the *Alabama* followed the steamer *Kwangtung* out of the harbor under the direction of a Malay pilot, the crew working around huge stacks of bagged coal amidships. Veering west, toward the Straits of Malacca, the Confederate ship passed the *Kwangtung* handily. Soon a bark came into view that bore an unmistakably American cut to her hull and rig, and a shot from one of the thirty-twos brought her to a halt. Master's Mate Fullam ferried over to inspect the vessel, which bore the name *Martaban* on her stern. He discovered that this was a product of Boston shipbuilders, and that she had once carried the name *Texan Star*. Like many shipowners whose craft might have to cross waters cruised by Confederate raiders, the proprietors of the *Texan Star* had sold their ship to a British firm. The master refused to return to the *Alabama* with Fullam, so the perplexed master's mate reported the case to his captain.

For the first time since the war had begun, Raphael Semmes cinched on his swordbelt and rode one of his boats over to a prize. The skipper of the *Martaban*, his mate, and some of his crew were Americans, he deduced, and the bill of sale proved rather recent. He concluded that the sale was fraudulent, as the American consul in Calcutta had evidently admitted. Such deceit was not difficult to understand, for marine insurance companies disputed the claims against captured vessels even when the proprietors had paid the exorbitant premiums, and prospective shippers hesitated to let their cargo sail in American holds. Semmes evidently believed it was time to discourage this farcical subterfuge, and to reinforce the vulnerability of even nominal neutrals. He ordered the *Martaban*'s crew to the deck of the cruiser and watched as the boarding party set fire to the fiftieth American sail the *Alabama* had destroyed or appropriated. That night the Southern steamer dropped anchor off Malacca, landing the prisoners Christmas morning.[2]

The flames that sank the *Texan Star* also sparked fires ashore. At first blush the governor at Singapore judged the *Martaban* a legitimate British vessel, considering her destruction a violation of international law. A week after the capture, the *Singapore Free Press* remarked that Semmes's action "savors very much of downright piracy." Semmes could still take satisfaction, though, for his stubbornness had worked the desired effect: nearly three months afterward, when he was long gone from these waters, a Boston captain wrote from Calcutta that "English houses are not disposed to Ship Cargo in Am*cn* Bottoms now at all—."[3]

To celebrate Christmas, Semmes ordered the grog tubs opened for a ritual splicing of the main brace. Southerners and British tars alike downed a draught to the health of their loved ones, and then it was back to the war. Late in the afternoon Mr. Fullam climbed into another boat to check the identity of a French ship, and at night Semmes ordered the *Alabama* near shore again, where he anchored rather than risk the narrow passage in the darkness.

Early the following morning the lookout called that two ships lay at anchor dead ahead, and both proved to be American. The first was the *Sonora*, which had dashed out of Singapore as soon as the *Alabama* arrived there; the second was the *Highlander*. Both sailed under the ownership of Massachusetts citizens, though the crew of the *Sonora* was composed mostly of Africans. Within hours the two ships lay ablaze at their anchors, while their crews pulled for shore or, in the case of one boat, for a French ship that hovered nearby. One boatload of the *Sonora*'s crewmen went astray in a squall before reaching land, but eventually everyone arrived safely at Pinang.

Toward noon that day the lightship at the northern mouth of the straits came into view, and Semmes discharged his Malay pilot. The quartermaster spun the *Alabama*'s engraved wheel to the west, through the Great Channel, between Sumatra and the Nicobar Islands, bearing generally along the fifth degree of latitude to skirt the Bay of Bengal.

The game grew thin in these waters. American ships could find no cargoes, especially after news of the *Martaban* flashed about Britain's eastern ports, and for the most part they clung to their safe harbors to await word of the Confederate ship's direction. Fullam and one of the Prussian master's mates, von Meulnier, boarded an American-looking ship the afternoon that they left the straits, but the *Ottone* proved to have been sold outright by its American owners the previous May, offering still more evidence of the cruiser's impact on Northern shipping. Captain, crew, and papers were all Dutch, so Semmes let it proceed to Rangoon unmolested. He ordered the engineers to blow off the steam and hoist the propeller; with all sails set, the *Alabama* bounded toward Ceylon in a heavy rain.[4]

Over the next week only one British ship, the *Thomas Blythe*, roused the lookout's suspicion. Mr. Fullam introduced himself to the *Blythe*'s commander as an officer from the USS *Wyoming* (which had not yet returned from its excursion to Manila); the English captain apparently believed the ruse, but British newspaper editors in Singapore were not fooled.

With nothing to interfere, Semmes appointed another court-martial to deal with the recaptured Singapore deserters. Three had been dragged back in irons. The ordinary seamen could not be reduced much further, so they drew confinement and loss of pay, but aging Russell Hobbs, that rare Southern recruit from deep in slaveholding Delaware whom Semmes had made a quartermaster, found himself sent back before the mast.

Growing tedium and the sense that the cruise would never end merely aggravated the insubordination aboard Semmes's tiring greyhound. More than a score of his trusty Terceira crew were gone, now—either through desertion, discharge, or transfer—and they had been replaced by some fifty-six men shipped from various prizes and ports, whose reliability seemed to diminish in direct proportion to the lateness of their enlistment. These recruits now composed nearly half the noncommissioned crew, and their rising insolence helped to infect the original crewmen, who had now spent sixteen months aboard the ship. The officers wore their sidearms on duty, as usual, but nowadays perhaps they touched their elbows to their holsters more frequently. The first Sunday after the courts-martial, Lieutenant Kell read the Articles of War to the crew, with all the attendant references to the penalty of death.[5]

Captain Semmes alternated the implied threat of punishment with a certain generosity, opening up the grog tubs for a celebratory dram on New Year's Day. On January 11, the anniversary of the *Alabama*'s victory over the *Hatteras*, the dipper plunged in again, this time for what Fullam called "a very long splice indeed!" Occasional treats like that and the deadening routine of the sea watches seemed to mollify the sailors, as did the westward course. If the helmsman did not turn about at the tip of India, that might mean a return to Europe, with either an end to the cruise or an opportunity to desert the ship near home.[6]

The cruiser lay virtually becalmed very near that southern extremity of India just after noon on January 14 when the lookout trained his glass on the ship *Emma Jane*, nine days out from Bombay. Many months from Bath, Maine, now, the *Emma Jane* was one of those American vessels that had experienced trouble finding a cargo, and the reason for that difficulty fired a blank warning round at about 3:00 P.M. Captain Francis Jordan hove to and waited for the armed boat's crew led by Mr. Fullam, while Mrs. Jordan amplified the bosom of her dress with what silver it would hold, tossing in as well two pocket watches belonging to her husband and the first mate. Captain Jordan followed Fullam back to the cabin of the *Alabama*, where a tired-looking Semmes, clad in his old Union blue and wearing "a terrible revolver," held his little admiralty court and condemned the ship, telling Jordan to bring back his ship's company with what personal possessions they could carry. By late evening the *Emma Jane* lay blazing in the dark water fifty miles off the Malabar coast.

Semmes lodged Captain and Mrs. Jordan in the wardroom, but the master at arms herded the twenty-one crewmen into the waist of the weather deck. The *Alabama* curved northward under light breezes to find a place where the prisoners might be dropped, and within forty-eight hours of leaving their ballasted merchantman the crew, the captain, and his lady found themselves looking through the gun ports at the Indian harbor of Anjenga. A lieutenant went ashore with an escort and scared up the son of the local Portuguese magistrate, who arrived aboard the Confederate ship and agreed to arrange the discharge of Semmes's passengers. Another officer led a detail back to the shore with the young man, but so many hours passed that Semmes grew nervous. Finally he heard a few shots fired, at which his concern for the detachment turned to alarm, and he dispatched another boat with more men under Lieutenant Kell. Kell, however, found everyone safely awaiting the return of the magistrate, who came back late that night and authorized the landing. With the dawn of the Sabbath the crew of the *Emma Jane* descended into the *Alabama*'s boats and returned to the land whence they had come less than a fortnight before—all save two, a German and an Englishman, who signed on with the *Alabama*.

Dark natives climbed aboard the strange visitor and perambulated the deck in their loincloths until the officers ushered them over the side at midmorning. The boatswain called all hands to the windlass and raised the anchor, and by noon the cruiser lay well to sea. Breezes remained light, though, and the land did not disappear until the following morning. Spirits doubtless rose despite the slow progress, for the prow held to the west, right through the Maldives and into the Arabian Sea.[7]

Stopping only briefly at Molocoy Island in a vain search for potable provisions, Semmes directed a course for the Horn of Africa. After seventeen days of fine, hot weather and steady breezes, without a trace of another sail, the lookout sighted the Comoro Islands, deep in the Somali Basin and at the entrance to the Mozambique Channel. Anchoring February 9 near an island known then as Johanna, Semmes sent ashore for provisions.

The inhabitants of these lush tropical islands caught Semmes's interest because they kept African slaves, though the natives were themselves black or Semitic Moslems. Enchanted by the political value that such a contradiction might offer to the Confederacy, the captain lingered a week in the vicinity, chatting occasionally with a turbaned mullah while Dr. Galt went ashore for fresh meat, fruit, limes, and oranges. Because of the Mohammedan sovereignty, once again the purser found no liquor, to the disappointment of officer and crewman alike.[8]

The *Alabama* had struck the Comoros at the commencement of Ramadan, and when Semmes ambled ashore in the town of Anzuan, he found most of the free population bent over their Korans in the porticoes of their homes. The stone and thatch houses crowded so closely against the narrow, winding passageways that a man could have touched a wall on either side with his outstretched hands. On a second visit two days later, Semmes relaxed at the homes of a couple of local princes, sipping rose syrup while a young black girl fanned his face.

Four recruits from the *Alabama* put a day's liberty to use by running into the steep hills that stood in the center of the island. Three of these ordinary seamen—Thomas Brandon, Thomas White, and a miscreant who signed under the name of John Adams—had boarded the ship when it left Simon's Bay the previous September; the fourth man, Henry Higgins, had shipped in Singapore barely seven weeks before. All probably expected to find passage back to Cape Town within a couple of weeks, but Semmes offered a reward for their capture, and the natives brought them back after nightfall of February 14. The next day, with some young bulls tethered to the deck and the storerooms bulging with fruit, the ship steamed away from the island to a cacophony of cheering boatmen.[9]

While a court-martial considered the fate of the four deserters beneath the wardroom skylight, the helmsman maintained his course for Cape Town under a broiling sun. The heat abated somewhat on February 19, and squalls began to kick up around the creaking cruiser. One ship passed within ten miles on the nineteenth, but nearly another week went by before Semmes chose to hail one, just as the *Alabama* eased out of the Mozambique Channel. The ship raised the British flag, which Semmes answered with the French tricolor.[10]

The wind picked up on February 27 and the sea turned rough. The weather worsened through the night, and Sunday, February 28, came off with squalls and heavy swells. The wind died a little in the afternoon, but the ship continued to pitch, her bows dipping under the froth as she dropped into a sea, then rising high in the air as the swell passed under. Henry Godson, a recruit from the *T. B. Wales*, chose that moment to make his way to the head, but he was not feeling very well, and when the prow of the *Alabama* pitched into a sea, Godson was swept to the side and over. The cry of "Man overboard" brought Captain Semmes to the deck, while the duty officer ordered the ship brought by the wind and the helm spun about to pick him up.

In such a turbulent sea everyone supposed Godson had been lost for good, and he would have been were it not for Michael Mars, the daredevil of the ship's company, who jumped to the taffrail and spotted him. Throwing a wooden grate over the side in lieu of a life preserver, Mars followed it into the water and swam to the drowning man, pulling him onto the floating grate. A boat dropped into the water from the ship, its crew pulling like demons, and soon enough both the middle-aged Mars and the choking Godson had reached the deck again. A week later Captain Semmes congratulated Mars in a general order read at the Sunday muster.[11]

The week that intervened between the rescue and the commendation told on the battered cruiser. Seas continued to wash over the decks, leaking into crevices that had opened under the glaring tropical sun. Only on February 26 had the ship crossed the Tropic of Capricorn, leaving behind the sweltering heat, and on March 4 the officers and men stood their watches bundled in their pea jackets.

Captain Semmes observed that day that the *Alabama* needed a complete overhaul as soon as he could find a drydock for her. Her captain had about run his course, too, and he noted in his private journal, "It is three years to day since I parted with my family in the City of Washington, on the day on which the great republic of Washington was humiliated by the inauguration as President of a vulgar, third-rate politician. . . . These three years of anxiety, vigilance, exposure, & excitement have made me an old man, & sapped my health, rendering repose necessary, if I would prolong my life."[12]

The Cape of Good Hope rose into view a week after Semmes scrawled that gloomy entry. Britain's ninety-day rule prevented him from coaling his vessel for another twelve days, counting from his purchase at the colony of Singapore, but rather than risk losing any crewmen on liberty he stood off Cape Town for over a week, stopping an occasional sail and keeping a glass to sea for any ominous steamers. Passing his ship off as the USS *Dacotah*, on its way to relieve the *Wyoming* in Southeast Asia, Master's Mate Fullam learned from two westbound merchantmen that the *Alabama* was "playing the mischief in the Java Sea." No civilized power had heard from the *Alabama* since the prisoners from the *Emma Jane* stepped ashore on January 17, leaving everyone to suppose that she might still be lingering in the East; such a belief served to decoy Federal warships away from the *Alabama*'s real position, but if some Goliath of the *Vanderbilt* class should take a notion to visit the Far East, it would probably follow the route around the Cape of Good Hope. The *Vanderbilt* lay somewhere on the American side of the North Atlantic just then, though.

At that moment the Cape Town newspapers were still carping over the capture of the British bark *Saxon* by the *Vanderbilt* the previous October. A junior officer from the *Vanderbilt* had "accidentally" shot and killed the first mate of the bark *Saxon*, which it had stopped near Penguin Island after the bark left Angra Pequeña. The *Saxon*'s hold was filled with wool that had come from the *Alabama*'s prize *Conrad*, or so the *Vanderbilt*'s skipper had supposed, and he had made a prize of the smaller vessel, sending it to New York.[13]

Relieved of its cargo, the *Conrad*, now the CSS *Tuscaloosa*, had cruised the South Atlantic for weeks under Lieutenant Low, capturing, meanwhile, only one American vessel that had to be ransomed because of a neutral cargo. With food and supplies running out, Low had put into Cape Town the day after Christmas. Colonial authorities there, still smarting over reprimands for their failure to seize the vessel in August, when it still contained its captured cargo, immediately detained the *Tuscaloosa*. Low had protested to no avail, and in January he had departed the ship along with his executive officer, William Sinclair. The two returned to Liverpool, and Sinclair continued on to the Confederate naval bureau in Paris.

Semmes learned all of this after he headed the *Alabama* into Cape Town on March 20; he came in flying the French flag, lest any anchored Federal warships steam out for him before he reached territorial waters. Under the shadow of the great cottony cloud that lay atop Table Mountain the ship dropped one anchor and then another, when the wind picked up. While his officers scattered about to look for coal and supplies, Semmes devoted most of his first two days in port to writing his own legal brief for the release of the *Tuscaloosa*. Unknown to either Semmes or the governor of Cape Town, Britain's secretary of state for the colonies had already decided that the seizure was illegal and had ordered the *Tuscaloosa* released to Semmes, or to any official representative of the Confederate government. That instruction came from Downing Street on March 4, with a full explanation following on March 10, but neither message reached Cape Town before the *Alabama* sailed. The *Tuscaloosa* remained in port for the rest of the war, waiting for a crew that never came.[14]

The legal document represented only Semmes's formal adherence to his duty; he probably realized that, even if the British yielded the little cruiser in time for him to man it again and send it to sea, his own ship's efficiency would be greatly diminished with little corresponding benefit to the Confederacy. The *Tuscaloosa* had accomplished precious little in its six months as a commerce raider, save to deprive the *Alabama* of some good officers and sailors. Semmes's disappointment at leaving the forlorn bark behind may not have been so deep as he portrayed it later. However discouraged he may have been, he was pleased to find that the proceeds from the sale of both the *Tuscarora*'s wool and the prize-ship *Sea Bride* had been collected for him on shore in gold; he took the strongbox aboard for future expenses.

A discernible shift in Britain's general political stance toward the Confederate States did, however, disturb the *Alabama*'s commander. The *Cape Argus* of March 22 reported that the U.S. minister to Great Britain, Charles Adams, had demanded damages from Parliament for the havoc wrought on American shipping by the cruisers built in England and Scotland. The *Argus* merely repeated an article in the London *Times*, the editors of which had scoffed at Adams's allegations, but the *Times* also suggested that sympathy for the Confederacy was waning in the British Empire. One February 12 piece told of a rumored steamer under construction by two British shipping firms whose owners intended it expressly for the destruction of the *Alabama*. The origin of that fable is not clear, but if Britons were willing to believe such a thing, it could only mean that American pressure had had some effect. England wanted no real trouble with the United States, and the chilling reduction of American shipping had worked against some British houses, all of which eroded the instinctive sympathy of the average Englishman for the struggling South.[15]

Semmes certainly recognized the change, railing against the perfidy of an England that he had once seen as the Confederacy's only ally. The disaffection at least did not seem to have infected many among the cape colonists. While lighters brought coal and provisions out to the cruiser, civilians crawled all over the deck. E. B. Rose, who had visited the ship with the civil service boat the previous August, hitched a ride with another contingent of admirers on March 24. This time Rose actually caught a glimpse of Captain Semmes, who had evaded him in August. The company included a number of ladies, whose presence naturally distracted crewmen who had not seen a white woman in at least three months. But Semmes and his officers greeted the visitors cordially, Rose recorded, and he seems not to have perceived the officers' aggravation at the confusion the civilians brought to the busy ship.[16]

The last of the supplies were stowed away late that night, and the *Alabama* readied for sea the next morning. Bitterly disappointed to see a Yankee steamer turn past the headland and into the bay just as the anchors came up, Semmes knew the lucky ship would not venture out again for days or weeks after such a close call, so he left the prospective prey behind and ordered the sails set.

Though the stay in port had filled the ship's brig again, no one had deserted this time. With every mile bringing them closer to the civilization that most of them called home, the crewmen evidently preferred to take the chance of reaching Europe and finding their long-awaited prize money. Four new faces worked the stays, as well: three ordinary seamen and a landsman had remained aboard from the last supply boat when it cast off, and Semmes signed them on as soon as they made open water.[17]

The *Alabama* groaned in every timber now. Beams of green English oak had begun to split, and some of the decks were sagging. With the boilers corroded by seawater, Semmes dared not tax the engines; with her bottom fouled with barnacles and seaweed, he found he could make no more than two knots under sail alone. At that sluggish pace the ailing raider made her way northward, her captain meanwhile reading his collection of newspapers in the relative comfort of his cabin.

Nearly another month passed with no sign of an American vessel. An Italian bark just from Buenos Aires helped to explain the poor hunting on April 17: only three or four American ships lay at anchor in the Argentinian port now, hoping in vain for customers who would ship freight aboard them.

A French ship bound home with guano from Peru's Chincha Islands reported not a single American sail there, where scores had been reported the previous July. Around the globe, U.S. shippers had either sold their vessels or laid them up to avoid losing them to the *Alabama* or her sister ships.

There must have been at least one American at the guano islands, though, for the *Alabama* ran her down six days later. The *Rockingham*, from Portsmouth, New Hampshire, had rounded Cape Horn a couple of weeks before on the voyage to Queenstown, her hold full of rich, black guano. The *Alabama*'s lookout spotted her near noon, off the lee bow, and the helmsman veered toward her. The chase continued through the afternoon, northward up the coast of Brazil, and the cruiser kept astern of her all night long. By dawn the chase lay only a couple of miles ahead, and Semmes ordered the U.S. flag up the mizzenmast. The leading vessel responded with the same colors, and a blank round brought the *Rockingham* around.

Despite unsworn documents purporting neutral ownership of the cargo, Semmes condemned the vessel and everything aboard. Captain Edward Gerrish, of Portsmouth, had brought along his wife, their child, and the child's nurse, and the family descended to the wardroom while the twenty-man crew clustered amidships. After the prisoners had been transferred and all the useful stores had been taken, Semmes ordered exercise at general quarters. The drum beat and the gun crews raced to their stations, dropping the starboard ports. The two pivot guns cranked around to bear, and four of the thirty-twos ran out at the prize, which sat 500 yards away over calm water. Each gun fired twice with round shot, then twice each with shells. Fullam pronounced it "some excellent firing," but even at that relatively short range only seven of the two dozen rounds took effect: four in the hull and three in the rigging. Captain Semmes noted particularly that the fuses of his shells did not seem to explode satisfactorily.

Leaving the flaming *Rockingham* behind, the *Alabama* continued northward, passing four foreign sails in the next three days. At midafternoon of April 27 a small bark ran straight into range of the cruiser's guns, one of which thudded a dull demand for the bounding merchant vessel to heave to. The bark did so, and that was the end of her. She was the *Tycoon*, on her way from New York to San Francisco with a general cargo for the mining country. No papers even pretended that there might be neutral cargo aboard, and Fullam's boarding party rifled the hold for the benefit of nearly every department on the *Alabama*—including New York newspapers barely five weeks old, for the captain's consumption. The *Tycoon*'s master and his fifteen crewmen came aboard to join the score of men from the *Rockingham* in the waist, and at 3:00 A.M. on April 28 the torches ignited the last prize that Raphael Semmes would ever destroy.[18]

From the last two prizes, Captain Semmes realized two final recruits. Robert Longshaw, the first mate of the *Rockingham*, claimed to be a resident of Savannah and thus a Southern sympathizer. Dr. Galt signed him to the crew, but only at the rate of an ordinary seaman despite his exalted position aboard the guano transport. Meanwhile Edward Burrell, an Englishman from the *Tycoon*, volunteered at the full pay of an able seaman.[19]

The equator passed beneath the *Alabama*'s bows for the fourth and last time on May 2. The North Atlantic wrought a miraculous transformation on the spirits of the crew, for now they were headed home for certain. The lowering glances of November and December disappeared, and the checkerboards came out again among the off-watch. The bearded old mariner Brent Johnson—the deposed chief boatswain's mate who now wore the quartermaster's wheel on his sleeve—lounged on the forecastle once more with his needles and thread, embroidering clothing for his "chicken," a Liverpool cabin boy named Thomas Parker. In the evenings, the ship's storytellers returned to their yarns, spun to an audience squatting about the forecastle, or the fiddler and piper would bring out their instruments, and sometimes Captain Semmes would wander up to the bridge to listen. As they climbed into the north latitudes, anxious sailors who had never managed to leave two sovereigns touching in their pockets calculated their prize money from the fifty-five vessels they had captured and the ten that Semmes had ransomed.[20]

The wind fell calm at mid-ocean, and the pace slowed. During four days in the middle of May the ship averaged less than twenty-eight miles per day. To occupy the time, Semmes ordered up a few shells and had them fired. During target practice on the *Rockingham* he had noticed that most of his shells had not exploded, so he tried a few over the open water. Not one of them burst, so he directed Gunner Cuddy to replace the fuses in the entire arsenal of shells. With a pencil he scribbled the words "Bad Fuses" in large letters along the margin of his journal.

The few ships that appeared before the *Alabama* glided handily past her. A blank shot failed to stop one vessel that flashed British colors as it sped by, leaving Semmes to complain that "our bottom is in such a state that everything passes us. We are like a crippled hunter limping home from a long chase." The cruiser could stop only those sails that bore directly down on her, and those were all neutrals. When one of them announced a satisfactory destination, Semmes would seek passage for his prisoners, but he found no willing carrier.

On the eastern edge of the Sargasso Sea, southwest of the Azores, Semmes supposed that he had reached a crossroads for southbound American commerce, but—as though in testimony of the success of his cruise—no Yankee ships came his way. Even with all his studding sails set, he could not overtake a couple of strange sails on May 23, but he supposed they were foreign, anyway. The next day he ordered the wheel about to chase a schooner that slid close by, but the little vessel ignored a blank cartridge. Next the *Alabama* threw a shell at the schooner. The shell did not explode, but the chase eventually drew up and submitted to a visit. Finding it to have English registry despite the American rig, the boarding officer offered his apologies and returned to the cruiser.

Semmes noted that the decks leaked badly now when the sea stirred. Both fore and aft the bilges collected far more water than they usually saw, and foul weather stuck with the ship for most of the final week in May. In that week the *Alabama* skirted the northwestern fringe of the Azores, crossing the route of her first voyage, and the coast of England lay less than a fortnight's sail away. Semmes could wait no longer, though, and on the second day of June he asked the carpenter to have the deck caulked above his cabin.[21]

Other sails hove into sight more readily now, as the *Alabama* trudged toward the English Channel. At least fifteen vessels passed within view between June 4 and 9, and eleven more appeared on June 10. Of these Semmes stopped only seven, learning almost nothing except from one English brig that carried newspapers as recent as ten days old. The greatest news from those journals concerned the recent fighting in Virginia, which Semmes characteristically interpreted as evidence of a Federal defeat. The leaky cabin had evidently contributed to a cold that wracked the captain as his ship entered the channel, and his brow burned with a fever; perhaps that fever accounted for his belief that the vicious encounters in Virginia would end in favor of his new nation. He may not have digested the myriad evidence that the Confederacy had begun to crumble. With no word from his naval or political superiors for at least a year, perhaps he did not yet understand how low the tide had sunk.

On June 9, a couple of hundred miles from Brest, Semmes sent the topmen into the mizzen rigging to disguise the *Alabama*. The world over she was known as a bark, and some had warned that her mainsail had so long a drop that she looked like a barkentine; to further confound any roving Union frigates, Semmes ordered spare yards fashioned on the mizzen. Using parts taken from prizes, the crew rigged mainsail and topsail yards, adding topgallant yards by scavenging the *Alabama*'s own mainroyal yards. When the men came down, the cruiser had the appearance of a full-rigged ship, rather than a bark.

The engineers raised steam well before dawn the next morning. The weather thickened in the afternoon, as the cruiser slid by the tip of Brittany, and Semmes had just begun to worry about picking his way through the treacherous channel at night when a pilot boat came alongside. He welcomed the pilot aboard and kept him there until morning, easing all the while toward Cap de la Hague, which loomed on the horizon at 10:00 A.M. on June 11. At noon the weary vagabond lay off the fortified breakwater of Cherbourg harbor, the copper peeling off her mossy bottom and her wheezing boilers leaking from pinholes that freckled their tubing. Ominously, Semmes recorded his cruise as having come to "a successful conclusion."

On deck, no one thought of these things. The crew simply lined the starboard forecastle rail and gazed at the seventeenth-century facade of Quai Alexandre III, and the chalk bluffs that rose so precipitously beyond the city. Above Cherbourg, on a steep slope to the right, a quartermaster with a telescope might have been able to make out the old cemetery. Others might have turned away from the breakwater to look toward the invisible coast of England. For dozens of Mersey sailors such as George Appleby, Frederick Johns, and William Crawford, home lay barely 250 miles to the north. For Brent Johnson, it was right across the channel.[22]

CHAPTER EIGHTEEN

Reception

Many a sailor lad foresaw his doom,

Roll, *Alabama*, roll,

When the *Kearsarge* it hove in view,

Oh, roll, *Alabama*, roll.

—Old sea shanty

U nusually vicious March winds blew the *Kearsarge* all over the throat of the English Channel, forcing the warship to seek shelter under the lee of any headland that came into sight. The latest French proclamation prevented the sloop from lingering more than twenty-four hours in any neutral port, which rendered coaling nearly impossible. The twenty-four-hour law also prevented Winslow from posting himself off Calais to keep a close eye on the *Rappahannock*, so he hired a little steam tug called the *Annette* and put James Wheeler in charge of her, telling him to watch for the Confederate cruiser's departure, and to signal that event to the *Kearsarge*. Meanwhile, the *Kearsarge* plied about the treacherous Straits of Dover for a few days—much to the aggravation of the engine-room crew, which would answer a call for coal only to blow off steam a few minutes later when the officer of the deck sent down a two-bell signal to stop engines.

Finally the *Kearsarge* dropped anchor in the roadstead off Dover, within spyglass distance of the white cliffs, atop which the red coats of British soldiers wound their scarlet way to the chapel overlooking the channel. Morale aboard the ship had slumped appreciably, though perhaps not so badly as it had on the *Alabama*, but in March a dozen crewmen went into confinement for varying degrees of insubordination. John Dempsey, who had now worked his way back up to a berth as a quarter gunner, spent a week in irons for mutinous language and threatening an officer. To ease the monotony that bred such behavior, Winslow allowed a boatload of men to row ashore each day. Each evening, one or more of them failed to return. Even Quartermaster William Smith, one of the most dependable men on the ship, took a couple of extra days in Dover with the ship's cook and Boatswain's Mate William Bond, and when they finally did come back, they went straight into irons. None of them lost their rates as a result, unlike another boatswain's mate, Thomas Burns, who deserted to Dover rather than serve as a common sailor. Two recruits went with him.[1]

The strain of so long a cruise had even begun to wear on the officers, and harsh words passed between Captain Winslow and his chief engineer. Winslow reprimanded Mr. Cushman for not apprising him of trouble that had developed in the boilers, and the proud Cushman rankled, declining to take the blame. Perhaps Winslow's tantrum had less to do with the pending repairs than with the fright he endured that same day, when smoke began billowing from the coal bunkers. Coal heavers jumped into the suffocating bunker with shovels, overhauling twenty tons of coal before they found the source of the smoke: the last coaling had included a wet pocket that had begun to smolder from spontaneous combustion, or from the friction of particles grating against one another as the ship shifted.[2]

The stay at Dover brought frequent visitors, many of whom were British soldiers who entertained the sailors with stories of Her Majesty's service. Among the redcoats were Scotsmen from a Highland regiment, replete in their kilts, which drew a low whistle of sympathy from Coal Heaver William Wainwright, who shivered to see bare legs in such raw weather. One of the Highlanders had served nearly two decades, including thirteen years in India. He wore a glass eye and medals for the Persian campaign and the relief of Lucknow, and the *Kearsarge* men crowded around him to hear his tales. A photographer called on the ship March 24, snapping some pictures of the men at their battle stations, and the newspapers carried an advertisement of a special excursion to the *Kearsarge* three days later. The excursionists never saw the ship, though, for that day Winslow ordered the engine room to raise steam for a run across the channel.

Winslow wished to look in on the *Rappahannock* once before running up the Thames for repairs. As he stopped off Boulogne, he learned that the Confederate cruiser would not be allowed to leave anytime soon, and that it might even be impounded by the French government. That seemed good enough for him, and he turned the *Kearsarge* back to England. Wishing to make the return trip hastily, the duty officer ordered up the foretopmast staysail, but the brisk channel winds strained it so that the foretopmast snapped off at the lower masthead, bringing down yards and all. Deck hands climbed into the tangle of splinters and rigging, cutting everything away in less than two hours.[3]

After another brief stop at Dover, the *Kearsarge* steamed up the coast to the mouth of the Thames on March 30, dodging smaller craft that floated downriver in droves. After the noon meal the off-duty crewmen saw Gravesend, the starting point for many a famous English voyage, but dock officials would not let the warship land its powder there. Farther upriver at Woolwich, past the stunning stench of a glue factory, crewmen began unloading the powder at midafternoon. Early the next morning the anchor came up for the last short haul to Victoria docks, London.[4]

Captain Winslow showed either audacity or ignorance of current affairs by bringing the ship to a British dockyard. Through the winter the queen's solicitors had discussed the assorted legal infractions posed by the recruiting efforts of both the Confederate and the Union navies, and it was only the inaccessibility of the perpetrators that discouraged them from recommending charges. While it was surely a violation of the Foreign Enlistment Act for native-born British subjects to fight for either side, the defendants on the *Alabama* lay beyond the reach of prosecution, but when the *Kearsarge* docked in London, it offered an opportunity to address the Queenstown incident. A Dublin shipping agent asked the undersecretary to Ireland about arresting the ship's officers, but so drastic an action drew no interest in official circles. There was, however, the matter of Michael Ahern.

Ahern had been born and raised in Queenstown, where he supported himself as a writing clerk. He had been one of the recruits smuggled aboard in that port the previous November, enlisting as a landsman, but before the ship left Brest to return the "stowaways," he had found a niche as Paymaster Smith's steward, doubling as a second clerk. Ahern was the only one of the Queenstown men who did not return ashore in the pilot boat. Come February Daniel O'Connell, one of the returned men, peached on Ahern in an affidavit that O'Connell probably hoped would win the judge's mercy, for he and the other *Kearsarge* recruits were bound for court after the middle of March. Their trial proceeded on schedule in Cork on March 21, and testimony such as O'Connell's clearly implicated the Federal naval officers in the breach, but Attorney General Roundell Palmer advised only that Ahern should be arrested, and that only if he were found ashore. Palmer warned that going aboard the ship to seize him "would be (to say the least) inexpedient."

Captain Winslow did his best to cover up the Queenstown affair. The names of the men who were carried away from Ireland that night were never recorded in the ship's log, although they were duly shipped, uniformed, and put to work. When, months later, Winslow submitted a list of his crew that was doctored to exaggerate the preponderance of American natives who served the ship during its encounter with the *Alabama*, he left only one name—Ahern's—from that list. Yet the Irishman was certainly aboard, for six days after the battle Winslow specially commended a number of crewmen in a dispatch to Washington, among them "Michael Ahern, paymaster's steward," who later received a Medal of Honor for his conduct.[5]

Palmer's recommendation to arrest Ahern came the day after the *Kearsarge* left London, but Ahern probably kept to the ship just in case. The rest of the crew suffered no such anxiety, and at least the engineer department enjoyed liberty in the fabled city of London. Others "ran the blockade" past the Marine guard, dropping over the side and climbing the fence to find a grog shop near the docks. Those officers who remained aboard seemed not to notice.[6]

The men on duty saw the *Kearsarge* lifted out of the water by a cast-iron pontoon. Inspection showed the bottom in good condition, and the engineers managed to fix the boilers within a couple of days, but the more extensive work that Winslow had wanted could not be accomplished. The U.S. minister to London, Charles Adams, relayed the British government's dissatisfaction with the *Kearsarge*'s sudden appearance in the capital, arguing that time enough had not been allowed for an answer to Winslow's request. Observing that he had first inquired about repairs weeks before, Winslow nonetheless consented to leave. The ship dropped back into the water late in the afternoon of April 6, sooner than anyone expected, and word sped to the dockside bars, from which crewmen came running. They clambered aboard even as their ship backed away from its slot, but no one appeared to take notice of their transgression. Only one ordinary seaman, Martin Roach, failed to return: after nearly two years of service, the sudden departure may simply have caught him too full of ale.

That night the *Kearsarge* lay in the river, at anchor. Firemen lighted the boilers early the next morning and started downstream, but the steamer *Great Republic* backed into the river and blocked the sloop's way for several hours. With a stop to reload the magazines, the *Kearsarge* returned to Dover's roadstead before midnight. The British had also objected to Winslow's use of Dover as a base of operations, however, so he started for France the next day. The tender *Annette* towed a collier along in the wake of the *Kearsarge*, anchoring five miles off Boulogne, and there the crew spent fourteen hours shoveling a hundred tons of dusty Cardiff coal into the sloop's bunkers. The work finished late on the evening of April 9, by which time some of the *Kearsarge* sailors had succumbed to liquor brought aboard by small-time speculators on the collier.[7]

While the deck hands transferred the coal, Charles Fisher went ashore at Ambleteuse to look for provisions. Except for a local bakery he had little luck, finding that the inhabitants brought their food home in small quantities that they did not care to sell at a convenient price. He did meet a French woman with two pretty daughters, however, and the daughters made up for the lack of groceries. Intrigued by this black stranger, they asked, in French, where he had come from, and he obliged them with imaginative explanations in his best New Orleans patois. They followed him back to the boat, where Charles Danforth pumped him about the girls, but Fisher feigned ignorance, letting the master's mate wonder about them. Fisher confessed that he was "sorter smit" by the pair.[8]

Charles Poole had no better luck a few days later. As caterer of his mess he roamed the waterfront in search of meat, but there was none to be found. He, too, saw women with baskets wandering to the beach for shells, and perhaps shellfish, but no such native encounter lifted his spirits, as it had for Fisher. Poole was growing dreadfully homesick nowadays, though his nature did not lead him to misbehave in the manner of so many others in the crew, whose increasing dissatisfaction drew official notice in the log. A court-martial disrated a couple of seamen on April 14, and the next day the officers again sent their cook ashore to increase their larder, this time landing him nearer Boulogne with a couple of seamen. All three took the opportunity to remain overnight without permission, though the distant booming of the *Kearsarge*'s gunnery practice reminded them of their duty. The ship weighed anchor and left Ambleteuse Roads the following morning, and the three might have been left for good, like Martin Roach, but someone saw their boat pulling from shore even as the propeller began to turn. Stopping the engines long enough for the laggards to come alongside, the officer of the deck promptly locked irons on all of them and lodged them forward for five days of bread and water.[9]

Early the next day the *Kearsarge* appeared off Ostend, Belgium, which had enacted no prohibitive proclamations against American vessels. A pilot came aboard to lead the ship between the two piers that marked the narrow inlet, and, once inside, the channel grew even tighter. A footbridge over a canal ran right alongside the ship's route, but the pilot seemed perfectly confident. He called for eight knots, and the incredulous engine crew gave him that much, but two minutes after passing the piers the ship fouled a fishing sloop, carrying away her two topmasts. Backing out of that tangle, the pilot ordered forward speed again only to run aground where the footbridge made a dogleg, knocking out fifty feet of the bridge, shearing off the *Kearsarge*'s head gear, and running the bow aground on the rocks.

A disgusted Eben Stoddard, who had just taken over the deck when the accident occurred, ordered the engines back again to no avail. The tide had started to run out, dropping the ship's stern so the deck sloped sharply backward, and Stoddard had to run chains from the masthead to a nearby pier to prevent the ship from rolling over on her beam ends. There was no sense trying to pull away with the tide out, so Stoddard started shifting weight away from the bows. All day the crew strained to move spare chains aft or lighter it away, and they took one anchor ashore, rowing the other into the river and sinking it while spectators gawked from shore. The tide started back in during the afternoon, and shortly after the evening watch every hand went to the capstan.

Winslow gave the word to sing—a practice common enough in the merchant service, but not allowed on a man-of-war. Jimmy Haley and Quartermaster Saunders led the shanties, and for twenty minutes their fellows strained to "Santa Ana fought his way," and "Haul away my Rosey" while the engine raced at sixty revolutions in reverse. That failed to do the trick, so Ezra Bartlett called the men aft, to see if their weight might raise the bows enough. That did not work, either, so it was back to the capstan. A little after 10:00 that night the bow finally dragged off the rocks, but the embarrassed pilot refused to guide the ship farther. A North Sea pilot therefore came aboard, and well before midnight the ship tied to the wharf at Ostend, a thousand yards from the site of the mishap.[10]

Here the *Kearsarge* underwent some spring cleaning. After satisfying himself that the bow had sprung no leaks from its brutal introduction to Belgium, Captain Winslow took the train for Brussels with Paymaster Smith and Surgeon Browne while the crew scrubbed hammocks and painted the ship. In the captain's absence, Charles Poole and a few others painted the cabin for him. Visitors came, as usual, including one couple from Winslow's native North Carolina. George Catlin, the painter of the American West, stopped by on April 20—looking rather shabby, according to William Wainwright. The usual miscreants brought themselves trouble with their fondness for liquor, and before the ship left Ostend, Quartermaster Saunders also found himself in irons. One man engaged in a fight with a local fisherman, returning to the ship with a black eye, and the police followed him. Those who earned no liberty and could not sneak away turned to singing sea shanties on the forecastle at night, their taste apparently whetted by their bout on the rocks.[11]

From an agent in Calais, Winslow learned by telegraph on April 22 that the *Rappahannock* was taking on coal and provisions, evidently in an effort to run for it. The captain wired Lieutenant Thornton to back the ship into the river while he, Paymaster Smith, and Surgeon Browne raced back from Brussels, and an hour after midnight the engine-room watch was awakened to get steam up. Thornton took the ship out three miles from the piers, and the next morning Winslow returned. Early that afternoon the *Kearsarge* stood for the Straits of Dover, reaching Calais at 8:00 P.M., but there sat the *Rappahannock*, as bulky and idle as ever. Winslow blamed the false alarm on the agents, whom he suspected of giving faulty information because there was no accurate news to transmit.[12]

Winslow had allowed the *Annette*'s charter to expire, since he believed the *Rappahannock* had been seized, but even now he doubted whether it should be hired again. The tender had done little but transport the mail, he told the London consul, and when that steamer pulled alongside that night, Winslow recalled Mr. Wheeler from her.

For three days the *Kearsarge* stood off Calais, waiting and watching. At night the deck watch kept their revolvers and cutlasses strapped on, in case the Confederates sent out a boarding party. By day, details descended into the bilges to pump them clear, clean them, and apply some whitewash in an effort to kill the moldy smell that pervaded the hold after collecting the ship's leakage for nearly twenty-seven months. At last Winslow turned back to Dover, where he picked up newspapers and communicated with the consul. He had asked the London consulate for eight or ten recruits, if they could be spirited out to the ship without trouble, but no recruits met him at the white cliffs.

The newspapers offered information that seemed more important than anything the paid agents had forwarded. Reports of the *Alabama*'s March stopover at Cape Town had finally reached England; she was said to be bound for the English Channel, too, while the *Florida* was reported at Madeira. Adding that news to his suspicion that the *Georgia* and the *Rappahannock* lingered deliberately in Europe, Winslow recalled the earlier rumors that Confederate cruisers aimed to attack his ship in concert. In fact the *Florida* anchored at Martinique the very day that Winslow recorded his suspicions, and the *Georgia* was starting from Bordeaux for Liverpool, where she would be sold to an English businessman. The *Rappahannock* lay alternately in the water and on the mud of Calais, depending on the tide, and her commander lacked both crewmen and armaments. Of the four fabled cruisers, therefore, only the *Alabama* followed the route Winslow had predicted. Within a week the papers would relieve him of anticipation over a combined attack, incorrectly reporting the *Florida* at Havana. More accurate rumors spoke of the *Georgia* in Liverpool as early as May 3, the day after its arrival there.[13]

This same shipment of papers carried news of special significance to Charles Fisher and the other black sailors on the *Kearsarge*. Just out of irons for his sally ashore and still griping over the lack of letters from his family, Fisher read of the slaughter of black soldiers at Fort Pillow, Tennessee, by Confederate cavalrymen who overran that earthwork overlooking the Mississippi. This was a place Fisher knew, for as a steward on the steamer *Fannie Bullitt* he had helped to carry Confederate guns to the bluffs that became Fort Pillow. Though doubtless outraged at the reports of Colored Troops murdered after they surrendered, Fisher seemed unsurprised; it was pride that showed most in his diary, for he had never supposed that men of his color would garrison such a place.[14]

By May 4 Captain Winslow felt safe enough to sail for Holland, where carpenters might have a look at the *Kearsarge*'s scraped forefoot without all the international complications that he would face in England or France. The next day the sloop dropped anchor in the Westerschelde, off Flushing, where the navy yard allowed Winslow to deposit his powder. Eben Stoddard again had the deck on May 6 when, just after noon, he ordered up the port anchor and started in for the inner harbor. The pilot ran the ship perilously close to the pier, striking a piling and running the *Kearsarge* aground again. A strong tide spun the stern around and impeded the rescue, but within a few minutes a fuming Stoddard, his chinstrap beard working madly, had succeeded in hauling a hawser behind the ship and towing her out of the mud. That was enough for one day, though, and Stoddard brought the ship back to the outer harbor, where she waited for the tide to return. The next morning he had no better luck, grounding half an hour into the harbor. All hands worked the windlass well into Ezra Bartlett's watch before the sloop slid free, and 3:00 had come before the ship tied up at the drydock.[15]

Cooperative officials and mechanics found the *Kearsarge*'s hull damaged only to the extent that fifty-one sheets of copper had been peeled off. The repairs required almost none of the crew, most of whom took liberty either with or without permission. The dock lay in the center of the town, and the ship's bowsprit shaded one of the streets, so the Marines found it almost impossible to keep anyone aboard. A plank thrown down for easy passage remained undisturbed all day, and even Charles Poole took an unauthorized holiday in the quaint little city.

The stone and brick buildings were undergoing their weekly scrubbing that first Saturday in May. Women cleaned not only their windows but their doorsteps, and even the sidewalks; Poole found it hard to escape a ducking, so freely did the soap and water flow. The next day he walked all the way to Middleburg, four miles away, taking in the tulip fields that lined the road most of the way. Poole returned to the ship each night for his meal, for he had expended all his own funds, but others stayed in Flushing. William Wainwright discovered barely a dozen men on the ship when he returned from a Sunday jaunt, so he turned back for town. George Williams, the cook they called "Ham Fat," found himself the only one in his mess at dinner, so he fried up the squad's entire beef ration and ate it all.

Dutch visitors crowded the ship in the crew's absence. They found a few sailors aboard who were willing to entertain them, and James Lee played hide-and-seek with a group of children that Sunday afternoon. Benjamin Button, the Guamanian coal heaver, ran about riotously drunk, chasing everyone with a bag as though he considered them wild game for the pot— an illusion that his Micronesian features may have enhanced. Captain Winslow had departed to visit Antwerp, and most of the officers seem to have followed him. Anarchy reigned.

All that ended May 10, when Winslow returned, finding thirty-five men absent besides those on liberty. He asked the police to bring his wayward children back, and that afternoon local constables presented him with six of them; sixteen more lay in the jail, they said, and might be retrieved later. As soon as the police turned the men over, they ambled forward, dropping right off the bowsprit again and starting back to town, but Winslow reacted by locking them up. The crew's clown, William Gowin, lay in irons in the bowels of the ship—along with the perennial tippler William Fisher; the carpenter's mate, Mark Ham; a couple of the Marines; and Benedict Drury. The Irish rowdy, John Dempsey, sat among those in the Flushing jail, all of whom came back aboard, under guard, the next morning. Only one of the recruits failed to turn up before the *Kearsarge* sailed, and Winslow replaced him with a Dutchman who signed the roll the day after they left port.[16]

The pleasant sojourn at Flushing left some of the crew even more discontented when they left than they had been before. Charles Poole observed that it seemed more difficult to pass time now: games gotten up on a whim died of disinterest, and reading became a bore, even with the addition of volumes bought in England a few weeks before. The common activity now may have been argument, as the repressed energy of so many young men turned to combativeness, and disputes over politics and the war effort waxed warm.[17]

Even the old man of the officers, David Sumner, showed some temper. The *Kearsarge* hastened back from Dover to look in on the *Rappahannock* the night of May 21, for that ship was reportedly planning her departure that evening, and on the crossing a stiff wind split the foretopsail. Sumner clewed up the fore- and maintopsails, evidently believing the wind too strong, and apparently Captain Winslow ordered him to unfurl the sails for greater speed, perhaps sending the message through Lieutenant Thornton. Sumner objected, and for the first time since the cruise began the captain suspended an officer of the deck, sent him below, and reported him to the Navy Department for refusal to perform his duty. Sumner went to his stateroom, where he remained for the next twenty-six days; the officers' cook heard that Sumner intended to resign, and that a sympathetic Wheeler might follow him. Indeed, both Sumner and Wheeler asked for a leave of absence.[18]

The *Kearsarge* came under surreptitious Confederate inspection during that long weekend's observation of the *Rappahannock*. Two Southern lieutenants from that beached cruiser, a master's mate, the ship's gunner, and the captain's clerk all donned civilian clothing and borrowed a fishing smack for a Sunday jaunt around the Federal sloop. They claimed to find the freshly scrubbed enemy vessel in a grimy condition, which they probably hoped was a sign of declining morale in the Union crew, but the daring officers seemed not to notice the bulging deal veneer over the chaincladding amidships. That same day the paymaster of the *Rappahannock* encountered the *Kearsarge*'s "dog of a Captain" as he ambled ashore with Midshipman Preble and the American vice-consul—who, the Southerner recalled, had once drunk to the health of the Confederacy.

The visit ashore produced papers carrying news from home, which spoke of vicious fighting in Virginia. Aboard the *Kearsarge* they interpreted that as a sign of impending victory, for it appeared the Federal army was driving Robert E. Lee back on his capital, as it was. The officers of the *Rappahannock* had undoubtedly paid more attention to the repulse of Nathaniel Banks's army from the border of Texas. They may have taken garbled early reports from Virginia as evidence of Confederate victory, or as proof that Lee could still stave off an overwhelming enemy, and on May 23 the tidebound cruiser raised a huge Confederate flag to its masthead, supported by numerous fluttering pennants. The *Kearsarge* replied the next day with Federal equivalents, and with the English flag at the foremast, in honor of Queen Victoria's birthday.[19]

Three days later Winslow heard from the Dover consul that the *Rappahannock* was taking her coal out again. No one could say why, but the information could only mean another delay for the unlucky Southern ship, so Winslow determined to go back to Flushing for the engine repairs he had tried to make in London. Leaving his destination with the consular agent at Calais, he turned the *Kearsarge* back up the straits and arrived at Flushing on the morning of May 31, to the great delight of his crew.

The officers fled the ship again, save for some token supervisors of the watch. In place of the suspended Sumner, the captain left Franklin Graham in command of the deck. This was the old gunner's first experience as watch officer, and he accepted it, one would expect, with an eye to the promotion it might entail, for it was seldom that a warrant officer earned a chance for a line commission.

While the officers frolicked, for the first three days it was nothing but work for deck hands and engineer department alike. Coal heavers and firemen scrubbed the flues, replaced corroded tubing in the boilers, and painted the engines and ash pits, while topside the sailors scraped the spars and tied in new rigging. Then, on Sunday, the captain granted liberty, and some of the lucky ones scampered ashore to the town they seem to have favored over all others. Charles Poole, who had often gone for months without leaving the ship, expressed uncommon gratitude at the chance to set foot on "Mother Earth" again, barely three weeks after his last jaunt ashore. William Gowin and a number of others who had misbehaved during the last stopover here also won permission to go ashore again, but Gowin had not learned his lesson; he stayed on shore overnight this time, too, and wound up in irons once more. The captain proved more sympathetic now, though, and instead of keeping him there a week he released the jovial seaman after only two days. Half a dozen others failed to return at the end of their liberty, and a couple of Netherlands natives who had shipped at Cadiz in February abandoned the ship altogether.

Unlike some of the crew, Poole returned to work Monday morning. When they finished painting on June 11, he remarked that they must have had the sharpest-looking engine room in the U.S. Navy. Poole felt somewhat more satisfied, but painting the engines did not strike him as an especially productive service for his country. More than anything else, he and his shipmates just wanted to go home. At night the strains of "Home, Sweet Home" on a concertina only made the ennui and the separation seem worse.[20]

Fiddles and accordions were squawking on the forecastle Sunday afternoon, June 12, when a messenger came aboard with a telegram for Captain Winslow from William Dayton, the U.S. minister to Paris. Winslow read it, ordered a gun fired to bring back the liberty men, and called for steam from the engine room. When the last man returned from shore, the *Kearsarge* started up the river, turned around, and headed for sea. Civilians lined the shore to wave goodbye, most of them probably as ignorant as the American sailors of the cause of their sudden departure.

Winslow satisfied their curiosity as they put to sea. The boatswain's whistle called them to muster, and when all but the duty watch had assembled on the quarterdeck, Winslow revealed the contents of the telegram. The *Alabama*, he said, had arrived in Cherbourg harbor, and the *Kearsarge* was ordered to stand off that port to wait for her. With that, he ordered Boatswain Walton to pipe the men down.

These men were not about to pipe down, however. They seemed to go wild, cavorting on the hatches and the aft pivot gun. At last—and inevitably, given the habits of that day—one of the boatswain's mates invited three cheers for the *Kearsarge*, and then three for Captain Winslow. Why the news should have affected them so does not seem clear. For months had they lain on the hated coast of Spain, watching the decrepit *Sumter* only to lose it in the end. The *Florida* had likewise given them the slip, after a long, unpleasant stay at Brest. The *Georgia* had escaped from this same port of Cherbourg. Before, some had greeted word of a nearby Confederate glumly, predicting the monotony and misery of the long vigil that would follow, and the presence of the *Alabama* guaranteed no opportunity for excitement. But this was the cruiser that Federal sailors coveted above all others, and no Union officer had yet put a spyglass on her, let alone come within broadside range. For the chance to see this ship, and perhaps have a crack at her, the bored and homesick crew might have given a great deal.[21]

Anchoring in Dover Roads the next morning, Winslow sent ashore for the ship's mail, and for the trysail and topsail he had ordered to replace those destroyed by channel gusts. He reported to the Navy Department through the consul, and telegraphed to Gibraltar for the old *St. Louis* to come up with some extra supplies and help keep watch over Cherbourg's two entrances, meanwhile ordering Master's Mate Yeaton to return from Cadiz with that ship. He also discharged the channel pilot he had just taken on. The pilot had been indiscreet enough to joke that he would not care to stand aboard the *Kearsarge* if it engaged the *Alabama*.

That night the black sloop slid away from Dover and sailed to the southwest, crossing the Greenwich meridian near midnight. By dawn the Cotentin Peninsula rose on the horizon, burnished a bright amber by the sun that rose behind the *Kearsarge*, and at 10:00 the helmsman turned for the long, fortified breakwater. At a distance off the eastern inlet Winslow called for the engines to shut down, and he readied a boat for shore. The crew clustered on the forecastle, leaning over the port rail, as the quartermasters passed their telescopes around. Beyond the breakwater, in Cherbourg's Grande Rade, lay what seemed to William Wainwright "a very fine looking ship," for at that distance her weaknesses went undetected. Tiny figures crawled her rigging, taking down the mizzen spars that had disguised the notorious bark as a full-rigged ship. A hundred men or more lined the port bow of the Yankee warship, straining their eyes or waiting for one of the glasses. From the deck of the *Alabama*, Confederate officers returned their stare.[22]

CHAPTER NINETEEN

Rendezvous

No more to rise for ever.
—Melville, *Moby Dick*

After the exchange of some telegrams between Cherbourg and Paris, thirty-eight paroled prisoners left the *Alabama* the night of Saturday, June 11—among them the captains of the *Tycoon* and the *Rockingham*, who carried news to the American consul of the poor target practice on the latter vessel. The next day Captain Semmes sent a request ashore for repairs to his hull and boilers in the Cherbourg dockyard, but Admiral Augustin Dupouy, the newly installed naval prefect at Cherbourg, also passed this request along to the marine minister in Paris. When Semmes came ashore to visit him on the morning of June 13, Dupouy pointed out that the Cherbourg docks all belonged to the French government, and he dared not issue authority for their use by a belligerent warship. The admiral implied that France had grown sensitive to all the Confederate warships that flocked to havens on her coast, and that Semmes might not find the government overly cordial. While Semmes awaited an answer from Paris, he passed the time composing a letter of explanation to an increasingly unsympathetic London *Times*, which had questioned his practice of burning his prizes. Meanwhile, Semmes and his officers feasted on fresh strawberries, mutton, and milk.

Semmes intended to put his ship in drydock for a couple of months and give his crew leave to go ashore until the repairs were completed. That probably meant they would desert for home with their pay, but he may have counted that little loss, for the men had grown so surly that they could offer little more good service anyway. If they deserted, it would diminish the navy's obligation to pay prize money. The *Alabama*'s officers needed rest, too, or replacement, and Semmes intended to ask for someone to take his own place. At fifty-four he was too old for much more service at sea; the chills and fever that had plagued him as they entered the English Channel continued to assail him.

A vessel from Dover brought word that the *Kearsarge* would come to pay a call within a day or two, and Semmes began to wonder about the repairs. If permission were refused, he would have to flee, and the condition of the *Alabama*'s bottom precluded escape from any steamer with moderate speed. Instead of sending his crew ashore, therefore, he called for general quarters and turned his men to practice at the guns, running unloaded muzzles out at the breakwater and the waterfront buildings.[1]

When the black sloop appeared off the eastern inlet, just before noon on June 14, Semmes decided to fight. Years later Lieutenant Kell remembered his captain calling him down to the cabin for a conference, in which he outlined their unenviable position if the French turned them away: a small fleet of Yankee ships would blockade the *Alabama*, probably for the rest of the war. It might be better to fight the single enemy, inflicting at least a little damage on her, and perhaps sinking her, instead of waiting to be bottled up. Kell said that he agreed, despite the Navy Department's instructions to avoid engagements with Union cruisers.

Such reasoning indicated that Semmes did not enjoy his usual familiarity with the disposition of enemy ships, for the next nearest U.S. man-of-war, the old *St. Louis*, lay at distant Gibraltar. Whether his real motive lay in logic, instinctive aggressiveness, or a reluctance to avoid what might be his last opportunity for a stand-up fight after destroying so many unarmed craft, Semmes decided to engage the *Kearsarge*. He ordered coal from shore, but a hopeful Admiral Dupouy asked if that meant the request for repairs was withdrawn—for both could not be allowed. Semmes conceded, though perhaps he had hoped to return to the dockyard after the fight, and from that point the die was cast. It would have been all the same, however, had Semmes taken the safer course and waited, for the next day the French marine minister wrote to Admiral Dupouy that the Confederate raider could not be accommodated in a French yard.[2]

Semmes likewise appears to have remained ignorant of the *Kearsarge*'s chain armor. Lieutenant Sinclair asserted in his memoirs that the port admiral told Semmes about it, though he did not explain how that information could have been conveyed; Dr. Galt reportedly admitted that the officers of the *Alabama* were all aware of it, despite their later denials; others suggested that the chaincladding should have been obvious. No contemporary source corroborates either of the first two stories, and the third suggestion wears thin in light of the close inspection of the *Kearsarge* performed on May 20 by a boatload of officers from the *Rappahannock*, who failed to detect the veneer of deal boards covering the chains.[3]

Perhaps the most preposterous story told to illustrate that Semmes knew of the *Kearsarge*'s chaincladding came from a British consular official who told the secretary of state in 1879 that Lieutenant Kell had gleaned the news from another Briton. Vice-Consul H. E. Huntington wrote that his friend, Sir John Burgoyne, was eating dinner at the Crown Hotel in Dover a few days before the battle when he was approached by "an agreeable stranger" who asked Burgoyne to tell him all about the U.S. warship sitting off Dover just then. Once the stranger had learned all the details of the *Kearsarge*'s armament and chain protection, he allegedly retreated with the announcement that he was "the First Lieutenant of the *Alabama*." For all of such obviously fabricated legends as that, though, the Yankee ship's chain armor does appear to have been an active rumor aboard the *Alabama*, or so recalled Semmes's clerk in a newspaper interview nearly half a century later. What is missing is any evidence that Semmes gave the rumor much credence.[4]

When a boat from the *Kearsarge* carried Captain Winslow ashore on the dark, dismal afternoon of June 14, Winslow learned of the *Alabama*'s prisoners and asked to take them aboard. Back on the *Alabama*, Raphael Semmes hoped that the French officials would not allow the Yankee to augment his crew that way, and he wrote a letter of protest on that point; he also hoped the Federal sloop would not sail away in disappointment. Having already surrendered his opportunity to repair and refit his ship, Semmes tantalized the *Kearsarge*'s captain with an old-fashioned challenge. He instructed the Confederacy's agent at Cherbourg to inform the American consul that he was prepared to duel with the Federal vessel on June 15, or June 16 at the latest. The next day that consul gleefully handed the message to Semmes's old friend and shipmate John Winslow, who rowed back to his ship with it. Recollecting Gideon Welles's admonition of the previous March, Winslow did not respond to the invitation.

Winslow ordered the decks cleared for action as soon as he stepped back aboard the *Kearsarge*. Loose materials that played no part in a battle were stowed below, and Ham Fat beat his drum to announce an exercise at repelling boarders. A French pilot who had come aboard just the previous day for night service misunderstood the great rush and ran aft as though for the gangway, knocking down sailors at every step. When that practice session ended, he demanded that Winslow call for his boat; he had had all he wanted of piloting a ship of war.

Well into the evening the crew practiced loading, running the guns out, and reloading. Surgeon Browne taught the gun crews how to apply the tourniquets he distributed to them; then he asked Lieutenant Thornton to have a space cleared away where he might treat the wounded. Their captain made his men a patriotic speech, if a rather stiff one, assuring them that Semmes was a worthy foe, and officers and men alike greeted the promised fight with the enthusiasm of the long-bored. They all wanted to go home, but most shared Ezra Bartlett's preference for seeing some action first.[5]

In token of his early determination to fight, Semmes took his treasury ashore, sending five bags of gold sovereigns worth nearly $25,000 to the Confederate agent at Cherbourg, a middle-aged man named Bonfils, leaving as well Paymaster Galt's records of the crewmen's accounts and the ransom bonds for all his unburned prizes. The *Alabama* started taking on coal the afternoon of June 15. The work continued all day June 16, even as visitors thronged the decks again. Several French and English yachts lay moored in the harbor, among them the *Hornet* (whose owner Semmes asked to transport the accumulated chronometers of his prizes), and the *Alabama* offered delightful diversion for the officers and owners of these pleasure craft. The week's cool, damp weather continued, with occasional rain, but from the crosstrees the lookout could still discern the *Kearsarge*, plying to and fro. Captain Winslow kept his ship under minimal steam, cruising slowly back and forth, swinging back into the channel sometimes for so long that land fell from sight. Hats in hand, some of his enlisted men came forward to beg him not to wander so far away from the breakwater, lest they lose their prey. Pleased with their spirit, he told them he would keep their caution in mind. He grew benevolent, even releasing Benedict Drury and the recalcitrant Marine John Batchelder, after thirty-two days in irons. No one had seen Acting Master David Sumner on deck since the affair during the storm of May 21, but he asked Winslow for permission to take part in the expected fight. When the midnight watch took over on June 16, Sumner had the deck.

On the evening of June 17 another steam yacht turned into the harbor and slid past the *Alabama*, anchoring a couple of hundred yards nearer shore. The next day a boat from this vessel came alongside to inquire if visitors were welcome, only to find that they were not, but from the gilt ribbons around the boat crewmen's hats the *Alabama* sailors learned that they were from the *Deerhound*. She had come in from the Isle of Jersey to pick up her owner, John Lancaster, who arrived with his family from St. Malo via Caen on the train late Saturday evening.

By dawn on Saturday, June 18, the seas had swollen noticeably, and the *Kearsarge* rolled heavily. Ashore at Cherbourg, William L. Dayton, Jr., approached Admiral Dupouy at the prefecture and asked for a pass to visit the Federal ship. Dayton, the son of the U.S. minister to Paris, carried a dispatch from his father to Captain Winslow. Dupouy had rebuffed Dayton the evening before, telling him to forget his fear that the *Alabama* would slip out that night, and this morning he exacted a guarantee that the young man would not remain to serve aboard the *Kearsarge*. Dayton promised to report to him when he returned, and with his pass he started for shore to hire a boat. Before the customs officers would allow him to leave they demanded that permit, and while he waited for passage out to the *Kearsarge*, he saw the gendarmes detain a couple of young men who wanted to go to the *Alabama*—evidently the two Prussian master's mates, who aborted their journey home when they heard of the impending combat. Midshipman William Sinclair and his father had also come out from Paris to join their country's most famous ship, but the police stopped them, allowing only the father to visit the cruiser briefly. The Prussians were finally allowed to board, since they had come into port with the vessel.[6]

The morning squall had apparently exhausted the clouds of the past week, for the sky had cleared when Dayton steamed out to the *Kearsarge*. He found her some eight or nine miles out, and at midafternoon he climbed aboard with his father's message. In that note, the minister cautioned Winslow against bringing his fight too close to the French shoreline: the old law of the three-mile limit was based on the limited range of eighteenth-century cannon, but the French foreign minister feared the effects of long rounds from the big pivots on the *Alabama* and the *Kearsarge*. Better to take their battle six or seven miles out in the channel, if possible, the senior Dayton wrote. Winslow asked the minister's son to go personally to Le Havre to ask the consul there for coal, machine oil, and some recruits. The youth left the *Kearsarge* at about five that afternoon, stopping in on the admiral as he had promised, and Dupouy mentioned that the *Alabama* would leave Cherbourg within twenty-four hours. Realizing the futility of his mission to Le Havre under those circumstances, Dayton checked into a local hotel.[7]

At 10:00 that night the Confederate agent, Bonfils, visited Semmes one final time. The captain observed that he would miss the next morning's mass, and he implored the agent to attend in his stead, asking prayers for the seamen who might go to their deaths. Bonfils, who had warned the Confederate minister at Paris of Semmes's intention to risk his ship in battle, and who still waited for instructions to stop him, nevertheless agreed to offer the mass for him.[8]

The morning of June 19 opened quite clear and warmer than any day that week, with a light breeze to assist the patient *Kearsarge* in prowling beyond the breakwater. A lookout on the French ironclad *Couronne* spotted the Yankee warship off the eastern entrance an hour before dawn, but, when the sun rose, the *Kearsarge* had disappeared into the channel again. At 5:45 the deck officer of that ironclad saw lights flickering aboard the *Alabama* as her crew came to life. Twenty-five minutes later sparks from her stack revealed that Miles Freeman had lighted fires under his boilers, and Captain Penhoat of the *Couronne* ordered his own fires started. The captain of the *Deerhound* also called for steam, for John Lancaster hoped to run out and observe the promised conflict. At 6:55 a boat from the *Couronne* pulled alongside the *Alabama* to explain the protocol: when Semmes started out to meet his adversary, the *Couronne* would escort him to the limits of territorial waters before turning back; anytime thereafter, the two ships might have it out.

Half an hour later the *Kearsarge* appeared again off the eastward passage, curving by on a westerly tack. She slunk to and fro, passing within view of the same entrance periodically, the masthead lookout peering toward the spot where he had last seen the *Alabama*. A light fog had settled rather late, but it failed to mask the seaward vessel from those at anchor.

By 7:50 the wheezing boilers on the *Alabama* had produced steam, and five minutes later the *Couronne*'s engineer announced that he, too, had raised sufficient pressure. The *Kearsarge* passed by again, outside the breakwater, but still the *Alabama*'s anchor lay on the bottom.[9]

William Dayton and the American consul at Cherbourg procured a telescope and hired a carriage to take them to Querqueville, a village four miles west of Cherbourg. The chapel of St. Germain, a 200-year-old stone building on the slope of a long hill behind Querqueville, overlooked both Cherbourg harbor and the English Channel beyond the breakwater, which obstructed the view from Cherbourg.

Other spectators began staking out their vantage points on the hill, and not only interested inhabitants: hundreds of tourists had come up from Paris. They had not come especially to see a naval duel, but to enjoy some beach weather, thanks to a new excursion route offered by France's Western Railroad Company. Starting that weekend, for a mere 16 francs (12 francs third class), Parisians seeking escape from their sweltering city might take an overnight train on Friday from Saint-Lazarre station and arrive at Cherbourg Saturday morning, returning Sunday early in the morning. With the news of imminent combat between the two American warships, many of the city's refugees let the train leave without them. From Querqueville, on the west, to Tourlaville, east of Cherbourg, beaver hats and parasols began to fringe all the higher elevations.[10]

After 9:00 the *Deerhound* got under way, just as the windlass began to squeal aboard the *Alabama*. Once the anchor had been secured, the creaking raider started to turn its bowsprit away from the waterfront and toward the sea. The *Deerhound* steamed in a wide counterclockwise circle around the famous cruiser before steering for the eastward entrance. From his perch on the hill above Querqueville, William Dayton evidently interpreted the

Deerhound's promenade around the *Alabama* as a form of communication between the two vessels. With the first churn of the *Alabama*'s propeller, at precisely 9:30, the *Couronne* prepared to get under way, but, once the bark had turned about, it lay still for a few minutes. Finally, at 9:45, the *Alabama* started forward from its anchorage before the navy yard, and the *Couronne* followed.[11]

In his pew at St. Clement's church on Rue du Val de Saire, Monsieur Bonfils listened to the service he had requested for the departing Confederates as they steamed toward the western passage. At 10:00, just as the bells of St. Trinity's basilica tolled the hour along the Cherbourg waterfront, the *Alabama* rounded the little battery at the western end of the breakwater, and the lookout sighted the *Kearsarge*, several miles off. The *Deerhound* hesitated, as though uncertain whether the spectacle might be too dangerous, until the *Alabama* surged past.

Aboard the *Kearsarge*, Captain Winslow had called his men to quarters for their Sunday inspection. The man at the masthead cried that he could see a steamer coming out, accompanied by an ironclad; she looked like the *Alabama*, he offered. Within a few moments an officer confirmed the suspicion, adding that a smaller bark bearing British colors—the *Deerhound*—had also emerged from behind the breakwater.

Captain Winslow called for the drum, which brought every man to his quarters. He turned the *Kearsarge* about and headed her deeper into the channel, to draw his opponent the desired distance away from French soil. To some of his crewmen it seemed as though they were running away.[12]

Raphael Semmes called his crew aft, to the quarterdeck, where he climbed atop a gun carriage and waved them to gather around him. Some of the original Liverpool crew had seen his other speech off Faial, but for those who had joined from the prizes and for the recruits of Cape Town and Singapore it was a new event to see Old Beeswax gamboling about so informally. Speaking to the British blood that flowed in most of their veins, he reminded them of their common heritage and the history of English victories in the channel. He invoked the memory of the *Hatteras*, and struck at their sympathy for a struggling young nation that fought against odds. Every man listened intently. Both old sailors as experienced as Brent Johnson, Michael Mars, George Appleby, and Frank Townsend, and youths as young as Frederick Johns, who should have stayed in a clerkship ashore, may have thought of the tales they would carry home in a few days or weeks. Russell Hobbs, the Delaware volunteer, perhaps hoped to win back his quartermaster's rate. Robert Longshaw and Edward Burrell, who had shipped from prizes within the last fifty days, may have entertained some last-minute regrets. David, the Delaware slave, could rightly have seen the *Kearsarge* as his best hope of freedom, though he had experienced the same limited measure of liberty as his shipmates during the past twenty months. Winding up his address, Semmes asked if they would let the *Alabama*'s good name go down in defeat, to which they responded with a resounding cheer of defiance, and the captain looked approvingly over their sun-darkened faces. "Go to your quarters," he said, ending it there.[13]

The *Couronne* stopped at the edge of international waters, but the *Deerhound* continued on at a distance from the *Alabama*. The *Kearsarge* ceased its run at six or seven miles from shore and turned about at 10:30, as the captain of the *Couronne* marked it (or 10:50, by Captain Winslow's faster watch). Lieutenant Thornton called ominously for sand on the gun deck and the forecastle, lest the battle's blood render them too slippery to maneuver, and the officers all shook each other's hands before taking position at their pieces. As the helmsman sheered slightly to port to avoid raking fire, his mates all stood to their battle stations, the gun ports down and the lanyards ready.[14]

With eight guns altogether, the *Alabama* carried one more than the *Kearsarge*, but both ships would present six muzzles in this action. On the *Alabama*, hands slid one of the thirty-twos from the port battery to an empty port on the starboard side, while the *Kearsarge*'s crew did the same. Captain Winslow tried to shift a second 32-pounder, but it could not be manned without obstructing the operations of other guns. With his 28-pounder rifle on the forecastle—not counting the little 12-pounder boat howitzer, with which Henry Cook and Quartermaster Charles Butts stood ready to throw canister at short range—Winslow matched the Confederate at least in numbers of weapons, and exceeded her in the weight of metal he could throw; still, the *Alabama* had that long-range Blakely rifle at the forward pivot. The wise course for Semmes would have been to keep his distance and use that piece exclusively, but he ran toward the *Kearsarge* until, at some 1,200 yards, he veered to port and let his first volley fly.

All six rounds passed high over the deck of the *Kearsarge*, doing no damage except to the rigging. The gunners reloaded and fired another volley that did little more harm, and a third volley flew high, as well. At that, Winslow directed his ship to turn to the port and delivered his first broadside. Less than a thousand yards apart, the two antagonists began circling in a clockwise rotation, firing constantly. The *Alabama*'s gun crews raced to reload each time, averaging one round a minute per gun, but the Yankee gunners paced themselves more carefully, reaching less than half that rate of fire.[15]

Each ship poured its greatest fire into the stern of the other. Early in the fight a shot from the *Kearsarge* struck the *Alabama*'s spanker gaff, bringing down both that spar and the Confederate colors, but Semmes ordered

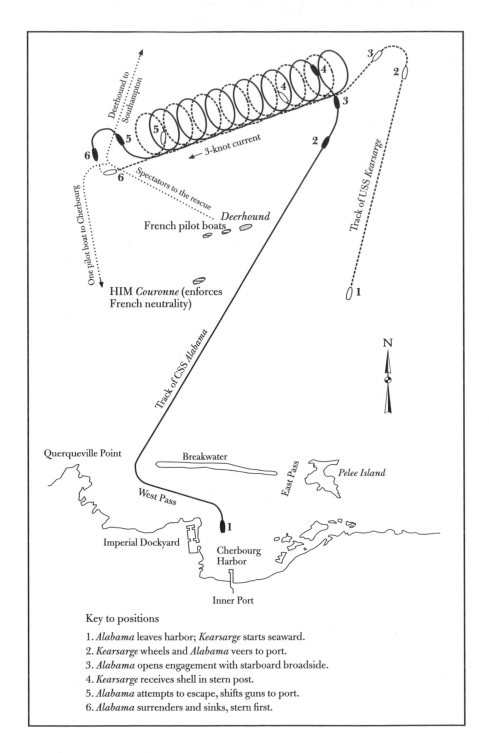

Map 3. Battle between the *Alabama* and the *Kearsarge*, June 19, 1864

Within the map:

Deerhound to Southampton

3-knot current

Spectators to the rescue

Track of USS *Kearsarge*

One pilot boat to Cherbourg

Deerhound

French pilot boats

HIM *Couronne* (enforces French neutrality)

Track of CSS *Alabama*

N

Querqueville Point

Breakwater

East Pass

Pelee Island

West Pass

Imperial Dockyard

Cherbourg Harbor

Inner Port

Key to positions

1. *Alabama* leaves harbor; *Kearsarge* starts seaward.
2. *Kearsarge* wheels and *Alabama* veers to port.
3. *Alabama* opens engagement with starboard broadside.
4. *Kearsarge* receives shell in stern post.
5. *Alabama* attempts to escape, shifts guns to port.
6. *Alabama* surrenders and sinks, stern first.

another flag up to the head of the mizzenmast before the *Kearsarge* even slackened its fire. At about the same time, a shell from the *Alabama*'s hundred-pounder rifle plowed into the sternpost of the *Kearsarge*, jarring the ship mightily, but the huge projectile lay there, smoldering harmlessly without the explosion that might have ended the battle—as well as ending the career of the pride of Portsmouth. At the helm, Quartermaster William Poole retained control of the ship, but the shell had bound the rudder so tightly that he needed three other men to help turn the wheel. After the fray this shell would be cut from the sloop's sternpost and sent to Washington as a curiosity. "It was the only trophy they ever got of the Alabama!" boasted Semmes.

Working his gun on the quarterdeck of the *Kearsarge*, Ship's Barber Martin Hoyt observed that he was the subject of a few close shaves himself, as most of the *Alabama*'s rounds seemed to veer his way. Mr. Sumner took pride in the men of his division, who worked these aft guns, and especially Joachim Pease, the black seaman who served as loader of his Number 1 gun: "One of the best men in the ship," Sumner called him.

A few moments later a shell from the *Alabama*'s aft pivot smashed through the oak bulwarks and exploded as it whirled past the corresponding pivot gun on the *Kearsarge*. When the smoke cleared, three of the gun crew lay bleeding on the sandy deck. William Gowin, the ship's jester, saw the bones of his left leg protruding, both above and below the knee, but he declined assistance and tried to drag himself toward the forward companionway. The Boston rowdy John Dempsey had been struck by big steel shards in the right arm, which hung in unrecognizable shreds below the tattoo on his bicep. James MacBeth, one of the Cadiz recruits of the previous winter, suffered from a painful compound fracture of the left shin, but his wound was the least serious. Surgeon Browne started working on Gowin, whose voluminous bleeding threatened to drain his life away; when he had finished binding up the Michigan minstrel, Browne turned to Dempsey, instinctively opening the lid to his box of knives and saws.[16]

Those two rounds from the pivot guns yielded the only good luck the *Alabama* saw that day. Most of the Confederate iron either missed its target entirely or embedded itself in the chain cables hung from the side of the Federal ship, of which Captain Semmes apparently still remained unconvinced. Either the powder or the fuses in his shells failed to ignite more often than not, recalling Semmes's journal entry about the fuses. He complained later that he lost the battle through defects in his ammunition, "which had been two years on board," but the ammunition of the *Kearsarge* had been at sea even longer. Puzzled that his shells wrought little damage, Semmes threw only solid shot for a time, then switched back to shell when that also failed to show any effects; Lieutenant Sinclair insisted that Semmes fired solid shot to pierce the rumored armoring. The real problem seems to have been poor marksmanship, for most of the *Alabama*'s rounds flew too high, despite Semmes's admonition to aim low.

Meanwhile, a single shell from one of the 11-inch Dahlgren guns leveled nearly the entire crew of the *Alabama*'s aft pivot—the 8-inch gun—killing several men and mangling more; Lieutenant Kell transferred Lieutenant Armstrong's crew from a 32-pounder to the shorthanded pivot. Another shell exploded in the *Alabama*'s bulging coal bunkers, interfering with the operation of the ship's weakened boilers. Now the long, boring practice sessions aboard the *Kearsarge* began to pay dividends.

Liverpool newspapers carried thrilling (and almost certainly exaggerated) reports of the action from the deck of the *Alabama*. According to one, an 11-inch shell broke through the bulwarks and struck something solid enough to stop its forward progress, after which it careened about the gun deck until Michael Mars and Frank Townsend pounced upon the sizzling projectile and wrestled it overboard. The home-port journals revealed that the wounded aboard the *Alabama* showed as much grit as William Gowin had, a thousand yards across the water: one petty officer (apparently misidentified by the *European Times* as Coxswain William McGinley) was said to have simply taken out his knife and sliced the thread of skin from which hung the mutilated wreckage of his arm before helping to run his gun back into place. Others ignored their wounds and kept to their guns, at least one man reportedly serving his piece and refusing to recognize his wounds until he dropped dead.[17]

The Confederate gunners' accuracy deteriorated early in the engagement, although—or perhaps because—they continued to load and fire madly. Of some 370 rounds that they had fired, only a dozen took effect in the hull of the *Kearsarge*, while ten more clipped away pieces of Yankee rigging. Taking more careful aim, the Union sailors riddled the *Alabama*. Only the Marines, fully exposed to enemy view at their post on the forecastle rifle, betrayed a nervous tendency to work quickly. They fired off forty-eight rounds in an hour, and after one shot Roscoe Dolley tried to unbend a kink in the outhaul rope, so it would not bind in the tackle when the gun discharged again. The gunner yanked his lanyard before Dolley could step back, and the loop tightened about his wrist when the gun recoiled, spraining his elbow. It would not begin to hurt until he stopped moving, though, so he stayed in his place as second sponger of the rifle.[18]

The tandem corkscrew courses of the dueling vessels carried them diagonally toward the waters off Querqueville, where stood the ancient chapel of St. Germain and hundreds of fascinated tourists. There young William

Dayton and the Cherbourg consul watched, and there waited Cherbourg photographer François Rondin, with his apparatus poised to capture an image of the two combatants. When the spiraling battle reached a point only five miles away, Rondin snapped the shutter.[19]

By now, forty-five minutes into the contest, water began pouring into the *Alabama* through the ragged pockmarks in her starboard planking. Lieutenant Sinclair recalled the death blow as an 11-inch shell that perforated the hull at the waterline, dousing all the starboard gun crews. Kell called for more steam, and Engineer William Brooks told him the boilers had reached the limits of their pressure; the ship would explode if he threw on more coal. Not long afterward a disconsolate Miles Freeman came up from the engine room to report that the water had flooded everything, and the fires had been drowned. As everyone could see, the game was about up.

As the ship began its seventh revolution, Semmes pulled it out of its arc, pointing hopelessly toward the French coast, five miles away. The helmsman heeled the listing craft to port, turning vaguely toward the crowded hills above Querqueville, and Semmes ordered a forecastle man to loosen the jib sail. As Arthur Sinclair remembered it three decades later, it was John Roberts who leaped on the jib boom and began untethering the canvas. A piece of shell sliced his belly open, but Roberts held his guts in place with one hand and finished his job with the other, working his way back to the forecastle deck before he collapsed with his bowels spilling out before him.

The crippled raider slid slowly toward the coast, but the *Kearsarge* raced to intercept its route. Kell dashed down the wardroom ladder to see how high the water had risen, returning to tell Semmes that they had perhaps ten minutes of buoyancy remaining. At that Semmes ordered the colors struck and sent the gig to the *Kearsarge* with a request for aid. Gaining rapidly on the *Alabama*, Captain Winslow thought it was his guns that had brought down the raider's flag; when the *Kearsarge* came abreast of the two guns still protruding from the *Alabama*'s port battery, he fired five more times, claiming later that he saw those two guns open on his ship. A hand-held white flag came fluttering from the stern of the *Alabama*, where two men stood on the spanker boom to display it, and the *Kearsarge*'s guns fell silent. About an hour had passed since the *Alabama* had fired that first long shot. Once the last volley had finished echoing across the water, George Fullam leaped into the gig, and brawny seamen started pulling him urgently toward their adversary.[20]

Fullam found the Federal ship positioned to rake the deck of the *Alabama* lengthwise. He yelled from alongside that Semmes had surrendered and their ship was sinking, asking the *Kearsarge* to send its boats. Winslow ordered his two undamaged boats into the water, and granted Fullam's request to return with the gig for those he could save. Fullam signaled his oarsmen to turn back, but the *Kearsarge*'s boats lagged behind him. Noting that the *Alabama* was settling by the stern, Winslow called to the *Deerhound*, which was closing in, to drop some boats; by now, Confederate crewmen were struggling in the water around their hapless ship.

Aboard the *Alabama*, officers and shipmates embarked as many of the wounded as the sole remaining boat could hold, placing Lieutenant Wilson in charge with Dr. Galt accompanying him. Dr. Llewelyn remained aboard, never complaining that he could not swim, and he was left to improvise a life raft from flotsam. Captain Semmes consigned his ship's papers to two reliable men, Michael Mars and Frank Townsend, then he and Lieutenant Kell joined the rest of the crew in stripping down to their underwear for the inevitable immersion while the steward Bartelli and the black wardroom boy, David White, looked on apprehensively: neither of them could swim, either. Kell, a great, beefy man with an immense red beard, stood near his captain, who suffered not only from age and exhaustion but from a wound in his hand. Kell found a wooden grate to support them, and into the water they went. It was every man for himself now, and crewmen leaped from the forecastle rail as it rose high above the sea, paddling frantically to pull away from the *Alabama* before she sucked them to the bottom with her.[21]

Kell saw two men, nonswimmers both, who clung to the slanting deck in terror of the water. Walter Van Ness, a seaman who had shipped from the schooner *Crenshaw* eighteen months before, never passed the rail. Carpenter's Mate Frederick Myers finally gathered enough courage to leap into the water, but once there, he lost his nerve and flailed his way back aboard.[22]

The prow pointed skyward as the stern filled rapidly. The mainmast snapped where it had been chewed away by a shot, and in an instant the fouled bottom with its peeling copper flashed in the midday sunlight. Then—by the count of three, according to Minister Dayton's son, who watched from Querqueville with his telescope—the *Alabama* slipped stern-first beneath the English Channel, five miles off the Cherbourg breakwater in forty fathoms, dragging Van Ness and Myers down with her. From the deck of the *Deerhound*, yachtsman John Lancaster marked the sinking at 12:50 P.M. Captain Winslow recorded the same incident on his unsynchronized watch at 12:24. Understandably, no Confederate recorded the exact moment that the *Alabama* went to her grave, though Captain Semmes and his first luff glanced back at the sad, spectacular sight.[23]

From the deck of the *Kearsarge*, sailors who had worked desperately to sink the *Alabama* turned their pity on the survivors who struggled in the salt water. As the *Deerhound* rounded the *Kearsarge*'s quarter, a voice from the sloop bellowed, "Yacht ahoy; lend a hand to save the people." At least one of the two *Kearsarge* boats hesitated to rescue just anyone, however, and when those cutters arrived on the scene, one of them ignored Lieutenant Armstrong while the officer in command searched intently for some special prisoner—doubtless Captain Semmes himself. While the *Kearsarge* boat's crew laid on its oars, Armstrong swam as well as he could with his bruised ribs to the pilot boat of a Frenchman named Mauger.[24]

One survivor refused rescue by the Federals. Charles Steeson, the Swedish captain of the forecastle who had signed on from the prize ship *Anna F. Schmidt* nearly a year before, told the Union sailors who waved at him to save their room for those more exhausted than he. Instead, he swam to the *Deerhound*, which is where Fullam took those he rescued in the gig. The *Deerhound*'s own gig plopped into the water with three oarsmen and a coxswain, picking up Semmes, Kell, and Frank Townsend, who carried the *Alabama*'s still-dry papers aboard with him. Within ten minutes the yacht's gig and cutter had gathered in the majority of the late cruiser's commissioned and warrant officers and more than two dozen men, for a total of forty-one survivors. Quartermaster James Dent, the last of the Savannah pilots, found a place on the yacht, as did Robert Longshaw, the Savannah-born first mate of the prize *Rockingham*, who had served the Confederacy now for less than two months. Quartermaster Brent Johnson crawled aboard, with an oak splinter through his foot. Both the midshipmen and all the master's mates found refuge under Lancaster's British flag, and all the lieutenants save Armstrong and Wilson. Wilson surrendered himself and his boatload of wounded aboard the *Kearsarge* with Dr. Galt, who offered his services to Surgeon Browne but proved too bruised and exhausted to be of much help.

Seaman Mars joined Lieutenant Armstrong, the engineer Brooks, Sailmaker Henry Allcot, and half a dozen others in Pilot Mauger's boat, which took them to Cherbourg. Lancaster asked Captain Semmes where he wished to go, and Semmes chose England. At 1:00 by the yachtsman's faster watch, the *Deerhound* turned for Southampton.[25]

An infuriated Captain Winslow saw the *Deerhound* slipping away, but he could hardly leave his own boats and the men still bobbing in the water, so the yacht escaped with the prisoners Winslow most wanted. When he put into Cherbourg, he claimed the *Deerhound* had acted as a tender for the *Alabama*, and he accused Lancaster of deliberately spiriting away legitimate prisoners of war. Both Mr. Dayton the younger and a repentant (and apparently mistaken) Brent Johnson later suggested that Semmes had communicated with the *Deerhound* before the battle. Including the wounded and the officers, Winslow steamed into Cherbourg two hours later with sixty-seven of the *Alabama*'s crew. Carpenter William Robinson had died of his wounds before the ship docked. Two more sailors—George Appleby and the James

King who enlisted from the Singapore docks—had been lifted, dead, from the *Alabama*'s boat.

Assistant Engineer William Badlam came ashore to seek permission for landing the wounded. Dayton met him at the dock, and together they approached Admiral Dupouy, who agreed to receive the maimed but warned that the Confederate wounded would cease to be prisoners as soon as they touched French soil. Winslow accepted those terms, and late that afternoon carriages took the wounded from both ships to the Marine Hospital on the Rue de l'Abbaye. The boats brought ashore a dozen of the mangled from the *Alabama* and the three from the *Kearsarge*—including John Dempsey, once Dr. Browne had sewn up the stump of his right arm.[26]

Before they ate dinner, most of the crew sat down to write home about the battle, or to record the greatest day of their lives in their journals. Probably coughing a bit between lines, the tubercular chief engineer, William Cushman, headed a letter to his mother from "US Victorious Steamer Kearsarge." Fresh from his duties in the shell room, Master's Mate Ezra Bartlett wrote to inform his brother that he was uninjured, and that the *Alabama* was no more. Martin Hoyt wrote a six-page letter recounting the fury of the fight, and such faithful diarists as Charles Poole and William Wainwright consulted one another—and evidently the ship's log—on details of the battle, in order that their personal records might ring true when their grandchildren read them.

While his crewmen scribbled and nursed ringing headaches, Captain Winslow turned to the question of his uninjured prisoners. These he dared not release without permission, so he telegraphed Dayton's father in Paris. Minister Dayton told him to keep his captives by all means, but Winslow had no room to house the prisoners aboard, so he paroled them all anyway; he retained only the four officers—Wilson, Miles Freeman, Boatswain McCaskey, and Third Engineer John Pundt—whom he also allowed ashore so long as they promised to return when he demanded them.[27]

At 10:00 that same evening, across the channel, the *Deerhound* steamed up the River Test and docked at Southampton. The forty-one passengers spilled ashore, enlisted men scattering for boardinghouses while the wounded were carried a short way down Canute Road to the Sailors' Home. Led by Lieutenant Kell, Captain Semmes made his way straight across the waterfront road to Queen's Terrace, where both of them took upstairs rooms at Robert Kelway's Oriental and Australian Hotel. A local physician left his fireside to tend the captain's wound. The day that had begun with these two commanding a renowned ship of war ended with them sleeping in beds for which they could not pay the first farthing. The cruise of the *Alabama* had ended.[28]

CHAPTER TWENTY

Exodus

Is this mine own countree?
—Coleridge, "Rime of the Ancient Mariner"

The *Alabama* had carried 146 men and boys out of Cherbourg harbor. Of those, Semmes counted 9 killed and 21 wounded. At least 4 were known to have drowned, including Dr. Llewelyn, though none of their bodies were pulled in. The *Deerhound* had scooped 41 men out of the water, and the pilot Mauger had saved 10. The *Kearsarge* picked up 2 dead bodies and 68 living men, including 13 of the wounded, of whom 1—Carpenter Robinson—perished from his injuries. That left 14 missing men, all of whom apparently suffered the same fate as their ship. Bartelli, the captain's steward, was not among those rescued, though he was still alive when the firing ceased, and David White, the suspected slave from Delaware, had not been dragged into the boats.

News of the sinking of the *Alabama* cast the towns along the Irish Sea into greater gloom than even their weather usually offered, and only partly because of the secret pride taken in so famous a local craft. As word of individual fates leaked back home, grieving relatives signed the probate register for the few pounds due their sons and husbands. Jane Roberts, of Llangadwalad, on Anglesea, accepted the pay of her heroic, disemboweled son John. The Reverend David Llewelyn, of Euston, Wiltshire, received a couple of hundred pounds in back pay on behalf of his doctor son, whose body had been spotted but not recovered. The Scottish third assistant engineer, William Robertson, was never seen again, and a few weeks later his uncollected pay was awarded to his father, in Glasgow. The probate court gave the effects of Paymaster's Steward Frederick Matthew Johns, Jr., the Liverpool clerk, to his father, who lived on Castle Street, and the senior Johns used it to erect a slate stone in his missing son's memory. The paltry estate of widower John William Welham went to his father, a grocer in Sudbury. And on July 21 one widow of questionable bereavement, Elizabeth Appleby, collected the money owed to the husband she had known barely eight weeks when he joined the *Alabama* at Liverpool; six days later Widow Appleby married a Fleet Street porter named Robert Payne.[1]

On June 21 strange hands carried the remains of George Appleby far up the ancient hillside cemetery overlooking Cherbourg harbor. There he was buried, near the edge of a crowded terrace alongside James King, and their impoverished shipmates put together a small fund to raise cheap limestone crosses over their graves. The same Cherbourg civil official recorded the death of William Robinson. If any other bodies came to shore from the *Alabama*, they were not identified, and no further burials were recorded.[2]

One funeral remained, however. The *Alabama* wounded all fared well in the baroque wards of the Marine Hospital, and James MacBeth, of the *Kearsarge*, recovered relatively quickly from his broken leg, but his two injured shipmates grew worse. John Dempsey had lost his right arm near the shoulder, and he had been wounded in the left arm, as well; when he fell ill with dysentery, he was therefore left in the embarrassing position of having to be helped with his clothing and cleaning at every call of nature. For a time his shipmates feared he might die of the intestinal ailment, which, in their ignorance, they attributed to his trauma. Dempsey would, in fact, succumb to this affliction, but not for another five years. It was William Gowin who fooled them all, giving up the ghost when his surgeon and friends saw no need for him to die. Gowin pined a few days for his poor widowed mother in Michigan, and for his lost leg, discounting the advice of those who assured him that he would survive. On June 27 he breathed his last, and two days later a procession of sailors followed the steps up the steep slope of the old cemetery to the unwanted corner where lay Appleby and King. They buried his casket in chalky soil right in front of Appleby's unsettled mound; before the day was finished, they had collected enough cash for a fat granite obelisk and a little wrought-iron fence, the construction of which they left to the consul at Cherbourg. Americans in Paris later sent Surgeon Browne money for a similar monument in the Michigan town where Gowin had been born, but no funds seem to have been raised for his mother's support. Three years later, a grateful but tardy government finally offered her $8 a month.[3]

The day after Gowin's funeral François Rondin, the photographer who had captured the battle on a glass plate, visited the *Kearsarge* in the harbor, bringing his cumbersome equipment along in the boat. While the crew stood to quarters as they had while approaching the *Alabama*, Rondin opened his tripod on the forecastle and immortalized them. Then he turned around and photographed the Marine guard at the forecastle rifle, with Master's Mate Charles Danforth at their side. Descending the forecastle steps, Rondin gathered Assistant Engineer Sidney Smith and thirty of the crew for a standing portrait before the smokestack, and finally he wandered aft, where he circled seven petty officers around the wheel, posed four officers in front of them, and stood the diminutive Spanish cabin boy, twelve-year-old Manuel José Gallardo, in the center of the scene.

There was talk that Rondin had made a print of his battle negative, but the only reliable witness to the photographer's masterpiece was an Englishman who came to interview the *Kearsarge* crew for a little book about their fight. Frederick Edge saw only the negative, which he thought "a fine image," but this would have been the most valuable picture Rondin ever produced, and no print appears to have survived. Rondin may have ruined the plate before he could reproduce it.[4]

The battle at Cherbourg continued long after the guns stopped. From his cabin Captain Winslow issued periodic letters lamenting the dishonorable behavior of the *Deerhound*'s owner and the perfidious actions of Semmes and his other officers, particularly Fullam, for escaping with the yacht after they had surrendered. Across the channel, in his room overlooking Queen's Park, Semmes the cavalier bewailed Winslow's "deception" in planking over the chainclad armor about the waist of his ship, which he declared he had known nothing of until George Fullam brought word of the huge chain mail that he had glimpsed beneath the ruptured deal planking when he delivered the news of surrender. Both captains detailed their versions of Winslow's notorious final volley into the *Alabama*, though the entire incident seems to have resulted from confusion aboard the sinking ship, some of whose zealous company fired the last two unused guns when the port side came into action. Unlike Semmes, Winslow also had to defend himself against his own Navy Department, which later criticized him for freeing the captured enlisted men.[5]

For the enlisted men of the *Alabama*, the war was over. Even the two Georgians, Quartermaster James Dent and Seaman Robert Longshaw, drew their final pay when Dr. Galt crossed over to Southampton with the paymaster's accounts, and Semmes discharged everyone but those who remained wounded at the Marine Hospital in Cherbourg. The only prize money they ever saw came from the sale of captured chronometers, which the *Hornet* carried back to Southampton. The Englishmen returned to their earlier callings, though for the majority of them it was still the sea. Most of the officers found other assignments, either on Confederate cruisers fitted out in

Europe or, like Semmes and Kell, on river gunboats back in the Confederacy. It was on the way back to service in the South from Liverpool that Gunner Thomas Cuddy drowned in the wreck of a blockade runner, exactly seven months after the fight off Cherbourg. The two Prussian master's mates, Schroeder and von Meulnier, returned to their native land, while George Fullam went home to Yorkshire. Though a resident of Liverpool, Sailmaker Henry Allcot accepted the same warrant on the cruiser *Shenandoah* a few months later, joining three old *Alabama* shipmates: Engineer O'Brien, Sailing Master Irvine Bulloch, and Boatswain George Harwood, who came out of retirement at Liverpool again to serve the Confederate nation on which he never laid eyes.

The crew of the *Kearsarge* enjoyed no such liberty of choice, but their celebrity berth at Cherbourg entertained them for a couple of weeks. Visitors swarmed over the ship, and from the day after the battle every seascape painter in Paris came to execute a rendition of the contest. One of the most memorable canvases appeared under the name of Edouard Manet, whose reported presence at the battle seems to have been misunderstood. Three decades later a friend claimed that Manet had ridden in a pilot boat during the combat, but Manet himself implied that his painting of the *Alabama* going down before a looming *Kearsarge* was done from hearsay and other people's sketches. He appears to have made his first eyewitness sketch of the Federal sloop at Boulogne, on July 17.[6]

Captain Winslow and his senior officers returned from their holiday in Paris in the evening of July 4. The following day the USS *Sacramento* arrived in the harbor from Lisbon. Winslow called in the four Confederate officers from their temporary parole, whereupon the two Federal ships raced each other across the channel to Dover.

The Dover consul delivered mail that forced a shuffling among the junior officers. Midshipman Preble found his commission as a lieutenant, along with orders to turn for home, so Captain Winslow moved Charles Danforth up from master's mate to acting master, as a reward for his performance in command of the forecastle rifle. William Smith, the rum-loving old quartermaster who had captained the aft pivot gun, suddenly found himself wearing an officer's cap and drawing $45 a month.

Such little surprises offered the only diversion in an existence that quickly resumed its former level of unbearable monotony. Men who had been commended for their courage and efficiency on June 19 reverted to the bottle again by August, deserting their boats en masse whenever the opportunity offered. They thundered ashore now, boasting of their victory while in their cups. Still anchored off England on August 5, Coal Heaver Charles Poole remarked that "our prospects of staying for life are pretty good," but a week later the *Kearsarge* left for Cherbourg, to retrieve Dempsey and McBeth. Rondin took the opportunity to scurry aboard with his photographs of the crew, and Lawrence Crowley stole ashore for a final frolic with one of Cherbourg's less discriminating ladies. The encounter afforded him a few moments' delight and a case of syphilis that would haunt him for three decades.

That evening all hands manned the capstan to raise the anchor from European water one last time. No one but Captain Winslow knew that they were heading home, although they all suspected it. The *Florida* had taken to the water again, capturing eight U.S. vessels in July alone, and Gideon Welles had ordered the *Kearsarge* to the coast of Brazil to close the noose about that raider. The crew expected a more direct route; when the Scilley lighthouse fell behind them, the men began to feel a little better, only to turn more despondent when weeks passed with no sign of a course for New England.[7]

The *Kearsarge* stopped at Faial at noon of August 22, taking on coal and, just before leaving on September 1, boarding a score of stranded whalers as part of the crew; their names found no place in the log, for they were merely working their way home. For the next five weeks they saw no land at all as the ship curved down the middle of the Atlantic Ocean. By September 23 a despairing William Wainwright expressed his ennui with a vague reference to suicide. "I can't tell how long I will last if we are out in this part of the world any longer," he wrote in his journal, "and I don't see any prospect of our getting away." The next day he began to show signs of real depression, describing himself as "almost too lazy" to bring his duffel bag on deck, where everyone was airing their clothing in the ratlines. By October 1 he revealed deep disappointment at the possibility that they might spend that month and the next at sea, after all.

The rocks of St. Peter and St. Paul offered the first sight of anything that might be called land on October 4. A sympathetic captain allowed men ashore to fish and collect birds' eggs, and three days later the anchor dropped off Fernando de Noronha, where the *Alabama* had once stopped to take aboard the fruits of its enterprise. Within a few hours a boat brought back all the fresh provisions the cooks could find, and by the evening of October 7 the sails were set for St. Thomas, and home.

That same evening, a day's cruise to the southwest, the USS *Wachusett* rammed and captured the *Florida* in the harbor of Bahia, Brazil, in blatant violation of Brazilian neutrality. Jubilantly towing his illicit prize northward, the commander of the *Wachusett* met the *Kearsarge* at St. Thomas on

October 30. Captain Winslow accepted seventeen prisoners from the *Florida*, making room for them by transferring his whalers to a Baltimore ship that sailed into St. Thomas in distress, suffering from scurvy.[8]

With the seventeen Confederates locked up forward and the hundred-pound shell from the *Alabama* still lodged in her sternpost, working her framework apart, the *Kearsarge* left port on Halloween. Seven days later, early in the second dog watch, James Wheeler had the deck when Cape Cod light came into sight. Half an hour later two guns boomed for a pilot, but none came, so the *Kearsarge* crept carefully into Massachusetts Bay. At 8:00 Ezra Bartlett took the deck, and three-quarters of an hour later he spotted Minot light; Bartlett fired another gun at 9:10, and by 9:30 a pilot crawled aboard. A rocket spiraled skyward, announcing to the city of Boston that the conqueror of the *Alabama* had come home, and a few minutes after midnight, November 8, 1864, the *Kearsarge* dropped her port anchor at the Charlestown Navy Yard.[9]

In the morning the four officers from the *Alabama* and the seventeen prisoners from the *Florida* left the deck of the *Kearsarge* for Fort Warren, where they spent the remaining six months of the war. Two days later a Marine band from the yard formed on the dock, and the crew of the *Kearsarge* lined up behind, marching to the blaring music through a cold rain, across the bridge to Boston and Faneuil Hall. There the people of Boston had prepared a reception, complete with a welcoming song written by the pastor of the First Baptist Mariners' church. When the meal ended, the bluejackets filed out of the hall and started homeward, leaving the Marines and officers behind. Three weeks later they would return for their final pay and discharges, but—except for the few who signed on for the next cruise—they never stood on the deck of the *Kearsarge* again. At last, nearly five months after the single hour's clash that had represented the purpose of their entire three years' service, their war was over, too. In time, most of them would forget how intensely they had grown to hate the vessel that had been their home.[10]

The returning veterans probably carried away an inordinate sense of accomplishment that the homecoming festivities only confirmed and perhaps augmented. Their three years' service may have included the destruction of the most famous of the enemy's cruisers, but from an international perspective the affair off Cherbourg had added only a splash of melodrama to the anticlimactic arrival of the ailing *Alabama* at that port. In the thirteen years that remained to him, Semmes wrote proudly of the *Alabama*'s record, and indeed his ship did the greatest damage to Union shipping of all the Confederate raiders—so much so that the international reparations case arising from Confederate depredations became known as the Alabama Claims. By the time the *Alabama* limped into the English Channel, however, that damage had reached its optimum extent. By the middle of 1864 so many American vessels had been sold to foreign owners or registered under other flags that the international lanes offered few victims for Confederate ships, and although 76 more were burned or scuttled after the *Alabama* went down, most were small domestic schooners, pilot boats, or whaling ships. Between 1860 and 1863 the annual number of U.S. ships sold to foreign nationals jumped more than eightfold, from 41 to 348. Some have argued that this "flight from the flag" blighted American shipping until the outbreak of World War II, but to blame that on the Civil War ignores economic, geographical, and political factors that played a greater role: interior development of the United States refocused transportation interests on railroad traffic at the same time that the rapid development of its colonies encouraged Great Britain to expand its own maritime industry. The cost and regulatory impediments of American registry, for which Confederate cruisers can claim no credit, continue to this day to send international shippers to other nations.[11]

The *Alabama*'s principal service to the Confederacy appears to have been its effect on Southern morale, for it offered false hope of victory at sea and spread sympathy for the cause around the globe. It diverted few Union vessels from the stifling blockade, which it never had any hope of breaking. And the *Kearsarge* crewmen achieved perhaps even less in a practical sense, despite their victory. Even Raphael Semmes had seemed to predict the end of his crippled ship's career as it approached the Cotentin Peninsula, and increasing European discomfort over Confederate vessels would have sealed its fate before long, anyway. The battle against the commerce raiders was really won by the foreign ministers, and no one needed to die in the channel except to appease Southern honor.

Our life is closed, our life begins,
The long, long anchorage we leave,
The ship is clear at last, she leaps!
—Whitman, "Joy, Shipmate, Joy!"

Austin Quinby, onetime corporal in the U.S. Marines but now a widower in his eighty-second year, seemed to enjoy the notoriety that his former association with the USS *Kearsarge* afforded. He offered interviews to all who would listen, and he collected a thick scrapbook of newspaper clippings about the old ship. In his leisure he seems to have transcribed a diary of his wartime experiences, apparently borrowing from official sources, shipmates' journals, and his vivid imagination to flesh it out. After he retired from a career that ran from millwork to real estate brokerage, his greatest glee came each June, when the Kearsarge Naval Veteran Association met at Boston's Quincy House on the anniversary of the battle with the *Alabama*.

Only three other comrades arrived to share with Quinby the fifty-fifth anniversary of their naval duel on June 19, 1919: John Bickford, Patrick McKeever, and William Giles, all of whom were approaching eighty or already beyond it. A dozen aging members had met on that date four years before, but fewer than a dozen even remained alive today. The wives, widows, and daughters of absent crewmen livened their dinner at the Quincy House, and, when the meal ended, the honored foursome composed a brief address for those who could not attend. With fresh crowds of young soldiers all about who had just returned from France themselves, the old sailors could see that the events that had excited their generation were now all but forgotten, so they tried to lash their memories to recent events, drawing what parallels they could between the navies of the Civil War and the World

War. With that, they closed their meeting with the perennial wish of old age: "May we meet again."[1]

Most of them would not meet again, and the greater part of the crew that had left Portsmouth harbor in 1862 was already long gone. Yeoman Carsten DeWit died at the Chelsea Naval Hospital early in 1865, and the chief engineer, Cushman, perished of tuberculosis on October 31 of that year. The telepathic Faial Portuguese, Francis Viannah, died shortly after his discharge from a second cruise, in 1868, while the consumptive carpenter, Mark Ham, succumbed to a pulmonary hemorrhage in March of 1869, just hours after finishing his day's work aboard the USS *Vandalia*; John Dempsey died at home in Boston the following July. Captain Winslow, promoted to rear admiral in 1870, resigned after an apparent stroke in 1872, and died from the effects of a second attack on September 29, 1873, at his home in Boston. Captain Pickering died of kidney disease on February 29, 1888. Within a quarter-century of leaving the *Kearsarge* most of the senior officers had found their graves, and once the century turned, the ranks of survivors began to dwindle quickly. Zaran Phillips died at the age of ninety, just before Christmas of 1914—more than half a century after he fell from the mizzen-mast onto the quarterdeck of the *Kearsarge*. Coal Heaver Charles Poole died five weeks later, on his seventy-fourth birthday; his fellow diarist and companion in the engine room, William Wainwright, passed away in 1920, as the battle anniversary approached. Paymaster Smith's first steward, Daniel Sargent, died in Omaha in the spring of 1921. Just a year later Corporal Quinby, the last of the Marine detail, took his long-cherished memories to his final rest, and the Kearsarge Naval Veteran Association ceased to exist. The last survivor of the *Kearsarge* crew lived out his days far away from the ocean. William Alsdorf, the German recruit who ran into so much trouble with shipboard discipline, migrated to the American West and lived out his days in New Mexico, where he died in an isolated mining town in 1935.[2]

None of Alsdorf's erstwhile antagonists appear to have outlasted him. The sailor's life had taken as severe a toll on the *Alabama*'s crew as it had on the career seamen of the *Kearsarge*, but for most of them their British nationality left them to live out their lives in obscurity. Occasionally the name of an *Alabama* survivor surfaced in English records, though generally without special notice, and many of them found unmarked paupers' graves. Thomas Potter, who deserted with John Latham in Jamaica but returned to fight against (and be rescued by) the *Kearsarge*, died at his Everton home less than three years later, at the age of thirty-two, and a Liverpool clerk recorded the disposition of his pitiful effects. The irrepressible Michael Mars was finally subdued—at fifty-seven—in the summer of 1878; except for the scribblings of the Confederate officers under whom he served, the only earthly remembrance of his life is the entry in the register of the cemetery where he lies, not far from the Thames docks where he stepped off his last ship. George Fullam had command of a Newcastle collier that went down with all hands late in 1879, and the tragedy earned official notice in both permanent records and newspaper headlines. When Sailmaker Henry Allcot died at his Liverpool home in 1891, two days after the death of his baby boy, his heirs commissioned a stone in their memory in Liverpool's Anfield Cemetery.[3]

Only such infrequent bits of evidence remain on European soil, but the Southern officers achieved a certain fame in their homeland. Semmes, who died in 1877, left his name on a statue and public buildings in his adopted Mobile. John Kell gave up the sea and took to farming, but, before he died in 1900, he served as adjutant general of his native Georgia. Lieutenant Armstrong sought asylum in Nova Scotia, where he died in 1904. Joseph Wilson, the hesitant Florida Confederate, dropped from public view. Arthur Sinclair returned to Baltimore, where he lived in poverty and engendered the dislike of his former fellow officers by criticizing the revered Captain Semmes. Dr. Galt established a private practice in Norfolk, his Old Dominion home, but later he married a woman from Loudoun County, where he died late in 1915.

When the *Confederate Veteran* noted the final survivors of the *Alabama* in 1918, it ignored Lieutenant Sinclair altogether. The magazine mentioned instead Adolphus Marmelstein, the signal quartermaster who transferred to the *Tuscaloosa*, and Midshipman Edward Anderson, both of whom lived in Savannah, as well as an Irish impostor residing in Texas. Marmelstein died just before Thanksgiving of 1922, and on the fourth Sunday of 1923 Anderson also drew his last breath. The pallbearers took him to Savannah's Laurel Grove Cemetery, where, sixty-two years before, the wayward Clarence Yonge had buried his first child. Paymaster Yonge survived his firstborn only five years, dying under an alias in a Washington boardinghouse immediately after the war ended.

Anderson's demise seemed to close the log on the *Alabama*, but Arthur Sinclair lingered on in Baltimore for nearly three years more, forgotten by all now that no other officers remained to quarrel with him over details of their ship or service. There, in November of 1925, amid squawking automobile klaxons and the bellowing foghorns of Chesapeake steamers, the last of those who had trod the fabled *Alabama*'s deck yielded quietly to the relentless tide of time.[4]

APPENDIX 1.
WHICH MOUNTAIN WAS IT?

Although Gideon Welles did not know it when he authorized the name of his new corvette, it happened that there were two mountains in the Granite State that were known as "Kearsarge." One, in Merrimack County, had been spelled "Kyar Sarga" and "Kyahsarg," while the taller one in Carroll County, which the wife of Assistant Secretary Gustavus Fox knew, was generally rendered "Kiarsarge." As soon as word reached New Hampshire that one of the new corvettes was to have that name, however, a Concord newspaper publisher named Henry McFarland jumped to take the credit for the suggestion, which he claimed to have made in honor of the Merrimack County mountain. Secretary Welles could remember no letter from McFarland, and none was ever found in department correspondence, but McFarland had a habit of assuming credit for such things. The publisher also alleged that he or his wife named the *Ossipee*, the christening of which she attended.

Years later McFarland kicked up a great fuss over it. In 1875 he tried to stir Welles's memory about the letter, but Welles recalled discussing the name with no one but Fox and Treasury Secretary Salmon P. Chase. As a lifelong New Hampshire resident Mrs. Fox must have known of both mountains, Welles reasoned, and she must also have known which of them she had in mind. Welles advised that it would "be meet and gallant to commemorate" the more prominent mountain "in accordance with the suggestions of a lady."[1]

McFarland did not care to be gallant, though, if he could get the credit. He provoked a controversy, enlisting the aid of the state historical society and its president, Nathaniel Bouton. Bouton—like most of the state's more influential politicians—lived near the Merrimack County mountain, and he embarked as though on a crusade. His first strategy, and ultimately his only one, was to cloud the issue by charging that the Carroll County peak was not known as Kearsarge, and he asked the state legislature to rename it Mount Pequawket.

Gustavus Fox spared no expense in defense of his late wife's own claim. He hired researchers in London to examine colonial maps, engaged a Catholic priest who was fluent in the Abenaki dialect to demonstrate how the two mountains could have derived the same name from different Indian words, and he interviewed dozens of Carroll County residents who had never known their mountain as anything but Kearsarge, including one who had been born there early in the Revolution. He need not have bothered with all of that, for it was necessary only to demonstrate that the mountain was known as Kearsarge when his wife proposed it in 1861. Several antebellum guidebooks referred to it as Kiarsarge, and North Conway's principal lodging facility in 1861 was the Kearsarge House, named for the nearby height. A village sitting at the town's northern boundary, at the foot of the mountain, also came to be called Kearsarge.

Fox convinced the Appalachian Mountain Club of his contention, but Bouton challenged him to do the same for the New Hampshire Historical Society. Fox dutifully appeared with his boxful of evidence, and Bouton appointed him to a three-member committee, one member of which was Bouton himself. Bouton and the other committeeman lived at the foot of the smaller Mount Kearsarge, and by a predictable vote of two to one the committee swept aside everything Fox presented, declaring that the Carroll County peak should be called Mount Pequawket.[2]

McFarland embraced the committee's decision as though it were somehow proof of his assertion, though it had no bearing on the question of who named the vessel. Eventually he published a booklet on the subject, in which he claimed for the first time that his 1861 letter proposing the ship's name had been addressed to Fox, rather than to Welles—thus implying that Fox had misappropriated the idea for Mrs. Fox's benefit.

Both Welles and Fox were dead by then, but that did not end the matter. Taking McFarland's self-serving story as their authority, numerous people who had been associated with the *Kearsarge* mentioned that the ship had been named for the Warner mountain, and these secondhand comments also became part of the "proof." An establishment called the Winslow House, after the captain of the *Kearsarge*, was constructed on the side of the Merrimack County mountain by those who presumed the height to be the source of the corvette's name. Admiral Winslow himself attended the dedication of the second Winslow House in 1868, after the first building burned, and Warner citizens donated a boulder from their mountain as Winslow's gravestone in 1873. Though all these actions arose from nothing more than the unfounded convictions of the participants, they, too, are cited as hard evidence.

As witnesses who could say otherwise died off, other claimants materialized, including an aging Baptist minister named Joseph Gilmore. Gilmore said his father and namesake had been governor of New Hampshire when he was asked by the Navy Department to come up with some local Indian names for the new warships. The father delegated the duty to him, said the son, and the first name he thought of was Kearsarge, for the Merrimack County mountain near his home. Reverend Gilmore's reputation as a theologian appears to have prevented anyone from pointing out that his father did not take office as governor until 1863—two years after the *Kearsarge* was first named.

In 1915 the U.S. Geographic Board took up the nomenclature of the two mountains. Operating without Fox's valuable firsthand evidence, a subcommittee scratched at the cold trail and heard the usual proportion of hearsay testimony and perjury from people like Gilmore; the oldtimers Fox had interviewed were all dead by then. The board ultimately ruled that the northernmost mountain should henceforth be known as Pequawket, but that carried no weight in Carroll County. Residents refused to call their peak anything but Kearsarge, and in 1958 the federal government caved in, redesignating it Kearsarge North. Even that did not satisfy those who live within sight of it, for whom it is still only Kearsarge.[3]

The geographic board also decided that the ship had been named for the Warner mountain, but it did not deign to certify any of those who claimed to have offered the name for the ship. The only credible candidates are Henry McFarland and Mrs. Fox. The only evidence that McFarland thought of the name is his own insistence on it, and perhaps he did, but it seems doubtful without the discovery of his original letter on that point. The man who compiled the report of the geographic board claimed that Fox "admits" receiving McFarland's letter, but he does not cite the source of that admission, or whether the alleged letter referred to the *Kearsarge* or the *Ossipee*, the name for which McFarland also took belated credit. Even if such a document does come to light, it is entirely possible that McFarland's suggestion came simultaneously with that of Mrs. Fox, in which case it appears unlikely that his suggestion was responsible for the choice. Whether or not McFarland submitted such a letter, Mrs. Fox had the better opportunity to influence the secretary of the navy, who could not remember talking about it with anyone but her husband. And if Mrs. Fox was the source, as both logic and evidence seem to suggest, then the ship carried the name of the Bartlett mountain.[4]

APPENDIX 2. SHIPS' ROSTERS

Abbreviations

BM	Boatswain's Mate
CH	Coal Heaver
CM	Carpenter's Mate
CT	Coal Trimmer
FM	Fireman
GM	Gunner's Mate
LM	Landsman
OS	Ordinary Seaman
QG	Quarter Gunner
QM	Quartermaster
SM	Able Seaman
USMC	U.S. Marine Corps

Roster offers name, rank, age at enlistment and birthplace (if known), date of enlistment, and any additional service record information. An asterisk (*) denotes those who took part in the battle of June 19, 1864.

USS *Kearsarge*

Enlisted men (other than Marines) were discharged November 30, 1864, unless otherwise stated.

Adams, Henry A., Officers' Steward; November 10, 1862; deserted.

*Ahern, Michael, Paymaster's Steward; Queenstown, Ireland; November 7, 1863; awarded Medal of Honor.

*Alloway, Thomas, SM; 21; New York; February 10, 1864.

*Alsdorf, William, OS; 20; Hamburg, Germany; January 27, 1863; reduced to LM July 9, 1863.

*Andrew, George A., OS; 23; Chile; March 23, 1862.

*Antoine, Clement, CH; 30; San Antonio, Azores; April 9, 1863.

Antoine, Fred, LM; June 5, 1863; deserted.

*Badlam, William H., 2nd Assistant Engineer; 21; Massachusetts; appointed October 8, 1861.

*Bailey, George, LM; Virginia; January 11, 1862.

*Baker, George, SM; 22; Baltimore, Md.; January 29, 1864; reduced to LM April 14, 1864.

*Barnes, William, LM; 21; Newfoundland; February 12, 1864.

*Barrows, John, OS; 30; Massachusetts; January 14, 1862.

*Barth, Jacob, LM; 17; December 12, 1861.

*Bartlett, Ezra, Acting Master's Mate; 29; Stratham, N.H.; appointed January 23, 1862; promoted to Acting Ensign November 23, 1864; died August 18, 1886, Stratham, N.H.

*Bastine, William H., LM; 22, New York; January 13, 1862.

*Batchelder, John G., Private, USMC; 21; New Hampshire; August 26, 1861; deserted December 16, 1864, Portsmouth, N.H.

Bell, William, OS; January 26, 1864; deserted.

Benson, Richard? (Mentioned in *Kearsarge* Log, December 23, 1862).

*Bickford, John F., OS; 18; Maine; rated SM December 17, 1862; rated Captain of the Top; awarded Medal of Honor.

*Blaisdell, Benjamin H., 1st Class FM; 32; Rhode Island; November 7, 1861.

*Blaisdell, Joel B., 1st Class FM; 25; Rhode Island; November 7, 1861.

Blake, Thomas; January 26, 1864; deserted.

Blees, Charles; January 26, 1864; deserted June 6, 1864.

Boener, Clement, CH; Prussia; died at sea August 26, 1863.

*Bond, William, BM; 23; Boston, Mass.; January 16, 1862; awarded Medal of Honor.

*Boyle, John, OS; 22; Troy, N.Y.; January 2, 1862.

*Brackett, Sylvanus P., CH; 19; Maine; December 2, 1861.

*Bradley, James, SM; 21; Maine; January 11, 1862.

*Bradley, John E., OS; 21; Rhode Island; January 9, 1862.

*Brier, Jonathan, LM; 19; Boston, Mass.; January 29, 1864.

*Briset, John, CH; France; February 2, 1864; deserted.

Brown, Charles, Supernumerary; August 2, 1862; deserted.

Brown, William; January 26, 1864; deserted.

*Browne, John M., Surgeon; 29; assigned December 18, 1861; retired as Surgeon General, U.S. Navy, May 10, 1893; died December 7, 1894, Washington, D.C.

*Buckley, Thomas, OS; 26; Wisconsin; January 19, 1862.

Burns, James, OS; 26; Dublin, Ireland; January 1, 1862; sent home from Spain April 6, 1862; discharged June 26, 1862.

Burns, Thomas W., SM; 29; Ireland; January 14, 1862; deserted March 25, 1864.

*Buttons, Benjamin, CH; 32; Guam; January 1, 1863.

*Butts, Charles, QM; 32; Rhode Island; January 15, 1862.

Cameron, William, OS; June 26, 1862; deserted.

*Canty, Timothy G., SM; 24; New Bedford, Mass.; February 10, 1864.

*Carey, Joshua, SM; 34; Maine; January 14, 1862; rated Sailmaker's Mate July 4, 1862.

Carroll, James, QM; disrated to SM September 19, 1862; sent home to the U.S. from Spain, June 18, 1863.

*Chappell, William D., LM; 27; Connecticut; January 11, 1862.

*Charles, Daniel, LM; 23; Philadelphia, Pa.; January 13, 1862.

Chase, John M., 1st Class FM; 25; Newburyport, Mass.; November 29, 1861; sent home from Spain May 13, 1862; discharged October 20, 1863.

Clark, William W., LM; deserted March 18, 1863.

Clarke, Daniel; deserted January 21, 1863.

Coalter, John, LM; 19; December 17, 1861; deserted January 28, 1862, before cruise began.

*Collins, Joshua, OS; 20; Ireland; January 26, 1864.

*Cook, Henry, Captain of the After Guard; 29; Connecticut; January 13, 1862.

*Conroy, Michael, SM; 25; Massachusetts; January 7, 1862.

*Crowley, Lawrence T., OS; 25; Boston, Mass.; January 14, 1862.

Cummings, William, OS; 22; Ireland; July 14, 1864.

*Cushman, William H., Chief Engineer; Pennsylvania; appointed October 16, 1861; died October 31, 1865.

*Dabney, José I., LM; May 8, 1863.

*Danforth, Charles A., Acting Master's Mate; Massachusetts; appointed December 19, 1861; promoted to Acting Ensign November 23, 1864.

*Davis, Benjamin S., LM; December 31, 1862.

*Dempsey, John W., Captain of the After Guard; 25; Boston; January 11, 1862; disrated to SM July 30, 1862; rated QG January 22, 1863; lost right arm, June 19, 1864; died July 24, 1869.

DeSanto, Sabine, Officers' Steward; Portugal; January, 1862; died at sea, March 11, 1862.

*Devine, James O., LM, 22; Boston; January, 1862.

*DeWit, Carsten B., Yeoman; 54; Maine; January, 1862; died 1865.

*Dolley, Roscoe D., Private, USMC; 24; Laconia, N.H.; September 10, 1861; injured left arm, June 19, 1864; discharged 1865; died August 29, 1906.

*Donnelly, William H., 1st Class FM; 25; Philadelphia, Pa.; November 17, 1861; lost tip of left middle finger.

*Drury, Benedict, SM; January 14, 1862.

*Dugan, John F., CH; 22; Philadelphia, Pa.; November 25, 1861.

*Dugan, Joseph, 1st Class FM; 27; Philadelphia, Pa.; November 20, 1861; lost left thumb in line of duty.

*Dwyer, John, 1st Class FM; 26; Ireland; January 31, 1862.

*Ellis, William, Captain of the Hold; 29; New York City; January 24, 1862.

Emery, Mark W., LM; 22; Bucksport, Maine; May 26, 1862; died at sea August 19, 1863.

*English, George, SM; 24; Italy; February 11, 1864.

*Evans, William Y., Nurse; 19; Portsmouth, N.H.; February 1, 1862.

*Fisher, Charles B., Officers' Cook; 23; Virginia; January 15, 1862; died January 27, 1903, Washington, D.C.

*Fisher, William, LM; 20; Virginia; January 18, 1862.

*Flood, Patrick, Private, USMC; 27; Ireland; October 31, 1861; discharged 1865.

*François, Vanburn, LM; 15; Belgium; February 7, 1864.

*Gallardo, Manuel José, 2nd Class Boy; 12; Spain; January 1, 1864.

*Giles, William, SM; 18; Massachusetts; January 6, 1862.

Gilson, Edward, SM; 35; Keene, N.H.; January 13, 1862; sent home from Spain August 25, 1862; discharged January 26, 1863.

Golden, James, Private, USMC; sent home from Spain August 25, 1862.

*Gowin, William, OS; Michigan; died June 27, 1864, of wounds received June 19.

*Graham, Franklin A., Gunner; Philadelphia, Pa.; appointed December 17, 1861; died July 28, 1873, aboard USS *Frolic*.

Griffin, J. W.; deserted May 28, 1862.

*Gurney, William W., QM; 21; Massachusetts; January 7, 1862.

*Haley, James, Captain of the Forecastle; 38; Ireland; January 17, 1862; awarded Medal of Honor.

*Ham, Mark G., CM; 42; Portsmouth, N.H.; January 23, 1862; awarded Medal of Honor; died March 11, 1869, Portsmouth, N.H.

 Harris, Thomas C., Lieutenant; 36; assigned November 11, 1861; returned to U.S. February 15, 1863; died January 24, 1875, Naval Asylum, Philadelphia, Pa.

*Harrison, George H., SM; 20; Massachusetts; March 19, 1862; awarded Medal of Honor.

*Hartford, Lyman H., CH; 35; Wilmot, N.H.; January 23, 1862; discharged as 2nd Class FM; died December 20, 1897, Portsmouth, N.H.

*Hartwell, Seth E., Captain's Clerk; 27; Middleboro, Mass.; reported July 1, 1863; died April 7, 1876, U.S. Navy Hospital, Mare Island, Calif.

*Hayes, James F., LM; 16; Charlestown, Mass.; December 12, 1861.

*Hayes, John, Coxswain; 30; Philadelphia, Pa.; December 31, 1861; awarded Medal of Honor.

*Henson, James, LM; 16; Rhode Island; January 15, 1862.

*Hill, Charles, LM; 23; New Hampshire; February 1, 1862.

*Hobson, Henry, Private, USMC; 21; England; October 3, 1861; promoted to corporal May 3, 1864; discharged 1865.

*Horrigan, Jeremiah, SM; 40; Ireland; March 19, 1863.

*Hoyt, Martin, LM; 21; Newington, N.H.; December 20, 1861.

*Hurley, Timothy, Ship's Cook; 23; Fall River, Mass.; January 7, 1862.

 Igo, Thomas W., Coxswain; disrated to SM July 4, 1862; disrated to OS December 17, 1862; deserted August 14, 1863.

 Iguacio, José, OS; February 6, 1864; deserted.

*Ives, Nathan, LM; 17; Connecticut; January 2, 1862.

*Jamison, Henry, 1st Class FM; 26; Ireland; December 30, 1862.

*Johnson, Augustus, SM; 30; Sweden; November 10, 1862.

*Jones, Charles, SM; 26; Massachusetts; January 10, 1862.

 Jones, Robert, Supernumerary; July 2, 1862; deserted.

 Jones, Thomas, OS; January, 1862; deserted October 16, 1862.

 Joseph, Alexander, OS; February 6, 1864; deserted.

 Kelly, John, LM; June 5, 1863; deserted November 4, 1863.

 Kelly, Norman J., SM; May 26, 1862; rated Captain of the Top July 4, 1862; deserted.

*Kerrigan, James, Private, USMC; 21; New York; October 28, 1861; discharged 1865.

*Kinne, George H., OS; 39; Maine; September 26, 1862.

 Lahie, Daniel, OS; January, 1862; deserted October 16, 1862.

 Lambert, John J., 2nd Class FM; 34; Cohasset, Mass.; January 10, 1862; sent home from Spain; discharged October 14, 1863.

 Langton, W. T.?; name appears only on the original roster.

*Lee, James H., SM; 22; New York; January 10, 1862; rated Captain of the Top; awarded Medal of Honor; died August 9, 1877, Oswego, N.Y.

 Lewis, Manuel; January, 1862; sent home from Spain April 6, 1862.

*Littlefield, Adoniram K., CH; 26; Wells, Maine; December 21, 1861.

 Locke, William; January, 1862; deserted 1862.

*Ludy, Peter, SM; 22; Austria; February 11, 1864.

*Lynch, Timothy, CH; 26; Portsmouth, N.H.; November 29, 1861; died May 20, 1893, Suncook, N.H.

*McAllen, John, Private, USMC; 21; Massachusetts; October 12, 1861; discharged 1865.

*McBeth, James, OS; January 26, 1864; fractured left leg, June 19, 1864.

*McCarthy, John H., 1st Class Boy; December 4, 1861; rated OS, but reduced to LM April 14, 1864.

*McCarty, Dennis, LM; 28, Ireland; January 2, 1862.

McClaymont, Archibald, Officers' Steward; May 11, 1862; deserted.

*McConnell, Henry L., 3rd Assistant Engineer; appointed 1861; died May 10, 1903.

*McKeever, Patrick, LM; 21; Ireland; January 2, 1862.

McNally, Mathew, OS; June 26, 1862; deserted.

*McPherson, Hugh, GM; 30; Nove Scotia; January 14, 1862.

*Magee, James, SM; December 24, 1861.

Maguire, Charles; January, 1862; deserted May 28, 1862.

*Marsh, Thomas, CH; June 17, 1862.

*Mattison, Charles, OS; January 29, 1864.

Meinsen, Heinrich, CH; February 6, 1864; deserted.

Mellus, James W.; January, 1862; deserted January 6, 1863.

Melvin, Thomas, LM; May 11, 1862; deserted.

*Miller, Frederick L., 3rd Assistant Engineer; Massachusetts; appointed October 21, 1861.

*Moore, Charles, OS; March 25, 1862; rated SM; awarded Medal of Honor.

*Morey, James, OS; December 30, 1861.

*Morgan, William S., Coxswain; January 14, 1862.

Motley, Robert; January, 1862; deserted December 23, 1862.

Mulhall, Peter, Corporal, USMC; sent to hospital February 2, 1862, before cruise began.

Murphy, Hugh, Supernumerary; March 24, 1863; deserted.

Murphy, John, SM; January, 1862; sent home from Spain August 25, 1862.

Muzzey, Charles O., Captain's Clerk; appointed November, 1861; returned to U.S. from the Azores, April 9, 1863.

Netto, John, LM; July 11, 1862; deserted January 24, 1864.

*Nye, Levi W., SM; 25; Maine; January 7, 1862.

*O'Connor, Patrick, 2nd Class FM; 24; Ireland; February 4, 1862.

*O'Halloran, William, SM; 29; Ireland; June 18, 1863.

*Ordion, John E., 2nd Class FM; 22; New Hampshire; November 13, 1861.

*Pease, Joachim, SM; 20; Long Island; January 13, 1862; awarded Medal of Honor.

*Perry, Thomas, SM; 26; New York; January 14, 1862; rated Captain of the Foretop 1862; rated BM 1863; awarded Medal of Honor.

*Phillips, Zaran, OS; 37; Massachusetts; January 7, 1862; died December 12, 1914.

Pickering, Charles W., Commander; 48; assigned November 1, 1861; promoted to Captain July 16, 1862; relieved April 8, 1863; died February 29, 1888, St. Augustine, Fla.

Pike, Jacob F.; sent home from Spain April 6, 1862.

*Poole, Charles A., CH; 20; Bowdoinham, Maine; November 26, 1861; died January 17, 1915.

*Poole, William B., SM; 29; Cape Elizabeth, Maine; February 1, 1862; rated Coxswain July 4, 1862; rated QM December 17, 1862; awarded Medal of Honor.

*Pope, John, CH; 21; England; January 26, 1864.

*Preble, Edward E., Midshipman; assigned December 17, 1861; promoted to Lieutenant February 22, 1864; detached from *Kearsarge* July 15, 1864.

*Priest, True W., 1st Class FM; 26; Portsmouth, N.H.; December 28, 1861; died February 20, 1909.

Quanstrum, G. T.; name appears only on original roster.

*Quinby, Austin, Private, USMC, 23; Sandwich, N.H.; October 13, 1861; appointed corporal December 21, 1861; discharged October 17, 1865; died April 22, 1922.

*Raymond, George A., Private, USMC; 21; New York; September 18, 1861; discharged 1865.

*Read, Charles A., SM; 25; Sweden; January 11, 1862; rated Coxswain; awarded Medal of Honor.

*Read, George E., SM; 24; Rhode Island; January 7, 1862; awarded Medal of Honor.

*Redding, Charles, LM; 22; Boston, Mass.; January 1, 1862.

*Remick, George W., 1st Class FM; 33; Newburyport, Mass.; January 17, 1862.

Roach, Martin, LM; May 11, 1862; deserted April 7, 1864.

Roland, Edward, LM; September 26, 1862; deserted.

Roney, Charles; name appears only on original roster.

Rousserz, Antonio, OS; February 6, 1864; deserted.

*Rowley, Andrew, QG; 34; Maine; January 11, 1862.

*Russell, George H., Armorer; 29; Massachusetts; January 1, 1862.

*Salmon, Thomas, 2nd Class FM; 27; Ireland; February 4, 1862.

*Sanborn, Joel L., 1st Class FM; 29; Epsom, N.H.; January 18, 1862; died April 11, 1906, Boston, Mass.

*Sanborn, John W., CH; 22; Newmarket, N.H.; December 13, 1862.

*Sargent, Daniel B., Paymaster's Steward; Maine; promoted to Paymaster's Clerk; died April 17, 1921, Omaha, Nebr.

*Saunders, James, QM; 53; Massachusetts; January 11, 1862; awarded Medal of Honor.

Scott, Robert T., Wardroom Steward; January, 1862; deserted August 19, 1862.

*Sheffield, James W., 2nd Class FM; 24; New York; November 26, 1861.

*Shields, John, SM; 22; Ireland; February 10, 1864.

Simpson, Martin T.; name appears only on original roster.

*Smart, George A., 2nd Class FM; 32; Portsmouth, N.H.; November 21, 1861.

Smith, Christian, QM; January, 1862; deserted January 1, 1863.

Smith, David M.; name appears only on original roster.

*Smith, Joseph Adams, Assistant Paymaster; Maine; promoted to Paymaster.

*Smith, Sidney L., 3rd Assistant Engineer; Massachusetts; appointed October 21, 1861; promoted to 2nd Assistant Engineer August 25, 1863; died May 25, 1914.

*Smith, Stephen, 2nd Class FM; 35; New Hampshire; November 19, 1861.

*Smith, William, 1st Class FM; 23; Ireland; November 28, 1861; died January 12, 1902.

*Smith, William, SM; 24; Ireland; rated Coxswain July 4, 1862; rated QM; rated Master's Mate July 8, 1864; awarded Medal of Honor.

*Smith, William M., LM; 17; Massachusetts; January 11, 1862.

*Sonius, John M., 1st Class Boy; 23; Netherlands; May 12, 1864.

Spencer, William C., OS; June 26, 1862; deserted March 17, 1863.

*Spinney, Lyman P., CH; 21; Eliot, Maine; November 25, 1861; died January 24, 1899.

*Stackpole, John T., 2nd Class FM; 35; Maine; January 21, 1862.

*Stanley, William, 2nd Class FM; 38; Vermont; January 22, 1862.

Stevens, P. E.; transferred to USS *Ino* April 29, 1862.

*Stoddard, Eben M., Acting Master; Massachusetts; appointed October 29, 1861.

*Stone, James O., 1st Class Boy; 16; Massachusetts; November 13, 1861.

*Strahan, Robert, SM; 26; New Jersey; January 20, 1862; rated Captain of the Maintop September 19, 1862; awarded Medal of Honor.

Sullivan, Thomas; name appears only on original roster.

*Sumner, David H., Acting Master; Maine; appointed December, 1861.

Taylor, James, OS; April 10, 1862; deserted.

Thompson, John, OS; January, 1862; deserted November 4, 1863.

*Thornton, Isaac, Private, USMC; 21; New York; October 28, 1861; discharged 1865.

*Thornton, James S., Lieutenant Commander; 36; New Hampshire; assigned December, 1862; reported April 8, 1863; died May 14, 1875, Philadelphia, Pa.

Tibbetts, Edward H. (real name Edward H. Sampson), OS; 19; Brunswick, Maine; January 1, 1862; killed by a shark July 13, 1862.

Tirnan, Charles; Ireland; January, 1862; sent home from Spain June 18, 1863.

*Tittle, George A., Surgeon's Steward; 39; New Hampshire; forefinger amputated for infection, March 12, 1862.

Trude, Francis M.; January, 1862; deserted May 27, 1863.

*Tucker, James, Private, USMC; 23; Ireland; October 8, 1861; discharged 1865.

Tupic, Andrew, SM; January, 1862; sent to hospital February 2, 1862, before cruise began.

Turner, Thomas, Supernumerary; August 25, 1862; deserted.

*Turner, William, SM; 32; Massachusetts; June 18, 1863.

Van Dyke, H. H.; January, 1862; sent home from Spain April 6, 1862.

*Viannah, Francis, SM; 43; Faial, Azores Islands; February 3, 1862; appointed Captain of the After Guard July 30, 1862; died August 1, 1868, Holmes Hole Marine Hospital, Mass.

Vincent, Richard H., CH; 30; Cornwall, England; January 13, 1862; deserted February 3, 1862, before cruise began.

*Wainwright, William, CH; 20; England; November 22, 1861; died April 13, 1920.

*Wallace, Edward, SM; 23; Ireland; March 28, 1862; rated QM but later disrated.

*Walton, James C., Boatswain; appointed May 9, 1859; died June 30, 1887, Naval Asylum, Philadelphia, Pa.

Wards, Henry, Supernumerary; discharged March 25, 1862.

*Watrus, Jason N., Master at Arms; 27; Ohio; January 9, 1862.

*Weeks, Phillip, SM; 26; Massachusetts; February 10, 1864.

*Wheeler, James R., Acting Master; England; appointed October 29, 1861.

*Whipple, George A., OS; 27; Millbury, Mass.; March 26, 1862.

White, Charles; January, 1862; deserted.

Whittaker, James W., 1st Assistant Engineer; detached from *Kearsarge* September 9, 1862; died March 9, 1881.

*Williams, Edward, Captain's Steward; 30; Boston, Mass.; January 17, 1862.

*Williams, George, Captain's Cook; 34; Maryland; January 18, 1862.

Wilson, Frank, OS; March 25, 1862; rated Captain of the Top July 4, 1862; rated Coxswain September 17, 1862; disrated to SM January 22, 1863; deserted March 17, 1863.

*Wilson, James, Coxswain; 27; New York; December 31, 1861.

Wilson, John; January, 1862; deserted March 24, 1862.

*Wilt, Edward, SM; 27; Pennsylvania; June 26, 1862.

*Winslow, John A., Captain; 51; North Carolina; assigned December, 1862; took command April 8, 1863; promoted to Commodore retroactively to June 19, 1864; promoted to Rear Admiral 1870; died September 29, 1873, Boston, Mass.

Wood, John, OS; April 10, 1862; deserted.

*Woodbury, John C., OS; 23; Massachusetts; January 6, 1862.

Yeaton, William H., Acting Master's Mate; December 17, 1861; left sick at Cadiz, Spain, February 12, 1864; ordered to return to U.S. from Cadiz August 11, 1864. Mistakenly carried on roll of *Kearsarge* during battle of June 19.

*Young, Charles T., Orderly Sergeant, USMC; 41; Massachusetts; October 9, 1858; discharged December 7, 1864.

*Young, Jere, 1st Class FM; 29; Newmarket, N.H.; January 18, 1862.

*Young, John W., CH; 22; Dover, N.H.; December 16, 1861.

Number of officers and men aboard *Kearsarge* during battle of June 19, 1864: 162.

Total number of officers and men who served aboard the *Kearsarge* at one time or another, during the cruise of 1862–64: 240 (includes four who deserted or were sent to the hospital before the cruise began, but does not include fifteen "stowaways" returned to Ireland in December of 1863, or twenty whalers transported from the Azores to St. Thomas in 1864).

CSS *Alabama*

All began their duties August 24, 1862, unless otherwise noted.

Adams, James, OS; shipped at Kingston, Jamaica, January 25, 1863; discharged by court-martial August 30, 1863, Angra Pequeña, coast of Africa.

*Adams, John, OS; shipped at Cape Town August 15, 1863; reduced to LM February 16, 1864; missing June 19, 1864.

*Adams, Nicholas, LM; shipped at Cape Town March 25, 1864; captured by *Kearsarge* and paroled.

*Addison, George, Armorer; Liverpool; missing June 19, 1864.

*Allcot, Henry W., Sailmaker; 24; Liverpool; rescued by pilot boat; later Sailmaker, CSS *Shenandoah*; died March 3, 1891, Liverpool.

Allen, John, SM; shipped from prize October 3, 1862; deserted December 24, 1863, Singapore.

Allman, Thomas J., OS; shipped from prize *Conrad* June 21, 1863; transferred to *Tuscaloosa* same day.

*Anderson, Edward Maffitt, Midshipman; Savannah, Ga.; rescued by *Deerhound*; died January 28, 1923, Savannah, Ga.

*Angel, Henry, OS; shipped at Cape Town, September 25, 1863; rescued by *Deerhound*.

*Appleby, George, Yeoman; 32; New Brunswick (resided in Liverpool); reduced to SM May 21, 1863; killed June 19, 1864.

*Armstrong, Richard F., 2nd Lieutenant; 19; Georgia; wounded June 19, 1864, and rescued by pilot boat; died 1904, Halifax, Nova Scotia.

*Bartelli, A. G., Captain's Steward; drowned June 19, 1864.

*Benson, John, CT; shipped from prize April 21, 1863; captured by *Kearsarge* and paroled.

*Bradford, William, OS; shipped from prize July 7, 1863; missing June 19, 1864.

*Bradley, Patrick, FM; Liverpool; captured by *Kearsarge* and paroled.

*Brandon, Thomas, OS; shipped at Cape Town September 25, 1863; reduced to LM February 16, 1864; captured by *Deerhound* and paroled.

Brewer, Samuel, SM; 23; Liverpool; shipped from prize November 8, 1862; transferred to *Tuscaloosa* June 21, 1863; died 1886, Liverpool.

*Bright, Maurice, Boy; shipped from prize April 18, 1863; rescued by pilot boat.

*Broderick, James, OS; shipped from prize July 7, 1863; rated SM December 20, 1863; rated Coxswain December 31, 1863; captured by *Kearsarge* and paroled.

*Brooks, William P., 2nd Assistant Engineer; Georgia; rescued by pilot boat.

*Brosnan, James, SM; Liverpool; rated BM March 1, 1863; Chief BM August 19, 1863; wounded June 19, 1864, and rescued by *Deerhound*.

*Buckley, John, OS; shipped at Cape Town March 25, 1864; missing June 19, 1864.

*Bulloch, Irvine S., Midshipman; Georgia; rescued by *Deerhound*; later sailing master of CSS *Shenandoah*.

*Burns, William, SM; shipped from prize November 8, 1862; rated QG April 12, 1864; captured by *Kearsarge* and paroled.

*Burrell, Edward, SM; shipped from prize *Tycoon* May 9, 1864; captured by *Kearsarge* and paroled.

*Caren, John, SM; Liverpool; wounded June 19, 1864, captured by *Kearsarge*, and paroled.

*Clark, William, SM; shipped from prize October 3, 1862; captured by *Kearsarge* and paroled.

*Clements, James, OS; shipped from prize October 12, 1862; rated Yeoman July 1, 1863; captured by *Kearsarge* and paroled.

Coles, Charles, OS; shipped from prize April 1, 1863; rated SM August 22, 1863; deserted September 19, 1863, Cape Town.

*Colson, Charles, OS; England; shipped from prize *Emma Jane* January 16, 1864; missing June 19, 1864.

*Columbia, Fred, OS; France; shipped from prize July 7, 1863; rated Captain of the Hold August 15, 1863; captured by *Kearsarge* and paroled.

*Connor, Joseph, SM; Liverpool; rated Captain of the After Guard February 1, 1863; rescued by *Deerhound*.

*Conroy, George, OS; shipped at Cape Town September 25, 1863; captured by *Kearsarge* and paroled.

Cosgrove, Henry, Boy; Liverpool; deserted December 23, 1863, Singapore.

*Crawford, William, QG; Liverpool; rated GM February 1, 1863; rescued by *Deerhound*.

*Cuddy, Thomas C., Gunner; Charleston, S.C.; rescued by *Deerhound*; drowned January 19, 1865, in the foundering of blockade runner Lelia.

Cummings, Simeon W., 3rd Assistant Engineer; New York; accidentally killed August 3, 1863, Saldanha Bay, South Africa.

*Curran, Frank, FM; Liverpool; captured by *Kearsarge* and paroled; 3rd Assistant Engineer, CSS *Shenandoah*.

*Dent, James G., QM; Savannah, Ga.; rescued by *Deerhound*.

*Devine, Robert, OS; shipped at Singapore December 24, 1863; wounded June 19, 1864, captured by *Kearsarge*, and paroled.

Doyle, John, SM; deserted December 23, 1863, Singapore.

*Duffy, Owen, FM; Ireland; rescued by *Deerhound*.

Duggan, John, SM; Liverpool; transferred to *Tuscaloosa* June 21, 1863.

*Duncan, Peter, CT; Liverpool; rated FM March 1, 1863; killed June 19, 1864.

*Dupois, Louis, OS (served as midshipmen's steward); France; shipped from prize *T. B. Wales* November 9, 1862; rescued by *Deerhound*.

Egan, Robert, Boy; England; deserted September 21, 1863, Cape Town.

*Egerton, George, LM; Liverpool; rated OS May 16, 1863; rescued by pilot boat.

*Emery, John, LM (engineers' steward); Liverpool; rated OS April 19, 1863; captured by *Kearsarge* and paroled.

*Eustachia, Henry, OS; captured by *Kearsarge* and paroled.

*Evans, James, Master's Mate; 27; England (resided Charleston, S.C.); rescued by *Deerhound*.

*Evans, Richard, OS; shipped at Cape Town September 25, 1863; captured by *Kearsarge* and paroled.

*Fisher, Henry, Coxswain; Liverpool; reduced to SM October 9, 1862; missing June 19, 1864.

Fitzmaurice, Edward, OS; Liverpool; discharged as an invalid November 26, 1862, Blanquilla.

Forrest, George, SM; captured aboard the *Dunkirk* October 8, 1862, and recognized as a deserter from the CSS *Sumter*; dishonorably discharged November 26, 1862, Blanquilla.

*Forrestal, William F., QM; Liverpool; captured by *Kearsarge* and paroled.

*Foxton, James, CT; Liverpool; rated FM April 21, 1863; rescued by *Deerhound*.

*Freeman, Miles J., Acting Chief Engineer; 30; Wales (resided New Orleans, La.); captured by *Kearsarge* and transported to Fort Warren, Boston Harbor, where he was held until the conclusion of the war.

*Freemantle, George, Captain's Coxswain; England; captured by *Kearsarge* and paroled.

*Fripp, Edgar, LM; London, England; rated OS April 19, 1863; captured by *Kearsarge* and paroled.

*Fullam, George T., Master's Mate; 21; England; rescued by *Deerhound*; lost at sea in December, 1879.

*Galt, Francis L., Surgeon; 30; Norfolk, Va.; appointed Paymaster January 25, 1863; captured by *Kearsarge* and paroled; died November 17, 1915, Upperville, Va.

Genshlea, Michael, FM; Ireland (resided in England); discharged as an invalid November 26, 1862, Blanquilla.

Getzinger, George, OS; shipped from prize April 18, 1863; discharged as an invalid August 12, 1863, Cape Town.

Gilman, Albert, OS; shipped from prize January 25, 1863; deserted July 31, 1863, Saldanha Bay.

*Godson, Henry, OS; shipped from prize November 8, 1862; captured by *Kearsarge* and paroled.

*Godwin, Charles, Captain of the After Guard; Liverpool; rescued by pilot boat.

Grady, John, Boy; Liverpool; deserted December 23, 1863, Singapore.

Halford, William, OS; shipped from prize October 9, 1862; deserted January 21, 1863, Kingston, Jamaica.

Hambly, Richard, OS; shipped at Cape Town September 25, 1863; deserted December 23, 1863, Singapore.

*Harrigan, John, FM; Ireland; captured by *Kearsarge* and paroled.

*Hart, James, OS; shipped at Cape Town September 25, 1863; rated SM December 30, 1863; killed June 19, 1864.

Harwood, George, Chief BM; Liverpool; enlisted for six months and discharged at sea February 27, 1863; later Boatswain of the CSS *Shenandoah*.

*Hearn, William, SM; Liverpool; rescued by *Deerhound*.

Henney, Peter, OS; Liverpool; deserted May 17, 1863, Bahia, Brazil.

*Henry, Samuel, SM; Liverpool; captured by *Kearsarge* and paroled.

*Higgins, Henry, OS; Liverpool; shipped at Singapore December 24, 1863; reduced to LM February 16, 1864; captured by *Kearsarge* and paroled.

*Higgs, James, Captain of the Hold; Liverpool; reduced to SM July 3, 1863; captured by *Kearsarge* and paroled.

*Hobbs, Russell B., OS; Georgetown, Del.; shipped at Cape Town August 15, 1863; rated QM same day; reduced to SM December 31, 1863; captured by *Kearsarge* and paroled.

*Howell, Becket K., Lieutenant of Marines; Louisiana; rescued by *Deerhound*.

Hughes, John, SM; shipped from prize March 27, 1863; deserted September 18, 1863, Cape Town.

*Hughes, Peter, Captain of the Foretop; Liverpool; rated Coxswain March 1, 1863; rated BM August 19, 1863; wounded June 19, 1864, captured by *Kearsarge*, and paroled.

Hyer, Albert, OS; shipped from prize March 26, 1863; rated SM November 1, 1863; reduced to OS November 16, 1863; deserted December 23, 1863, Singapore.

Jack, John, FM; England; deserted September 18, 1863, Cape Town.

Jackson, Peter, OS; shipped from prize March 26, 1863; deserted September 19, 1863, Cape Town.

James, Thomas, OS; shipped from prize November 17, 1862; deserted August 12, 1863, Cape Town.

*Johns, Frederick M., Paymaster's Steward; 22; Liverpool; missing June 19, 1864.

*Johnson, Brent, BM; England; rated Chief BM March 1, 1863; disrated to SM August 18, 1863; rated QM December 24, 1863; wounded June 19, 1864, and rescued by *Deerhound*.

Jones, Edwin, SM; England; transferred to *Tuscaloosa*, June 21, 1863.

*Jones, William, OS; England; shipped from *Agrippina* January 4, 1863 (from Sinclair's roster; not on muster roll of July 7, 1863); missing June 19, 1864.

*Jonson, John, OS; shipped from prize *Emma Jane* January 16, 1864; captured by *Kearsarge* and paroled.

*Kehoe, Thomas S., OS; shipped at Cape Town September 25, 1863; rescued by *Deerhound*.

*Kell, John M., 1st Lieutenant; 39; Georgia; rescued by *Deerhound*; died October 5, 1900, in Georgia.

*King, James, OS, shipped at Singapore December 24, 1863; killed June 19, 1864.

King, James W. S., QM (Master at Arms); 28; Savannah, Ga.; deserted May 20, 1863, Bahia, Brazil.

*King, Martin, CT; England; rated FM September 25, 1863; wounded June 19, 1864, captured by *Kearsarge*, and paroled.

King, William R., QM; Savannah, Ga.; deserted December 23, 1863, Singapore.

*Lanerty, Peter, FM; England; captured by *Kearsarge* and paroled.

Latham, John, FM; 28; Manchester, England; deserted January 21, 1863, Kingston, Jamaica.

*Leggett, David, SM; shipped from prize October 8, 1862; captured by *Kearsarge* and paroled.

Legris, H., SM; transferred to *Tuscaloosa*, June 21, 1863.

*Lennon, Fred, OS; shipped at Cape Town March 25, 1864; rescued by *Deerhound*.

*Levins, William, CT; rescued by *Deerhound*.

*Llewelyn, David Herbert, Assistant Surgeon: 25; Wiltshire, England; drowned June 19, 1864.

*Longshaw, Robert, OS; Savannah, Ga.; shipped from prize *Rockingham* April 30, 1864; rescued by *Deerhound*.

Low, John, 4th Lieutenant; 26; Aberdeen, Scotland (resided Savannah, Ga.); transferred to *Tuscaloosa* June 21, 1863; died September 6, 1906, Liverpool.

McAlee, John, OS; England; deserted January 21, 1863, Kingston, Jamaica.

*McCaskey, Benjamin P., Boatswain; Louisiana; captured by *Kearsarge* and transported to Fort Warren, Boston Harbor, where he was held until the end of the war.

*McClellan, William, OS; shipped from prize March 26, 1863; rescued by *Deerhound*.

*McCoy, Henry, OS; shipped at Cape Town March 25, 1864; captured by *Kearsarge* and paroled.

McFadden, James, FM; Liverpool; enlisted for six months; discharged at sea February 27, 1863.

*McFarland, Malcolm, CT; Scotland; rated FM December 20, 1863; wounded June 19, 1864, and rescued by *Deerhound*.

*McGinley, William, SM; England; rated Coxswain July 1, 1863; wounded June 19, 1864, captured by *Kearsarge*, and paroled.

*McMillan, Thomas, Coxswain; England; reduced to SM May 21, 1863; rescued by *Deerhound*.

*Maffitt, Eugene Anderson, Midshipman; North Carolina; rescued by *Deerhound*.

*Maguire, James, CT; shipped at Kingston, Jamaica, January 25, 1863; captured by *Kearsarge* and paroled.

Mahany, Frank, OS; shipped at Cape Town August 15, 1863; deserted December 23, 1863, Singapore.

*Mair, James, FM; England; killed June 19, 1864.

Maling, Nicholas, OS; shipped at Cape Town August 15, 1863; deserted September 21, 1863, Cape Town.

Marmelstein, Adolphus Frederick, QM; 25; Baltimore, Md. (resided Savannah, Ga.); transferred to *Tuscaloosa* June 21, 1863; died November 21, 1922, Savannah, Ga.

*Mars, Michael, SM; 41; Ireland (resided at Bristol, England); rescued by pilot boat; died August, 1878, London, England.

Martin, James, SM; shipped from prize November 8, 1862; discharged as an invalid August 12, 1864, Cape Town.

*Mason, James, CT; England; rated FM May 26, 1863; wounded June 19, 1864, and rescued by *Deerhound*.

*Masters, Ralph, QG; Ireland; reduced to SM April 5, 1864; reduced to OS April 12, 1864; rescued by *Deerhound*.

*Mehan, John, OS; shipped at Cape Town September 25, 1863; rescued by *Deerhound*.

Mesner, Valentine, OS; shipped from prize October 27, 1862; deserted January 21, 1863, Kingston, Jamaica.

*Midich, Martin, OS; shipped from prize October 27, 1862; captured by *Kearsarge* and paroled.

Miller, John, OS; shipped from prize June 21, 1863; deserted September 21, 1863, Cape Town.

*Miller, William, OS; shipped at Kingston, Jamaica, January 25, 1863; captured by *Kearsarge* and paroled.

Minor, Joseph F., SM; Virginia; shipped from prize March 25, 1863; transferred to *Tuscaloosa* June 21, 1863.

Molk, Martin, OS; England; shipped from *Agrippina* November 25, 1862; transferred to *Tuscaloosa* June 21, 1863.

*Morgan, William, Captain of the Maintop; Liverpool; reduced to SM July 3, 1863; Captain of the Foretop December 23, 1863; wounded June 19, 1864, captured by *Kearsarge*, and paroled.

Morris, Alfred, OS; shipped from prize October 28, 1862; deserted August 12, 1863, Cape Town.

*Murphy, Thomas, FM; Ireland (resided in England); rescued by pilot boat.

*Myers, Frederick, OS; shipped from prize March 25, 1863; rated CM April 26, 1863; missing June 19, 1864.

Neal, Joseph, OS; England; shipped from prize November 8, 1862; deserted January 21, 1863, Kingston, Jamaica.

*Neil, John, SM; Liverpool; wounded June 19, 1864, captured by *Kearsarge*, and paroled.

Nordstrom, William, OS; shipped from prize March 27, 1863; deserted August 1, 1863, Saldanha Bay.

*Norhoek, Abram, Ship's Corporal; shipped from prize September 15, 1862; missing June 19, 1864.

*O'Brien, Matthew, 3rd Assistant Engineer; 25; Limerick, Ireland (resided in Louisiana); rescued by *Deerhound*; later Chief Engineer, CSS *Shenandoah*.

*Ochoa, Juan, OS; shipped from prize November 10, 1862; rated SM August 22, 1863; captured by *Kearsarge* and paroled.

*Olsen, Charles, OS; shipped from prize March 25, 1863; rated SM November 1, 1863; killed June 19, 1864.

Owens, Robert, OS; shipped from prize April 18, 1863; transferred to *Tuscaloosa* June 21, 1863.

*Pajorva, Karl, OS; shipped from prize November 11, 1863; killed June 19, 1864.

*Parker, Thomas L., Boy; England; captured by *Kearsarge* and paroled.

*Parkinson, Richard, Wardroom Steward; captured by *Kearsarge* and paroled.

*Pearson, Joseph, SM; Liverpool; rated CT May 26, 1863; captured by *Kearsarge* and paroled.

*Percy, George, OS; shipped from prize *Conrad* June 21, 1863; captured by *Kearsarge* and paroled.

*Pfeiffer, Andrew, OS; shipped at Cape Town September 25, 1863; rescued by *Deerhound*.

*Potter, Thomas, FM; 27; Liverpool; deserted January 21, 1863, Kingston, Jamaica; returned January 25, 1863; captured by *Kearsarge* and paroled; died February 3, 1867, Liverpool.

Price, William, OS; English; discharged as an invalid November 26, 1862, Blanquilla.

*Pundt, John M., 3rd Assistant Engineer; 31; Charleston, S.C.; captured by *Kearsarge*.

*Purdy, William, Sailmaker's Mate; Ireland; rescued by *Deerhound*.

*Pust, Christian, CT; Germany; killed June 19, 1864.

Raleigh, James, SM; shipped from prize November 8, 1862; deserted September 19, 1863, Cape Town.

*Rawse, Edward, Ship's Corporal; England; rated Master at Arms June 1, 1863; captured by *Kearsarge* and paroled.

Ray, Richard, OS; shipped at Cape Town August 15, 1863; deserted September 21, 1863, Cape Town.

*Riley, John, FM; disrated to CT November 17, 1863; captured by *Kearsarge* and paroled.

Rinton, William, Carpenter's Mate; England; wounded in cheek January 11, 1863; reduced to SM January 31, 1863; transferred to *Tuscaloosa* June 21, 1863.

*Roach, David, FM; England; deserted January 21, 1863, Kingston, Jamaica.

*Roberts, John, SM; Wales (resided in England); killed June 19, 1864.

*Robertson, William, 3rd Assistant Engineer; England; missing June 19, 1864.

*Robinson, William, Carpenter; 28; Boston, Mass. (resided in Louisiana); killed June 19, 1864.

*Robinson, William, SM; England; shipped from prize November 26, 1862; rescued by pilot boat.

Ross, George, OS; shipped from prize December 1, 1862; deserted September 17, 1863, Cape Town.

*Russell, John, OS; shipped at Cape Town August 15, 1863; captured by *Kearsarge* and paroled.

Saunders, Henry, OS; shipped from prize *Express* July 7, 1863; deserted September 21, 1863, Cape Town.

*Schroeder, Julius, Master's Mate; Hanover, Prussia; appointed at Cape Town, September 25, 1863; rescued by *Deerhound*.

Schwalbe, Gustave, OS; shipped from prize September 20, 1862; deserted January 21, 1863, Kingston, Jamaica.

*Semmes, Raphael, Commander; 52; Maryland (resided in Mobile, Ala.); promoted to Captain September 8, 1862; died August 30, 1877, Mobile, Ala.

*Seymour, Charles, Captain of the After Guard; England; rated QG February 1, 1863; rescued by *Deerhound*.

*Shields, Michael, SM; shipped from prize November 8, 1862; captured by *Kearsarge* and paroled.

*Shilland, Adam, FM; Liverpool; missing June 19, 1864.

*Sinclair, Arthur, Jr., Sailing Master; 25; Norfolk, Va.; promoted to 4th Lieutenant June 21, 1863; rescued by *Deerhound*; died November 15, 1925, Baltimore, Md.

Sinclair, William H., Midshipman; Virginia; transferred to *Tuscaloosa* June 21, 1863.

Smith, James, Captain of the Forecastle; Liverpool; deserted December 23, 1863, Singapore.

*Smith, John, OS; shipped at Cape Town September 25, 1863; captured by *Kearsarge* and paroled.

*Smith, William Breedlove, Captain's Clerk; Louisiana; rescued by *Deerhound*; later Paymaster, CSS *Shenandoah*.

*Steeson, Charles, SM; Sweden; shipped from prize November 8, 1862; rated Captain of the Hold July 3, 1863; disrated to SM August 15, 1863; rated Captain of the Foretop December 24, 1863; rescued by *Deerhound*.

Thomas, George, OS; shipped from prize *Conrad* June 21, 1863; deserted September 19, 1863, Cape Town.

*Thurston, David, SM; shipped from prize October 3, 1862; captured by *Kearsarge* and paroled.

*Townsend, Frank, SM; England; reduced to OS November 16, 1863; wounded June 19, 1864, and rescued by *Deerhound*.

*Tucker, Henry, Officers' Cook; England; captured by *Kearsarge* and paroled.

Valens, Samuel, OS; shipped at Cape Town August 15, 1863; deserted September 21, 1863, Cape Town.

*Van Ness, Walter, OS; shipped from prize October 27, 1862; rated SM August 22, 1863; drowned June 19, 1864.

*Verber, Jacob, OS; shipped from prize February 21, 1863; rated SM August 22, 1863; wounded June 19, 1864, captured by *Kearsarge*, and paroled.

Vial, John, OS; shipped from prize February 21, 1863; deserted September 17, 1863, Cape Town.

*Von Meulnier, Maximilian, Master's Mate; Bremen, Prussia; appointed at Cape Town September 25, 1863; rescued by *Deerhound*.

Wallace, James, OS; shipped from prize April 18, 1863; deserted August 1, 1863, Saldanha Bay.

Walsh, Thomas, OS; England; discharged as an invalid November 26, 1862, Blanquilla.

*Watson, Thomas, OS; shipped at Singapore December 24, 1863; captured by *Kearsarge* and paroled.

Weir, Thomas, GM; Liverpool; rated QM July 1, 1863; deserted August 11, 1863, Cape Town.

*Welham, John, OS; shipped at Cape Town September 25, 1863; drowned June 19, 1864.

*Welsh, James, OS; shipped at Cape Town August 15, 1863; rated CT September 25, 1863; rescued by pilot boat.

*Wharton, Philip, OS; shipped at Cape Town August 15, 1863; rescued by *Deerhound*.

*White, David Henry, Boy; 17; Delaware; black servant, ostensibly a slave, taken from prize *Tonawanda* October 9, 1862; missing June 19, 1864.

*White, Thomas, OS; shipped at Cape Town September 25, 1863; reduced to LM February 16, 1864; missing June 19, 1864.

*Williams, David, OS; shipped from prize October 3, 1862; wounded June 19, 1864, captured by *Kearsarge*, and paroled.

Williams, James, SM; shipped from prize November 8, 1862; rated Captain of the Foretop July 3, 1863; deserted December 23, 1863, Singapore.

*Williams, John, OS; shipped from prize *Conrad* June 21, 1863; rated SM August 22, 1863; missing June 19, 1864.

Williams, John, OS; shipped from prize *Express* July 7, 1863; deserted September 21, 1863, Cape Town.

Williams, Robert, SM; England; transferred to *Tuscaloosa* June 21, 1863.

*Williams, Samuel, FM; Wales (resided in Liverpool); wounded June 19, 1864, captured by *Kearsarge*, and paroled.

Williams, Thomas, SM; Liverpool; transferred to *Tuscaloosa* June 21, 1863.

*Wilson, James, Boy; captured by *Kearsarge* and paroled.

*Wilson, John, Boy; shipped at Cape Town September 25, 1863; captured by *Kearsarge* and paroled.

*Wilson, Joseph D., 3rd Lieutenant; 20; Florida; captured by *Kearsarge*; exchanged late in 1864; commanded CS gunboat *Hampton*, 1865.

*Wilson, William, SM; shipped from prize *Conrad* June 21, 1863; rated Coxswain August 19, 1863; captured by *Kearsarge* and paroled.

*Winter, Thomas, CT; Liverpool; rated FM March 1, 1863; wounded June 19, 1864, captured by *Kearsarge*, and paroled.

*Wright, Robert, SM; England; rated Captain of the Maintop March 1, 1863; wounded June 19, 1864, and captured by *Kearsarge*.

*Yates, Henry, SM; reduced to OS January 30, 1863; rated SM November 1, 1863; captured by *Kearsarge* and paroled.

*Yeoman, George, OS; England; shipped from prize November 26, 1862; wounded June 19, 1864, and rescued by *Deerhound*.

Yonge, Clarence Randolph, Paymaster; 29; Savannah, Ga.; deserted January 24, 1863, Kingston, Jamaica; later served as a recruit in the 25th New York Cavalry under the alias J. Edward Davies; died about 1866, Washington, D.C.

Total in battle: 146; total to serve on ship: 213.

GLOSSARY OF
NAVAL TERMINOLOGY

Abaft: Astern; toward the stern of a vessel.

Aft: Toward the stern of a vessel.

Bark: A three-masted vessel with square-rigged foremast and mainmast and fore-and-aft rigged mizzenmast.

Barkantine: A three-masted vessel with square-rigged foremast and fore-and-aft rigged mainmast and mizzenmast.

Brig: A two-masted vessel with square-rigged foremast and mainmast.

Brigantine: A two-masted vessel with square-rigged foremast and mainmast, except for the mainsail, which is fore-and-aft rigged.

Bulkhead: Partitions between compartments in a vessel.

Capstan: An upright winch situated near the fore part of a ship, used principally to weigh the anchors.

Chicken: A boy aboard ship; usually one who has been "taken under the wing" of an older sailor.

Davits: Curved stanchions from which boats are suspended over the sides of a vessel.

Forecastle: The forwardmost part of the upper deck, or the portion beneath it, where the enlisted sailors sling their hammocks; the *Kearsarge* had a raised forecastle deck, while the *Alabama* did not.

Foremast: The forwardmost mast of a vessel carrying two or more masts.

Frigate: An older, three-masted sailing ship, usually with two gun decks.

Galley: The kitchen where the crew's meals are prepared.

Gun Deck: The deck of a warship on which the guns are carried; on a sloop, synonymous with "spar deck."

Hermaphrodite Brig: A brig with a fore-and-aft rigged mainmast.

Keel: The timber that constitutes the spine of a ship, extending from stem to stern.

Mainmast: The second mast of a vessel carrying two or more masts.

Mizzenmast: The mast nearest the stern of a vessel carrying three masts.

Port: The left side of a vessel as one faces forward; originally called "larboard" but changed to avoid confusion with "starboard."

Powder Monkey: Informal term for the youngest members of a ship's crew.

Ship: Technically, a three-masted vessel with all masts square-rigged.

Shroud channels: Plates on the sides of a vessel to which the shrouds are anchored.

Shrouds: The cables or ropes running from the mastheads to the sides of a vessel, which support the masts.

Sloop: A smaller warship, usually with one gun deck.

Spar Deck: The upper deck, except in the case of a raised forecastle.

Splice the Main Brace: Slang term for taking a drink.

Starboard: The right side of a vessel as one faces forward.

NOTES

Abbreviations

ADAH	Alabama Department of Archives and History, Montgomery, Ala.
Alabama log	John Low's log of the *Alabama*, William S. Hoole Collection, University of Alabama, Tuscaloosa, Ala.
DL	William L. Dayton Letters, Princeton University, Princeton, N.J.
DU	Thomas H. Dudley Collection, Huntington Library, San Marino, Calif.
Kearsarge log	Log of the USS *Kearsarge*, 1862–64 (RG24), National Archives, Washington, D.C.
LC	Library of Congress, Washington, D.C.
LRO	Liverpool Registry Office, Liverpool, England
MHS	Massachusetts Historical Society, Boston, Mass.
MSM	Mystic Seaport Museum, Mystic, Conn.
NA	National Archives, Washington, D.C.
ND	Navy Dependents' Pension Files, M-1279, National Archives
NHHS	New Hampshire Historical Society, Concord, N.H.
OR	*War of the Rebellion: A Compilation of the Official Records of the Union and Confederate Armies.* 128 vols. Washington, D.C.: Government Printing Office, 1880–1901.
ORN	*Official Records of the Union and Confederate Navies in the War of the Rebellion.* 31 vols. Washington, D.C.: Government Printing Office, 1894–1927. All citations from series 1 unless otherwise noted.
PM	Peabody Museum, Salem, Mass.
SHC	Southern Historical Collection, Wilson Library, University of North Carolina, Chapel Hill, N.C.
SHSP	*Southern Historical Society Papers.* 52 vols. Richmond, Va.: Southern Historical Society, 1876–1959
UA	University of Alabama, Tuscaloosa, Ala.
USAMHI	U.S. Army Military History Institute, Carlisle, Pa.
WBL	William Brown Library, Liverpool, England

Chapter 1

1. Semmes journal, June 18, 19, 1861, ADAH; John McIntosh Kell to Blanche Kell, June 20, 1861, quoted in Kell, "Life and Letters," Kell Papers, Duke University.

2. Semmes, *Memoirs*, 75; Abstracts of Service Records, reels 5–9, NA; Morgan, *Recollections*, 129–30.

3. *ORN* 1:614–15; Semmes to Mallory, April 29, May 1, 1861, *Sumter* letterbook, folder 15, box 43, ADAH; Semmes journal, June 25, 1861, ADAH; Abstracts of Service Records, reels 6–9, NA.

4. Semmes journal, June 19–21, 1861, ADAH; *ORN* 1:615.

5. Semmes journal, June 21–25, 1861, ADAH.

6. *ORN* 1:618–19.

7. Semmes journal, June 25–30, 1861, ADAH; Semmes to Lts. Kell, Chapman, and Stribling, June 30, 1861, *Sumter* letterbook, folder 15, box 43, ADAH; *ORN* 1:34.

8. Semmes journal, June 30–July 4, 1861, ADAH.

9. *Portsmouth Chronicle*, May 26–30, June 21, 1861. Shipyard records indicate that work on the *Kearsarge* was begun June 17 (see Barnard, "Timbers of the Kearsarge," 147).

10. Welles to G. V. Fox, September 29, 1875; Welles to S. D. and S. W. Thompson, June 27, 1876; and Welles's endorsement on Fox's notation, undated, all in Fox Papers, NHHS. See Appendix 1 for the origin of the *Kearsarge*'s name.

11. Hale to Welles, May 29, 1861, reel 19, Welles Papers, LC; *Portsmouth Chronicle*, July 13, 30, August 20, September 12, 14, 1861; Barnard, "Timbers of the Kearsarge," 147–48; *ORN*, series 2, 1:118–19.

12. *Portsmouth Chronicle*, July 30, September 16, 1861.

13. Bulloch, *Secret Service*, 1:48, 53–58; *ORN* 1:363, and series 2, 1:252.

14. Bulloch, *Secret Service*, 1:58–63, 68; *ORN*, series 2, 1:247; *Alabama* Contract and Specifications, SHC.

15. Bulloch, *Secret Service*, 1:68.

Chapter 2

1. *Portsmouth Chronicle*, October 18, 26, 1861; *ORN*, series 2, 1:118–19.

2. Loose clipping, Pickering letterbooks, NHHS; Abstracts of Service Records, reels 5–9, NA; Mary W. Pickering's original application for widow's pension, May 14, 1888, Charles W. Pickering pension file, certificate 3860, ND; *Portsmouth Chronicle*, November 18, 1861.

3. Gideon Welles to George F. Pearson, November 8, December 20, 1861, Pickering letterbooks, 1:9, NHHS; Cushman's certificates as third, second, and first assistant engineer, Cushman Papers, LC; Poole journal, November 27, 1861, MSM.

4. Welles to Pearson, November 13, 1861, Letters Sent, reel 67, NA; *Portsmouth Chronicle*, November 18, 1861.

5. Wainwright journal, November 21–28, 1861, MSM; Eighth U.S. Census, reel 678, 256, NA; declarations for pension dated November 21, 1905, January 25, 1906, May 18, 1912, William Wainwright pension file, certificate 2999, Records of the Pension Office, NA.

6. Poole journal, November 27–28, 1861, MSM; affidavit of June 14, 1907, Charles A. Poole pension file, widow's certificate 789868, ND.

7. *Portsmouth Chronicle*, December 12, 1861; Poole journal, November 29–Decem-

ber 16, 1861, January 2, 1862, MSM; Wainwright journal, December 15, 1861–January 10, 1862, MSM; *ORN,* series 2, 1:88, 159.

8. Poole journal, November 30–December 1, 1862, MSM; Wainwright journal, December "15," 1861, MSM.

9. Poole journal, December 7–31, 1861, January 17, 1862, MSM; Wainwright journal, January 17, 1862, MSM.

10. *Portsmouth Chronicle,* December 30, 1861, January 1, 10, 14, 15, 17, 1862.

11. Wainwright journal, January 14–16, 1862, MSM; Tucker, "U.S. Navy Gun Carriages," 114, 118.

12. Abstracts of Service Records, reels 6, 9, NA.

13. Poole journal, April 5, 1862, MSM; Higginson, *Massachusetts in the Army and Navy,* 2:10, 38, 102, 134, 138, 152; W. H. Yeaton's appointment, Yeaton Family Papers, NHHS; Pickering to George F. "Pierson," December 17, 1861, Pickering letterbooks, 3:1, NHHS; Bartlett diary, January 18, 1862, LC.

14. Welles to Pickering, January 10, 21, 1862, and undated fragments of a letter, Pickering letterbooks, 1:3, 6, 3:2, NHHS.

15. Affidavit of Lyman H. Hartford, December 27, 1888, Mary A. Hartford pension file, widow's certificate 12417, ND; Welles to William L. Hudson, January 24, 1862, Letters Sent, reel 67, NA; *Portsmouth Chronicle,* January 25, 1862.

16. Pickering to Pearson, February 3, 1862; Pearson to Welles, February 4, 1862; Welles to Pickering, undated; and reward notice, all in Pickering letterbooks, 1:10, 2: unpaginated, 3:4, NHHS.

17. Poole and Wainwright journals, January 27, 28, 1862, MSM; reward notice dated January 28, 1862, Pickering letterbooks, 2: unpaginated, NHHS; *Kearsarge* log, January 28, 1862.

18. Quinby journal, January 24–February 4, 1862, PM; Poole and Wainwright journals, January 25–29, 1862, MSM.

19. Quinby journal, January 24–February 4, 1862, PM; Poole and Wainwright journals, January 30–February 3, 1862, MSM.

20. Pickering to Pearson, January 29, February 3, 1862; Pearson to Welles and reply, February 4, 1862, all in Pickering letterbooks, 3:2–4, NHHS; Quinby journal, February 5, 1862, PM.

21. Quinby journal, February 5, 1862, PM; Poole and Wainwright journals, February 5, 1862, MSM; *Kearsarge* log, February 5, 1862.

22. Log of Blockade Runners at Bermuda, CSA Papers, Navy Department, reel 19, LC; Bulloch, *Secret Service,* 1:127–40, 149; *ORN,* series 2, 2:113–14, 130, 132–35, 138–39.

23. Bulloch, *Secret Service,* 1:113; *ORN,* series 2, 2:132. Low is described in Sinclair, *Two Years on the Alabama,* 262–63, and more accurately in Hoole, *Four Years in the Confederate Navy,* 2–9.

24. *ORN,* series 2, 1:322, 2:132; Eighth U.S. Census, reel 115:358, NA.

25. "Records Relating to Confederate Naval and Marine Personnel," Carded CS Navy service records, NA; Sinclair, *Two Years on the Alabama,* 278–79.

26. *ORN* 7:217, and series 2, 2:139; Bulloch, *Secret Service,* 1:149–50.

27. Bulloch, *Secret Service,* 1:150; *ORN* 6:545.

28. *ORN* 1:744.

29. Semmes journal, January 3–18, 1862, ADAH.

30. Ibid., January 21–30, 1862; Semmes, *Memoirs*, 315.

31. Semmes journal, February 2–12, 1862, ADAH; *ORN* 1:358, and series 2, 1:227.

Chapter 3

1. *ORN* 1:284; Welles to George F. Pearson, January 24, 1862, Letters Sent, reel 67, NA.

2. *Kearsarge* log, February 5–7, 1862.

3. Ibid., February 7, 1862; DeWit journal, 2, MSM; Quinby journal, February 5–17, 1862, PM; Poole journal, February 7, 1862, MSM; *ORN* 1:320–21. The DeWit journal is dated only sporadically, but its pages are numbered and it is cited by page; the Quinby journal is erratically dated and paginated in an obvious transcription that appears heavily edited.

4. Quinby journal, February 5–17, 1862, PM; DeWit journal, 3–4, MSM; Poole and Wainwright journals, February 8, 1862, MSM.

5. Bartlett diary, February 7–10, 1862, LC; *Kearsarge* log, February 7–10, 1862; Quinby journal, February 5–17, 1862, PM; *ORN* 1:321; William H. Cushman to Pickering, February 25, 1862, Pickering letterbooks, 1:7, NHHS; DeWit journal, 3, MSM.

6. *Kearsarge* log, February 10, 11, 1862; Bartlett diary, February 10–12, 1862, LC.

7. Muster rolls of the *Kearsarge*, February 5, November 20, 1862, NA; death certificate, Charles W. Pickering pension file, certificate 3860, ND. The only two surviving muster rolls for the *Kearsarge* are torn, and several personal physical descriptions are missing; some have been reconstructed from pension files.

8. Muster rolls of the *Kearsarge*, February 25, 1862, NA; DeWit journal, 11, 29, MSM.

9. *Kearsarge* log, February 13, 1862; Poole journal, February 15, 1862, MSM; *ORN* 1:321.

10. *Kearsarge* log, February 16–19, 1862; Poole journal, February 16, 1862, MSM; *ORN* 1:320; Quinby journal, February 17–19, 1862, PM.

11. *Kearsarge* log, February 17–19, 1862; Poole journal, February 18, 19, 1862, MSM.

12. DeWit journal, 3, MSM; Quinby journal, February 5–17, 1862, PM; Wainwright journal, February 17–22, 1862, MSM; Poole journal, February 22, 1862, MSM.

13. DeWit journal, 3, MSM; Quinby journal, February 21, 22, 1862, PM; Poole and Wainwright journals, February 21, 22, 1862, MSM; *ORN* 1:320.

14. Wainwright journal, February 22, 1862, MSM; *ORN* 1:320; Cushman to Pickering, February "25" [22], 1862, Pickering letterbooks, 1:7, NHHS.

15. Poole and Wainwright journals, February 22–24, 1862, MSM.

16. *ORN* 1:320; DeWit journal, 5, MSM; Quinby journal, February 23–26, 1862, PM; Poole and Wainwright journals, February 23–26, 1862, MSM.

17. Quinby journal, February 26–March 4, 1862, PM; Poole and Wainwright journals, February 26–March 4, 1862, MSM.

18. "Diary of Charles B. Fisher," 5, USAMHI; Quinby journal, March 5, 6, 1862, PM; Poole and Wainwright journals, March 5, 6, 1862, MSM.

19. Quinby journal, March 7, 1862, PM; Poole and Wainwright journals, March 7, 1862, MSM.

20. Quinby journal, March 7, 1862, PM.

21. Poole and Wainwright journals, March 8, 1862, MSM; DeWit journal, 8, MSM; "Diary of Charles B. Fisher," 6, USAMHI. Fisher (76) mentioned having served on the steamer *Fannie Bullitt*, which he said delivered Confederate ordnance to Randolph, Tennessee, in "'62 in May" [April, 1861]; J. B. Roden described the same journey on the *Fannie Bullitt* in his "Trip from New Orleans to Louisville in 1861."

22. *ORN* 1:310–17, 665, 687; *OR*, series 2, 3:473–75.

23. *ORN* 1:310, 670–79.

24. Pickering to Horatio Perry, March 8, 1862, and to DeLong, March 21, 1862, Pickering letterbooks, 2: unpaginated, NHHS; Bartlett diary, March 10, 11, 1862, LC; Quinby journal, March 10, 11, 1862, PM; Poole and Wainwright journals, March 10, 11, 1862, MSM; DeWit journal, 9, MSM. Quinby's entry for March 10 is one of several in which he includes anachronisms that cast doubt on the wartime vintage of his journal: in this case he refers to the first lieutenant of the *Kearsarge* as "Mr. Thornton," although James Thornton did not join the ship until thirteen months later.

25. Bartlett diary, March 11–13, 1862, LC; Quinby journal, March 11–13, 1862, PM; DeWit journal, 11–12, MSM.

Chapter 4

1. Semmes journal, February 17–24, 1862, ADAH.

2. Ibid., February 23–March 1, 1862; *ORN* 1:663–64, and series 2, 2:148; *OR*, series 2, 4:441, 5:612, 651.

3. *ORN* 1:676, 681–82; Semmes journal, March 14–30, 1862, ADAH.

4. *Kearsarge* log, March 26, 1862; Whipple's affidavit, dated April 5, 1862; Horatio Sprague to S. Freeling, March 31, 1862; and Freeling to Sprague, March 29, 1862, 1:42–45, 47, 49; Pickering to Sprague, March 29, 1862, 2: unpaginated; and Pickering to Welles, March 29, 1862, 3:30, all in Pickering letterbooks, NHHS; *ORN* 1:682–83.

5. Semmes journal, April 9–11, 1862, ADAH; Semmes, *Memoirs*, 347.

6. Poole journal, February 7, 14, March 13, May 17, 19, 1862, MSM; Wainwright journal, March 2, July 30, 1862, January 1, 1863, MSM; Bartlett diary, February 5–March 13, 1862, LC.

7. Ezra Bartlett to Josiah Bartlett, May 20, 1862, reel 7, Bartlett Family Papers, LC; Poole journal, June 27, 1862, December 23, 1863, MSM.

8. Poole journal, March 16, 23, 30, 1862, MSM.

9. Ibid., April 14, 16, July 31, 1862.

10. Ibid., April 16, 1862; Muster rolls of the *Kearsarge*, February 5, 1862, NA; "Diary of Charles B. Fisher," 63, 79, USAMHI.

11. DeWit journal, 10–11, MSM.

12. Ibid., 43.

13. Ibid., 46; "Diary of Charles B. Fisher," 15, USAMHI.

14. DeWit journal, 20, MSM; *Kearsarge* log, March 26, 1862.

15. Poole and Wainwright journals, April 2, 3, 1862, MSM.

16. Poole journal, April 5, 1862, MSM; DeWit journal, 27–28, MSM; Quinby journal, April 4, 1862, PM.

17. Poole journal, April 5, 6, 1862, MSM; DeWit journal, 28, MSM; *Kearsarge* log,

April "5," 1862. Entries in the log of the *Kearsarge* often do not correspond to the actual dates of the events they record, and they sometimes appear to be added from memory after the fact; some important information of an embarrassing nature was never recorded at all.

18. Poole journal, April 4, 1862, MSM; Quinby journal, April 3, 1862, PM; DeWit journal, 29, MSM; *Kearsarge* log, April 6, 1862.

19. Quinby journal, April 7, 1862, PM; Wainwright journal, April 7, 1862, MSM; DeWit journal, 53, MSM; Poole journal, April 8, 10, May 19, 1862, MSM.

20. Quinby journal, April 8–10, 1862, PM; Wainwright journal, June 5, 1862, MSM; Poole journal, April 9, 11, 18, 1862, MSM.

21. Poole journal, April 21, May 19, 1862, MSM; Quinby journal, April 10–20, 1862, PM; Pickering to Welles, March 18, 1862, Pickering letterbooks, 3:24, NHHS.

22. Poole journal, April 30, May 6, 1862, MSM; DeWit journal, 55–56, MSM; Wainwright journal, May 1, 6, 28, 1862, MSM; *Kearsarge* log, May 30, 1862.

23. *Kearsarge* log, March 24–26, April 11, May 11, 13, 26, June 4, 1862; Poole journal, May 13, June 4, 1862, August 19, 1863, MSM; DeWit journal, 53, MSM.

24. Poole and Wainwright journals, June 3–8, 1862, MSM.

25. Wainwright journal, June 11, 1862, MSM; Poole journal, June 10, 1862, MSM; DeWit journal, 57, 69, 72, 75, MSM.

26. Poole and Wainwright journals, June 12, 1862, MSM; "Diary of Charles B. Fisher," 9, USAMHI.

27. Poole journal, June 15, 16, 1862, MSM; Wainwright journal, June 14, 15, 1862, MSM.

28. Poole and Wainwright journals, June 15–24, 1862, MSM; *Kearsarge* log, June 17, 25, July 4, 1862.

29. Poole journal, June 27–29, 1862, MSM; Wainwright journal, June 28, 1862, MSM; "Diary of Charles B. Fisher," 10, USAMHI.

30. Poole journal, July 2–11, 1862, MSM; Wainwright journal, July 10–30, 1862, MSM; *Kearsarge* log, July 4–20, 1862; "Diary of Charles B. Fisher," 13, USAMHI; Reports of Surgeon John M. Browne and Captain Charles W. Pickering, Pickering letterbooks, 3:58–59, NHHS.

Chapter 5

1. Semmes, *Memoirs*, 348–52; *ORN* 7:432, 465, and series 2, 2:238.

2. *ORN* 1:771; Semmes, *Memoirs*, 351.

3. *ORN*, series 2, 2:128, 130, 133, 167, 176–77, 188, 206–7, 209–10, 215.

4. Kell, *Recollections*, 180–82; Semmes, *Memoirs*, 352–54; *ORN* 7:48, and series 2, 2:172, 3:461.

5. *ORN*, series 2, 2:184, 382.

6. "Messrs. Laird Brothers and 'The Alabama,'" Gladstone Papers, Additional Collection 44610, folios 45–48, British Library; *ORN*, series 2, 2:381–84.

7. *ORN*, series 2, 2:386–87; *Case of Great Britain*, 3:411–13; *Alabama* expense account, DU, cited in Maynard, "Union Efforts," 51.

8. *Correspondence Respecting the "Alabama,"* 25–29; *The Alabama: A Statement of Facts*, 8; Isabella Harding to Layard, July 27 (2), 31, 1862, and John D. Harding to

Layard, July 31, 1862, Layard Papers, Additional Collection 39103, folios 273, 274, 288, 289, British Library; "Messrs. Laird Brothers," Gladstone Papers, Additional Collection 44610, folios 45–48, British Library.

9. Bulloch, *Secret Service*, 1:238–41; Bourne and Watt, *British Documents*, 6:152; *ORN*, series 2, 2:387–89. *Alabama* log indicates that the *Enrica* stopped for only an hour in the Mersey on July 28, putting to sea at 10:00 that morning, and William Hoole's biography of Low repeats this error (*Four Years in the Confederate Navy*, 48). All other witnesses date the departure on July 29, while Low apparently combined the two days in a single entry. Charles M. Robinson III, *Shark of the Confederacy*, 25, remains vague about the hour of the *Enrica*'s departure and does not mention the error shared by Hoole and Low, although Robinson adopts their erroneous contention that the ship left its dock at 9:00 A.M. on July 28, instead of that evening.

10. *ORN* 1:398–99, 414; Bulloch, *Secret Service*, 1:239–42; Bourne and Watt, *British Documents*, 6:152–53; *Liverpool Evening Mercury*, July 31, 1862.

11. Bulloch, *Secret Service*, 1:242; *Alabama* log, July 29–31, 1862.

12. Bourne and Watt, *British Documents*, 6:69; *Case of Great Britain*, 3:414, 416; *Birkenhead and Cheshire Advertiser*, August 9, 1862; *Liverpool Weekly Mercury*, August 9, 23, 1862; *ORN* 1:414.

13. Bourne and Watt, *British Documents*, 6:153; *ORN* 1:771–72.

14. *ORN* 1:773–74.

15. Calendar of Grants of Probate, 1864, William Brown Library; Marriage Records, LRO.

16. *Case of Great Britain*, 1:478, 481–82; *Alabama* muster roll, Confederate Subject File, NA; Clarence R. Yonge affidavit, April 2, 1863, 4481A, DU.

17. *Alabama* log, August 1–5, 1862.

18. *ORN* 1:771; Eighth U.S. Census, reel 457, 793–99, NA; Abstracts of Service Records, reel 10, 603, 1651, 2213, 2215, 2245, 2250, NA.

19. *ORN* 1:684, 776, 783–84; Clarence R. Yonge affidavit, April 2, 1863, 4481A, and Yonge to "Esteemed Friend," January 20, 1863, 4479, DU; *Case of Great Britain*, 1:475; Summersell, *Journal of George Townley Fullam*, 6, 10–11.

20. *Alabama* log, August 18–22, 1862; *Case of Great Britain*, 3:417, 476.

21. Semmes journal, August 21, 24, 1862, ADAH; *Case of Great Britain*, 3:417–18, 426, 475–76; *Alabama* log, August "25" [24], 1862. Fullam (Summersell, *Journal of George Townley Fullam*, 29) mentions that the *Alabama* was first decorated with the Stars and Bars, which the Confederacy had since replaced with the Southern Cross as the union of a white field. The French inscription on the *Alabama*'s wheel means "Help yourself, and God will help you."

Chapter 6

1. Semmes journal, August 24–29, 1862, ADAH; Yonge to "Sir," undated, 4480A, DU.

2. Clarence R. Yonge affidavit, April 2, 1863, 4481A, DU; *Alabama* muster roll, Confederate Subject File, NA; *Case of Great Britain*, 1:470, 478; Semmes, *Memoirs*, 418.

3. *Hampshire Independent*, June 25, 1864; Clarence R. Yonge affidavit, April 2, 1863, 4481A, DU. Summersell, *Journal of George Townley Fullam*, viii–xxx, sketches Ful-

lam's life. The locations of the *Alabama*'s various accommodations are detailed in *Willmer's & Smith's European Times*, June 27, 1864.

4. Pickering to Gideon Welles, March 18, 1862, Pickering letterbooks, 3:24, NHHS; Sinclair, *Two Years on the Alabama*, 268–69; Semmes journal, September 2, 1862, ADAH.

5. Semmes journal, August 29–30, 1862, ADAH.

6. Ibid., August 31–September 6, 1862; *Alabama* log, September 6, 1862; Semmes, *Memoirs*, 423–24; *ORN* 3:677; *Case of Great Britain*, 3:425, 451.

7. Semmes journal, September 7–8, 1862, ADAH; Semmes, *Memoirs*, 429–30, 1862; *Case of Great Britain*, 3:424–26.

8. Semmes journal, September 8–11, 1862, ADAH.

9. Ibid., September 13–16, 1862; *Alabama* muster roll, Confederate Subject File, NA.

10. Hoole, "Log of the Bark *Virginia*," 52–62; Semmes journal, September 17, 1862, ADAH; *Alabama* log, September "18" [19], 1862; *ORN* 3:678; *Case of Great Britain*, 3:447–49.

11. Semmes journal, September 18–24, 1862, ADAH; Semmes, *Memoirs*, 446; *Case of Great Britain*, 3:447–49. Schwalbe appears only in the roster appended to Sinclair's *Two Years on the Alabama*, unpaginated [296].

12. Semmes journal, September 20–October 3, 1862, ADAH; *Alabama* log, October "4" [3], 1862; *New York Times*, October 17, 1862; *Case of Great Britain*, 3:429–31; Summersell, *Journal of George Townley Fullam*, 29; New York Chamber of Commerce, *Proceedings*, 7–8.

13. Semmes journal, October 4–10, 1862, ADAH; Summersell, *Journal of George Townley Fullam*, 33–34; *Alabama* muster roll, Confederate Subject File, NA.

14. Semmes journal, October 10–13, 1862, ADAH; *Alabama* muster roll, Confederate Subject File, NA; Sinclair, *Two Years on the Alabama*, unpaginated [295].

15. Semmes journal, October 14–15, 1862, ADAH; *ORN* 3:677–78.

16. Semmes journal, October 16–19, 1862, ADAH; *Alabama* log, October 16, 1862; Summersell, *Journal of George Townley Fullam*, 38.

17. Semmes journal, October 20–23, 1862, ADAH; *Alabama* log, October "21" [20] to "24" [23], 1862.

18. Semmes journal, October 24–29, 1862, ADAH; *ORN* 1:509–10, 526, and series 2, 1:230; *Alabama* log, October "30" [29], 1862.

19. Semmes journal, October 30–November 9, 1862, ADAH; *ORN* 3:678; *Alabama* muster roll, Confederate Subject File, NA; Sinclair, *Two Years on the Alabama*, unpaginated [295–96]. Semmes recalled having shipped eight men from the *T. B. Wales* in his memoirs (496), but mentioned nine men in his journal; Sinclair's roster includes a tenth man who signed on November 9, and Fullam counted eleven (Summersell, *Journal of George Townley Fullam*, 49). Comparison with the *Alabama* muster roll indicates that Fullam was correct.

Chapter 7

1. Poole journal, July 23, 28, 1862, MSM; "Diary of Charles B. Fisher," 15, USAMHI; *Kearsarge* log, July 24, 28, 1862; Order for Dempsey's demotion, Pickering letterbooks, 3:61, NHHS.

2. Wainwright and Poole journals, July 30–August 16, 1862, MSM; *Kearsarge* log, August 6, 1862; DeWit journal, 71–72, MSM; John A. Little to Horatio J. Sprague, July 30, 1862; Horatio Perry to Sprague, August 5, 1862; Little to Perry, August 8, 1862; and Sprague to Pickering, August 7, 11, 15, 16, 1862, all in Pickering letterbooks, 1:59–61, 65–66, 75–80, NHHS; *ORN* 1:570, 17:346.

3. Wainwright journal, August 17, 1862, MSM; Poole journal, June 27, July 4, September 14, 1862, MSM.

4. Pickering to James DeLong, March 21, 1862; Robert Forman to Pickering, September 7, 1862; Pickering's reply, September 8, all in Pickering letterbooks, 1:80, 2: unpaginated, and 3:71–74, NHHS; "Diary of Charles B. Fisher," 17, 19–20, USAMHI; *Kearsarge* log, August 3–19, 1862.

5. Pickering to Cushman, August 19, 1862, Pickering letterbooks, 3:66, NHHS.

6. Poole and Wainwright journals, August 23, 1862, MSM; Quinby journal, August 24, 1862, PM; "Diary of Charles B. Fisher," 11–12, USAMHI. Curiously, Fisher misdates this event July 11, and it is recorded in the ship's log under August 19, in what appears to be an ex post facto insertion.

7. Quinby journal, August 24, 25, 1862, PM; Poole journal, August 24, 25, 1862, MSM; Wainwright journal, September 9, 1862, MSM; Pickering to Whittaker, September 8, 1862, Pickering letterbooks, 3:70, NHHS. Whittaker's invention fizzled, and was never produced.

8. DeWit journal, 69, 70, 74, 75, MSM; Poole journal, June 10, 21, 1862, MSM; Wainwright journal, September 7, November 19, 1862, MSM; "Diary of Charles B. Fisher," 75, USAMHI; John W. Dempsey to "Dear Sister," December 14, 1863, MHS.

9. Poole and Wainwright journals, September 14, 1862, MSM; *ORN* 7:583–84.

10. *Kearsarge* log, September 14, 1862.

11. Poole journal, September 15, 16, 1862, January 11, 1864, MSM; Wainwright journal, June 8, September 14, 1862, MSM; "Diary of Charles B. Fisher," 20, USAMHI.

12. Poole journal, September 18–October 2, 1862, MSM; Wainwright journal, September 30–October 2, 1862, MSM; *ORN* 1:490.

13. Poole and Wainwright journals, October 2–7, 1862, MSM; *ORN* 1:490.

14. Poole journal, October 7, 1862, MSM; Cushman to Pickering, Pickering to Charles D. Kiersted et al., and their reply, all October 7, 1862, Pickering letterbooks, 3:78–80, NHHS.

15. "Diary of Charles B. Fisher," 21, USAMHI; Poole and Wainwright journals, October 8, 9, 1862, MSM; DeWit journal, 80, MSM; *Kearsarge* log, October 8, 1862.

16. Poole and Wainwright journals, October 11–17, 1862, MSM; *ORN* 1:521; *Kearsarge* log, October 16, 1862; DeWit journal, 82, MSM; "Diary of Charles B. Fisher," 24, USAMHI.

17. Poole and Wainwright journals, October 16, 1862, MSM; DeWit journal, 82, MSM; *Kearsarge* log, October 16, 1862.

18. Poole and Wainwright journals, October 19, 1862, MSM; "Diary of Charles B. Fisher," 25, USAMHI.

19. *ORN* 1:521; Poole journal, October 17, 20, 1862, MSM; *Kearsarge* log, October 23, 30, 1862.

20. Poole journal, October 21–26, 1863, MSM; *ORN* 1:521.

Chapter 8

1. *Kearsarge* log, October 30, 1862; *ORN* 1:508–9, 523–24, 688–90, 15:564.

2. *ORN* 1:524–25; Poole and Wainwright journals, November 2, 3, 1862, MSM; *Kearsarge* log, November 4, 1862.

3. Poole journal, March 17, August 8, October 9, 30, November 5, 23, 1862, January 27, 1863, MSM; DeWit journal, 10, 17, 72, MSM; *Kearsarge* log, November 10, 1862; Gideon Welles to Charles Pickering, January 21, 1862, Pickering letterbooks, 1:6, NHHS.

4. Poole journal, November 6, 8, 9, 18, 1862, MSM; *ORN* 1:537, 540–41.

5. *ORN* 1:576.

6. *Kearsarge* log, September 2, October 30, November 1, 13, 19, 24, December 10, 20, 1862; Poole journal, November 1, 1862, MSM.

7. Poole and Wainwright journals, November 29, 1862, MSM; *Kearsarge* log, November 30–December 20, 1862; "Diary of Charles B. Fisher," 27, USAMHI.

8. Wainwright journal, December 1–4, 1862, MSM; Poole journal, December 1–18, 1862, MSM.

9. *Kearsarge* log, December 23, 1862, January 1, 5, 6, 1863; Wainwright journal, January 5, 1863, MSM; Poole journal, December 22, 1862, January 1, 5, 1863, MSM.

10. Poole journal, December 25, 1862, MSM; *Kearsarge* log, December 25, 1862.

11. Poole and Wainwright journals, December 30, 1862–January 1, 1863, MSM; *Kearsarge* log, January 1, 1863.

12. Poole journal, November 27, 1862, MSM.

13. Ibid., January 18, 21, 30, 1863; Wainwright journal, January 22, 29, 1863, MSM; *Kearsarge* log, January 21, 1863.

14. Poole journal, January 30, 1863, MSM; Wainwright journal, January 29, 1863, MSM.

15. Wainwright journal, January 31, 1863, MSM; *ORN* 1:382, 2:74, 77–78; Pickering to Thomas C. Harris, February 14, 1863, Pickering letterbooks, 2: unpaginated, NHHS.

Chapter 9

1. *Uniform and Dress*, 3–7; Semmes journal, November 16, 1862, ADAH.

2. Semmes journal, November 17–19, 1862, ADAH; Summersell, *Journal of George Townley Fullam*, 50–55; Clarence R. Yonge memorandum book, 4495, DU; *ORN* 1:549–51; *Case of Great Britain*, 1:476.

3. Semmes journal, November 20–24, 1862, ADAH; Edward Maffitt Anderson to Mrs. Edward C. Anderson, December 22, 1862, Anderson Papers, SHC; Summersell, *Journal of George Townley Fullam*, 56–57.

4. Semmes journal, November 25–26, 1862, ADAH; Sinclair, *Two Years on the Alabama*, 34 and unpaginated roster; Summersell, *Journal of George Townley Fullam*, 57–58; *Case of Great Britain*, 1:476; Edward Maffitt Anderson to Mrs. Edward C. Anderson, December 22, 1862, Anderson Papers, SHC.

5. Semmes journal, November 28, 1862, ADAH.

6. Ibid.; Summersell, *Journal of George Townley Fullam*, 57; *Alabama* muster roll, Confederate Subject File, NA; Sinclair, *Two Years on the Alabama*, 23.

7. Semmes journal, November 29–30, 1862, ADAH; Summersell, *Journal of George Townley Fullam*, 58–59.

8. Semmes journal, November 30–December 2, 1862, ADAH.

9. Ibid., December 3, 1862; *ORN* 1:559, 568, 571–72, 574.

10. Semmes journal, December 5–7, 1862, ADAH; *ORN* 1:577–78; Summersell, *Journal of George Townley Fullam*, 61–62.

11. Undated newspaper clipping, Solomon scrapbook, Duke University; Edward Maffitt Anderson to Mrs. Edward C. Anderson, December 22, 1862, Anderson Papers, SHC; Semmes journal, December 7–12, 1862, ADAH; Summersell, *Journal of George Townley Fullam*, 62–67; Read, *Pioneer of 1850*, 130–38.

12. Semmes journal, December 13–19, 1862, ADAH; Clarence R. Yonge memorandum book, 4495, and Yonge to Raphael Semmes, undated, 4480, DU.

13. Semmes journal, December 21–24, 1862, ADAH; Summersell, *Journal of George Townley Fullam*, 68.

14. Semmes journal, December 24–25, 1862, ADAH; Edward Maffitt Anderson to Georgia Anderson, December "24," 1862, Anderson Papers, SHC.

15. Semmes journal, December 25–29, 1862, ADAH; Clarence R. Yonge affidavit, April 2, 1863, 4481A, DU.

16. Semmes journal, December 30, 1862–January 4, 1863, ADAH; *Case of Great Britain*, 1:476; *ORN* 2:5–6; Summersell, *Journal of George Townley Fullam*, 69.

17. Summersell, *Journal of George Townley Fullam*, 69–70; Semmes journal, January 5, 1863, ADAH.

Chapter 10

1. Semmes journal, January 11, 1863, ADAH; *ORN* 2:18, 19:506–7, 510.

2. Summersell, *Journal of George Townley Fullam*, 70–79; *ORN* 2:19, 19:506–7; Semmes journal, January 11, 1863, ADAH; *Alabama* log, January 11, 1863; Clarence R. Yonge to "Esteemed Friend," January 20, 1863, 4479, DU. Fullam (76) said the *Alabama* was struck seven times, and Lieutenant Low counted six (*Alabama* log, January 11, 1863); but a sketch of the actual shot holes in the National Archives, "Subject File of the Confederate Navy" (M-1091), reel 7, shows thirteen.

3. Semmes journal, January 13–19, 1863, ADAH; Summersell, *Journal of George Townley Fullam*, 79–80; *ORN* 2:38–40; Welles, *Diary*, 1:217; Wilkes's commission, dated March 27, 1863, Wilkes Family Papers, Duke University.

4. Semmes journal, January 20–21, 1863, ADAH; Bourne and Watt, *British Documents*, 5:147–48.

5. Semmes journal, January 22–24, 1863, ADAH; Summersell, *Journal of George Townley Fullam*, 81; Clarence Yonge to "Esteemed Friend," January 20, 1863, 4479, DU.

6. Semmes journal, January 24–25, 1863, ADAH; Summersell, *Journal of George Townley Fullam*, 81–82.

7. Semmes journal, January 25, 1863, ADAH; Clarence Yonge to Semmes, undated, 4480, DU; London *Times*, June 24, 1863; *Case of Great Britain*, 1:476.

8. Semmes journal, January 25–28, 1863, ADAH; *Case of Great Britain*, 1:476; Summersell, *Journal of George Townley Fullam*, 82–85.

9. Semmes journal, January 29–31, 1863, ADAH; Summersell, *Journal of George Townley Fullam*, 85.

10. Semmes journal, February 2–20, 1863, ADAH; Summersell, *Journal of George Townley Fullam*, 86–87.

11. *ORN* 2:86–87, 94; Semmes journal, February 21–27, 1863, ADAH; Summersell, *Journal of George Townley Fullam*, 87–91.

12. Semmes journal, March 1–25, 1863, ADAH; Summersell, *Journal of George Townley Fullam*, 92–101.

13. Semmes journal, March 26–April 11, 1863, ADAH; Summersell, *Journal of George Townley Fullam*, 102–4.

14. Semmes journal, April 11–12, 1863, ADAH.

15. Ibid., April 13, 1863.

16. Ibid., April 14–15, 1863; Summersell, *Journal of George Townley Fullam*, 105–6; Semmes, *Memoirs*, 603.

17. Semmes journal, April 15–17, 1863, ADAH; Summersell, *Journal of George Townley Fullam*, 106–7.

18. Semmes journal, April 1, 18–26, 1863, ADAH; Summersell, *Journal of George Townley Fullam*, 107–8. Pernambuco is now known as Recife.

19. Semmes journal, April 27–May 11, 1863, ADAH; Summersell, *Journal of George Townley Fullam*, 108–11. The city of Bahia has been renamed Salvador.

Chapter 11

1. Poole journal, February 18–25, 1863, MSM; Wainwright journal, March 5, 1863, MSM.

2. Poole and Wainwright journals, February 15, 1863, MSM; Quinby journal, February 15, 1863, PM; Joseph A. Smith to C. E. Smith, April 16, 1863, U.S. Navy Papers, Duke University.

3. Pension records of Mary L. Harris, certificate 2081; Frances Cushman, certificate 1041; Elizabeth Graham, certificate 2218; Elvira Hartwell, certificate 2246; Frances Ham, certificate 4286; Julia G. Lee, certificate 5573; and Mary Viannah, certificate 1845, all in ND.

4. Poole and Wainwright journals, March 1–15, 1863, MSM; *Kearsarge* log, March 15, 1863.

5. Poole journal, March 13–17, 1863, MSM; Quinby journal, March 13–17, 1863, PM; *ORN* 2:103; *Kearsarge* log, March 25, June 26, September 19, 1862, March 17, 18, 1863; court-martial sentences, January 22, 1863, Pickering letterbooks, 3:103, NHHS.

6. Ezra Bartlett to "My Dear Sis," March 19, 1863, reel 7, Bartlett Family Papers, LC.

7. Ibid.; *Kearsarge* log, March 22–26, 1863; Pickering to Horatio Sprague, March 23, 1863, Pickering letterbooks 2: unpaginated, NHHS; Poole journal, March 24–26, 1863, MSM.

8. Poole and Wainwright journals, March 29, 1863, MSM; Quinby journal, March 29, 1863, PM; *Kearsarge* log, March 29, 1863; Joseph A. Smith to C. E. Smith, April 22, 1863, U.S. Navy Papers, Duke University.

9. Poole journal, March 30, 1863, MSM.

10. Poole and Wainwright journals, March 31–April 5, 1863, MSM.

11. Ellicott, *Life of John Ancrum Winslow*, 99–102; *ORN* 1:460, 2:146; *Nashua Gazette*, May 20, 1875.

12. Quinby journal, April 7, 1863, PM; Wainwright journal, April 8, 1863, MSM; DeWit journal, 96, MSM; "Diary of Charles B. Fisher," 33, USAMHI; Joseph A. Smith to C. E. Smith, April 16, 1863, U.S. Navy Papers, Duke University; *ORN* 15:332.

13. *ORN* 2:811; Poole and Wainwright journals, April 9, 10, 1863, MSM; *Kearsarge* log, April 9, 10, 1863. In chap. 6 of his 1849 work *White Jacket*, Herman Melville provides a good description of the social strata aboard an antebellum man-of-war.

14. Poole and Wainwright journals, April 11–19, 1863, MSM.

15. Poole and Wainwright journals, April 20–23, 1863, MSM; "Diary of Charles B. Fisher," 39, USAMHI; *Kearsarge* log, April 20–23, 1863; *ORN* 2:269.

16. Poole and Wainwright journals, April 23, 24, 1863, MSM; Joseph A. Smith to C. E. Smith, April 24, 1863, U.S. Navy Papers, Duke University.

17. Poole journal, April 27–30, 1863, MSM; Wainwright journal, April 27–May 4, 1863, MSM; Badlam, "First Cruise of the Kearsarge," 12. The *Kearsarge* log mistakenly records the commencement of this project on May 1, and Badlam evidently follows that source.

18. Muster rolls of the *Kearsarge*, November 30, 1864, NA; Poole journal, May 8–15, 1863; *ORN* 2:269; DeWit journal, 102, MSM; Wainwright journal, May 13, 1863, MSM.

19. Poole journal, May 16–26, 1863, MSM; Wainwright journal, May 26, 1863, MSM; *Kearsarge* log, May 21–26, 1863.

20. Poole journal, May 27–29, 1863, MSM; Wainwright journal, May 23, 1863, MSM.

Chapter 12

1. *Kearsarge* log, May 27, June 5, 7, 1863; Poole journal, June 1, 4, 7, 1863, MSM.

2. Elizabeth Graham pension application, undated, certificate 2218, ND; Muster rolls of the *Kearsarge*, November 30, 1864, NA.

3. Poole journal, June 7–14, 1863, MSM; Quinby journal, June 7–14, 1863, PM; *Kearsarge* log, June 6–9, 1863; Wainwright journal, November 8, 1863, MSM.

4. Poole and Wainwright journals, June 15–19, 1863, MSM; Quinby journal, June 15–19, 1863, PM; *ORN* 2:269–70.

5. *ORN* 2:269, 390–91; Poole journal, June 23, 1863, MSM.

6. *ORN* 20:595; Poole journal, June 23, 1863, MSM; Quinby journal, June 23, 1863, PM.

7. Poole journal, June 24–28, 1863, MSM.

8. Poole and Wainwright journals, June 29, 1863, MSM; *Kearsarge* log, June 29, 1863; "Diary of Charles B. Fisher," 39, USAMHI.

9. Poole and Wainwright journals, June 30–July 6, 1863, MSM; *ORN* 2:391; "Diary of Charles B. Fisher," 39–40, USAMHI.

10. Poole and Wainwright journals, July 5, 14, 15, 1863, MSM; *ORN* 2:391.

11. Poole and Wainwright journals, July 17–18, 1863, MSM; Quinby journal, July 17–18, 1863, PM; *Kearsarge* log, July 17–18, 1863; DeWit journal, 112, MSM; "Diary of Charles B. Fisher," 41–42, USAMHI; *ORN* 2:413.

12. Poole, and Wainwright journals, July 19–23, 1863, MSM; Quinby journal, July 19–23, 1863, PM; *Kearsarge* log, July 19–23, 1863; *ORN* 2:413, 9:213, 216; DeWit journal, 112–14, MSM; "Diary of Charles B. Fisher," USAMHI.

13. Poole and Wainwright journals, July 24–30, 1863, MSM; "Diary of Charles B. Fisher," 44, USAMHI.

14. Wainwright journal, August 17, 1863, MSM; *Kearsarge* log, July 17, August 9, 15–19, 1863; Muster rolls of the *Kearsarge*, November 30, 1864, NA; Quinby journal, August 2, 13–15, 1863, PM; Poole journal, August 14, 1863, MSM; "Diary of Charles B. Fisher," 45–46, USAMHI.

15. Poole journal, November 15, 1863, MSM.

16. Poole and Wainwright journals, August 15–19, 1863, MSM; *Kearsarge* log, August 15–19, 1863; "Diary of Charles B. Fisher," 46–47, USAMHI; DeWit journal, 109, MSM.

17. Poole and Wainwright journals, August 19–26, 1863, MSM; *Kearsarge* log, August 19–26, 1863; "Diary of Charles B. Fisher," 47–48, USAMHI; DeWit journal, 110, MSM.

Chapter 13

1. Semmes journal, May 11–14, 1863, ADAH; Summersell, *Journal of George Townley Fullam*, 113; *ORN* 2:680, 811–13.

2. Semmes journal, May 12–13, 1863, ADAH; *Case of Great Britain*, 1:532–36; Summersell, *Journal of George Townley Fullam*, 113–15; *ORN* 2:679, 813.

3. Semmes journal, May 14–15, 1863, ADAH; Summersell, *Journal of George Townley Fullam*, 113–15; Kell to Miss Louisa Tremlett, May 20, 1863, Museum of the Confederacy; Morgan, *Recollections*, 128–29.

4. Semmes journal, May 17–19, 1863, ADAH; *ORN* 2:813.

5. Semmes journal, May 15–20, June 26, 1863, ADAH; Summersell, *Journal of George Townley Fullam*, 115.

6. Semmes journal, May 21, 1863, ADAH; Summersell, *Journal of George Townley Fullam*, 115; marriage certificate 197 (1862), LRO; *Alabama* muster roll, Confederate Subject File, NA; *ORN* 2:813.

7. Semmes journal, May 24, 1863, ADAH.

8. Ibid., May 25–June 5, 1863; Summersell, *Journal of George Townley Fullam*, 119.

9. Semmes journal, June 5, 1863, ADAH; Summersell, *Journal of George Townley Fullam*, 119–20.

10. Semmes journal, June 6–16, 1863, ADAH; Summersell, *Journal of George Townley Fullam*, 120–21.

11. Summersell, *Journal of George Townley Fullam*, 121–22; Semmes journal, June 20–21, 1863, ADAH.

12. *ORN* 2:713, 3:781–82; *SHSP* 35:243.

13. *ORN* 2:713; *Alabama* muster roll, Confederate Subject File, NA; Semmes journal, June 21, 1863, ADAH; Summersell, *Journal of George Townley Fullam*, 122.

14. Semmes journal, June 21, 1863, ADAH; Summersell, *Journal of George Townley Fullam*, 123.

15. Summersell, *Journal of George Townley Fullam*, 123; Sinclair, *Two Years on the Alabama*, 263–64; *ORN* 7:48; Richard F. Armstrong to Blanche Kell, August 1, 1894, Kell Papers, Duke University.

16. Semmes journal, September 1, 1863, ADAH.

17. Ibid., June 26, 1863. Damaging comments about his officers are deleted from the

version of Semmes's journal that is published in *ORN*, as are some of the more inflammatory references to Abraham Lincoln and "the Yankee race" in general.

18. Armstrong to Blanche Kell, March 24, 1897, Kell Papers, Duke University.

19. Semmes journal, June 27–July 3, 1863, ADAH; Summersell, *Journal of George Townley Fullam*, 124–26. A somewhat fictionalized account of the capture of the *Anna F. Schmidt* appears in *American Neptune*, January, 1965, 18–28.

20. Semmes journal, July 2–3, 1863, ADAH; Summersell, *Journal of George Townley Fullam*, 125–26; London *Times*, August 21, 1863. Semmes identified the frigate as the *Diomede*; copying his error, so did Fullam and Sinclair (*Two Years on the Alabama*, 118), but it was the captain of the *Clio* who reported the incident to authorities in England.

21. Semmes journal, July 6–27, 1863, ADAH; Summersell, *Journal of George Townley Fullam*, 126–28.

22. Semmes journal, July 28–August 1, 1863, ADAH; *Cape Mercantile Advertiser*, August 8, 1863; *Alabama* muster roll, Confederate Subject File, NA.

23. Semmes journal, August 1, 1863, ADAH; Summersell, *Journal of George Townley Fullam*, 140; *Papers Relating to Foreign Affairs*, pt. 2, 327–28. Sinclair describes Johnson's physical appearance in *Two Years on the Alabama*, 119.

24. Semmes journal, August 3, 1863, ADAH; Summersell, *Journal of George Townley Fullam*, 128. Semmes originally thought that Cummings hailed from New York (Semmes to Stephen Mallory, May 16, 1861, *Sumter* letterbook, folder 15, box 43, ADAH), but Sinclair claimed he was a native of New London, Connecticut (*Two Years on the Alabama*, 276).

25. Summersell, *Journal of George Townley Fullam*, 129; Semmes journal, August 4, 1863, ADAH; *Cape Argus*, August 18, 1863.

26. Semmes journal, August 5, 1863, ADAH; Summersell, *Journal of George Townley Fullam*, 130.

27. Semmes journal, August 5, 1863, ADAH; Summersell, *Journal of George Townley Fullam*, 132.

28. Semmes journal, August 5–7, 1863, ADAH; Summersell, *Journal of George Townley Fullam*, 133–35; *Cape Argus*, August 8, 1863; diary of E. B. Rose, August 5, 1863, South African Library, copy in Bradlow notebooks, Transcripts of Articles (microfilm B28), UA.

29. Semmes journal, August 9–12, 1863, ADAH; *South African Advertiser and Mail*, August 12, 19, 1863; *Cape Mercantile Advertiser*, August 15, 1863.

30. J. M. Kell to Blanche Kell, July 27, August 12, 1863, quoted in Kell, "Life and Letters," Kell Papers, Duke University; Semmes journal, August 13–15, 1863, ADAH; Summersell, *Journal of George Townley Fullam*, 138–39; *Alabama* muster roll, Confederate Subject File, NA; Tenth U.S. Census, reel 117, enumeration district 46, sheet 15, NA.

Chapter 14

1. J. M. Kell to Blanche Kell, August 13, 1863, quoted in Kell, "Life and Letters," Kell Papers, Duke University; Semmes journal, August 14, 1863, ADAH; London *Times*, June 24, 1863; Clarence Yonge to Dudley, various dates in 1863 and 1864, 4483–93 and 4496–4506, DU.

2. *English News*, September 21, 1863.

3. *ORN* 2:426–27, 429–31, 475.

4. Semmes journal, August 16–31, 1863, ADAH.

5. Ibid., September 1, 1863.

6. Ibid., September 2–8, 1863.

7. Ibid., September 16–19, 1863.

8. Ibid., September 17–21, 1863; *Cape Mercantile Advertiser*, August 15, 1863; *Cape Argus*, August 18, September 3, 1863; *Correspondence Concerning Claims Against Great Britain*, 4:181–201.

9. Semmes journal, September 21–24, 1863, ADAH; *Alabama* muster roll, Confederate Subject File, NA; Kell, *Recollections*, 231–32; Summersell, *Journal of George Townley Fullam*, 146.

10. *ORN* 2:469; Semmes journal, September 25–October 6, 1863, ADAH.

11. Semmes journal, October 7–16, 1863, ADAH; Summersell, *Journal of George Townley Fullam*, 147.

12. Semmes journal, September 27–October 21, 1863, ADAH.

13. *ORN* 2:473–74, 494–95, 502.

14. Semmes journal, October 26, 31, November 6–10, 1863, ADAH; Summersell, *Journal of George Townley Fullam*, 151–54.

15. Semmes journal, November 11, 1863, ADAH; Summersell, *Journal of George Townley Fullam*, 156.

16. Semmes journal, November 13–17, 1863, ADAH; *Alabama* muster roll, Confederate Subject File, NA. Fullam maintained (Summersell, *Journal of George Townley Fullam*, 160) that Seaman Michael Mars was also court-martialed at this time, but the muster roll mentions formal sentences only for Townsend, Riley, and Hyer, and Semmes specifically stated that only three men were tried by that court.

17. *ORN* 2:562.

18. Semmes journal, November 19, 1863, ADAH; *ORN* 2:474.

19. Semmes journal, November 20–December 3, 1863, ADAH; *ORN* 2:560–61.

20. Galos, "L'Expédition de Cochinchine," 180.

21. Semmes journal, December 2–15, 1863, ADAH; Summersell, *Journal of George Townley Fullam*, 164; Semmes, *Memoirs*, 705.

22. *ORN* 2:561, 591; Lepotier, *Les Corsairs du Sud*, 146; Semmes journal, December 15–22, 1863, ADAH.

23. Semmes journal, December 22–23, 1863, ADAH; *Singapore Free Press and Advertiser*, December 10, 17, 24, 1863, January 21, 1864; *Overland Singapore Free Press*, January 8, 1864.

Chapter 15

1. *ORN* 2:449, 660; *Kearsarge* log, September 7–15, 1863; Poole and Wainwright journals, September 7–15, 1863, MSM.

2. *Kearsarge* log, September 17, 1863; Poole journal, September 17–19, 1863, MSM; *ORN* 2:458–59; DeWit journal, 115, MSM. DeWit's journal contains two pages numbered 115; this refers to the first.

3. *Kearsarge* log, September 18–26, 1863; *ORN* 2:680; DeWit journal, 116–17, MSM. The perfidious recruit's name was never entered in the log.

4. Quinby journal, September 21–October 1, 1863, PM; Poole and Wainwright journals, September 21–October 1, 1863, MSM; DeWit journal, 117, MSM; "Diary of Charles B. Fisher," 52, USAMHI; various declarations for pension, Zaran Phillips pension file, certificate 3163, Records of the Pension Office, NA.

5. Poole, and Wainwright journals, October 3, 1863, MSM; Quinby journal, October 3, 1863, PM; *Kearsarge* log, October 3, 1863; "Diary of Charles B. Fisher," 53, USAMHI.

6. *ORN* 2:470–71, 680; Poole and Wainwright journals, October 6–9, 1863, MSM; Quinby journal, October 11, 1863, PM; *Kearsarge* log, October 20, 25, 1863.

7. Poole journal, October 11, December 2, 1863, MSM; Wainwright journal, October 11, 1863, MSM; Quinby journal, October 11, 1863, PM; *Kearsarge* log, October 20, 25, 1863; *ORN* 9:213, 20:595.

8. *Kearsarge* log, October 8, 13, 1863; Poole and Wainwright journals, October 23–25, 1863, MSM.

9. DeWit and Wainwright journals, October 26–27, 1863, MSM; Surgeon General, U.S.N., to Commissioner of Pensions, January 12, 1886, Sarah B. McConnell pension file, certificate 15930, ND.

10. *ORN* 2:479, 818.

11. *ORN* 2:494; Poole, and Wainwright journals, October 31–November 3, 1863, MSM; Quinby journal, October 31–November 3, 1863, PM; John Dempsey to "Dear Sister," December 14, 1863, MHS; *Kearsarge* log, November 4, 1863; *Correspondence Concerning Claims Against Great Britain*, 2:419.

12. *Cork Examiner*, November 4, 1863; Poole, and Wainwright journals, November 4, 1863, MSM; Quinby journal, November 4, 1863, PM.

13. *Correspondence Concerning Claims Against Great Britain*, 2:419; *Cork Examiner*, November 4, 6, 1863; *Cork Daily Herald and Advertising Gazette*, November 6, 7, 1863; Poole, and Wainwright journals, November 5–6, 1863; Quinby journal, November 5–6, 1863, PM; *Kearsarge* log, November 6, 1863; affidavits of Daniel O'Connell, February 23, March 8, 1864, box 50, HO48, Home Office Records, Public Record Office; *ORN* 2:494, 564–65.

14. Poole and Wainwright journals, November 7, 1863, MSM; *Kearsarge* log, November 7, 1863; *ORN* 2:564–65. Winslow told the British naval commandant at Queenstown that he kept the refugees aboard at Brest to prevent them from augmenting the crew of the *Florida*, which seems inconsistent with the mock landing and offer of freedom.

15. *ORN* 2:494, 505, 510–11.

16. Wainwright journal, November 26, 27, 30, 1863, MSM; DeWit journal, 120, MSM; *Kearsarge* log, November 25, 1863.

17. *ORN* 2:498–99, 564, 9:338; *Cork Daily Herald and Advertising Gazette*, December 7, 1863; Poole, and Wainwright journals, December 5–7, 1863, MSM; Quinby journal, December 5–7, 1863, PM.

18. *ORN* 2:563–65; affidavit of Daniel O'Connell, February 23, 1864, box 50, HO48, Home Office Records, Public Record Office; *Kearsarge* log, December 7, 1863; *Cork Examiner* and *Cork Daily Herald and Advertising Gazette*, December 8, 1863.

19. *ORN* 2:562; Poole and Wainwright journals, December 9–11, 1863, MSM.

20. *ORN* 2:562; Poole and Wainwright journals, December 11–20, 1863, MSM; *Kearsarge* log, December 20, 1863.

21. *Kearsarge* log, November 12–December 23, 1863; DeWit journal, 118–22, MSM; Wainwright journal, December 22, 1863, MSM; Poole journal, December 26, 1863, MSM.

22. Poole journal, December 12, 25, 1863, February 1, 1864, MSM; Wainwright journal, November 25, December 20, 25, 1863, MSM.

Chapter 16

1. Poole and Wainwright journals, December 26–31, 1863, MSM; *ORN* 2:681, 808.

2. Poole and Wainwright journals, January 1, 2, 1864, MSM; *Kearsarge* log, January 2, 1864.

3. Poole journal, January 2–11, 1864, MSM; Wainwright journal, June 8, 1862, November 23, 1863, January 3, 1864, MSM; "Diary of Charles B. Fisher," 61, USAMHI.

4. Poole journal, January 8, 11, 1864, MSM; Wainwright journal, January 11, 1864, MSM.

5. *ORN* 2:586, 663–64.

6. *Kearsarge* log, December 24, 1863–January 19, 1864.

7. Poole journal, January 5–February 3, 1864, MSM; Wainwright journal, January 22–February 2, 1864, MSM; *Kearsarge* log, January 29–February 1, 1864.

8. Poole journal, February 2–6, 1864, MSM; *Kearsarge* log, January 26–February 2, 1864.

9. Poole journal, January 27–February 12, 1864, MSM; Wainwright journal, February 1, 10, 1864, MSM; *ORN* 2:583, 589, 596–98; *Kearsarge* log, January 26–February 12, 1864; "Diary of Charles B. Fisher," 57, USAMHI. Muster rolls of the *Kearsarge* for November, 1864, list the cabin boy Gallardo as having enlisted at Algeciras, his birthplace, on January 1, 1864, but the ship then lay at Brest.

10. *ORN* 2:596–98, 624.

11. Quinby journal, February 12–18, 1864, PM; Poole and Wainwright journals, February 12–18, 1864, MSM; *ORN* 2:606–8.

12. Poole and Wainwright journals, February 19–24, 1864, MSM; *Kearsarge* log, February 19–24, 1864; *ORN* 2:632.

13. Poole and Wainwright journals, February 24–25, 1864, MSM.

14. Poole and Wainwright journals, February 25–27, 1864, MSM; *ORN* 1:768, 2:632, 673, 681, and series 2, 2:819–20. A single reference to an engineer named William H. Jackson aboard the *Florida* on its final cruise (*ORN* 3:624) appears to be an error or sheer coincidence, as that Jackson could not have returned to France in time to receive a September appointment to the *Rappahannock*.

15. Poole and Wainwright journals, February 28–March 2, 1864, MSM; "Diary of Charles B. Fisher," 66–67, USAMHI; *Kearsarge* log, March 1–8, 1864.

16. Poole and Wainwright journals, March 3–8, 1864, MSM.

17. Wainwright journal, March 3, 1864, MSM; "Diary of Charles B. Fisher," 67–68, USAMHI.

Chapter 17

1. Semmes journal, December 23–24, 1863, ADAH; Summersell, *Journal of George Townley Fullam*, 166; *Alabama* muster roll, Confederate Subject File, NA.

2. Semmes journal, December 24–25, 1863, ADAH; [Brown and Colby], "The *Sonora* and the *Alabama*," 34; Summersell, *Journal of George Townley Fullam*, 166–69; Nathaniel Jacobs to F. W. Seward, May 23, 1863, cited in Logan, "*Alabama* in Asian Waters," 148; *Bengal Hurkaru*, February 4, 1864; *Overland Singapore Free Press*, January 8, 1864; captain of the *National Eagle* to Messrs. Fisher & Co., March 19, 1864, Matthews Papers, Duke University.

3. Charles W. Cook to Charles E. Cook, September 17, 1863, Cook Papers, Duke University; *Singapore Free Press and Advertiser*, December 31, 1863.

4. Semmes journal, December 25–26, 1863, ADAH; [Brown and Colby], "The *Sonora* and the *Alabama*," 36; *Singapore Free Press and Advertiser*, January 7, 1864; Summersell, *Journal of George Townley Fullam*, 169–71.

5. Semmes journal, December 30–31, 1863, ADAH; Summersell, *Journal of George Townley Fullam*, 171–72; *Alabama* muster roll, Confederate Subject File, NA; Hancock, *Delaware*, 164; Sinclair, *Two Years on the Alabama*, muster roll, unnumbered pages; *Times of India*, February 4, 1864.

6. Summersell, *Journal of George Townley Fullam*, 172–74; Semmes journal, January 1–11, 1863, ADAH.

7. Summersell, *Journal of George Townley Fullam*, 174; Semmes journal, January 11–20, 1864, ADAH; *Case of Great Britain*, 1:624–25, 628–29; *Cochin Chronicle*, January 23, 1864; *Times of India*, February 4, 1864; Kell, *Recollections*, 239.

8. Semmes journal, January 21–February 9, 1864, ADAH; Summersell, *Journal of George Townley Fullam*, 175; *ORN* 3:681.

9. Semmes journal, February 9–14, 1864, ADAH; Summersell, *Journal of George Townley Fullam*, 176.

10. Semmes journal, February 16–19, 1864, ADAH; Summersell, *Journal of George Townley Fullam*, 176; *Alabama* muster roll, Confederate Subject File, NA.

11. Semmes journal, February 19–March 6, 1864, ADAH; Summersell, *Journal of George Townley Fullam*, 177–78.

12. Semmes journal, March 4, 1864, ADAH. The quoted passage was deleted from the journal when it was published in *ORN*.

13. Semmes journal, March 11–19, 1864, ADAH; Summersell, *Journal of George Townley Fullam*, 178–79; *Cape Argus*, March 15, 21, 1864; *ORN* 2:480–88, 708–19.

14. Semmes journal, March 20–22, 1864, ADAH; Summersell, *Journal of George Townley Fullam*, 179–80; *ORN* 2:708–19.

15. *Cape Argus*, March 22, 1864; London *Times*, February 12, 15, 1864; Semmes journal, March 29, 1864, ADAH.

16. Semmes journal, March 29, 1864, ADAH; E. B. Rose diary, March 24, 1864, South African Library, Bradlow notebooks, Transcripts of Articles, UA.

17. Semmes journal, March 24–29, 1864, ADAH; Summersell, *Journal of George Townley Fullam*, 180–81.

18. Semmes journal, April 3–28, 1864, ADAH; Summersell, *Journal of George Townley Fullam*, 182–85.

19. *ORN* 3:53; *Alabama* muster roll, Confederate Subject File, NA.

20. Summersell, *Journal of George Townley Fullam*, 184; Sinclair, *Two Years on the Alabama*, 104–5, 192–97. Brent Johnson, whom both John Latham and Paymaster Yonge believed to be a member of the Royal Naval Reserve, did not appear on the

Reserve enrollment, at least under that name. He may have used an alias on the *Alabama* in order to avoid the summary discharge that the Reserve had meted out to Michael Mars (see *Case of Great Britain*, 1:482–83), but in September of 1864 he signed an affidavit as Brent Johnson (see *Papers Relating to Foreign Affairs*, pt. 2, 327–28).

21. Semmes journal, May 11–June 2, 1864, ADAH.

22. Ibid., June 4–11, 1864; Summersell, *Journal of George Townley Fullam*, 188–90; *Phare de la Manche*, June 14, 1864.

Chapter 18

1. *ORN* 2:632–33; Wainwright journal, March 9, 1864, MSM; *Kearsarge* log, March 8–26, 1864.

2. Poole and Wainwright journals, March 16, 1864, MSM.

3. Poole journal, March 18–28, 1864, MSM; Wainwright journal, March 18, 20, 28, 1864, MSM; *ORN* 3:7.

4. Poole journal, March 30–31, 1864, MSM.

5. Opinions of Roundell Palmer and R. P. Collier, February 2, April 8, 1864; William Karraghan to Thomas Larcorn, April 4, 1864; and affidavits of Daniel O'Connell, February 23, March 8, 1864, all in box 50, Home Office Records, Public Record Office; *Dover Chronicle*, March 19, 1864; *Executive Documents*, 6:674–75; *ORN* 3:68; *Above and Beyond*, 323. Winslow's list of crewmen who fought the battle also included Master's Mate William Yeaton. Yeaton was still at Cadiz at the time, having just recovered in time to be ordered back on the *St. Louis*, but, as that ship did not come to Cherbourg, neither did Yeaton (*ORN* 3:54). Still in Cadiz nearly eight weeks after the battle, Yeaton was ordered to find his own way home from there, but as late as forty-five years afterward Yeaton's daughter and son-in-law were still trying to get his *Alabama* prize money from the government (Winslow to Yeaton, August 11, 1864; S. W. R. Diehl to Edward Lasell, December 6, 1905; and G. O. Vass to Lasell, May 31, 1910, all in Yeaton Family Papers, NHHS).

6. Poole and Wainwright journals, April 2–6, 1864, MSM.

7. Poole and Wainwright journals, April 6–9, 1864, MSM; Quinby journal, April 9, 1864, PM; *ORN* 3:7–9.

8. "Diary of Charles B. Fisher," 72, USAMHI.

9. Poole journal, April 12, 16, 1864, MSM; *Kearsarge* log, April 14, 16, 1864.

10. Poole and Wainwright journals, April 17, 1864, MSM; *Kearsarge* log, April 17, 1864; "Diary of Charles B. Fisher," 73, USAMHI; *ORN* 3:15.

11. Poole and Wainwright journals, April 18–22, 1864, MSM; *Kearsarge* log, April 18–22, 1864.

12. Poole journal, April 22, 1864, MSM; *Kearsarge* log, April 22, 1864; Wainwright journal, April 21, 1864, MSM; *ORN* 3:18–19.

13. *ORN* 3:18–19; Wainwright journal, April 22–27, 1864, MSM; Poole journal, April 23–26, May 3, 1864, MSM; "Diary of Charles B. Fisher," 75–76, USAMHI.

14. "Diary of Charles B. Fisher," 76, USAMHI.

15. Poole journal, May 5–6, 1864, MSM; *Kearsarge* log, May 6–7, 1864.

16. Poole journal, May 7–11, 1864, MSM; *ORN* 3:37; Wainwright journal, May 8,

1864, MSM; "Diary of Charles B. Fisher," 78–79, USAMHI; *Kearsarge* log, May 6–12, 1864.

17. Poole journal, March 21, May 12, 14, 1864, MSM; Wainwright journal, May 26, 1864, MSM.

18. Poole journal, May 21, 1864, MSM; *Kearsarge* log, May 21, 1864; "Diary of Charles B. Fisher," 81, USAMHI; *ORN* 3:67.

19. Forrest diaries, May 20, 1864, SHC; Poole journal, May 23, 1864, MSM; Wainwright journal, May 21, 23–24, 1864, MSM; *ORN* 3:39.

20. *Kearsarge* log, June 1–13, 1864; Poole journal, May 30–June 11, 1864, MSM; Wainwright journal, May 27, 31, June 6–7, 1864, MSM.

21. Poole, and Wainwright journals, June 12, 1864, MSM; Quinby journal, June 12, 1864, PM; "Diary of Charles B. Fisher," 82, USAMHI.

22. Poole and Wainwright journals, June 13–14, 1864, MSM; *ORN* 3:50–51; *Kearsarge* log, June 14, 1864; Semmes journal, June 14, 1864, ADAH.

Chapter 19

1. *Phare de la Manche*, June 14, 1864; Semmes journal, June 11–13, 1864, ADAH; London *Times*, June 16, 1864; *ORN* 3:53, 647–48, 651; Ingouf, *Coulez l'Alabama!*, 16, 19.

2. Semmes journal, June 14–15, 1864, ADAH; Branham, *Interview*; *ORN* 3:58; Forrest diaries, May 20, 1864, SHC.

3. Sinclair, *Two Years on the Alabama*, xvii, 234; Delaney, *John McIntosh Kell*, 220.

4. H. E. Huntington to William Hunter, September 4, 1879, copy included in a letter from Richard F. Armstrong to Blanche Kell, January 16, 1896, Kell Papers, Duke University; *Daily Picayune*, September 29, 1912.

5. Semmes journal, June 14, 1864, ADAH; *ORN* 2:624, 3:55, 69; *Kearsarge* log, June 14–15, 1864; Poole and Wainwright journals, June 14–15, 1864, MSM; Ezra Bartlett to George Bartlett, June 14, 16, 1864, Bartlett Letters, Boston Public Library.

6. *ORN* 3:67, 651; Semmes journal, June 15–16, 1864, ADAH; Poole and Wainwright journals, June 17–18, 1864, MSM; *Kearsarge* log, June 15–16, 1864; William L. Dayton, Jr., to William L. Dayton, Sr., June 22, 1864, DL; Semmes, *Memoirs*, 755.

7. William L. Dayton, Jr., to William L. Dayton, Sr., June 22, 1864, DL.

8. *Phare de la Manche*, June 20, 1864; *ORN* 3:661–62.

9. Poole journal, June 19, 1864, MSM; Leland, "French Official Report," 120; Ingouf, *Coulez l'Alabama!*, 58.

10. William L. Dayton, Jr., to William L. Dayton, Sr., June 22, 1864, DL; Ingouf, *Coulez l'Alabama!*, 15; Leland, "French Official Report," 122.

11. Leland, "French Official Report," 120; William L. Dayton, Jr., to William L. Dayton, Sr., June 22, 2864, DL.

12. Ingouf, *Coulez l'Alabama!*, 59; *Kearsarge* log, June 19, 1864; Poole and Wainwright journals, June 19, 1864, MSM. Ingouf dispels the tradition that it was the steeple clock of St. Clement's church (which M. Bonfils attended) that tolled the departure of the *Alabama*. That clock was not installed until July 27, 1864, says Ingouf; it was the bell at St. Trinity that rang as the cruiser left port.

13. The speech appears in no contemporary source, but Semmes quotes it in his

Memoirs, 756, as does Kell in his *Recollections*, 246–47, and Sinclair in *Two Years on the Alabama*, 227–28, both of whom take it directly from Semmes.

14. Leland, "French Official Report," 120–22; *Kearsarge* log, June 19, 1864; Poole journal, June 19, 1864, MSM.

15. *ORN* 3:64, 79, 649; *Kearsarge* log, June 19, 1864; Poole journal, June 19, 1864, MSM; William L. Dayton, Jr., to William L. Dayton, Sr., June 22, 1864, DL.

16. London *Times*, June 23, 1864; *ORN* 3:63, 67–69, 78–80, 650; Semmes, *Memoirs*, 762; Martin Hoyt to "Dear Uncle," June 19, 1864, Portsmouth Historical Society.

17. *ORN* 3:80, 650; Semmes, *Memoirs*, 761; Sinclair, *Two Years on the Alabama*, 230; Kell, *Recollections*, 247–48; *Willmer's & Smith's European Times*, June 27, 1864. The *Mercury*, June 25, 1864, lists McGinley as only "slightly" wounded.

18. *ORN* 3:63–64; statement dated February 19, 1877, Roscoe G. Dolley pension file, certificate 4912, Records of the Pension Office, NA.

19. Edge, *Englishman's View*, 18.

20. Kell, *Recollections*, 148; Sinclair, *Two Years on the Alabama*, 231; *Willmer's & Smith's European Times*, June 27, 1864; ; *ORN* 3:80, 650; Wainwright journal, June 19, 1864, MSM.

21. *ORN* 3:70, 80, 650; London *Times*, June 20, 1864; Wainwright journal, June 19, 1864, MSM; *Hampshire Independent*, June 25, 1864; Semmes, *Memoirs*, 764. Summersell (*Journal of George Townley Fullam*, 196, and *C.S.S. Alabama*, 84) maintains that the papers were carried by Michael Mars and George Fremantle, and that Fremantle delivered his share of them to Semmes on the *Deerhound*, but Fremantle was instead taken prisoner by the *Kearsarge* (*Mercury*, June 25, 1864); Townsend, however, was rescued by the *Deerhound*. Evidently confused by the unreliable Sinclair memoir (*Two Years on the Alabama*, 244), Charles M. Robinson III (*Shark of the Confederacy*, 145–46) maintains that Mars alone carried the papers, and that he jumped from a *Kearsarge* boat, swam to the French pilot boat, then "transferred" to the *Deerhound*, although the pilot boat and the yacht did not meet after picking up survivors. Mars did leap from the *Kearsarge* boat to the pilot boat, but did not reach the *Deerhound*: see Lieutenant Armstrong's account, *ORN* 3:653.

22. Branham, *Interview*.

23. Ibid.; William L. Dayton, Jr., to William L. Dayton, Sr., June 22, 1864, DL; London *Times*, June 20, 1864; *Kearsarge* log, June 19, 1864.

24. Wainwright journal, June 19, 1864, MSM; *ORN* 3:653; London *Times*, June 20, 1864.

25. London *Times*, June 21, 1864; *Mercury*, June 25, 1864; *Papers Relating to Foreign Affairs*, pt. 2, 328; *Phare de la Manche*, June 20, 1864.

26. *ORN* 3:60–61, 69–70; William L. Dayton, Jr., to William L. Dayton, Sr., June 22, 1864, DL; *Papers Relating to Foreign Affairs*, pt. 2, 327; Wainwright journal, June 19, 1864, MSM; *Mercury*, June 25, 1864.

27. William H. Cushman to Francis Cushman, June 19, 1864, Cushman Papers, LC; Ezra Bartlett to George Bartlett, June 19, 1864, Bartlett Papers, Boston Public Library; Martin Hoyt to "Dear Uncle," June 19, 1864, Portsmouth Historical Society; Poole and Wainwright journals, June 19, 1864, MSM; William l. Dayton, Jr., to William L. Dayton, Sr., June 22, 1864, DL.

28. *Hampshire Independent*, June 25, 1864; *Post-Office Directory of the Borough of Southampton*, 142.

Chapter 20

1. Calendar of Grants of Probate, 1864, WBL; marriage certificates 197 (1862) and 71 (1864), LRO.

2. Entries 562–64, Actes de Decès, Archives Municipales de Cherbourg. While the graves of Appleby, King, and *Kearsarge* seaman William Gowin are a well-visited curiosity in Cherbourg's *ancien cimitière*, the location of Robinson's grave was unknown to the cemetery superintendent in August of 1993.

3. *ORN* 3:69–70; application dated December 8, 1864, John W. Dempsey pension file, certificate 1786, Records of the Pension Office, NA; undated application and affidavit, Margaret Dempsey pension file, certificate 1786, ND; Poole and Wainwright journals, June 27, 29, 1864, MSM; *Kearsarge* log, June 29, 1864; Margaret Gowin pension certificate 1924, ND.

4. Poole and Wainwright journals, June 30, 1864, MSM; *ORN* 3:62; Edge, *Englishman's View*, 18. As Norman Delaney notes in "Showdown at Cherbourg," 21, Marine Corporal Austin Quinby insisted in his journal that Rondin brought many copies of the battle print aboard to sell to the crew; Quinby claimed the image shows the *Alabama* going down with the *Kearsarge* standing by. Quinby's handwritten journal, however, was obviously doctored heavily after the war, and his statement about the pictures is not especially reliable. No other diarist mentions seeing the battle print, although William Wainwright said of Rondin, "I understand the same man has got a view of the fight," raising the question of why Wainwright never actually saw the photograph, if—as Quinby claimed—"the most of the ship's company bought one."

5. *ORN* 3:73–81, 650; London *Times*, June 23, 1864; *La Presse*, June 30, 1864.

6. *La Presse*, July 18, 1864; Proust, "Edouard Manet," 174; Manet to Felix Bracquemond, undated (but late July, 1864), quoted in "Les Lettres de Manet à Bracquemond," 149.

7. Poole journal, June 30, August 5, 12, 1864, MSM; Wainwright journal, July 4–11, August 11–13, 1864, MSM; *ORN* 3:124, 136; Abstracts of Service Records, reel 11, 568, NA; *Kearsarge* log, July 4–10, August 8–9, 1864; Surgeon General, U.S.N., to Commissioner of Pensions, October 25, 1880, Margaret Crowley pension file, certificate 11197, ND.

8. *ORN* 3:192, 350; Poole journal, August 31, October 31, 1864, MSM; Wainwright journal, September 1, 23, 24, October 1, 4, 7, 29–31, 1864, MSM.

9. *ORN* 3:350; *Kearsarge* log, November 7–8, 1864.

10. *Boston Evening Transcript*, November 8, 10, 1864; Poole journal, November 10, 1864, MSM.

11. Dalzell, *Flight from the Flag*, 239–49.

Epilogue

1. Affidavits of April 14, 1906, March 26, 1916, Austin P. Quinby pension file, certificate 10845, Records of the Pension Office, NA; *Boston Globe*, June 20, 1919.

2. J. Edward Bates to the Secretary of the Interior, July 30, 1882, Anna E. DeWit pension file, widow's application 995 (disapproved); original application, undated, Frances H. Cushman pension file, mother's certificate 1041; original application, undated, Mary Viannah pension file, widow's certificate 1845; statement of June 12, 1889, Frances Ham pension file, widow's certificate 4268; original application, undated, Margaret Dempsey pension file, widow's certificate 1786; death certificate, Mary P. Pickering pension file, certificate 3860; affidavit of September 19, 1916, Helen D. Poole pension file, widow's certificate 789868; original application, undated, Fannie Sargent pension file, widow's certificate 909312, all in ND; note of December 12, 1914, Zaran Phillips pension file, certificate 3163; note of June 4, 1920, William Wainwright pension file, certificate 2999; note of April 22, 1922, Austin P. Quinby pension file, certificate 10845, all in Records of the Pension Office, NA; Ellicott, *Life of John Ancrum Winslow*, 273–74; Taylor, "Showdown off Cherbourg," 138.

3. Calendar of Grants of Probate, 1867, WBL; burial register of St. Patrick's Cemetery, Leytonstone, London, entry of August 5, 1878; Summersell, *Journal of George Townley Fullam*, xxviii; Allcot headstone, Anfield Cemetery, Liverpool.

4. *Confederate Veteran*, 9 (January, 1901): 35; 12 (July, 1904): 356–57; 24 (March, 1916): 127; 26 (March, 1918): 133; 31 (January, 1923): 27; 31 (May, 1923): 184; *Savannah Morning News*, June 26, 1861; *Boyd's Directory*, 220; *Baltimore Sun*, November 17, 1925.

Appendix 1

1. Welles to G. V. Fox, September 29, 1875; Welles to S. D. and S. W. Thompson, June 27, 1876; and Welles's endorsement on Fox's notation, undated, all in Fox Papers, NHHS; *Boston Journal*, June 4, 1861; *New Hampshire Statesman*, June 8, 1861; *Portsmouth Chronicle*, June 10, November 18, 1861.

2. Albert Hatch to Fox, July 12, 1876; numerous letters to Fox from Conway, Bartlett, and Chatham residents; Fox's undated protest to the New Hampshire Historical Society; and *Facts About the Carroll County Kearsarge Mountain, of New Hampshire, Read Before the Appalachian Mountain Club by G. V. Fox*, n.p., n.d., all in Fox Papers, NHHS; King, *White Hills*, 157, 164, 167, 172–74. The postmaster of the village of Kearsarge, at the foot of the Carroll County mountain, was invited to the christening of the aircraft carrier *Kearsarge* in 1944.

3. McFarland, *Kearsarge Mountain*, 14; U.S. Senate, S. Doc. 307, 11–14; Hixon and Hixon, *Place Names*, 96. According to S. Doc. 307, 12, Fox later admitted receiving McFarland's 1861 letter, but the source of that alleged admission is not identified.

4. *Dictionary of American Naval Fighting Ships*, 3:609, credits the Merrimack County mountain, but the director of the Naval History Center in Washington, D.C., has conceded that both mountains merit recognition, saying the matter "defies a definitive conclusion by the Navy" (Dean C. Allard to the author, April 2, 1993).

BIBLIOGRAPHY

Manuscripts

Alabama Department of Archives and History, Montgomery, Ala.
  Semmes Family Papers
    Raphael Semmes journal
    CSS *Sumter* letterbook
Archives Municipales de Cherbourg
  Actes de Decès
Boston Public Library, Boston, Mass.
  Ezra Bartlett Letters
British Library, London, England
  Additional Collection
    William Gladstone Papers
    A. H. Layard Papers
William Brown Library, Liverpool, England
  Calendar of Grants of Probate
Duke University, Durham, N.C.
  Charles E. Cook Papers
  John McIntosh Kell Papers
    Correspondence
    Blanche Munroe Kell, "Life and Letters of John McIntosh Kell"
    Sketch of CSS *Alabama*
  George Matthews Papers
  Eugenius Aristides Nisbet Papers
  M. J. Solomon scrapbook
  U.S. Navy Papers
  Wilkes Family Papers
Huntington Library, San Marino, Calif.
  Thomas H. Dudley Collection
Langdon Library, Newington, N.H.
  Martin Hoyt Papers
Library of Congress, Washington, D.C.
  Bartlett Family Papers
    Ezra Bartlett diary and letters
  C.S.A. Papers, Navy Department
  William H. Cushman Papers
  Registry Papers of the *Conrad*, "Captured by the Alabama"
  Gideon Welles Papers
  John A. Winslow Papers
Liverpool Registry Office, Liverpool, England
  Marriage Records

Massachusetts Historical Society, Boston, Mass.
  John W. Dempsey letter
Museum of the Confederacy, Richmond, Va.
    John McIntosh Kell Letters
Mystic Seaport Museum, Mystic, Conn.
    G. W. Blunt White Library
      Carsten DeWit journal
      Charles A. Poole, "Journal of the Cruise of the U.S.S. Kearsarge in Serch [*sic*] of
        Rebel Privateers"
      William Wainwright journal
National Archives, Washington, D.C.
    Abstracts of Service Records of Naval Officers, 1798–1893, M-330
    Carded C.S. Navy service records (RG109), M-260
    Confederate Subject File (RG45), M-1091
    Letters Sent by the Secretary of the Navy to Officers, 1798–1868, M-149
    Log of the USS *Kearsarge*, 1862–64 (RG24)
    Muster rolls of USS *Kearsarge* (RG24)
    Navy Dependents' Pension Files, M-1279
    Old Subject File, 1776–1910 (RG24)
    Plan of the CSS *Alabama*, October 9, 1861, including profile of inboard works and
      plan of the lower deck (RG 109)
    Records of General Courts Martial and Courts of Inquiry of the Navy Department,
      1799–1867, M-273
    Records of the Bureau of the Census (RG29)
      Seventh United States Census, M-432
      Eighth United States Census, M-653
      Tenth United States Census, T-9
    Records of the Pension Office (RG15)
Naval Historical Center, Washington, D.C.
    Operational Archives
      Kearsarge file
New Hampshire Historical Society, Concord, N.H.
    Gustavus V. Fox Papers
    Charles Whipple Pickering letterbooks
    Yeaton Family Papers
Peabody Museum, Salem, Mass.
    Austin Quinby, "Kearsarge Journal"
Portsmouth Historical Society, Portsmouth, N.H.
    Martin Hoyt letter
Princeton University, Princeton, N.J.
    William L. Dayton Letters
Public Record Office, Richmond, Surrey, England
    Home Office Records
      Law Officers Correspondence
University of Alabama, Tuscaloosa, Ala.
    William S. Hoole Special Collections

John Low's log of the *Alabama*
Transcripts of Articles in Various Newspapers and Periodicals Relating to the
Alabama
University of North Carolina, Chapel Hill, N.C.
Southern Historical Collection
Alabama Contract and Specifications
Edward Clifford Anderson Papers
Chisholm Family Papers
James Heyward North Letters
Forrest Family Papers
D. F. Forrest diaries
Nisbet Family Papers
U.S. Army Military History Institute, Carlisle Barracks, Pa.
"Diary of Charles B. Fisher" (typescript)

Newspapers

Athenaeum and Statesman, Madras, India
Baltimore Sun
Bengal Hurkaru, Calcutta
Birkenhead and Cheshire Advertiser
Boston Evening Transcript
Boston Journal
Cape Argus, Cape Town, South Africa
Cape Mercantile Advertiser, Cape Town, South Africa
Cork Daily Herald and Advertising Gazette
Cork Examiner
Daily Picayune, New Orleans
Dover Chronicle and Kent and Sussex Advertiser
English News, London
Hampshire Independent
Illustrated London News
Liverpool Evening Mercury
Liverpool Weekly Mercury
Mercury, Liverpool
Nashua (N.H.) Gazette
New Hampshire Statesman, Concord
New York Herald
Overland Singapore Free Press
Phare de la Manche, Cherbourg
Philadelphia Weekly Times
Portsmouth (N.H.) Chronicle
La Presse, Paris
Punch
Savannah Morning News
Singapore Free Press and Advertiser

South African Advertiser and Mail, Cape Town
Southampton Times
Straits Times, Singapore
Times, London
Times of India, Bombay
Tribune and Daily Advertiser, Kingston, Jamaica
Willmer's & Smith's European Times, Liverpool

Published Sources

Above and Beyond: A History of the Medal of Honor from the Civil War to Vietnam.
    Boston: Boston Publishing Co., 1985.
Adams, Charles Thornton. *The Family of James Thornton, Father of Matthew Thorn-
    ton.* New York: Privately published, 1905.
Ahmat, Sharom bin. "The *Alabama* in Singapore Waters." *Peninjau Sejarah* (Malaya)
    2 (January, 1967): 25–29.
The Alabama: A Statement of Facts from Official Documents. London: John Snow &
    W. Tweedie, 1863.
"The Alabama and Her Doings and Crew." *Nautical Magazine*, March, 1864, 135–41.
[A. M. G.]. "The Pride of Mr. Laird." *Blackwood's Magazine*, September, 1963.
Badlam, William H. "The First Cruise of the Kearsarge." *Civil War Papers Read Be-
    fore the Commandery of the State of Massachusetts, Military Order of the Loyal
    Legion of the United States.* 2 vols. Boston: Loyal Legion, 1900, 1:11–26.
———. "The Kearsarge and the Alabama." *Personal Narratives of the War of the Re-
    bellion.* 10 vols. Providence, R.I.: Rhode Island Soldiers and Sailors Historical So-
    ciety, 1878–1905, 5:2.
Baker, Mark. "David Herbert Llewelyn, 1837–1864." *The Wiltshire Archeological and
    Natural History Magazine* 68 (1973): 108–15.
Barbet, Paul. "Naval Encounter Between the *Kearsarge* and *Alabama* Fought in Sight
    of Cherbourg, France, on June 19, 1864." *U.S. Naval Institute Proceedings* 52 (Au-
    gust, 1926): 1681–86.
Barnard, Joseph. "The Timbers of the Kearsarge." *Granite Monthly* 15 (May, 1893):
    145–48.
Booth, Alan R. "The *Alabama* at the Cape." *American Neptune* 26 (April, 1966): 96–
    108.
Bourne, Kenneth, and D. Cameron Watt, eds. *British Documents on Foreign Affairs:
    Reports and Papers from the Foreign Office Confidential Print.* 49 vols. N.p.: Uni-
    versity Publications of America, n.d.
Boyd's Dictionary of Washington and Georgetown. Washington, D.C.: Hudson Taylor,
    1867.
Bradford, Gamaliel, Jr. "Raphael Semmes: A Last Confederate Portrait." *Atlantic
    Monthly*, October, 1913, 469–80.
Bradlee, Francis Boardman Crowninshield. "The *Kearsarge-Alabama* Battle; The
    Story as told to the Writer by James Magee of Marblehead, Seaman on the *Kear-
    sarge*." *Historical Collections of the Essex Institute* 57 (1921).

Bradlow, Edna, and Frank Bradlow. *Here Comes the Alabama: The Career of a Confederate Raider*. Cape Town: A. A. Balkena, 1958.

Branham, Alfred Iverson. *Story of the Sinking of the Alabama 290: Interview with Capt. John McIntosh Kell*. Atlanta: Cornell, 1930.

[Brown, Laurence, and Isaac Colby]. "The *Sonora* and the *Alabama*." *Civil War Times Illustrated* 10 (October, 1971): 32–39.

Browne, John M. "The Duel Between the *Alabama* and the *Kearsarge*." In *Battles and Leaders of the Civil War*, edited by Robert U. Johnson and Clarence C. Buel, 4:615–24. 4 vols. New York: Century Co., 1884–88.

——. "The Kearsarge and the Alabama: A New Story of an Old Fight." *Overland Monthly* 14 (1875): 105–11.

——. *The Story of the Kearsarge and Alabama*. San Francisco: Henry Payot & Co., 1868.

Bulloch, James D. *The Secret Service of the Confederate States in Europe*. New York: Thomas Yoseloff, 1959.

The Career of the Alabama, No. 290, From July 29, 1862 to June 19, 1864. London: Dorrell, 1864.

The Case of Great Britain as Laid Before the Tribunal of Arbitration Convened at Geneva. 3 vols. Washington, D.C.: Government Printing Office, 1872.

Chandler, Porter L. "How My Grandfather Nearly Lost the Civil War." *American Neptune* 33 (January, 1973): 5–15.

Chase, Lew A. "The *Alabama* and the *Emden*." *Nation*, December 3, 1914, 99.

——. "The Search for the *Alabama* and the New Era in Naval Warfare." *Sewanee Review* 18 (July, 1910): 344–58.

Correspondence Concerning Claims Against Great Britain, Transmitted to the Senate of the United States. 5 vols. Washington, D.C.: Government Printing Office, 1869–70.

Correspondence Respecting the "Alabama;" Also Respecting the Bark "Maury," at New York, During the Crimean War. [London]: n.p., [1865].

Dalzell, George W. *The Flight from the Flag: The Continuing Effect of the Civil War upon the American Carrying Trade*. Chapel Hill: University of North Carolina Press, 1940.

Delaney, Norman C. *John McIntosh Kell of the Raider Alabama*. University: University of Alabama Press, 1972.

——. "Showdown at Cherbourg." *Civil War Times Illustrated* 15 (June, 1976): 16–21.

"Destruction of the British Ship *Martaban* by the *Alabama*." *Nautical Magazine*, March, 1864, 141–44.

"Destruction of the Confederate Ship *Alabama* by the United States Ship *Kearsage* [sic]." *Nautical Magazine*, July, 1864, 375–82.

Dictionary of American Naval Fighting Ships. 8 vols. Washington, D.C.: Government Printing Office, 1981.

Dillon, Richard H., ed. "First Word from the *Kearsarge*." *American Neptune* 19 (April, 1959): 126–28.

Duret, Théodore. *Histoire de Edouard Manet et de Son Oeuvre, avec un Catalogue des Peintures et des Pastels*. Paris: Bernheim-Jeune, 1926.

Edge, Frederick Milnes. *An Englishman's View of the Battle Between the Alabama and the Kearsarge: An Account of the Naval Engagement in the British Channel, on Sunday, June 19, 1864*. New York: A. D. F. Randolph, 1864.

Ellicott, John M. *The Life of John Ancrum Winslow, Rear Admiral, United States Navy*. New York: G. P. Putnam's Sons, 1902.

Executive Documents Printed by the Order of the House of Representatives During the Second Session of the Thirty-Eighth Congress. 15 vols. Washington, D.C.: Government Printing Office, 1865.

[Fullam, George Townley]. *The Cruise of the Alabama, Raphael Semmes, Commander, from Her Departure from Liverpool, July 29, 1862*. London: N.p., 1864.

Galos, Henri. "L'Expédition de Cochinchine." *Revue des Deux Mondes* 51 (May, 1864): 173-207.

Goodrich, Albert M. *Cruise and Captures of the Alabama*. Minneapolis: Wilson, 1906.

Gould, James W. "The Civil War in the Far East." *U.S. Naval Institute Proceedings* 88 (September, 1962): 160-64.

Hancock, Harold Bell. *Delaware during the Civil War: A Political History*. Wilmington, Del.: Historical Society of Wilmington, 1961.

Handford, Stanley W. "Again the *Alabama*." *U.S. Naval Institute Proceedings* 90 (June, 1964): 172-74.

Haywood, Philip D. *The Cruise of the Alabama, by One of Her Crew*. Boston: Houghton, Mifflin, 1886.

Higginson, Thomas Wentworth. *Massachusetts in the Army and Navy during the War of 1861-65*. 2 vols. Boston: Wright & Potter Printing Co., 1896.

Hixon, Robert, and Mary Hixon. *The Place Names of the White Mountains: History and Origins*. Camden, Maine: Down East Books, 1980.

Hobson, Henry S. *The Famous Cruise of the Kearsarge: An Authentic Account in Verse of the Battle with the Alabama off Cherbourg, France, on Sunday, June 19, 1864*. Bonds Village, Mass.: N.p., 1894.

Hoole, William S. "The C.S.S. *Alabama* at Cape Town: Centennial Celebration, 1863-1963." *Alabama Review* 17 (July, 1964): 228-33.

———. *Four Years in the Confederate Navy: The Career of Captain John Low of the C.S.S. Fingal, Alabama, Florida, Tuscaloosa, and Ajax*. Athens: University of Georgia Press, 1964.

———, ed. "The Log of the Bark *Virginia* Sunk by the C.S.S. *Alabama*, 1862." *American Neptune* 33 (January, 1973): 52-62.

———. *The Logs of the CSS Alabama and CSS Tuscaloosa, 1862-63, by Lieutenant (Captain) John Low, C.S.N.* University, Ala.: Confederate Publishing, 1972.

Ingouf, Paul. *Coulez l'Alabama!: Un Episode de la Guerre de Secession en Contentin*. Cherbourg: La Dépêche de Cherbourg, 1976.

Jarvis, Rupert. "The Alabama and the Law: A Reconsideration." *Journal of Southern History* 33 (August, 1967): 360.

Jeffries, William W. "The Civil War Career of Charles Wilkes." *Journal of Southern History* 11 (August, 1945): 324-48.

Jenkins, Brian. *Britain and the War for the Union*. 2 vols. Montreal: McGill-Queen's University Press, 1974, 1980.

Kell, John McIntosh. "Cruise and Combats of the 'Alabama.'" In *Battles and Leaders*

of the Civil War, edited by Robert U. Johnson and Clarence C. Buel, 4:600–614. 4
    vols. New York: Century Co., 1884–88.
——. *Recollections of a Naval Life; Including the Cruises of the Confederate Steamers
    Sumter and Alabama*. Washington, D.C.: Neale Co., 1900.
King, Thomas Starr. *The White Hills; Their Legends, Landscapes, and Poetry*. Boston:
    Crosby, Nichols, 1860.
Laugel, Auguste. "Les Corsaires Confédérés et le Droit des Gens." *Revue des Deux
    Mondes* 52 (July, 1864): 224–48.
Leary, William M., Jr. "*Alabama* versus *Kearsarge*: A Diplomatic View." *American
    Neptune* 29 (July, 1969): 167–73.
Leland, Waldo G. "The *Kearsarge* and *Alabama*: French Official Report, 1864."
    American Historical Review 23 (October, 1917): 114–22.
Lepotier, Lieutenant de Vaisseau ——. *Les Corsaires du Sud et Le Pavillon Étoilé*.
    Paris: Société d'Éditions, Géographiques, Maritimes, et Coloniales, 1936.
"Les Lettres de Manet à Bracquemond." *Gazette des Beaux Arts* 6 (April, 1983): 146–
    60.
*List of Claims Filed with the Department of State, Growing Out of the Acts Committed
    by the Several Vessels Which have Given Rise to the Claims Generally Known as the
    Alabama Claims*. Washington, D.C.: Government Printing Office, 1871.
Littleton, William G. *The Battle Between the Alabama and the Kearsarge, off Cher-
    bourg, France, Sunday, June 19, 1864*. Philadelphia: Pennsylvania Commandery,
    Military Order of the Loyal Legion of the United States, 1930.
Logan, Frenise A. "Activities of the *Alabama* in Asian Waters." *Pacific Historical Re-
    view* 31 (May, 1962): 143–50.
McFarland, Henry. *Kearsarge Mountain and the Corvette Named for It*. Concord,
    N.H.: Rumford Printing Co., 1906.
Maynard, Douglas H. "The Confederate Super-*Alabama*." *Civil War History* 5
    (March, 1959): 80–95.
——. "Plotting the Escape of the *Alabama*." *Journal of Southern History* 20 (May,
    1954): 197–209.
——. "Union Efforts to Prevent the Escape of the *Alabama*." *Mississippi Valley Histor-
    ical Review* 41 (June, 1954): 41–60.
Merli, Frank J. *Great Britain and the Confederate Navy, 1861–1865*. Bloomington: In-
    diana University Press, 1970.
Morgan, James Morris. *Recollections of a Rebel Reefer*. Boston: Houghton Mifflin, 1917.
*Narrative of the Cruise of the Alabama, and List of Her Officers and Men, By One of
    the Crew*. London: N.p., 1864.
Nash, Howard P. "The C.S.S. *Alabama*: Roving Terror of the Seas." *Civil War Times
    Illustrated* 2 (August, 1963): 5–8, 34–39.
Naval Historical Foundation. *Captain Raphael Semmes and the C.S.S. Alabama*.
    Washington, D.C.: The Foundation, 1968.
Navy Register for 1861.
Newell, Robert R. "Capture and Burning of the Ship *Anna F. Schmidt* by *Alabama*."
    American Neptune 25 (January, 1965): 18–28.
New York Chamber of Commerce. *Proceedings on the Burning of the Ship Brilliant,
    by the Rebel Pirate Alabama, October 21, 1862*. New York: The Chamber, 1862.

Official Records of the Union and Confederate Navies in the War of the Rebellion. 31 vols. Washington, D.C.: Government Printing Office, 1894–1927.

Our Cruise in the Confederate States War Steamer Alabama. The Private Journal of an Officer. London: A. Shulz, 1863.

Papers Relating to Foreign Affairs, Accompanying the Annual Message of the President. 3 parts. Washington, D.C.: Government Printing Office, 1865.

Poolman, Kenneth. *The Alabama Incident.* London: William Kimber, 1958.

The Post-Office Directory of the Borough of Southampton. Southampton: Forbes & Bennett, 1861.

Prentice, E. Parmelee. "An American Battle in Foreign Waters." *Harper's Monthly Magazine,* November, 1910, 873–88.

Proust, Antonin. "Edouard Manet: Souvenirs." *La Revue Blanche* 88 (February, 1897): 125–84.

Raphael Semmes, Rear Admiral, Confederate States Navy, Brigadier General, Confederate States Army. Mobile, Ala.: Museum of the City of Mobile, 1978.

Read, George W. *A Pioneer of 1850: Adventures of George Willis Read, 1819–1880.* Boston: Little, Brown, 1927.

Roberts, Walter A. *Semmes of the Alabama.* Indianapolis: Bobbs-Merrill, 1938.

Robinson, Charles M., III. *Shark of the Confederacy: The Story of the CSS Alabama.* Annapolis, Md.: Naval Institute Press, 1994.

Robinson, William M., Jr. "The *Alabama-Kearsarge* Battle: A Study in Original Sources." *Essex Institute Historical Collections* 60 (April–July, 1924): 97–120, 209–18.

Roden, J. B. "Trip from New Orleans to Louisville in 1861." *Confederate Veteran* 18 (May, 1910): 236.

Rowe, William H. *The Maritime History of Maine.* New York: Norton, 1948.

Semmes, Raphael. *The Cruise of the Alabama and the Sumter, From the Private Journals and Other Papers of Commander Raphael Semmes, C.S.N., and Other Officers.* 2 vols. in one. New York: Carleton, 1864.

——. *Memoirs of Service Afloat: During the War Between the States.* Baltimore: Baltimore Publishing Co., 1887.

——. *Service Afloat and Ashore During the Mexican War.* Cincinnati: Wm. H. Moore, 1851.

Sinclair, Arthur. *Two Years on the Alabama.* Annapolis, Md.: Naval Institute Press, 1989.

Smith, Joseph A. *An Address Delivered Before the Union League of Philadelphia on Saturday Evening January 20, 1906, at the Presentation by the Art Association of the Painting Representing the Battle Between the Kearsarge and Alabama.* Philadelphia: Lippincott, 1906.

——. "The Battle Between the *Kearsarge* and the *Alabama.*" *Magazine of History* 5 (January, 1907): 1–26.

Spencer, Warren F. *The Confederate Navy in Europe.* University: University of Alabama Press, 1983.

Standing, P. C. "Boarding Officer of the *Alabama.*" *Cornhill Magazine* 75 (May, 1897): 592–603.

Summersell, Charles G., ed. *C.S.S. Alabama: Builder, Captain, and Plans.* University: University of Alabama Press, 1985.

———. *The Journal of George Townley Fullam, Boarding Officer of the Confederate Sea Raider Alabama*. University: University of Alabama Press, 1973.

Taylor, John M. "The U.S.S. *Kearsarge* Versus the *Alabama*: Showdown off Cherbourg." *Yankee* 48 (July, 1984): 72–77, 133–38.

Tucker, Spencer C. "U.S. Navy Gun Carriages from the Revolution through the Civil War." *American Neptune* 47 (Spring, 1987): 108–18.

Uniform and Dress of the Navy of the Confederate States (Naval War Records Office Memoranda No. 7). Washington, D.C.: Government Printing Office, 1898.

U.S. Congress. Senate. S. Doc. 307, 64th Cong., 1st sess., 1916.

U.S. Executive Branch, Doc. No. 282, 42nd Cong., 2nd sess., 425–30.

Valuska, David L. *The African American in the Union Navy, 1861–1865*. New York: Garland, 1993.

War of the Rebellion: A Compilation of the Official Records of the Union and Confederate Armies. 128 vols. Washington, D.C.: Government Printing Office, 1880–1901.

Welles, Gideon. *Diary of Gideon Welles*. 3 vols. Boston: Houghton Mifflin, 1911.

Wilson-Barbeau, Juliet, ed. *Manet by Himself: Correspondence and Conversations*. London: Macdonald Illustrated, 1991.

Emery, Mark W., 47, 169

Emily Farnham, 74

Emma Jane, 222, 223, 225

English News, The, 185

Enrica, 55–62, 152, 297 (n. 9). See also
    Alabama, CSS

Evans, James, 123

Evans, Robley, 59

Express, 179

Fannie Bullitt, 239, 295 (n. 21)

Farragut, David, 124, 155

Fingal, 19, 20

Fisher, Charles B.: voyage on *Fannie
    Bullitt*, 32, 239, 295 (n. 21); as enter-
    tainer, 47, 90; and women of Algeci-
    ras, 82–83; relations with white sail-
    ors, 83; lack of mail, 84–85; as officers'
    cook, 95; on Mr. Yeaton, 97; on Capt.
    Pickering, 153; at small arms drill, 163;
    as captain's cook, 217; and French
    women, 236; on Fort Pillow massacre,
    239; misdates Scott's desertion, 299
    (n. 6)

Fisher, Henry, 59, 75

Fisher, William, 97, 98, 100, 206, 240

Fitzmaurice, Edward, 185

Florida, CSS, 238, 243; construction of,
    10, 20; at Nassau, 51; at Pernambuco,
    171; meets *Agrippina*, 172; at Brest,
    196–200, 202, 204–7, 208–11; flags of,
    199; crewmen of, fighting with USS
    Kearsarge sailors, 206–7; and sus-
    pected fleet attack upon *Kearsarge*,
    213–14; escapes Brest, 215; captured,
    263; *Kearsarge* takes prisoners from,
    264. See also *Manassas*; *Oreto*

Foi, 66

Foreign Enlistment Act, 55, 185, 203, 234

Forrest, George, 74–75, 102–3, 104–5

Fort Jackson, La., 3, 5, 157

Fort St. Phillip, La., 3, 5, 157

Fox, Gustavus, 8, 269–70

Fox, Mrs. Gustavus, 8, 269–71

Franklin, USS, 14

Fraser, Trenholm & Co., 55, 112

Freeman, Miles, 78; joins *290* (*Enrica*),
    60; and dispute over rank, 66; disman-
    tles *Ariel* machinery, 108; repairs CSS
    Alabama machinery, 109, 119; paroled,
    258

Fremantle, Arthur, 22

Fremantle, George, 312 (n. 21)

Fullam, George Townley: appointed
    master's mate, 65; as boarding officer,
    175, 190, 220, 221, 222, 225; as prize
    master, 181; rescues CSS *Alabama* sur-
    vivors, 255–56; brings Semmes news
    of USS *Kearsarge* chaincladding, 261;
    returns to England, 262; drowning of,
    268

Gallardo, Manuel José, 214, 261, 308
    (n. 9)

Galt, Francis L.: in Nassau, 52–53; as
    surgeon of CSS *Alabama*, 65; as pay-
    master of *Alabama*, 118, 122, 123, 172,
    176, 188, 194, 223, 229, 247, 261;
    allegedly acknowledges awareness of
    chaincladding on USS *Kearsarge*, 245;
    accompanies wounded to *Kearsarge*,
    256, 257; later career and death, 268

G. Azzopadi, 175

Genshlea, Michael, 59, 65

Georgia, CSS, 209, 243; escapes from
    Great Britain, 152; commissioned, 154;
    at Bahia, 171–73; at Simons Town, 187;
    at Cherbourg, 202, 204, 206, 208; and
    suspected attack upon USS *Kearsarge*,
    213–14; leaves Cherbourg, 215; reports
    of, 238

Gerrish, Edward, 228

Gibraltar, 100, 205. See also *Sumter*,
    CSS

Gildersleeve, 174

Giles, William, 161, 211, 213, 266

Gilmore, Joseph, 270

Godwin, Charles, 65

Godwin, Henry, 224

Golden Eagle, 120

Golden Rocket, 7, 21

Golden Rule, 118

bumboat vendors, 91; on Spanish beef, 94; as caterer of his mess, 95, 236; on rations, 98; on liberty in Cadiz, 98, 160, 213; and baseball, 147; on Spaniards, 149–50; on calm seas, 155; and "hoax," 158; disgust with Spain, 160; and *Smoker*, 163; and Coal Heaver Boener's funeral, 170; on beer, 197; on liberty in Brest, 200–201; at Queenstown, 202; on living conditions, 207; at target practice, 210; supplements rations, 211; recreation aboard ship, 212; on Coal Heaver Briset, 213; on general quarters drill, 218; paints captain's cabin, 237; absent without leave, 239; on liberty in Flushing, 239–40; records victory over CSS *Alabama*, 258; death of, 267

Poole, William, 168, 253

Port Hudson, La., 184

Portsmouth, USS, 14

Potter, Thomas, 118, 267

Powhatan, USS, 5–6, 16

Preble, Edward E., 59, 96, 163–64, 206, 262

Pundt, John M., 258

Punjaub, 121, 187

Quarters: assignment according to rank, 16–17, 65; conditions of, aboard USS *Kearsarge*, 18, 25–26, 84, 207; conditions of, aboard CSS *Alabama*, 64, 110

Queen of Beauty, 175

Queenstown affair: "stowaways" taken aboard, 202–3; recruits uniformed and assigned to duty, 203–4; British authorities object and consider prosecution, 204, 234–35; Capt. Winslow returns recruits to Queenstown, 205; Capt. Winslow covers up violation of Foreign Enlistment Act, 234–35, 307 (n. 14)

Quinby, Austin: joins USS *Kearsarge*, 18; on rough seas, 25, 27; on Sgt. Young and Surgeon's Steward Tittle, 30; at Tangier, 33; and *Smoker*, 163; and

Juno, 167; and postwar reunions, 266; death of, 267; questionable vintage of journal, 295 (n. 24); on photograph of battle between USS *Kearsarge* and CSS *Alabama*, 313 (n. 4)

Rank: privileges accorded to, 46, 66; discrimination by, 96–97; functions of various grades, 154–55

Rappahannock, CSS, 204, 241; and suspected fleet attack upon USS *Kearsarge*, 213–14, 238; at Calais, 216, 217, 218, 232, 233, 237–38, 240

Release, USS, 47, 84

Remick, George W., 83

Riley, John, 192

Rinton, William, 115, 119

Rising Sun, 60

Roach, David, 59

Roach, Martin, 235, 236

Roberts, Jane, 259

Roberts, John, 58, 255, 259

Robertson, William, 58, 259

Robinson, William, 60; repairs battle damage to CSS *Alabama*, 117; death of, 257, 259, 260; grave site unknown, 313 (n. 2)

Rockingham, 228–29, 244, 257

Rondin, François, 255, 260–61, 263, 313 (n. 4)

Rose, E. B., 227

Rowley, Andrew, 90, 91, 211

Royal Naval Reserve, 59, 62, 105, 180, 310 (n. 20)

Russell, George, 86

Russell, John, 57

Sabine, USS, 8, 14, 120

Sacramento, USS, 262

St. Louis, USS, 45; reaches Azores, 89; arrives at Cadiz, 96; returns to Azores, 156, 157; Capt. Winslow wishes to borrow guns from, 213; ordered to Cherbourg, 243; at Gibraltar, 245

Sampson, Edward H. *See* Tibbetts, Edward H.

Sanborn, Joel L., 83

San Jacinto, USS, 103, 107

Santee, USS, 8, 14

Sargent, Daniel B., 41, 267

Saunders, James: age, 26; height, 27; absent without leave, 157; and bottle of brandy, 168–69; confined, 237; leads shanty, 237

Saxon, 225

Schroeder, Julius, 248, 262

Schwalbe, Gustave, 73

Scott, Robert, 84, 86, 95

Scott & Co., 203, 205

Sea Bride, 181–83, 186, 188, 226

Sea King, 151

Sea Lark, 124

Semmes, Raphael, 55, 58, 59, 203; as commander of CSS *Sumter*, 3–7, 21–23; background, 4; and Tangier incident, 32–33, 37–38; at Gibraltar, 37–39; leaves Gibraltar for London, 39–40; in London, 51–52; in Nassau, 52–53; assumes command of *290* (*Enrica*), 60, 61–62; first prizes as commander of CSS *Alabama*, 63–79; rumors of whereabouts, 95; and discipline, 101–3, 106, 192, 316 (n. 16); and mutiny, 102–3; and California steamers, 105–10; health of, 109, 187, 245; plans to raid Banks expedition, 110–12; and battle with USS *Hatteras*, 113–15; in Jamaica, 117–18; at Santo Domingo, 119; seeks *Agrippina*, 120, 121, 125; at Fernando de Noronha, 122–24; interprets newspaper articles on progress of war, 124, 184, 230; at Bahia, 171–74; fooled by burning wreckage, 174; on female "passenger" aboard *Conrad*, 175; and seaworthiness of *Alabama*, 175, 225, 227, 229; on Lt. Sinclair, 177; on Lt. Wilson, 178; photographed, 182; uniform of, 183, 222; at Cape Town, 184–86, 226–27; reprimands Lt. Sinclair, 187; at Singapore, 195; boards prize, 220; appoints court martial, 221; discharges pilot, 221; intrigued by African slave owners, 223; commends Seaman Mars, 224; on Abraham Lincoln, 225; captures last prize, 228; and bad shell fuses, 228, 229, 253; requests repairs at Cherbourg, 244; decides to fight USS *Kearsarge*, 245; and chaincladding of *Kearsarge*, 245–46, 253, 254, 261; challenges Capt. Winslow, 246; sends treasury ashore, 247; interview with M. Bonfils, 248; speech to crew before battle, 250–51; fires first volley, 251; orders new flag up, 251, 253; on shot in *Kearsarge*'s sternpost, 253; orders colors struck, 255; escapes *Alabama*, 256; rescued by *Deerhound*, 257; arrives Southampton, 258; tallies casualties, 259; discharges crew, 261; subsequent service, 262; and *Alabama*'s effectiveness, 264–65; on number of recruits, 298 (n. 19); expunges damaging remarks from journal, 304–5 (n. 17)

Seward, William H., 70

Shamrock, HMS, 83

Simpson, Martin, 47, 90

Singapore Free Press, 220

Sinclair, Arthur, III, 56

Sinclair, Arthur, IV, 176; assigned to *290* (*Enrica*), 53; promoted, 177; photographed, 183; reprimanded by Semmes, 187; on chaincladding of USS *Kearsarge*, 245, 254; later life and death, 268

Sinclair, Hamilton & Co., 58

Sinclair, William H., 176, 226, 248

Smith, Christian, 98

Smith, James, 76

Smith, Joseph A., 94, 205, 267; opinion of Lt. Harris, 148; on chase, 151; on Capt. Pickering, 153; on beauty of Azorean women, 157; condemns supplies, 212; seeks drydock privileges, 217–18; visits Brussels, 237, 238

Smith, Sidney L., 84, 170, 261

Smith, William, 97, 197, 233, 262

offers liberty, 160, 161, 200; and *Smoker*, 162–63; aggressiveness of, 164–65; and *Juno*, 165–67; and the lost anchor, 168; reads burial service, 169; learns whereabouts of CSS *Florida*, 196; at Brest, 197–202, 204–5, 206–7; allows card-playing, 199; and dream, 199; at Queenstown, 202–3, 206–7; and recruits, 203–5; crewmen question sanity of, 206; at Ushant, 209–11; recruiting sailors, 211, 212–13; extends enlistments of crewmen, 211–12; correspondence with secretary of navy, 214; leaves Cadiz, 215; on escape of *Florida*, 215; at Cherbourg, 215–16, 243; arranges for coal tender, 216; seeks drydock, 217–18; general quarters drill, 218; blames Chief Engineer Cushman for boiler malfunction, 233; at London, 234; cover-up of Queenstown affair, 234–35, 307 (n. 14); falsifies crew list, 235; visits Brussels, 237, 238; and suspected fleet attack upon *Kearsarge*, 238; at Flushing, 239; visits Antwerp, 240; correspondence with William L. Dayton, 242, 247–48; and Capt. Semmes's challenge, 246; calls crew to quarters, 250; delivers first broadside, 251; and

final volley from CSS *Alabama*, 255; orders rescue of survivors, 255–56; complains of *Deerhound*'s flight, 257, 261; paroles prisoners, 258; visits Paris, 262; promotes officers, 262; turns for home, 263; death of, 267; attends dedication of Winslow House, 270

Winslow House, 270

Wyoming, USS, 190, 193–95; CSS *Alabama* passes as, 221

Yeaton, William H.: Capt. Pickering selects for assignment to USS *Kearsarge*, 16; drunk on duty, 97; left behind at Cadiz, 215; ordered to Cherbourg, 243; absence from *Kearsarge* during battle with CSS *Alabama*, 310 (n. 5)

Yonge, Clarence R.: background, 20; and escape of *Enrica*, 55–56; and recruiting of sailors, 58; suspicious correspondence, 60; enrolls sailors, 62; complains of quarters, 64, 110; assigned steward, 65; completes pay allotments, 112; leaves CSS *Alabama* at Port Royal, 117–18; testifies about *Alabama*, 184–85; death of, 268

Young, Charles T., 29–30, 42, 99, 163